THE MAKING OF OLIVER CROMWELL

THE MAKING OF
OLIVER CROMWELL

RONALD HUTTON

YALE UNIVERSITY PRESS
NEW HAVEN AND LONDON

For information about this and other Yale University Press publications, please contact:
U.S. Office: sales.press@yale.edu yalebooks.com
Europe Office: sales@yaleup.co.uk yalebooks.co.uk

Set in Adobe Garamond Pro by IDSUK (DataConnection) Ltd
Printed in Great Britain by TJ Books, Padstow, Cornwall

Library of Congress Control Number: 2021935455

ISBN 978-0-300-25745-8

A catalogue record for this book is available from the British Library.

10 9 8 7 6 5 4 3 2

CONTENTS

◈

ILLUSTRATIONS

PLATES

1. 'A perfect list of the many victories obtained (through the blessing of God) by the Parliaments forces under the command of his excellency, Robert Earl of Essex and Ewe, Viscount Hereford, Lord Ferrers of Chartley, Bourchier and Lovaine', 1646. © British Library / Bridgeman Images.

2. Huntingdon, *c.* 1770–90. Maps K.Top.16.6.1. Album / Alamy Stock Photo.

3. Ely, by an unknown artist, *c.* 1800. incamerastock / Alamy Stock Photo.

4. The school of Oliver Cromwell. © Charles O'Brien.

5. Elizabeth Cromwell (née Steward), by Charles Turner, published by Samuel Woodburn, 1810. © National Portrait Gallery, London.

6. Portrait of Sir Oliver Cromwell, circle of Hieronimo Custodis, *c.* 1580. Courtesy of the Cromwell Museum, Huntingdon.

7. Miniature of Elizabeth Cromwell (née Bourchier), by Samuel Cooper, seventeenth century.

8. Bird's-eye view of Sidney Sussex College, Cambridge, by David Loggan, 1690.

9. The marriage of King Charles I and Henrietta Maria, after an unknown artist, late eighteenth century. © National Portrait Gallery, London.

MAPS

ILLUSTRATIONS

ACKNOWLEDGEMENTS

In the writing of this book, I owe two great debts to two different institutions. The first is my own university, of Bristol, which I have served for forty years, and which has always treated me well. In particular, I am very grateful to its School of Humanities for granting me a full year of research leave in which to carry out the primary source work and commence the writing.

The other institution is Yale University Press, for publishing the result, and this is always personified for me in Heather McCallum, whose presence in the firm is the reason why I have written four successive books for it to date. Her mixture of hard-headed professionalism and genuine kindness and solicitude is one which invites loyalty. I am also beholden to the two readers of the manuscript for the press, and the helpful suggestions that they made for improvement.

A NOTE ON STYLE

Because of a desire to maximize text within a word count, I have not added a bibliography to this book, but have instead given full publication details for each work cited during its first appearance in the notes to each chapter, no matter how often it has been recorded before. In keeping with the convention for works on this period I have used dates according to the old (pre-1752) calendar, but taken the year as beginning on 1 January.

When dealing with the work of colleagues, of whom there are many both for anybody who writes on this period in general, and on Cromwell in particular, I have observed a dual system. Whenever I have drawn a conclusion on a specific matter on which I accord with what (to my knowledge) another historian has written, I have attempted to give that person full credit for the view. Conversely, however, I have not usually signalled a point at which I dissent from another author over a matter of detail. Experts in the subject will recognize such moments automatically, and students spot them as they get to know the field, while more general readers are unlikely to be interested. I have only the highest of respect for previous biographers of Cromwell, as for the many others who write upon the events in which he was engaged, and a large number are personal friends (while none are foes). I have therefore no desire to signal differences from them over petty matters, while over major issues – the pivotal importance of Oliver's times and the enduring fascination of his character – we all agree.

General readers were mentioned above and remain dear to me because I started out as one, in boyhood, and remain one in any field other than the handful in which I have expertise. I am accordingly profoundly grateful to anybody who tries to write accessibly on scholarly subjects. This work is designed therefore both as a monograph which will contribute to academic debate and as an introduction to those new to the subject and with a broad interest in history. Hence the notes are full of information intended to be of interest to experts, while the text is at times written in a style designed to bring out my own sense of the beauty and variety of the English landscape and its seasons, and the immediacy of recreated history. My hope of course is that each of these aspects will complement one another rather than jarring on the opposite audience; but my books are always experiments, and it remains to be seen, if I continue to deal with Cromwell's life, whether this is the right approach to take.

THE EASTERN ASSOCIATION

Core territory from December 1642

Counties added in late 1643

York

Ouse

Kingston upon Hull

Humber

LINDSEY

North Sea

NOTTINGHAMSHIRE

Lincoln

LINCOLNSHIRE

Newark

KESTEVEN

Nottingham

Boston

Grantham

HOLLAND

King's Lynn

RUTLAND

Stamford

Wisbech

NORFOLK

Norwich

Leicester

Peterborough

Great Yarmouth

Lowestoft

NORTHAMPTONSHIRE

ISLE OF

ELY

Ely

HUNTINGDON-

SHIRE

Huntingdon

Northampton

Cambridge

Bury St Edmunds

SUFFOLK

CAMBRIDGE-

SHIRE

BEDFORD-

SHIRE

BUCKINGHAMSHIRE

HERTFORDSHIRE

Hertford

Oxford

St Albans

ESSEX

London

Reading

Thames

80 km

50 miles

N

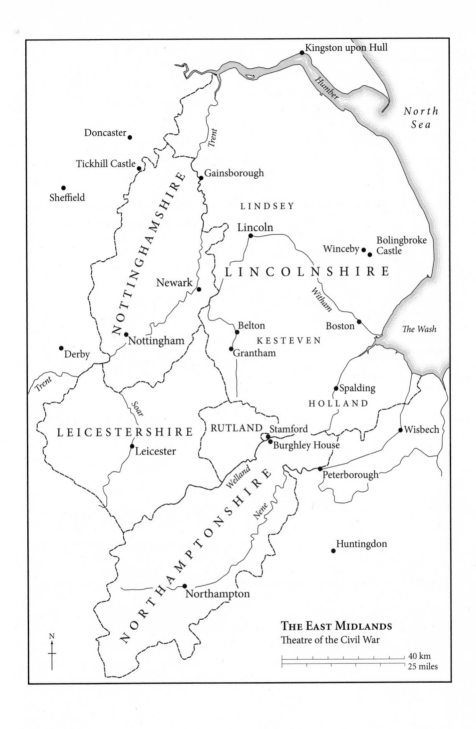

Kingston upon Hull

Humber

North Sea

Doncaster

Trent

Tickhill Castle

Gainsborough

Sheffield

LINDSEY

Lincoln

Winceby • Bolingbroke Castle

N O T T I N G H A M S H I R E

L I N C O L N S H I R E

Newark

Witham

Belton

Boston

The Wash

Derby

Nottingham

K E S T E V E N

Grantham

Trent

Soar

Spalding

H O L L A N D

L E I C E S T E R S H I R E

RUTLAND

Stamford

Wisbech

Leicester

Burghley House

Welland

Peterborough

N O R T H A M P T O N S H I R E

Nene

Huntingdon

THE EAST MIDLANDS
Theatre of the Civil War

N

40 km
25 miles

Northampton

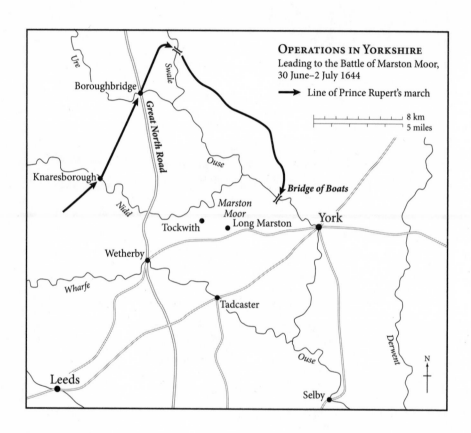

OPERATIONS IN YORKSHIRE
Leading to the Battle of Marston Moor,
30 June–2 July 1644

→ Line of Prince Rupert's march

8 km
5 miles

Ure

Swale

Boroughbridge

Great North Road

Knaresborough

Ouse

Nidd

Bridge of Boats

Marston
Moor

Tockwith

Long Marston

York

Wetherby

Wharfe

Tadcaster

Derwent

Leeds

Ouse

Selby

N

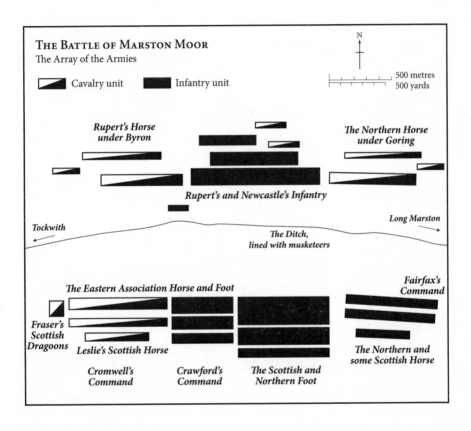

THE BATTLE OF MARSTON MOOR
The Array of the Armies

Cavalry unit   Infantry unit

N

500 metres
500 yards

*Rupert's Horse
under Byron*

*The Northern Horse
under Goring*

Rupert's and Newcastle's Infantry

Tockwith

Long Marston

*The Ditch,
lined with musketeers*

The Eastern Association Horse and Foot

*Fairfax's
Command*

*Fraser's
Scottish
Dragoons*

Leslie's Scottish Horse

*The Northern and
some Scottish Horse*

*Cromwell's
Command*

*Crawford's
Command*

*The Scottish and
Northern Foot*

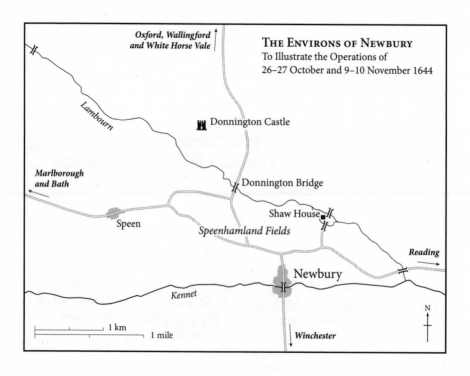

Oxford, Wallingford
and White Horse Vale

THE ENVIRONS OF NEWBURY
To Illustrate the Operations of
26–27 October and 9–10 November 1644

Lambourn

🏰 Donnington Castle

**Marlborough
and Bath**

Donnington Bridge

Shaw House

Speen   *Reading*

Speenhamland Fields

Newbury

Kennet

1 km
1 mile

N

Winchester

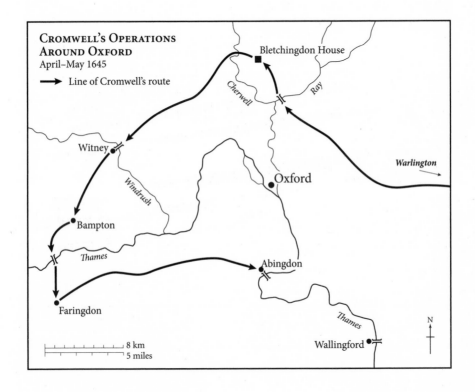

CROMWELL'S OPERATIONS
AROUND OXFORD
April–May 1645

➤ Line of Cromwell's route

Bletchingdon House

Cherwell

Ray

Witney

Windrush

Oxford

Warlington

Bampton

Thames

Abingdon

Faringdon

Thames

8 km
5 miles

Wallingford

N

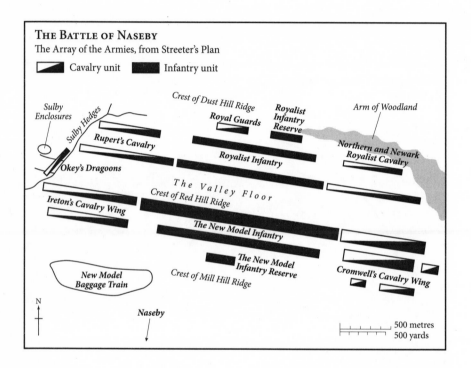

THE BATTLE OF NASEBY
The Array of the Armies, from Streeter's Plan

Cavalry unit   Infantry unit

Sulby
Enclosures
Sulby Hedges
Crest of Dust Hill Ridge
Royal Guards
Royalist Infantry Reserve
Arm of Woodland
Rupert's Cavalry
Okey's Dragoons
Royalist Infantry
Northern and Newark Royalist Cavalry
The Valley Floor
Crest of Red Hill Ridge
Ireton's Cavalry Wing
The New Model Infantry
The New Model Infantry Reserve
New Model Baggage Train
Crest of Mill Hill Ridge
Cromwell's Cavalry Wing

N

Naseby

500 metres
500 yards

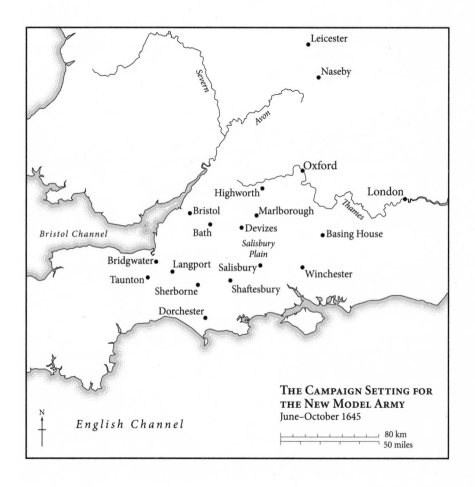

Leicester

Naseby

Severn

Avon

Oxford

Highworth

Thames

London

Bristol

Marlborough

Bath

Devizes

Basing House

Bristol Channel

Salisbury Plain

Bridgwater

Langport

Salisbury

Winchester

Taunton

Sherborne

Shaftesbury

Dorchester

THE CAMPAIGN SETTING FOR THE NEW MODEL ARMY
June–October 1645

N

English Channel

80 km

50 miles

OPERATIONS IN SOMERSET
5–10 July, Leading to the
Battle of Langport

Bridgwater

Parrett

Wagg Rhyne

Langport ✕ *Site of battle*

Taunton

Ilchester

Yeo

Isle

Parrett

Yeovil

N

5 km
4 miles

Crewkerne

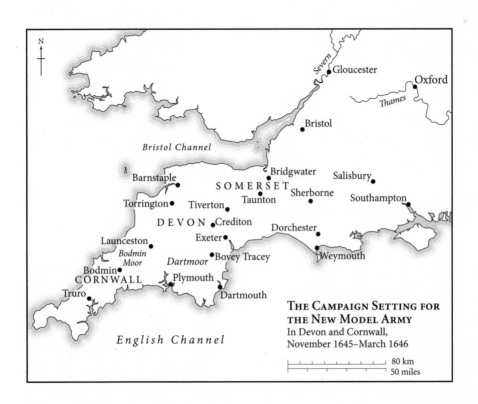

N

Severn

Gloucester

Oxford

Thames

Bristol

Bristol Channel

Bridgwater   Salisbury

Barnstaple   S O M E R S E T   Sherborne

Torrington ●   Tiverton   Taunton   Southampton

D E V O N   Crediton

Launceston   Exeter   Dorchester

Bodmin   *Dartmoor*   Bovey Tracey

Moor   Weymouth

Bodmin   Plymouth

C O R N W A L L

Truro   Dartmouth

English Channel

**The Campaign Setting for
the New Model Army**
In Devon and Cornwall,
November 1645–March 1646

80 km

50 miles

INTRODUCTION

Why another book about Oliver Cromwell? The question is one which may readily occur to anybody familiar with the history of his period. There can be few other figures from the British and Irish past about whom as much has already been published as on him: indeed, he seems to be the most heavily studied ruler in the whole story of these islands, and in recent years the pace of publication on him has accelerated markedly. Since 1990 there have already been five successive full-scale biographies by distinguished academic scholars.[1] In addition, the same period has seen the long and important entry by John Morrill in the *Oxford Dictionary of National Biography*, three book-length studies of Cromwell as a soldier, and three major collections of essays upon his career and its impact.[2] Around these may be piled the essay-length surveys of his life and character, and the books, articles and chapters which have concentrated on particular episodes of his story, let alone those on individual events and personalities involved in it, which in turn reflect upon him. It is perfectly in order to suggest that changing historical preoccupations mean that a leading historical figure needs to be considered anew in each generation: but such considerations hardly justify a new life of this one in on average every five years.

Such a phenomenon might be the more explicable if these recent biographers had disagreed fundamentally, and created a controversy which has provoked further interventions: but the exact opposite has been true.

Although differing slightly in preoccupation and nuance, all of them since 1990 have given us essentially the same man, an intensely courageous, devout and high-principled one whose most important relationship was with his God and whose main political goal was to bring to fruition that God's intentions for the English. The corollary of this view, common to all these recent writers, is to make Cromwell's own mighty, complex and conflicted personality the driving motor of events, subordinating contextual factors to its will on a personal journey of revelation and implementation.[3] So why, with such apparent consensus, has this stream of books continued, and why does it continue here?

Part of the reason must lie in the sheer importance and allure of their subject, that of the only English commoner to become the overall head of state, and so arguably the greatest commoner of all time. Moreover, Cromwell's story is as sensational as his eventual achievement, for he spent the first two-thirds of his life as an obscure, minor and apparently unambitious provincial gentleman before some of the most dramatic events in world history pitched him into supreme military and then political power in around a dozen years. He was, in addition, a soldier who never lost a battle or failed in a siege, despite taking up the trade of arms only in middle age and learning it entirely on the job. The harvest of national memory which he has reaped as a result has been proportionate. His is the statue past which anybody walks on the most direct route from the outside world to the British House of Commons. He has more than two hundred and fifty streets and roads named after him in England, beating any other historical character with the exception of Queen Victoria and – perhaps – the Duke of Wellington. When the British Broadcasting Corporation held a poll to mark the new millennium by identifying the greatest British figure of the passing one, Cromwell came in third, after Shakespeare and Churchill but ahead of any monarch. He has joined that select band of historical personalities who have become legendary, in the sense that they are best known for words they never actually spoke or actions they never took. Just as there is no evidence that King Alfred ever burned any cakes, Sir Francis Drake played bowls on Plymouth Hoe, Sir Walter Raleigh dropped his cloak over a puddle or Marie Antoinette suggested that the French should eat cake, so there is none that Cromwell ever told his men to 'trust in God and keep your powder dry': the phrase was popularized by the immensely influential Victorian scholar Samuel Rawson Gardiner, to sum up his character as Gardiner saw it.[4]

Oliver Cromwell is, therefore, a big, alluring subject, one of the clearest examples of the way in which an individual personality can credibly sway history and so justify historical biography as a meaningful sub-discipline. This is not in itself, however, the most compelling apparent reason for the persistence of new lives of the man. There is, I would suggest, an uneasy feeling among experts in his period that Cromwell is still somehow eluding them, and that nobody has as yet quite managed to get to grips with him. Back in 1937 the compiler of the fullest edition of documents yet associated with him moaned that 'what we have gained in truth we have, in a sense, lost in certainty', when dealing with Cromwell.[5] Since then this unease has increased. One of his recent biographers has commented that despite the huge number of preceding lives, 'many of the historical problems concerning him have never been satisfactorily answered'.[6] Another added that 'there is general agreement, first, that Cromwell is one of the great figures of British history, and yet also, second, that the nature of that greatness is shrouded in paradox'.[7] Some of that paradox lies in the chasm between his own representations of himself, in private as well as public, and the views taken of him by the majority of his contemporaries, including many who knew him well, and found him to be ruthless, devious and self-promoting, for many of them to the point of hypocrisy. More can be found in the manner in which he either abandoned or turned savagely against institutions, ideas and people whom he had previously professed solemnly to uphold and admire. There is no doubt that he was both godly and wily, and the two seem at times to jar with each other. There is equally little doubt that he spoke, alternately, a language of healing, conservation and preservation, and one of charismatic and apocalyptic reform, and could be deliberately vague in defining concrete goals in either case. He was at once an outstanding success in achieving and maintaining power and a dismal failure in obtaining the ultimate aims which he set himself in taking it.

Nonetheless, his recent biographers, while acknowledging these problems, have all resolved them in much the same way, which is why their portraits of the man are so similar. They have ended up by discounting the criticisms and condemnations of Cromwell made by contemporaries, and taking him essentially at his own evaluation. This is largely because ultimately they have taken him, literally, at his own word, because so many of his words have been preserved. The quantity and quality of them surpass those of any other ruler of England before Victoria, and they have been offered up in ever more capacious editions since the early nineteenth century. As a result, while the quality can beguile biographers, as it apparently provides direct access to the true workings of his mind, so the quantity can overpower them. It is too easy to use the letters and speeches as the scaffolding on which the rest of the book can be hung, and Cromwell's self-representation as the objective test of validity against which other historical records may be measured. Over the past three decades there has been a growing sense of this problem among experts. In 1990 the editor of a distinguished collection of new studies of Cromwell could introduce them by declaring that 'the essays in this volume have quite properly allowed him to speak for himself. They have not been insouciant or uncritical, but they have projected a picture of a man very close to the image he projected of himself.'[8] By contrast, the editor of another important collection, in 2009, emphasized that his contributors were careful not to take Cromwell at his own word, but to try to see him through the eyes of others.[9] The first contributor in order of appearance criticized biographers for their tendency to 'view the Great Man in isolation'.[10] Certainly, the person who emerged as a result of this treatment was sometimes less admirable than the one in the biographies.

It is possible that this shift in opinion may have been slightly influenced by my own work, in that for thirty years I have advocated a better contextualization of Cromwell in the surrounding events and pressures of his time. I have also suggested that this process reveals a man who was more pragmatic and more devious than the one represented by his own speeches and writings.[11] Colleagues have accordingly encouraged me to undertake a proper biography. When considering this, I was daunted by two aspects of the task as I saw it. The first was the sheer scale of the enterprise needed to carry out a close reading of Cromwell's own words in the setting provided by the records of the time and the testimonies of his contemporaries. The exercise represented by the collection in 2009 had consisted of administering this treatment to slivers of his career, which could each fit into an essay. To undertake the whole would probably result in a book massive, congested and unwieldy enough to deter both publishers and readers. My other concern was with what would result if I found that – as I suspected would happen – in many cases the conflict of evidence was such that the historical truth could never be recovered with certainty. The outcome, in a full-length life, would be a chaos of possibilities bereft of both narrative power and psychological insight – the two qualities which can make biography a compelling form – however effective the demonstration might be of the difficulties of writing history in a postmodern age. My eventual solution has been to undertake the enterprise for the part of Cromwell's life until the end of the Great Civil War, his first forty-eight years in which he established himself as a national figure. This seemed to represent engagement on a scale which could be managed in a book of normal size, especially as I was already very familiar with many of the events, personalities and sources. To be able to treat developments in detail, through a more focused study, would also enable insights which would not be possible in more broad-brush coverage. Such, at any rate, has been my framework for the enterprise, as developed through the middle years of the 2010s and put into action in the last few. With a trepidation that can be imagined, I now launch it onto the ocean of publication.

1

THE PREHISTORIC CROMWELL

THE PROBLEM

It has already been mentioned that Cromwell passed the first two-thirds of his life in relative obscurity. This is a fact which has vexed his biographers literally since the time of his death, at which point accounts of his life immediately began to appear. For a few months, when his son Richard had succeeded him as head of state, they were slavishly admiring, and for a year after that, with the republic over which Cromwell had presided still in place, generally warm. Then came the restoration of most parts of the political system which he and his allies had overthrown, and biographies of him turned vitriolic. What all these early accounts have in common, however, is how little the authors could dig up about his first forty years, even though most of those were within the living memory of many people at the time. Moreover, some of the apparent facts which they did establish turn out almost certainly to have been wrong.

One of the very few pieces of information about Cromwell's youth of which his first biographers were sure was that he had studied law at Lincoln's Inn, one of the London 'Inns of Court' which were the schools of the profession. It was included in the summary of his life posted above his body as it lay in state before his funeral, and so must have been believed by people close to him; and it popped up regularly in eulogies of him over the following year.[1] Lincoln's Inn, however, has good enrolment records, and his name is not in them, although his father and other relatives did study there.[2] It may therefore have been natural to somebody at his death to assume, wrongly, that he had studied there too, and to record it as a means of emphasizing his credentials as a conventionally educated gentleman. His detractors liked to emphasize instead that he, or in some versions one of his parents, had run a brewery when he was young, and this became so much part of received belief that under the restored monarchy visitors to his home town were shown what was supposed to have been the brewhouse concerned.[3] The assertion was clearly intended to undermine his claims to social respectability, and was first made by political enemies soon after he had become prominent. It looks, then, like a satirical and libellous false-hood, but cannot be conclusively disproved.[4]

Occasionally enemies seem to have tried to deceive posterity by falsifying records. The register of the parish church he attended in his thirties twice cites him as having to do penance for moral misdeeds, but these are the only such entries in it, and penances were not usually put into registers; so they look like insertions intended to defame him.[5] A similarly hostile hand seems to have erased the record of Cromwell's baptism in the same register, only for a more kindly one to re-enter it, adding a date of birth for him – raising some slight doubt over whether either of these subsequently interpolated dates can entirely be trusted.[6] Furthermore, later seemingly unbiased contemporary commenta-tors sometimes made assertions about Cromwell's early career which would overturn accepted accounts of it if they were true, but which can neither be verified nor disproved. For example, when Cromwell was leading the nation in 1655 the current ambassador from Venice reported that a Jew had come to visit him from Antwerp, having known Cromwell when he was travelling in Flanders in his youth.[7] No other source mentions such a visit, and none credits Cromwell with any travel to the Continent at all, at any point of his life. Flanders, a province under Spanish and Roman Catholic rule at the time, would be an unlikely destination for a young Protestant. So, the statement looks like a mistake; but this also cannot be conclusively demonstrated.[8]

When all such probable false trails are disregarded, the solid records for Cromwell's first forty years remain a sparse collection of legal and official documents, with a few letters and a single speech. This is the rickety and incomplete skeleton which successive biographers have fleshed out according to their own tastes. The rest of this chapter will be devoted to a fresh inspection of it, in the light of accumulated scholarly knowledge and with a greater scepticism regarding the degree of certainty with which a story can be constructed.

THE SETTING

Whatever the difficulties of Cromwell's early life for a historian, its setting can be reconstructed with a fair amount of confidence.[9] Through the heart of this flows a river, the aptly named Great Ouse, the biggest watercourse of the East Midlands. It is indeed the only river in Britain to pass successively through three county towns, Buckingham, Bedford and Huntingdon, and then a cathedral city, Ely. Before the modern processes of dredging and embankment it was – like most English rivers – a much more complex and wilful waterway, with a greater number of islands, bends and channels. In high summer its waters would have been a mass of quivering reflections. Kingfishers would have drawn azure lines of flight across its banks and nested in round holes bored into them. Its edges would be crowded with coarse clumps of comfrey and figwort, giant dock leaves and fragrant foamy meadowsweet, and with moorhens, bumblebees, dragonflies, orange-billed swans with cygnets, bright beetles and lizards. The lush meadows along its banks would have had grazing bullocks and sheep, singing skylarks, circling rooks, and grasshoppers, cowpats and caterpillars. Twisted pollard willows would dip their toes in its waters like old grey men, and elders would spill the heavy, heady scent of their creamy blossoms. The Ouse was, however, prone to flood, even in July, and in winter regularly turned into a single huge stream the colour of gun metal, burying its banks and islets and carrying a flotsam of torn planks and wrecked hayricks. It was also in quieter moods a great industrial and commercial highway. Watermills ground out flour along its banks and in its smaller channels, and barges of every shape and size sailed or were hauled along it, piled with goods and thronged with passengers from its vast hinterland, and from London and the ports all around the North Sea.

Ashore, the young Cromwell's world was divided into two halves. The western one consisted of an undulating clay plateau with nucleated villages set in a largely open countryside, like much of the East Midlands. Farming in most of it was still based on the medieval system of three enormous fields, each shared out into strips of which individual farmers held several in each, ranging across the best and the worst land to provide a rough parity. Crops rotated between these, so that in any one year typically one would grow grain, one vegetables – especially peas, lentils and beans – and one be left to grass and weeds on which livestock would be grazed. The system was designed to ensure that the land was regularly fertilized, with nitrogen from the vegetables and manure from the animals, to withstand the depleting effect of cereals. The field under grazing was almost ideal territory for walkers and riders, with nothing to impede them except the gentle corrugation of the green surface by the strip-holdings bounded by their slight ditches, a pattern which still shows up in the modern landscape long after the system has been abandoned. The cereal and vegetable fields were, however, heavy going in summer and early autumn when the crops caught at feet and hooves. For a period after harvest they could be easily traversed, but as soon as they were ploughed the thick and heavy brown soil would become a serious impediment. It would be given an added dimension of nastiness by the fact that most human excrement from the villages and towns was spread across it as extra fertilizer, after being carried thither in carts from the cesspits and tubs.

Nowhere in this region did woodland represent more than a fifth of the ground cover, but woods and copses were still an important part of the landscape and economy. There were stands of oaks, with their dark, ridged bark and full crowns of lobed leaves; of ashes, with paler, straighter and more slender trunks and sprays of spear-like foliage; of beeches, smooth grey pillars with knobbly roots and leaves which turned the woodland floors into a red-gold fire at the end of autumn; and of elms, with furrowed bark, papery leaves and sweeping branches. The East Midland oak woods were one of the main haunts of the most magnificent of British dryland butterflies, the purple emperor, and the woods in general had an additional, auditory, beauty in the songs of blackbirds, robins and nightingales. They were also, in their way, a crop as intensively protected, managed and exploited as those of the fields, as out of them had to come the materials for most fuel, buildings, furniture, household utensils, and the construction of boats and shipping. In autumn acorns and beech mast provided a crucial fattening food for pigs. Outside woods individual great trees studded fields and thoroughfares, though hedges were relatively rare, except on boundaries such as those of parishes where they were grown tall and thick, often of hawthorn or blackthorn, with few openings. This complex landscape would have been of importance to the young Cromwell during the brief period in his life when he became directly involved in farming; but it would have a different and more acute kind of vital significance to him later in life, when he had to wage war over it.

The clay lands through which the Ouse flowed for the first half of its length represented a terrain familiar across much of lowland England, but after it had passed Huntingdon, and then the little town of St Ives, the river plunged into an utterly different world. This comprised the great marshes known as the Fens, a landscape found elsewhere in Britain only rarely and in miniature. It was almost completely flat, save for occasional islands of which the largest and most important was that of Ely. In winter much of it flooded, and these waters were echoed at many other times by dense mists and fogs. Eight rivers crossed it, of which the Ouse was the mightiest, and their banks, and those of the many ditches which seamed it, were formed of glossy black peat soil. In summer much of it was a vast water meadow, golden with buttercups and marsh marigold in early summer and waving with pollen heads at the season's height, with the occasional apple tree.

Large areas, however, remained under water, as meres, marsh or channels, and these waved with tall stands of whispering feathery sedge, spiked teasels, dark brown bullrush heads, and the thin green spears of reeds.

Much of the fauna of this land was as strange to outsiders as its flora. There were huge flocks of wildfowl, some coming for the winter such as geese of different kinds, cream-crested wigeons and whooping yellow-billed swans. Others nested there in summer, or were resident, like glossy brown mallards, little streak-winged teals with metallic green eye-patches, and garganeys, their heads striped in lemon. Tall grey cranes danced and trumpeted, bitterns sounded their booming cry from reed beds, ruffs displayed their great salmon-pink collars, harrier hawks planed above the sedge and rushes, and black and white ospreys, fish eagles, swooped above the open waters. Also flying about these green wetlands were distinctive and magnificent butterflies, yellow and black swallowtails and large coppers with their burnished wings. When darkness fell, yet stranger apparitions sometimes danced through the air above the water and the greenery: the small pale flames known as will-o'-the-wisps or jack-o'-lanterns, which tradition held variously to be either nature spirits or souls of the restless dead.

Like the clay-land oak woods, these apparent nature reserves were sites of intense and valuable economic activity, the rights to which were zealously guarded and contested. Cattle and sheep grazed abundantly in the summer grasslands, yielding milk, cheese, butter and wool, and huge crops of hay were mown there. Fish and eels were taken in great quantity from the waters, and rushes provided both cattle fodder and coverings for house floors. Reeds and sedge made thatching for their roofs and some of the wetland plants – red mace and yellow flag iris – were woven into mats, baskets and horse collars. Peat was cut for fuel, and waterfowl were lured or driven into nets, trapped upon sticky limed twigs, or knocked down with poles when moulting, before being sold for their meat and feathers. Teasels were used in cloth-making, and flax and hemp harvested on the edge of marshland. The wetland trees, willow and alder, provided baskets, hurdles and jetties. The inhabitants of the region, whose settlements clustered on the islands and the fen edge, were accordingly both more prosperous and more independent than those who lived on the clay land to the south and west.

Cromwell himself, however, was a townsman. From birth to death he lived in urban centres, though sometimes small, and when in later life he became the owner of large country estates with fine mansions and castles, he showed no interest in retreating to them. He was born in Huntingdon, and stayed there until his thirties, when he moved east to St Ives, and then further east to Ely. All were on the Ouse, but were very different one from another. Huntingdon was the capital of its shire, a proper chartered corporation which sent representatives to Parliament, situated where the most important highway in England, the Great North Road which the Romans had built to link London to York, crossed the river. Like a lot of English river towns Huntingdon was basically a high street running down to a bridge, with a marketplace halfway along and a few other streets poking out.[10] By Cromwell's time it had long been in decline, having lost three-quarters of the parishes it had possessed at its medieval high point; and the one in which he himself was baptized would not last out the seventeenth century. Huntingdon lacked paving for its streets and virtually all of the buildings were of timber and thatch. Nonetheless it retained the social and economic as well as the political trappings of an important town, with inns, taverns, shops, industries and some large private dwellings. Perhaps two thousand people lived there, almost half of whom could vote in borough elections, put their beasts to graze on the common lands and send their sons to the grammar school.[11] Today, Huntingdon remains infused with the memory of its most famous son, whose name appears there repeatedly, on businesses, surgeries and local government buildings.

St Ives was a miniature of Huntingdon about five miles downstream, with the same layout but no corporation and one parish church. What made it a place of any note was its annual market, frequented by Dutch merchants. Still, it had about half the population of Huntingdon, and contained clothiers, metalworkers, grain merchants and leatherworkers who all sent their produce off down the Ouse. Oliver Cromwell remains the most celebrated resident and has a statue there.[12] In contrast to both Huntingdon and St Ives, Ely was dominated, in every respect, by its cathedral, the tall golden western tower of which, shining like a lantern in sunlight, acted as a landmark for travellers of the Fens, as it still does. Its bishop, dean and chapter controlled the appointment of local officials and supervised the economy of the small town (which the cathedral made technically a city) and large island around, with their trade along the river, the good farming on the greensand soil of the isle, and the natural riches of the marshes around. In times of flood or fog, the great cathedral and its surrounding settlement floated above the water and vapour like a ship.[13]

Many aspects of the physical environment of the young Cromwell would seem alien to a modern person, and two of those were its darkness and its peace. Both would have a bearing on his experience as a soldier. Homes were illuminated by fires and (mostly tallow) candles, but the outside world at night was largely unlit by humans.[14] Huntingdon required innkeepers to hang lanterns outside their doors during business hours after dark, but otherwise there seems to have been no obligation to light the streets even in this important local centre.[15] This would have had the effect of increasing the menacing and disturbing reputation of the night for contemporary humans.[16] As a species we are not equipped to deal well with low light or darkness, which make us vulnerable, and it is not surprising that the belief systems of most of the English of Cromwell's time populated the night with ghosts, demons and other malevolent spirits. Lack of artificial light also made the heavenly bodies of the night all the more conspicuous and important. The stage of the moon would have made a considerable difference to the degree of visibility, and the lack of human light pollution would have powdered a clear night with stars, so that the flesh as well as the bones of constellations was apparent. This would in turn have made anomalies in the sky, such as comets or supernovae, all the more conspicuous and laden with possible divine portent.

As for quietness, this was a world in which the loudest regular natural sounds were the murmuring and sighing of the wind and the songs and cries of birds. The loudest sounds in the human world were church bells, giving the latter a prominence which their centrality to the community deserved, whether as calls to pray together or to gather in arms to face threats. In the natural world, storms, with screaming or roaring gales or claps of thunder, would have been especially impressive, and possible manifestations of divine wrath. In the human one, the hubbub of a market day or the tumult of an angry crowd would have been all the more disruptive and dramatic, and the most striking embodiment of both those qualities of sound was war, based on the relatively new gunpowder technology. The crash of field and siege artillery, the reports of massed muskets, the accumulating thunder of horses' hooves and the roaring of attacking soldiers and the screaming of the injured, would, according to one's viewpoint, echo either the might and fury of God himself or the horrors of Hell.

FAMILY AND EARLY LIFE

The vital facts concerning Cromwell's family background, family life and youth were first pieced together by an eighteenth-century clergyman, Mark Noble, who went about his task with the dedication and precision of a modern genealogist.[17] The family tree commences with a minor Welsh landowner from just north of Cardiff, Morgan ap Gwilym, who entered the service of the Tudors before they fought their way to power at the battle of Bosworth in 1485 and received his reward with a job at the royal court. Duly anglicized as Morgan Williams, he married his son Richard to the daughter of another upwardly mobile family, that of Walter Cromwell, a brewer and innkeeper at Putney, on the south bank of the Thames upstream from Westminster. It was apparently a good deal for both, as the Cromwells hovered near the top of the yeoman class, the most prosperous division of the English middling sort, while the Williamses were undoubtedly genteel, but relatively poor and from a people whom the English had traditionally despised.[18] In fact Richard had struck gold, because Walter's son Thomas Cromwell rose to become the chief minister of Henry VIII, carrying his nephew to fortune with him as a trusted and able lieutenant. Richard duly showed his appreciation by adopting the family name Cromwell in 1538, though in legal terms it always remained an alias and documents continued to give both surnames as alternatives down to and after the time of Oliver himself. At moments when the name Cromwell became politically toxic, down to the end of the seventeenth century, members of the family reverted to being Williams, and the whole dynasty retained a pride in its Welsh ancestry. Like the Tudors themselves, they turned a nationality which could in some respects be a social and political liability into an asset, by claiming descent from medieval Welsh princes.[19]

Richard Cromwell (alias Williams) displayed his intelligence and dexterity again in managing to retain royal favour after the spectacular fall and execution of his mighty brother-in-law. He ended his life peacefully in possession of a large collection of landed estates, with a particular concentration in Huntingdonshire which made him the leading magnate of that county and yielded him £3,000 a year, the income of a lord. That local dominance passed down to his grandson, Sir Oliver, who led the family in the first decades of the seventeenth century: his portrait shows a self-confident man in an expensive black suit and fancy lace collar, with the large bulbous nose which was a family hallmark and which our Oliver duly inherited.[20] The Cromwells were fertile as well as rich, and Sir Oliver had five brothers and five sisters who survived to adulthood. Most of these married into leading gentry families across south-eastern England – three of the girls wedded knights – and so established a web of potentially useful connections and alliances.[21]

Our Cromwell was the son of Sir Oliver's next brother, called Robert, who was set up by their father as one of the most important inhabitants of Huntingdon. He was established in a fine house in the high street, with an income of around £300 a year, roughly that with which Morgan had started out, which put him at the lower end of the gentry class. On the other hand, it was a genteel income, in that Robert did not have to earn any of it because it was based on rents and a share of local tithes, the regular payment made by parishioners for the upkeep of their minister, of which since the Reformation secular landowners creamed off part in many parishes. Moreover, he punched above his economic weight, representing his town in Parliament and serving in the county as a justice of the peace and the high sheriff, offices normally associated with the greater gentry. This was probably because of the importance of his father, continued in his elder brother, who both dominated not only the county but the town. Their main seat was Hinchingbrooke, a Tudor confection of grey stone and red brick with pepper-pot chimneys, a mile west of Huntingdon.[22] Sir Oliver duly became godfather to his brother's only son, who was therefore named after him. Robert Cromwell has left no recorded words and no authenticated portrait, and nobody remembered anything that he had actually done.[23] He therefore seems like a nonentity, but that may be a harsh expression for a contented and unambitious man.

Robert married locally and into his own class, of urban gentry, by choosing Elizabeth, the daughter of William Steward of Ely, who owned and leased a substantial landed estate, to judge from that subsequently held by his son Thomas. Robert and Elizabeth duly produced a large family, with one son but six daughters who survived childhood: Elizabeth, Catherine, Margaret, Anna, Jane and Robina. Oliver was born after Elizabeth and Catherine, on 25 April 1599 if the register entry can be trusted, and given the education of a gentleman's heir. He was sent to the town grammar school, where he would in theory have been taught English grammar, Latin, Greek, philosophy and mathematics.[24] This qualified him to matriculate on 23 April 1616 at Sidney Sussex College, Cambridge, a new and relatively poor but fashionable foundation. It was built of rose-red brick with stone facings, around a courtyard. He was enrolled as a 'fellow commoner', paying higher fees to get a room to himself and the same food as the dons, and so again underlining his gentility. The syllabus offered more Greek, Latin and philosophy, with rhetoric and logic.[25]

Young Oliver could, however, spend no more than fourteen months there before he was plucked out by the first climactic event of his life, the death of his father in June 1617. It is in keeping with the minimal presence of Robert Cromwell in history that we do not know how sudden and unexpected this was, or how much of an impact it made on Oliver, and we do not indeed know what relations between them were like at all. We do, however, know the economic consequences, from Robert's will, which bequeathed two-thirds of his estate for twenty-one years to his widow Elizabeth, to provide for their daughters. She was also willed a £600 debt owed to Robert by a relative, and all his goods, and made sole executrix. Oliver was left with the remaining third of his father's estate, and so had somehow to carry on his father's position on about £100 a year, which put him, at best, onto the lowest border of gentility.[26] It was perhaps a sensible step to ensure dowries of the five daughters who were as yet unmarried, as well as to secure the position of Elizabeth. It apparently testifies to Robert's love or concern for his wife, but may also reflect a distrust of his son. Alternatively, it might have been a tax dodge, to try to reduce the liability of Oliver's inheritance to wardship, the levy made by the Crown on the estates of heirs who were still legally minors by selling third parties the right to administer and exploit the estates until those due them came of age.[27] Oliver would get his full inheritance on the verge of middle age, or sooner if his mother decided to hand it over before then. Moreover, he had a good expectation of becoming in addition the heir of his mother's childless brother, now Sir Thomas Steward. Nonetheless, for the time being he was financially pinched. It is a striking proof of the strength of the emotional bond between Oliver and his mother that the arrangement does not seem to have caused any known tension between them. Indeed, she remained a supportive but not meddling background figure for most of the rest of his life, and impressed observers with her prudence and common sense.[28]

Our Cromwell now vanishes from history for three years, to reappear on 22 August 1620 at St Giles's Church, Cripplegate, in the old City of London, where he got married. His bride was Elizabeth, the eldest daughter of a London fur and leather merchant called Sir James Bourchier who was prospering and had leased a landed estate in Essex.[29] The event, once again, shows how little we know of Oliver's youth. His courtship of Elizabeth may have been the product of a lengthy residence by him in the capital, in the course of which he might have had all sorts of experiences and adventures. It could have resulted from a shorter sojourn there, or he might not have gone near the city at all before the wedding but met his wife through a provincial connection: for example, his aunt Joan had married an Essex gentleman. Oliver's union with Elizabeth could have been preceded by a long courtship or a whirlwind romance, and may initially have been a love match or an arranged one. For a financially strapped gentleman like Cromwell to marry into the family of an upwardly mobile City merchant was a classic way of obtaining a much-needed injection of cash in the shape of a dowry. On the other hand there is no surviving record of such an agreement: on the contrary, we find Cromwell himself signing over a significant part of his paltry immediate inheritance to provide a jointure to support his wife. Nor did the wedding beget a lasting alliance between the families: we hear no more of the Bourchiers in Cromwell's affairs. One of the most important developments in his young life, therefore, may be read in various different ways, from a mutually enthusiastic partnering between two houses, perhaps brokered by friends and relatives, to an unexpected love match of which the father of the bride disapproved.

What is certain is that it was a successful marriage, which lasted until the end of Oliver's own life and never displayed any sign of tension, ennui or infidelity. Elizabeth's portrait, made in middle age, shows a woman run to plumpness but preserving signs of unmistakable prettiness in youth, with soft features and a lingering sweetness about the mouth.[30] The passion of their physical relationship, coupled with the fecundity of the Cromwell genes in an age without reliable contraception, is displayed in the steady succession of children which followed the wedding: Robert in 1621, Oliver in 1623, Bridget in 1624, Richard in 1626, Henry in 1628, Elizabeth in 1629 and James in 1631.[31]

As the latest generation of Cromwells emerged, and the oldest was starting to die off, the middle one, Oliver's own, was being settled as his sisters also began to marry. Robert Cromwell's inferior status, as a comparatively poor younger son, shows in the matches that his daughters found. Whereas Robert's sisters had wed major gentry from a wide geographical area, Oliver's found less prominent young men in the local region. Margaret did best, getting Valentine Walton, an important Huntingdonshire landowner who subsequently represented the county in Parliament. Anna married a lesser gentleman from the same shire, Catherine one from a Fen settlement to the north of it, and Robina a clergyman. Jane found John Desborough or Disbrowe, the younger son of the squire of a village in Cambridgeshire south of Huntingdon, who had set himself up as a lawyer.[32] Some of these new in-laws were going to rise with Cromwell himself, and more glamorous matches would lie in store for some of his sisters as he did rise, but for the time being he was getting tied into a respectable but limited local network.

Can any more flesh be put onto these scraps of archival bone? Do we have any sense of what the young Cromwell was like as a person? Here there is an obvious problem with the early biographies of him: that, naturally, enough, the sycophantic accounts produced just after his death represented him as a paragon of sagacity, preparing for a great future, and those written later by political enemies make him an exemplar of most follies and vices, including financial irresponsibility, peevishness and irritability, theft from orchards and pigeon cots, violent aggression, drunkenness and lechery.[33] Various anecdotes from childhood or adolescence were repeated later which presaged his ambition or his greatness.[34] All or none of these portraits and accounts may be true. We are on safer ground when both the admiring and hostile accounts agree on the occasional detail, such as his lack of interest in academic study; but that could have been deduced anyway from his later character. It was noted (in his defence, by a eulogist) that he retained enough Latin to be able to converse in it with foreign ambassadors as head of state.[35] Nevertheless, as an adult he never showed any personal interest in scholarship, and he was markedly free of that devotion to the Greek and Roman classics which characterized so many of his educated contemporaries and peppered their speeches. Nor did he ever talk like a lawyer, common or civil, which is another indication that he did not study law. All that can be said with reasonable certainty of Cromwell as a youth is that he would have been impulsive, and given to fits of savage temper, brooding withdrawal and boisterous good humour; because that is what he was like all his life.

EARLY POLITICAL ACTIVITY

The trail of references to Cromwell gets no greater in the course of the 1620s. The sequence of baptisms of his children shows that he stuck close to home and family in Huntingdon, and a few other records show him playing his part as one of its leading inhabitants. In 1621 his name led the list of citizens, after the bailiffs who presided, witnessing the election of Members of Parliament for the town, and the decade culminated in his own service as an MP in 1628. He probably held urban office and sat on the council, though the archives are too imperfect to prove this. His economic situation remained parlous for somebody operating at this sort of political level, his tax assessment matching that of forty other households in the town. Whether he was so prominent because of his own qualities, the honour paid to his father's memory or the continuing influence of his uncle at Hinchingbrooke, nobody can say. He shows no sign in the 1620s of any especial distinction, ambition, ideology or activity. He appears to be, in fact, remarkably like his father.[36]

Nonetheless, his arrival in Parliament placed him briefly at the centre of one of the biggest political storms in early modern English history. For almost three decades, since the accession of the Stuart royal family to the throne, tension had been growing, and in 1628–9 it finally produced political breakdown. The causes were various. One was simply that the Stuarts came from Scotland, a kingdom always independent of England and occupied by a people whom the English traditionally despised as inferior and disliked as frequent enemies. The first of them to hold both thrones, James VI of Scotland and I of England, therefore automatically ran up against anti-Scottish prejudice, and suffered from the unprecedented burden of having to run both kingdoms at once. To compensate the Scots for the removal of their royal court, he awarded English titles, money and offices to many of them, so incurring English resentment and disapproval. Moreover, his accession coincided with the conclusion of the English conquest of Ireland, landing him with a third burden, a divided land full of resentful natives, which could not meet the costs of an expensive English occupation that the English themselves did not want to fund. In addition, James inherited from the previous monarch, the very popular, long-lived and successful Tudor queen Elizabeth, a state financial system which had been allowed to run down near to the point of collapse, and which needed complete reform by a political nation unaware of the problem and disinclined to believe in it. After failure to work with a Parliament to find a solution, the royal government was only able to survive by putting up the customs rates on its own authority, which it had no clear constitutional right to do.

To these functional problems, James and his son Charles I, who succeeded him in March 1625, added misjudgements. Both, and especially Charles, pursued controversial religious policies, which will be discussed below. James, who had functioned effectively in Scotland, did not understand the rules of English parliamentary politics and puzzled and alarmed many of his new subjects. He increasingly relied on unpopular favourites, who were often suspected of exerting an inappropriate influence over his judgement for their own personal profit. Charles was a well-intentioned but obstinate and formulaic conviction politician, with poor personal skills and a tendency to indecision punctuated by fits of desperate action following panic. He initially continued reliance on his father's least popular favourite, and started two disastrous foreign wars simultaneously, which lessened the military reputation of the English and plunged the royal finances into a huge deficit. Within a decade of taking the throne, King James had found it difficult to work with Parliaments in a way true of no Tudor monarch, and this remained the case until his death. Charles's wars made the situation still worse, as Parliaments in 1625 and 1626 increasingly lost faith in his government and demanded changes to it, as the price of financial support, which he was not prepared to make. At the same time, the continuing decay of an unreformed national fiscal system meant that when war taxes were voted, they yielded much less than MPs believed that they would. Once again, the royal regime survived by bending constitutional rules, and levying a 'Forced Loan' on wealthier subjects, which seventy-five refused to pay. The Parliament which Cromwell joined in 1628 was called in a desperate attempt to mend relations and get the normal system working again. After a promising first session, it ended in catastrophe in 1629, when a majority of the House of Commons condemned the king's ministers for both his financial and his religious policies. Charles dissolved the Parliament in fury and settled down to rule without one for what turned out to be an unprecedented length of time.[37]

Naturally, we do not know what the still obscure Oliver Cromwell thought of any of these events, including the climactic series in the Parliament. Six of his cousins had refused to pay the Forced Loan, but being a Cromwell he had a lot of cousins, and we can only guess at whether he sympathized with these.[38] He was one of the majority that refused to adjourn the House of Commons as the king had initially ordered when the crisis came in 1629, and so presumably shared its anger with royal policies. Otherwise, he made just one recorded speech, which will be considered later.[39]

He returned to Huntingdon, but the town was now in the throes of dramatic change, which was to end his familiar life there. His uncle, the flamboyant Sir Oliver, had one serious weakness, financial extravagance, and by the late 1620s this was eroding his inherited role as the county magnate. In 1627 it collapsed, as he was obliged to sell his seat of Hinchingbrooke and retreat north to his lesser mansion of Ramsey on an island in the Fens. The gap created by his withdrawal was filled immediately by a rising gentry family, the Montagus, which had made fortunes in the law and already dominated eastern Northamptonshire from Boughton and Kimbolton Castles. In the 1620s the head of the family was made Lord Montagu of Boughton and his still more successful younger brother, who had entered royal service, became the earl of Manchester. The earl was now expanding the family power eastwards. In 1624 and 1625 Montagus represented Huntingdonshire in Parliament alongside Sir Oliver, but from 1626 they controlled both county seats. It was the earl who bought Hinchingbrooke from the knight and planted his younger brother there to oversee Huntingdon and the south and centre of the shire. Our Oliver was elected MP for the town in 1628 alongside one of the earl's younger sons, and it is not known whether this was because of his popularity there, or the last gasp of his uncle's influence, or a goodwill gesture towards the Cromwells by the new magnate.[40]

The change seems, nonetheless, to have destabilized Huntingdon's politics, as well as leaving Oliver more vulnerable in them even while his economic position had not improved: in 1627 he had sold two closes of land, a sign of financial pressure.[41] In 1630 the town's leaders petitioned the king for a new charter, which would replace an elected common council with aldermen who served for life, as the town government. It was granted, and Cromwell was not among the new aldermen, although he was made a justice of the peace. He then got into a heated quarrel with the new town leadership, together with another man who had been snubbed by the new arrangements. Both were reported to the king's Privy Council for misconduct, summoned to London, deemed culpable by the council, and committed to custody while the earl of Manchester investigated the matter. The targets of Cromwell's abuse had been the current mayor and a slick lawyer called Robert Bernard who served as the borough's recorder (legal officer) and had drawn up the new charter. The occasion of Cromwell's outburst had not been the charter itself, which had been supported by both Sir Oliver Cromwell and the earl himself, and not opposed in the town, but the power it gave the new town rulers to levy fines on those who refused to serve as aldermen, dispose of town property and graze extra cattle on the common land. The earl removed two of these powers and reduced the third, but also ruled that Cromwell and his companion had expressed themselves with language unacceptable in public life and forced both men to make a public apology. Cromwell duly offered it, pleading that the offending words were uttered 'in heat and passion' and asking for pardon. To rub salt into Cromwell's wounds, the earl also praised Bernard, by contrast, for his conduct.[42] A mixture of misfortune, political folly and emotional intemperance had cast Oliver out of power in his home town and inflicted a bruising humiliation upon him.

His reaction has long been famed among his modern biographers, and was as impulsive and furious as that which had got him into trouble in the first place: within a few months, by 7 May 1631 and with the consent of his mother, wife and uncle, he had sold almost all of his property in and around Huntingdon, and moved away.[43] This brought in £1,800, which would mean that Cromwell's income at that time was where he had started at his father's death, at around £100 a year: but we do not know whether his mother had released any of her share of the inheritance to him, and so what financial losses may have been disguised by this. His house was included in the sale, but his mother rented it back immediately from the new owner, and so continued to live there herself. The rest of the family moved with him to nearby St Ives, and it is not known why they chose that town. It may have been because the minister there was an old friend from Cambridge, as will be discussed, or because the lord of the manor, Henry Lawrence, was another of Oliver's numerous relations, or because their new home was closer to Ely and Sir Thomas Steward, whose principal heir Oliver now seemed to be.

Around this time, Cromwell was in trouble with the royal authorities again, because of one of the gambits adopted by the government to repair the dreadful financial problem left by the failure of its wars and parliamentary sessions. This was to revive the medieval custom whereby substantial landowners had either to present themselves at a royal coronation to be knighted or pay a fine. The custom had apparently not been active for over a century, but was still legally in existence, and as nobody had presented himself at Charles's coronation in accordance with it, this meant that all defaulters could be fined. The bar of eligibility was officially where it had been around 1500, at an income of forty pounds a year from property. Since then there had been a monetary inflation of around 400 per cent, and so thousands of minor gentlemen and yeomen, now far below the economic threshold of a knight, were caught in the fiscal trap, including Cromwell. It was another blow to befall him during this dreadful period, and it is not surprising, given his preoccupations, which may have included financial difficulties, that he initially defaulted. There is no sign that he had any principled objection to the levy, although he may have done. He was duly listed for defaulting by a county commission led by his uncle Sir Oliver and Sir Sidney Montagu, but agreed to pay up and eventually did so, handing over a minimal ten pounds and not being treated as a resister.[44]

The fine imposed was that given to a yeoman and not a gentleman, and is one signal of how much Cromwell's social position had declined. At St Ives he became a working tenant farmer, renting a large house, Slepe Hall, and some of the rich meadows along the Ouse, where he apparently kept livestock and grew willows for building and furniture. His new status was apparent in legal documents. At Huntingdon, he had been addressed, despite his relatively low income, as 'esquire', the mark of somebody from the upper rank of gentry, who filled county offices. At St Ives he became 'Mr', the title of a minor gentleman or prosperous yeoman.[45] He seems to have joined the vestry, the body which appointed most of the town's officials, because he was apparently recorded at its annual appointment of them in 1633 and is likewise apparently recorded at that in 1634, heading the list of signatories and so suggesting that he had already assumed some role of local leadership. However, in the first case the place where his name should be has been cut out and the signature in the second may be a fake, interpolated later.[46] Even if he became a big fish in a small Huntingdonshire pond, he was clearly now far below the level of the county elite, represented locally by the Lawrences who owned the manor and the Montagus, whose tentacles now reached St Ives where the earl of Manchester gained control of the profits of the market, the bridge and the manorial court, in which 'Mr' Cromwell was punished in October 1633 when his shepherd drove a flock onto the wrong land.

One of the most telling signs of the trauma of this period lies in Oliver's reproductive history. Until 1632 the almost annual arrival of a new baby to him and Elizabeth had continued steadily: then it ceased, for five years. This being, as said, an age without reliable contraception, such a break is a strong indication of a cessation of physical marital relations. It may have been the result of personal grief, as the last child to arrive before the gap was James, who was christened on 8 January 1632 and buried the next day.[47] The loss of a baby, the first of their offspring to die young, may have left the Cromwells disinclined to venture into parenthood again for a long time, especially if the birth had been dangerous to Elizabeth. Alternatively, financial hardship may have propelled an exercise in family limitation, if there was no certainty that Oliver's farm would prosper. In addition it is possible that the shock of his political and social humiliation may have left him in a state of prolonged depression. Whatever the reason, there were no more children during the St Ives years.

There is a chance that Cromwell's mental state was more generally disturbed at this time, and had been for a while. In 1628 the renowned physician Sir Theodore Mayerne, based in London, recorded that he had treated a 'Monsieur Cromwell' and found him *valde melancholicus*, which could be translated as 'very depressed' or even 'severely unbalanced'.[48] Decades later, a memoirist recalled that another medical man, John Simcott, had told him that in his Huntingdonshire years Oliver would sometimes lie abed 'all melancholy', and was neurotic enough to send for Simcott in the middle of the night because he thought himself to be dying. On other occasions Cromwell had 'strange fancies' about Huntingdon's medieval stone cross, said that a spirit had predicted that he would be 'the greatest man in the kingdom' or became 'most splenetic'.[49] It would be easy to link these pieces of evidence to his change of fortunes and suggest that increasing financial and political insecurity during the late 1620s generated a tendency to depressive illness which developed in the early 1630s into a full-scale nervous breakdown.

The evidence, however, loses solidity on closer inspection. Mayerne was actually treating his patient for dry skin, stomach aches after eating and a pain in the side, and a phlegmy cough. The sufferer may simply have been cast down by his (temporary) afflictions. Alternatively, by 'melancholia', the doctor may have signified a literal meaning, of a surfeit of black bile on which, according to medieval medical convention, such symptoms might be blamed. Furthermore, the Cromwell concerned may not have been our man at all, but one of his cousins.[50] Simcott's account is an overtly hostile one, recorded second-hand by a political enemy of Cromwell, and combines experiences which the doctor was claimed to have had himself with the story of the spirit's prediction, which was acknowledged to be reported by others. In later years, Cromwell showed none of the hypochondria and melodrama alleged against him here. Simcott's actual case-book has survived and does not contain any of this information, only the rather delightful snippet that Cromwell had taken a medicine alleged to ward off the plague and accidentally cured the pimples from which he had suffered.[51] There is, however, a more credible account of his physical ill-health in this period, recorded in the eighteenth century from the parish clerk of St Ives, who had been told it by very old people surviving from the time when Cromwell had lived there. It described how he attended church with a piece of red flannel wrapped around his neck, as he was subject to sore throats.[52] This is the kind of trivial and inconsequential visual detail which seems authentic. Apparently the life of a farmer was hard on Oliver.

If so, he may have made a desperate attempt to escape from it in 1635, with an action as impulsive and precipitate as his quarrel at Huntingdon and his subsequent flight from the town. In July of that year his maternal uncle, Sir Thomas Steward, was accused before the authorities of being mentally unfit to manage his own affairs, a charge which is overwhelmingly likely to have originated within his family. Had it been upheld, then use of his possessions would have passed to guardians, normally appointed from among his closest relatives. There were three of those: his wife, his sister, and her only son, Cromwell; and suspicion naturally falls upon the latter, as the person with the most to gain from the action. Moreover, after his death two hostile commentators directly accused him of instigating it, and the very next year after the action an opponent of Cromwell in a lawsuit alleged that Cromwell and his uncle had recently been on bad terms. Whoever did launch the suit, it failed. Sir Thomas's portrait, now in the Cromwell Museum, shows a weak-faced, anxious man with a flamboyant beard and moustache – perhaps a credible subject for such an accusation – but after three months an inquisition at Cambridge pronounced him sane.[53] The evidence therefore points very strongly to Cromwell as involved in the attempt, and quite strongly suggests that he was its driving force: but neither suspicion can quite be proved.

If either is true, then Steward showed an astonishing capacity to forgive, because when he made his will upon his deathbed on 29 January 1636, he still named Cromwell as his principal heir. However, there was a sting in it: the bequest included part of Sir Thomas's freehold, and most of his lease-hold, land, but none of his moveable goods, and Oliver was not allowed to inherit anything until his uncle's debts were paid, which totalled at least £1,300. He had to buy the goods back for £2,000, and after an unsuccessful attempt to overturn the unattractive aspects of the will by a lawsuit, took until the end of 1638 to gain possession of all the land due to him, and so presumably to pay off the debts. After that, he could at last enjoy the whole of the income that his new estate provided, which came to around £450 a year.[54] It was derived mainly from urban property, but also some farm and fen land, and the collection of church tithes. Cromwell seems to have moved immediately to the new home in Ely which was at the heart of the inheritance, a fine brick, stone and tile townhouse surrounded by a complex of offices and storehouses, including a large barn.[55] Even before it was all secured, his new income would have been better than any he had personally enjoyed before, and when it was fully delivered it made him richer than his father and unequivocally one of the urban gentry of the region. Like a gentleman, he did not have to work to earn most of it. Within the year he had leased more land from Clare College, Cambridge, and had been appointed to his uncle's place on the board of trustees of Ely's most important charity. In its official papers he was restored to the rank of

'esquire', and his return to this rank was signalled further b
ment in 1638 as a justice of the peace – one of the local r
tried minor offences and carried out much local administratio..
Isle.[56] The effect of Cromwell's change of fortune on his marital life i.
signalled by the immediate resumption of the appearance of children: Mary
in 1637 and Frances in 1638.[57] It is important not to overstate his newly
acquired prosperity – the Ely tax returns list him as the eighteenth richest
inhabitant – but it was a great improvement.[58]

Meanwhile the wider affairs of the nation unfolded, and the Crown
pursued its objective of finding ways to stabilize its finances without
recourse to parliamentary taxation. The most important and controversial
of these was Ship Money, originally a rate levied on maritime counties to
strengthen the navy during a military emergency, which was extended to
the whole nation and made annual from 1635. It caused a great deal of
disquiet concerning the constitutional implications, and in 1637–8 was
submitted to a direct legal challenge by one of Cromwell's cousins, the
Buckinghamshire squire John Hampden. He was ably defended in court by
another of Oliver's cousins by marriage, Oliver St John, and eventually lost
by a slight majority of all the royal judges, who were called collectively to
determine the case. Despite these family connections, the true significance
of the issue in our Cromwell's life is its apparent irrelevancy. He paid his
share of the rate promptly, and his views on its wider significance are not
recorded. Six months after the determination of Hampden's case, he wrote
a long letter to St John's wife, his cousin in blood, which will be considered
below, and in which he made no reference to these recent momentous
events. He appears, indeed, indifferent to national politics throughout the
1630s, and his compliance with Ship Money makes it more likely that his
failure to pay his distraint of knighthood fine was the result of financial
dislocation, and not principle.[59]

It is noteworthy that the single political issue in which he can be proved
to have involved himself in the later 1630s was purely a local one: that of
drainage and enclosure. The economy of the Fens depended on the expectation

.hat, even if they flooded each winter, the pastures which covered most of the region would dry out to be grazed or mown each summer; but it would appear that increasingly this was not happening. It is possible that this was one effect of the Reformation, in removing the religious houses which had maintained the traditional drainage works. It is also true, however, that the early seventeenth century saw the climax of a long period of deteriorating climate, the weather overall becoming colder and wetter. Whatever the cause, the effect was perceived as a serious problem, and in 1630 many years of debates, plans and small-scale local initiatives culminated in a grand scheme led by the most important nobleman of the south-east Midlands, the earl of Bedford, to drain over 300,000 acres of the South Fens. The main method adopted was to cut a new channel for the Ouse, straight across the huge bend that it made in the fenlands east of St Ives, of which Ely lay in the apex. The river water would then flow down both courses, taking pressure off the land between and around.[60]

Nobody had much objection to reduced flooding, but the problem with the scheme was that Bedford and his fellow projectors treated the fenland as if it were a virgin wilderness, and proposed to divide much of it between themselves once drained, with a share going to the Crown and some of the reclaimed area set aside so its profits could maintain the drainage works. The public benefit was advertised as increasing the nation's productivity and agricultural resources in an era of rising population pressure. The provocative aspect of the scheme was that it ignored the long-established rights of the commoners of the Fens and the settlements on their edge to pasture their beasts on the summer meadows and harvest the rich natural resources of the marshes, pools and watercourses. Similar schemes, with the same kind of rationale and the same shortcoming, were launched at places all over the eastern English marshlands in the 1630s, though Bedford's was the largest. Accordingly, most of them were challenged, by legal action, in print and by rioting. To complicate matters further, in 1638 the king upheld local complaints that the works of Bedford's consortium were imperfect, and took them over directly, greatly increasing the Crown's share of the anticipated new farmland and reducing that of the original investors. There the matter rested as it was overtaken by the ensuing national crisis which led to the English Civil War.

The controversy over the project involved the Isle of Ely as much as other places in the South Fens, and that became the setting for some of the largest protests. The bishop and cathedral chapter, and some of the justices of the peace, supported the commoners in appealing to the Privy Council against the scheme in 1637: their case was that the people of the Isle were expected to lose two-thirds of their fenland pastures even though the latter had not been badly affected by flooding, and so did not need drainage at all. The king and council supported Bedford and his friends, and one Huntingdonshire JP was removed for his attempt to start a fighting fund to oppose them. Near the end of a report to the council about this man's activities we find the assertion that it was 'commonly reported' that 'Cromwell of Ely' (who must be our man) had promised to launch a lawsuit against the drainers which would hold them up for five years, if the people of the Isle who had common rights in the Fens funded it by paying him a set sum for every cow they grazed on the fenland.[61] There is no corroborating evidence for this statement, for the truth of which the author himself could not vouch, but it has been given further weight by the assertion made almost half a century later, by one of Cromwell's enemies, that Oliver had spoken against the scheme at a meeting at Huntingdon in April 1638.[62] These pieces of information together caused historians for most of the twentieth century to portray Cromwell as becoming a popular hero in the area at this time, because of his defence of commoners' rights, so laying the basis for his later political and military following.[63] It was a view that went into the 1970 film about him, starring Richard Harris.

More recently, biographers have recoiled from it, emphasizing that there is no corroboration for either statement of his opposition to drainage, and that there is no sign that he ever opposed it in principle.[64] It has been noted that when an investigation was launched into riots led by Ely men in 1638, produced by opposition to the drainage works, Cromwell was not mentioned in its report.[65] Emphasis has been placed on the fact that legal opposition to the works was led by the authorities of the Isle, from the bishop downwards, and that if Cromwell was a part of that, he was playing his role as a member of this establishment, rather than acting as a demagogue.[66] This seems correct. Many years later, when he was the most powerful person in the land and his views were solicited on another fen reclamation project, it was recorded that he thought that drainage in general was a good idea, as long as the drainers did not claim too great a proportion of the land and fail to provide for the poor.[67] This seems entirely consistent with his behaviour in the 1630s, if he did indeed oppose Bedford's project.

Taken as a whole, there is no sign at all that in the 1630s Cromwell either took much interest in national politics or regarded himself as a champion of the common people. His concerns seem to have been local and pragmatic, continuing the pattern of the previous decade, of an unambitious individual with limited horizons, contented with the life of a provincial gentleman based in a small town.

RELIGION

Cromwell grew up in a world littered with the physical remains of the early English Reformation, above all the carcasses of medieval religious houses. Both his Cromwell and Steward ancestors had been closely involved in the dissolution of these, and gained most of their wealth from the process, in lands, tithes and buildings. Of the main Cromwell family seats, Hinchingbrooke had been a nunnery and Ramsey a Benedictine monastery. Oliver's own childhood home was adapted out of an Augustinian friary and he went to school in a building which had been part of a hospital. St Ives had grown up around the shrine of the holy man whose name the town embodied, and which had been demolished as part of the same process of reform.[68] It was the theological consequences of the later Reformation, however, rather than the physical traces of the first, which were really to shape his career, as will be shown.

In 1559–63 the official Church of England was made permanently Protestant by the Elizabethan settlement of it; but that was a rushed compromise produced by a clash between reformers and conservatives in Parliament which left nobody entirely satisfied. The result retained a Catholic structure, with bishops, cathedrals, archdeacons and the full medieval system of church courts, alongside a Protestant theology and service. Moreover, the last two were themselves a compromise, mixing elements of the main Continental Protestant traditions: the Lutheran in northern Germany, and the various other strains, especially Calvinist, in southern Germany, Switzerland and France. The result was – for the age – a quite astonishing amount of confusion concerning doctrine. Among the points which the settlement left unclear were whether the English Church was an improved version of the medieval one or a complete departure from it, allied to Continental Protestants; whether human beings could save themselves from sin by their own efforts; whether clergy had a sacred status which clearly divided them from the laity; whether the royal supremacy over the Church was vested in the monarch alone or in the monarch in Parliament; and whether bishops had absolute power over lesser clerics. Initially everybody expected that this situation would not last, and that the English Church's government would be altered and its doctrine clarified, most probably to bring it more into line with the Continental Protestant denominations. To general surprise, Elizabeth soon made it clear that she would not countenance any further alteration in the settlement, perhaps because of a tendency in her nature to preserve any situation with which she had become familiar, and perhaps because she realized that the existing one gave her additional power and flexibility as the Church's governor.[69]

When Elizabeth's attitude became obvious, from the mid-1560s, it produced a division among convinced English Protestants. Most, including the majority of her bishops, ministers and councillors, conformed to her wishes, however reluctantly and unhappily. A minority refused to do so, expressing active and vocal opposition to what they regarded as Catholic elements surviving in the English Church which differentiated it from the most thoroughly reformed Continental denominations such as Calvinism. These individuals rapidly acquired the derisory nickname of 'Puritans'. In the course of the 1560s and 1570s they waged a campaign to induce the queen to accept further reform, which foundered upon her refusal to oblige and the lack of any credible Protestant alternative to her as ruler. From the 1580s she found more active support for her stance, and her muddled compromise of a Church, for two reasons. One was that by then a generation had grown up which was accustomed to it, and so less inclined to see it as anomalous. The other was that religious conservatives were abandoning hope that Catholicism would be restored, and were coming to support Elizabeth's religious order as a barrier against more radically Protestant forms. By the time of Cromwell's birth, it seemed that the Puritan challenge had been defeated, and a nationally prescribed religion had been achieved which was exceptionally dynamic and disparate, its lack of strict definition allowing for a wide range of individual interpretation and expression.

Two serious weaknesses remained within it. One was that there were still large numbers of Puritans left, at all levels of society, forming a distinctive religious sub-culture. They were united by a desire to see the Church further reformed, though they differed greatly over the ideal extent of this or the features to which they at present objected; but they were also characterized by a remarkably uniform culture. It was marked by strenuous piety infused with intense introspection and a profound preoccupation with personal salvation; a reliance on the authority of the Bible as absolutely paramount in Christianity; and a conviction that the majority of humans, including of the English, were predestined to damnation. Puritans were found to a greater or lesser degree across most of the country, often forming distinctive enclaves within counties or even parishes. The other weakness was the appearance of a rival tendency by the end of the century, of English Protestants who wished the Church in some respects actually to become more Catholic. It sprang from different sources, such as a desire to believe that all humans might ultimately have a potential for salvation; a feeling that the now established religion represented a uniquely improved form of Catholicism rather than a national variant of a Continent-wide Protestant movement; and a hunger for a greater physical beauty, and larger element of ceremony and sanctity, in parish churches. By the time of Cromwell's childhood, opponents were giving those who embodied these attitudes the insulting label of 'Arminians', after the followers of a heretical Dutch theologian.

Puritans, Arminians and those who were broadly content with Elizabeth's Church formed a huge spectrum rather than a trio of distinct and coherent parties. There was no doubt, however, that the first two were now pulling English religion in opposite directions, and that a potential had developed for serious conflict if animosities could not be damped down. In addition, England still retained a small minority of the population – from 1 to 5 per cent – which adhered secretly or openly to the outlawed faith of Roman Catholicism, remaining loyal to the Pope and the traditional sacraments of his Church. Although few in number, they included many wealthy and influential nobles and gentry, especially in the north, who could be linked to the powerful Catholic states which still dominated much of the Continent, and they could provide the essential personnel for a reconversion of England should a Catholic ruler ever again come to the throne. In facing all these problems, Elizabeth's successor, James I, did fairly well according to the opinions of most recent scholars. He reaffirmed the essentials of the Elizabethan settlement, and picked off the most troublesome Puritans and Catholics while allowing the more peaceable a de facto toleration, the latter as long as they paid regular fines. He produced a bench of bishops which always had a majority committed to the existing settlement, but included a few who sympathized with Puritans and a growing minority of Arminians; the purpose of the latter was largely to ensure the king a continued freedom of manoeuvre and deter the mainstream majority if it tried to combine to push him into particular policies. Abroad, James displayed a consistent wish to reconcile the Protestant and Catholic faiths. All this was in many ways admirable, and in some respects sensible, but it had one major flaw: that it completely failed to defuse religious tensions in his realm. On the contrary, by its end, and Cromwell's achievement of maturity, animosities and suspicions between different kinds of English

Protestant were greater than ever, while suspicion and fear of Catholicism remained widespread at all levels of society.

It therefore mattered the more that on his succession in 1625 Charles I overturned his father's balancing act by manifesting a personal conversion to Arminianism. This immediately intensified the trouble which he experienced in working with Parliaments, where Puritans united with the former Elizabethan and Jacobean mainstream to express alarm at his promotion of Arminian-bishops and acceptance of their policies: it was the major factor in producing the final breakdown in 1629. Thereafter, ruling without Parliaments through the 1630s, Charles was free to promote an Arminian takeover, led by his new archbishop of Canterbury, William Laud. The Laudian programme included a re-endowment of the Church's wealth to render it stronger, more effective and more independent of the laity; a more rigorous enforcement of the prescribed ceremonies and clerical dress on Puritans who had been ignoring aspects of them; a repair and beautification of churches, as settings for ritual and for sanctity; and the generation of a better-educated and better-behaved clergy, under tighter central control ultimately wielded by the monarch. In the eyes of Charles, Laud and their followers, Puritans replaced Catholics as the most serious perceived menace to the established religious order, a shift signalled by the fact that as a last manifestation of James's conciliatory policy and a critical need for powerful foreign allies, Charles had married a Catholic princess, Henrietta Maria, sister of the king of France. This reintroduced Catholicism into the heart of the royal court. As not all bishops were yet followers of Laud, his reforms were patchily enforced, but taken together, these developments naturally induced horror in Puritans, and in many who had been more or less contented with the Church as it was under James. Moreover, the prospect of a more independent and powerful body of clergy, less responsive to the laity and more centrally directed, was alarming to a wider body of nobility, gentry and merchants than those concerned with the religious issues alone. By the end of the 1630s, the king's religious policy was producing serious unease among a great many of his subjects.

This, then, was the context within which Oliver Cromwell grew up and passed to the brink of middle age. His extended family, represented by his father's siblings, in-laws, and nieces and nephews, seems to have spanned most of the English religious spectrum. It contained no apparent Catholics or Arminians, but several people who were or became Puritans and many representatives of more mainstream Elizabethan and Jacobean Protestantism.[70] The head of the family, the flamboyant, extravagant and genial Sir Oliver, seems to have been conservative and conformist in religion as in other respects, while Sir Thomas Steward was apparently quite comfortable in his position as a neighbour, tenant and tithe-farmer of the powerful churchmen of Ely. On the other hand, there are hints that Oliver's father Robert Cromwell, while apparently a conforming member of the established Church, leaned more towards the Puritan end of the spectrum than his brother. One sign of this is the choice of a Cambridge college for his son Oliver which was different from his own or his elder brother's (Queens' College). Sidney Sussex was a recent foundation, specifically designed to train a godly Protestant preaching ministry. It demanded an exceptionally pious and austere lifestyle from its students, forbidding them flamboyant clothes and hairstyles, visits to taverns, and card or dice games. Unsurprisingly, Puritans were attracted to study there. Its master, Samuel Ward, was noted for his friendship with Puritan clergy, attachment to the Calvinist doctrine that salvation was restricted to a predetermined spiritual elite, covert dislike of bishops, and overt hostility to Catholics and Arminians.[71]

Then there was the identity of Robert's parish minister at Huntingdon, who was also Oliver's schoolmaster there. Thomas Beard was the leading churchman of the town and something of a national figure because of his writings. He may have shared a personal friendship with Robert as well as playing a pastoral role, because he witnessed his will. Beard was no Puritan, being (like Ward) a greedy pluralist, amassing multiple appointments to livings in order to maximize his income in a way of which Puritans disapproved. Nonetheless, he expressed attitudes which were also hallmarks of Puritan belief. One was an intense providentialism, a conviction that the Christian

God planted signs in the mortal world to convey his attitudes and intentions to the faithful, which to Beard especially took the form of punishments meted out to evildoers. Another was a sense of that world as a battleground between God and the Devil, with humans lined up on either side and Catholics in particular being in Satan's party. A concomitant of this was Beard's animosity towards Arminians, whom he viewed, in the manner of most of their opponents, not as Protestants with different religious tastes, but as covert Catholics seeking to destroy English Protestantism. All of these attitudes were to be shared by Cromwell as he emerges fully into history from 1640.[72]

The clearest evidence of Beard's impact on the young Oliver is provided by Cromwell's only recorded speech in Parliament during his stint there in 1628–9, delivered on 11 February 1629. The context was the attack launched by the House of Commons on the king's religious policy, and it is telling that it was this issue which should have drawn out the young MP rather than any other. Cromwell reported that over a decade before, Beard had made a public reply to a sermon delivered prominently in London by an Arminian cleric, and a bishop who favoured Arminians, Richard Neile, had attempted to silence him. This was presented as an example of the grip which that party was already attempting to get on the Church, and also as evidence against Neile, who had since been promoted to the powerful position of archbishop of York. Cromwell's intervention made an impression: it was noted in all three of the surviving accounts of the debate, and the House concluded that Beard should be summoned as a witness.[73]

This said, we have no real knowledge of the nature of Cromwell's relationship with his former schoolmaster, or of how it ended, although there is no sign of it after Oliver pulled out of Huntingdon. At the end of the 1620s Beard got himself embroiled in a dispute in the town over the best use of a large sum of money left to it for charitable uses in a bequest. The common council which then ran the town wanted to save money by using it to pay Beard's existing stipend as a preacher, which was in addition to his income as a parish minister. The London Mercers' Company which administered the bequest, however, and was allied to a party in Huntingdon, wanted that money to endow a new preacher instead. A lengthy wrangle resulted which dragged in the king and the local bishop, ending when Beard was bought off with a lump sum and the rest of the money was used to endow a new man. Cromwell later had dealings with the Mercers, as we shall see, and it is likely that he sided with them and their allies in his town, and against Beard, but the surviving records do not seem to make clear his part in the affair.[74] When Oliver had his fatal quarrel with the mayor and the lawyer Robert Bernard in 1630, Beard provided a statement that neither Cromwell nor the man charged with misconduct alongside him had made any objection to the new town charter when it was proposed.[75] This may have been intended to make Oliver look unreasonable, by suggesting that his objections to the revised arrangements had been lodged only after he had already accepted the latter. On the other hand, it may have been supportive, as an attempt to show that Cromwell was not a dangerous radical, but somebody who merely opposed particular details of the new form of town government which had only subsequently become apparent. The puzzle is a further illustration of how little can be understood of his relationships at this time.

A further indication of his early religious sympathies may be provided by his marriage: his father-in-law, Sir James Bourchier, leased his country estate in Essex from the earl of Warwick, one of the most prominent aristocratic patrons of Puritans. Moreover, Cromwell subsequently sent his four surviving sons to Felsted School, which was in the same Essex parish and controlled by the earl.[76] Unhappily, there is no evidence for a personal relationship between Cromwell and Warwick at this time, nor between the earl and Bourchier, and indeed no firm indication of the religious affiliations of the Bourchiers. Sir James's choice of a country seat may have been primarily due to economic and opportunistic factors, and Cromwell's choice of a school may initially have been down to its good reputation and its situation where his father-in-law could keep a kindly eye on the boys. Likewise, the choices of husbands for Cromwell's sisters reveal a striking pattern: of the five husbands, three do not have known religious attitudes at this time, but two, Valentine Walton and John Desborough, were or became staunch Puritans. All told, there is a consistent pattern in what little can be surmised of Oliver's religious milieu before 1630: it was not Puritan, conforming to the established national Church with seeming good grace, but consisted of an evangelical, Calvinist, strain of English Protestantism which had marked similarities to Puritanism. It was a soil from which Puritanism could easily grow.

In this case, grow it certainly did, and by the late 1630s, Oliver Cromwell was an absolutely stereotypical Puritan. His emergence as one has long been obvious from two of his surviving letters. The first was addressed from St Ives on 11 January 1636 to a member of the Mercers' Company called Storie. It began by praising him and his fellows for their pious work in founding a lectureship – an endowed position for a preacher – in his neighbourhood and installing a good man in it, a Dr Wells. Now, however, it was in danger of failing, at a time when so many lectureships were being suppressed by 'the enemies of God his truth'. This was a clear reference to the Laudian campaign to bring all clergy under the direct control of the national Church by eliminating all who did not hold a parish living in it. Lectureships, in particular, which had been founded in large numbers during the previous sixty years to improve the standard of local preaching, had come to represent almost an alternative body of clerics, and one which with some justice was thought to be disproportionately Puritan. Cromwell therefore implored Storie to ensure that the preacher concerned continued to be paid, and asked him to convey Cromwell's best wishes to a number of named fellow Mercers.[77] In one sense, this could be represented as a continuation of Oliver's former views: he had always been hostile to Arminians, as had those involved in his education, and that would have intensified as they came to dominate the Church and started to reshape it. Nonetheless, Cromwell now sees the world as fiercely divided between the friends and enemies of his God, and places an emphasis on the direct intervention of the deity in human affairs, and on true believers as a gathered group of 'God's children' – views which are quintessentially Puritan.

The second, and yet more famous, letter was written on 13 October 1638 to his cousin Elizabeth, the new teenage wife of Oliver St John, the defending lawyer of John Hampden. The St Johns were clearly also firm Puritans by then, for Cromwell wrote to Elizabeth in exactly that idiom, his subject matter being a meditation on passages of the Bible which are mostly concerned with the resilience of true believers under persecution. The use of Scripture is very extensive, comprising thirteen quotations (from eight psalms, three epistles, St John's Gospel and a Book of Samuel), drawn from two different English translations, the Calvinist Geneva one and the official one authorized by King James: Cromwell had clearly been studying both hard and comparing them.[78] He emphasized his sinful nature and the unworthiness of her regard, and gratitude to God for divine mercies bestowed notwithstanding. He reaffirmed his passionate devotion to his deity, and bewailed his situation repeatedly as one of enforced residence in 'a dry and barren wilderness', '*Blackness*' and 'a dark place': this could have been a reference to the general travails of mortal life or to the particular consequences of living among the churchmen of Ely. He affirmed his identity as a member of a Christian spiritual elite, 'the congregation of the firstborn', and represented that as something only recently found; reminding his (teenage) correspondent of his former life – as she had known it – as 'the chief of sinners'. He ended, without any apparent sense of bathos, by thanking his cousin for looking after one of his sons and chiding her husband for not obliging Cromwell yet by doing a favour for another cousin living in their county – which may have been the whole point of the missive. In a sense, Oliver Cromwell was born to history not in April 1599 but in October 1638, when he suddenly emerges as the personality by which he is known to it, fully formed and ready for action.

It is possible that his reference to his former life of sin was to a misspent youth, of the sort charged against him by hostile biographers, but the context, as indicated, suggests something more recent. It could have acknowledged a particular misdeed (such as his attempt to have his uncle certified insane, if he had ever made it) or a general manner of living: we can never know. What is significant is that Cromwell portrayed his piety as the product of a conversion experience. This was, again, a Puritan trope, because a sudden call to an enhanced sense of the workings, and majesty, of God, and of one's own innate wickedness, following the example of St Paul, was a major sign that a person could be one of the elect predestined for salvation. Nonetheless, in Cromwell's case it is given more credence by the fact that his hostile biographers in the Restoration period, cited above, asserted he had at some point between the early 1620s and late 1630s undergone a change of behaviour in which he had become (at least outwardly) both more godly and more moral. Modern biographers have agreed that his fervent Puritan faith was acquired in the course of a dramatic conversion, but not on when this occurred.[79] It is tempting to link it to the evidence for Cromwell's mental instability between 1628 and 1635, as part of a protracted process of breakdown and recovery: but that evidence is itself unreliable. Nevertheless, when the various dates put forward by modern scholars for his conversion are collated, they show a clear majority in favour of the idea that the St Ives years were in some way pivotal.

One piece of evidence for that lies in an earlier letter written by Cromwell, to a friend made at Cambridge who had entered the clergy, Henry Downhall. It was written on 14 October 1626 and invited Downhall, eloquently and graciously, to act as godfather to Cromwell's third son, Richard.[80] The occasion was one on which, had Oliver been the man he was ten years later, a use of pious language would have been very appropriate; and yet it is entirely lacking in the text. Most scholars, therefore, have agreed that his conversion must have taken place subsequently. Downhall became vicar of St Ives in 1631, when Cromwell and his family moved there, and it is hard not to believe that the prospect of having his old friend as minister played a part in his decision to choose that town as his new home. The same folk memory there which preserved the image of Cromwell nursing a sore throat with a piece of flannel also recorded that he indeed regularly attended the parish church.[81] Downhall appears to be another non-Arminian conformist clergyman, for his patrons were the earl of Holland and the local bishop, John Williams, both opponents of Laud's policies.[82]

Once installed at St Ives, however, Cromwell's friend found himself propelled into support for the government's religious policy and into conflict with Puritans. Downhall's predecessor in the parish, Job Tookey, had been ejected because of Puritanism, and was then intruded back into its church as the holder of a new lectureship sponsored by London merchants. Tension developed between the old and new incumbents, the conformist and nonconformist clergymen, with the parish dividing over the matter, and in 1635 Bishop Williams prevented Tookey from preaching. By that time (to judge from the letter to Storie) Cromwell was on the opposite side from his old friend, and no more is heard of Downhall in his life. When civil war came, the two of them again supported rival causes, and Downhall was ejected from St Ives by Cromwell's party and replaced with Tookey's son.[83] How and when Oliver switched his sympathies is not known. He may have been converted by one of the lecturers in the district at his time, such as Tookey himself or Wells.[84] On the other hand he may have been radicalized before moving to St Ives, and attracted there because the young lord of the manor, Henry Lawrence, was an extreme Puritan who actually emigrated to Holland in the late 1630s to join a sectarian church.[85] Alternatively, Lawrence may have been the key figure in Cromwell's conversion while at St Ives. Against both ideas is the apparent fact that the Lawrences did not reside much in the town at this time.[86] It is even possible that the context of Oliver's new religious commitment lies not in the Huntingdonshire town at all, but in his wider family affinity which included Elizabeth St John.

Taken altogether, the most probable conclusion to draw from these meagre scraps of evidence is that Cromwell became a Puritan at St Ives, but we do not know how or why. It is easy to construct a narrative whereby he left Huntingdon precipitately in anger and sorrow, having lost the community in which he had grown up and thought of as his own for so long – and found a replacement community of Puritans while living in the smaller town. This development would have afforded him both a new sense of worth, as a member of a spiritual elite, and also a channel for his anger and resentment. Such a plausible scenario, however, remains mere speculation.

What is certain is that having made this commitment, Cromwell held to it firmly for the rest of his life, including the next stage of it, when, moving to the cathedral city of Ely, it would have been more comfortable and practical for him to have had other loyalties. There he was to be not only a prominent inhabitant of a place controlled by higher churchmen, but as a tithe farmer and holder of lands leased from the cathedral chapter, closely bound up with them in his livelihood. Moreover, the bishop during the time of his residence there was Matthew Wren, one of the most ferocious of Arminian bishops, whose zeal even outran that of Archbishop Laud himself: a place of darkness indeed for a Puritan.

With Cromwell, however, things are rarely simple, and, as shown, he and Wren seem to have co-operated well over matters like riots: as the person who chose the JPs of the Isle, Wren must have favoured Oliver for this office. It is unlikely that he would have done this for a religiously suspect individual.[87] This said, the Puritans of the Ely diocese under Wren's rule were adept at concealing their beliefs, aided by the fact that they included in their number many of the parish officials who were supposed to report disaffection and nonconformity.[88] The great majority of them seem to have attended their parish churches obediently, and even comfortably if they did not have an Arminian minister. In Cromwell's case, this would have been St Mary's, in Ely, where his last daughter Frances was baptized in 1639.[89] As a Puritan, however, he would certainly have attended informal meetings outside the hours of church services, at which like-minded people could discuss religion and pray together. They had done this since Elizabeth's reign, and it would have been all the more necessary to do so in the time of Laudian dominance.[90] It was one of the means by which Puritan networks were maintained and extended.

Such gatherings probably lie behind the stories which were circulated after Cromwell's death, and the Restoration, that in the 1630s he had attended a 'conventicle' in the Isle of Ely or other places in the Ouse Valley and preached there.[91] Such assertions had a particular resonance in the Restoration period, when 'conventicle' signified an illegal gathering outside the national Church to conduct a rival religious service: by then many such meetings were held by sects which rejected the notion of a national religious body altogether, and were ministered to by lay preachers. Back-projected onto the 1630s, such a language carried connotations which were almost certainly alien to that earlier period and misleading. In addition, however, there are two other pieces of gossip which may at first sight seem to bear out these later reports. One was published in 1693 by a biographer of Bishop Williams, who claimed that the bishop had warned King Charles in 1645 that he had known Cromwell when the latter resided in his diocese but had not been aware of his religious beliefs. He then told the king that nonetheless Oliver was 'a common spokesman for sectaries, and maintained their part with stubbornness' and disliked the king's ministers, and was disgruntled because of the failure of his attempt to have his uncle committed as a lunatic.[92] That last reference dates the alleged conversation(s) to 1635, when Cromwell was at St Ives. It must be pointed out that there is no way of determining the accuracy of this second-hand and retrospective testimony. If true, then it is quite possible that at the time concerned Cromwell was defending Puritan lecturers (as he did to Storie) and that Williams later elided this with a defence of people who wanted to worship outside the Church altogether, which Cromwell was certainly providing by 1645.

The second source consists of notes made in the late 1650s by a political enemy of Cromwell, quoting a Cambridgeshire man reporting a story from his father-in-law, a supporter of Laud, who had a brother who was a Puritan minister. The story was that this brother had met with fellow believers, including Cromwell, in a barn twenty years before, to pray for the further reformation of the Church and the downfall of the government.[93] This is, therefore, a third-hand assertion, filtered through at least two hostile sources, but there is nothing inherently unlikely in the idea that Cromwell had met fellow Puritans to discuss the current official campaign by Laud and his supporters and pray that it might end. What may be doubted again is that the setting was a full-blown illegal religious gathering of the sort implied by the later account, written in different times. All told, it is virtually certain that Cromwell attended meetings with other Puritans during his Ely years, at which they prayed together and talked about religion and current affairs; but there is no clear evidence that any of these constituted formal religious services of the kind common in subsequent decades, nor that he took it upon himself to preach at any.[94]

It remains to deal with one other set of retrospective assertions about Oliver Cromwell in the 1630s: that at some point he attempted to emigrate to one of the Puritan colonies in America, and was prevented by government action or some other twist of fate. The implication of these stories is that had he departed, then the history of the British Isles would have been completely different. The assertion first appears in a hostile narrative of his life published in 1660, and was then repeated in other poison-pen accounts until taken up and elaborated by other authors, some now sympathetic, in the eighteenth century, until the story achieved its full-blown form, amplified into the greatest and most confident detail, about a century after the events it purports to describe.[95] A gentle verdict upon it is there is no contemporary evidence for the story, but no way of refuting it, so that it remains possible. A harsher one is that it has all the trappings of a retrospective legend. Both are tenable.

By 1639 Cromwell's life had a dual aspect. On the one hand, he was under the rule of a royal government employing religious policies with which he was thoroughly out of sympathy, and living in a place where the consequences of those were especially evident. On the other, he was financially secure and prosperous at last, and a member of a Puritan network which must have given him a feeling of community and companionship, with a religious devotion that provided him with a sense of purpose, excitement and personal value. It was at this point that the divine providence in which he so fervently believed dealt him an apparent severe blow: near the end of May his eldest son, Robert, died of smallpox at school in Essex aged seventeen, and was buried at the parish church of Felsted. Many contagious diseases of the time were most prevalent among the poor, while the more prosperous members of society, with better diets, cleaner houses and easier lives, were less vulnerable. Smallpox was the greatest exception; highly infectious and no respecter of rank, it was a scourge to royalty as much as to all other classes. The wound left on Cromwell was lifelong, and the pain of it palliated, in part, by Scripture, in this case specifically a text of St Paul's which encourages readers to put trust in Christ both in prosperity and adversity. On his own deathbed he found consolation in it again, while recalling that it 'did once save my life, when my eldest son died, which went as a dagger to my heart'.[96] Not for the last time in his life, he was to find that the widespread Christian sense of divine providence actually seemed to work, and an appalling misfortune was to be followed by a series of seemingly fortuitous events which were to bring him public fame and success.

2

❖

MEMBER OF PARLIAMENT AND
CAPTAIN OF HORSE

During the late 1630s Cromwell must have become aware, with the rest of the English political nation, that a major challenge was developing to Charles I's rule. It came from Scotland, on which, in 1637, the king attempted to impose a new church service which was both more uniform than before and more influenced by its English counterpart, bringing the two realms more closely into alignment. He did so without submitting it to discussion and approval either by the Scottish Parliament or by the national assembly of the Scottish Church, or Kirk. The majority of Scots, especially in the more densely populated and politically significant Lowlands, viewed this as a final insult to national pride by a ruler who, in contrast to his father, seemed to treat Scotland with neglect and disdain. A powerful protest movement developed, which rejected the new service and, as the king seemed to offer concessions too slowly and reluctantly, developed during 1638 into a rejection of much royal authority over the Kirk. This entailed the removal of bishops and cathedrals from its structure.

Charles treated this as a declaration of war and set out during 1639 to crush the opposition in Scotland with armies raised in his two other kingdoms. The Irish one never played a part in the ensuing campaign, but by a huge effort a large one was raised in England without need for parliamentary supply, and the king himself led it to the border. There he realized that the Scottish rebels, who have acquired the name of Covenanters from the national agreement, or Covenant, which they had signed to affirm resistance to his religious policy, were approaching him with a force that seemed at least as large as his. He also realized that his English advisers had little appetite for battle or enthusiasm for his cause, and when the Covenanters offered a compromise agreement, the king's nerve broke and he accepted it and called off the war. Each army was disbanded, but during the winter Charles and the Covenanters both recovered their nerve and failed to reach a settlement. They reaffirmed their changes in the Kirk and he decided to attack them again. This time it seemed apparent that he would not be able to do so without a vote for a war tax from an English Parliament. It was this expectation which produced one of the decisive turning points in Oliver Cromwell's career.

ELECTIONS

That development commenced on 7 January 1641, at the end of the Christmas holidays, when he was sworn in as a freeman of the town of Cambridge, at the behest of the mayor.[1] Cambridge lay fifteen miles south of Ely, up a tributary of the Ouse called the Cam. It was the administrative centre of its shire, within which the Isle of Ely formed a semi-autonomous unit, and in many respects was another typical English river-town, with the usual bridge, high street and marketplace, surrounded by more rolling clay lands, with small woods, cornfields, villages and gentry seats. In one respect it was highly unusual, however, because during the thirteenth century a group of scholars at Oxford's embryonic university had fled disturbances in that town and chosen the quiet eastern local capital as their new home. As a result, England's second centre of academic study had grown up there, and like that at Oxford had organized itself into colleges. The otherwise standard freshwater port and crossing accordingly found brick and stone monsters sprouting among the more regular timber and clay houses of its two main streets, running up from and along the river. These were filled with clergymen and their pupils, who came in the course of the Tudor period to consist increasingly of young gentry seeking educational polish, as well as trainee clerics. The townspeople quite rapidly came to view this alien community, much of the time, as a giant cuckoo growing within their nest, a complex of people independent in privileges and jurisdiction who intermittently jostled with the urban folk for space and power.

Cromwell had no known links with the town before 1640, and no economic or administrative activity there. An answer to the puzzle of how he became a freeman was provided by a section added to a revised edition, in 1665, of the longest and most relentlessly hostile of the biographies of him published after the Restoration, called *Flagellum* (the lash) and originally written by a hack called James Heath. It is not clear who compiled this passage, which consisted of a quite circumstantial account of how Cromwell had become admired by a group of Cambridge Puritans after one of them had come across him speaking at weekly meetings of co-religionists in the Isle of Ely. They formed the plan of getting him elected to represent their town in Parliament, for which he would be eligible if he had the legal freedom of it. The mayor was duly persuaded by them to use his power to create new freemen to bring in Cromwell, with the agreement that the mayor would simultaneously grant the same status to a candidate of his own. Cromwell was sworn in the next day, wearing a red coat with gold lace to signal his genteel status and tactfully plying the corporation with a gift of wine and confectionary.[2]

Recent careful research has revealed that the Cambridge townsmen named in this account all existed, with the occupations and religious views credited to them there, and that some of the detail in it, notably the mayor's sponsorship of Cromwell's attainment of freeman status, can be proved correct.[3] Letters survive by one of the other men in the story, written three years later, which demonstrate both his Puritan piety and his loyalty to and admiration for Cromwell.[4] It is also true that some of the information in the account can be shown to be garbled, and that the context in which it was published was one of vilification and persecution of the surviving Cambridge Puritans, who had been driven from the corporation and out of the national Church after the Restoration. To accuse them of having got the now officially hated Cromwell onto his road to power through a shoddy back-room intrigue would be an additional smear, and so its striking amount of local detail may have just been intended to make a falsehood plausible.[5] Nonetheless, there is some supporting evidence for the statements in *Flagellum*, even though it is also retrospective and hostile. In an attack on Cromwell's memory published two years earlier, it was stated that he was chosen as an MP for Cambridge because of the recommendation of some of his relatives, especially John Hampden, and of the Puritan faction at Cambridge: 'the town was generally infected with the same disease [of Puritanism], and therefore it was no hard matter to effect it'.[6]

Cambridge certainly had a powerful Puritan lobby by this date, largely focused on the lectureship at Holy Trinity church and allied with some elements in the university.[7] Hampden was another Puritan, Cromwell's cousin, and a national hero to those who disliked royal policies because of his stand against Ship Money. Had he added his recommendation to those of local citizens of like mind, that would have strengthened Oliver's position. Almost twenty years after *Flagellum*, another account of Cromwell's career, by his long-term political enemy Sir William Dugdale, declared that the choice of him to represent Cambridge was inspired by his earlier stand against fen drainage, which had given him fame as a speaker and campaigner.[8] In recent years, as said before, it has become accepted that Cromwell's role in opposing drainage was both limited and specific, and part of a more general opposition to it by the authorities of the Isle of Ely. Nor was Cambridge in the Fens or closely connected with them.[9] Nonetheless, it is interesting to see what Dugdale said next, which was that Cromwell's reputation as an effective campaigner in the Fens recommended him to the Puritans at Cambridge, who made him their parliamentary candidate. There was thus a powerful post-Reformation tradition that he became a parliamentary candidate for the town because his total opposition to the Crown's ecclesiastical policies, coupled with personal qualities of leadership and eloquence, made him seem an excellent champion to a strong party of people there who shared his views. They would have come across him because of the networks which Puritans maintained across the county and beyond it.

This is plausible: indeed, it is really the most credible explanation for his candidature at Cambridge. The only other way in which a minor gentleman of his kind could have got into that position would have been because of the patronage of a powerful noble; and there is absolutely no sign of that in his case. It looks as if the freemen of Cambridge (who elected Members of Parliament) were sufficiently disenchanted by royal policies, especially concerning the Church, to agree with the local Puritans to adopt a prospective MP who could be relied upon to oppose them. At any rate, Cromwell's admission procedure worked, and when the king called a Parliament in the spring he was duly elected unopposed, alongside a government candidate, Thomas Meautys, a clerk to the Privy Council: the town had split the difference politically by sending up a supporter and a critic of the regime.[10] The resulting assembly has gone down in history as the Short Parliament, which met in April and was dissolved three weeks later, after the Commons had refused to vote any war taxes until the king abandoned the policies of his personal rule. There is no record of Cromwell having said or done anything in the Short Parliament; but his record clearly pleased his electors at Cambridge enough for him to be made a candidate for a subsequent parliamentary election.

That was forthcoming, though nobody could have been sure of it in the early summer of 1640, as Charles I decided obstinately to renew his war against the Scottish Covenanters without the resources to wage it. The lack of a parliamentary grant meant that the army he put back together was short of pay, arms and ammunition, and only half of it was ready to be sent north when the campaign began. Furthermore, many of the king's subjects were even less certain of the necessity of the conflict, especially after the wasted expedition of the previous year. An increasing number, bolstered by a stream of shrewd propaganda sent into England by the Covenanters, were becoming convinced that the Scots rebels, far from being natural enemies, might well be natural allies against Laudian innovation and aggression. By contrast, the Covenanters were united by both religious and nationalist zeal, and supported by an efficient and sufficient system of war taxation and administration, devised for such an emergency. Charles was only persuaded to launch another attack on them with the assurance that he would be supported by a second army sent from Ireland, which in the event was not ready in time.

Instead the Covenanters decided to attack first, launching a large and well-equipped force across the border and overwhelming the king's advance guard on the Tyne. They then rapidly occupied the counties of Northumberland and Durham, which controlled the coal supply that kept London warm, and Charles was forced to sue for peace. The terms his victorious opponents imposed were to pay them a huge sum each month to support their occupying force in England until a permanent settlement could be worked out. This could only be provided by a Parliament, and so the king was not only forced to call one again but would have to comply with its demands until the treaty with the Scots was made. He therefore faced the new assembly not only in a weak position but with his existing government now saddled with the tremendous opprobrium of having been rapidly and resoundingly defeated by a nation whom many of the English had traditionally regarded as a foe, and furthermore one who had usually been overcome in battle. The fact that most of them thought the wars with the Covenanters to have been unnecessary in the first place would have reinforced public anger and contempt for the king and his advisers, and the more religious would have concluded that God had witnessed decisively against royal policies in both kingdoms.[11]

While these dramatic and transformative events were unfolding at the national level, Cromwell was going through an equivalent personal change: he left Ely, in the same apparently sudden and impulsive manner as he had quit Huntingdon almost ten years before. It is extremely likely that his now close and public association with the Puritans of Cambridge, and his open stance as a campaigner against Laudian religious innovations, had made life uncomfortable for him in a place dominated by a Laudian bishop and a cathedral chapter. Almost the whole estate which he had finally acquired, with such effort, under the terms of Sir Thomas Steward's will, was sold up and converted into ready cash, as a huge lump sum of between two and three thousand pounds. The one probable exception seems to have been the house itself, which was apparently still used by his wife and family during the next half a decade.[12] This move left him free for any action and opportunity, with considerable liquid resources, as events proved whether the king or his opponents would gain the upper hand. Cromwell's movements are not clear in the immediate aftermath of the sale. Cambridge is one obvious location for his activities, and Huntingdon another, now he could face it anew with status and wealth. Certainly he was involved in Huntingdonshire affairs by May, acting as arbitrator in a legal dispute at the behest of a local man.[13]

By autumn the drift of political events had become plain: a defeated king, leading a discredited ministry, was about to face a Parliament which he could no longer dissolve if it proved recalcitrant, as long as the Scottish army needed payment along with his own army which had to be kept on foot at York in case the Scots broke the truce. That meant further elections, and once more Cromwell stood at Cambridge, in what became a contest between government and opposition candidates. Meautys was running again, this time with a teammate, which put them into a fight with Cromwell. Traditionally, Cambridge tried to ensure that its interests were heeded by central government (especially in disputes with the university) by appointing the keeper of the king's Great Seal, one of the key royal ministers, to the honorific post of its High Steward. Its current holder was the principal judicial officer of Charles's personal rule, Sir John Finch, and he was the sponsor of Meautys. Either as a sign of aggression or insecurity, Finch now put up his own brother for the town's other seat. He himself had become one of the least popular of the royal ministers, and Cromwell ran against his candidates with a Cambridge townsman and fellow Puritan, John Lowry. In a pattern which was to be repeated in many places across the nation at that time, the court's nominees were defeated, and Oliver was on his way back to Westminster, to sit in what would go down in history as the Long Parliament, of which he was to be a part for over a dozen years.[14]

THE SETTING

The House of Commons into which Cromwell walked back on 3 November 1640 was accommodated in one of the most striking buildings of the medieval palace of Westminster, a royal residence abandoned for over a hundred years and left as the setting for meetings of the central law courts and of Parliaments. Like most of the larger royal palaces of Europe it was a huddle of structures, brick, stone or both, of different ages, sizes and designs. The Commons had met since the mid-Tudor period in the main chapel of the former palace, dedicated to St Stephen and rebuilt magnificently in the fourteenth century. It had a very high roof, with a timber vault and a whitewashed wooden ceiling, probably 27 feet and 5 inches (8.37 metres) from the floor. There was a double tier of large Gothic windows in the longer walls, and at the eastern end three small and narrow pointed windows and then a single huge one, above these, divided into three long and narrow panes. All these had plain glass, replacing the medieval stained panes that were destroyed during Edward VI's Reformation when the college of priests which served the chapel was dissolved and the MPs invited in.

The building was 62 feet and 5 inches (19.04 metres) by 32 feet and 2 inches (9.8 metres) inside. It had had five bays and along the final three of these it was furnished with rows of wooden stalls, facing each other along the side walls four deep. A broad aisle ran between them down the centre of the chamber. There was a raised dais at the eastern end where the medieval altar had been, now occupied by the Speaker's chair, and below and in front of this was the table for the two clerks. Above the Speaker were fixed the royal arms, to which MPs were supposed to bow on entering. The walls seem to have been mostly covered in wainscot panelling, which concealed the gold leaf coating and paintings of the medieval chapel. A thick ornamental screen ran across the interior at the end of the second bay in from the door, which had divided the chapel from its antechapel, the latter now forming the lobby of the Commons. This was pierced by a door which allowed all entry and exit from the chamber. The screen had steps leading up to a gallery which originally had been designed for the musicians who played during services. Above the lobby were now a committee room, and one for the serjeant, the main executive official of the House.[15]

The Commons usually met for around three hours in the morning, with afternoon sessions only during times of exceptional business or political crisis. Their numbers had grown so much since the time of Edward VI that there was now only space in the chamber for about half of those elected. This did not generally matter, as the average attendance was less than half the total, but for important and contentious discussions, when members crowded in, many of them had to stand on the floor or in the gallery.[16] The atmosphere of seventeenth-century Commons debates was frequently unruly, with members talking among themselves, and also laughing, hissing and heckling, and occasionally shouting speakers down.[17] There was no fireplace and so no heating, and therefore it was normal in the colder months to wear hats and cloaks in the chamber.[18] Members were also allowed the swords which were a visible mark of gentility.

If the House could not reach agreement over an issue, the Speaker put the point of contention to it as a question, and the two sides shouted assent or dissent in turn, after which the Speaker declared which was louder. Any MP could challenge his decision, whereupon he would ask one of the contending groups to leave the chamber. The convention was that the one to leave should be that which wanted to alter the legal status quo, as a subtle deterrent to challenging that; but rows about which should go were frequent. The Speaker appointed two tellers from each side to make the count, each bearing a staff as a symbol of his office. They reckoned the number left in the chamber and then stood two on each side of its door to count those who had walked out as they came back in. The doors leading outside from the lobby were locked before a division so that members could not swell the group which had left the chamber by coming in from outside. Abstention was not allowed, and MPs who left the House shortly before a question was put, to avoid taking sides, were regarded as dishonourable. If the discrepancy in numbers was obvious after a division, then one side would concede defeat. If not, the tellers would line up at a bar which stood in the centre of the chamber, in front of the clerks' table, the two representing the majority on the right and those for the minority on the left. This made the result obvious immediately, and they would specify it by pacing up to the bar, bowing to the Speaker and having the one standing furthest to the right announce the figures. The Speaker would then repeat them and confirm the result. Tellers were usually prominent advocates of a policy option, who had spoken for it during the preceding debate.[19]

The afternoons following meetings of the House were often taken up by those of committees which it appointed to consider issues in depth, usually with regard to clarifying legal technicalities and collecting information. Members shouted out the names of potential members of these, being limited to a total of two such suggestions each. The size of the resulting bodies could vary greatly, according to the importance and complexity of the matter under consideration: in the first two months of 1642 the smallest appointed numbered four, and the largest fifty-six.[20] They met, correspondingly, not just over the lobby but in other spaces of the former palace. A similar process selected members to represent the Commons to the other chamber of the English Parliament, that of the Lords, and chose the delegations which met those of the Lords for conferences to discuss matters over which the Houses disagreed. The principal setting for these meetings, connected to the doors of the Commons' lobby by a long gallery, was the Painted Chamber. This was a large rectangular room with a ceiling of oak boards, and walls covered in whitewash which now concealed most of the richly painted and gilded medieval murals that had given the place its name.[21] Conveniently next to the Painted Chamber was the House of Lords, where the hereditary aristocracy of the nation met. Their room had been built in the thirteenth century as the private apartment of the queen, and accordingly was more comfortable than that of the Commons, with a fireplace to keep it warm in winter. There was also more space, because the area inside was roughly the same as that of St Stephen's Chapel, and even in the impossible situation in which every peer of the realm was old and fit enough to attend Parliament and did, their total numbers would be less than a third of those of the Commons. The chamber was decorated in crimson and was hung with tapestries, for further decoration and warmth, and lit by a large lancet window at one end. Set into the floor near that end was a bar, also covered in crimson, where petitioners and MPs bearing messages could stand. At the other end was a raised dais where the king sat enthroned when he visited Parliament.[22]

From above, the palace of Westminster resembled a jumble of two-storey buildings with sharply sloping roofs ending in triangular gables. A few larger structures stood out among them, of which the slender tower of St Stephen's Chapel was one. The monster among them, although lower than the chapel, was the rectangular stone bulk, its sides covered in buttresses, of Westminster Hall, the main feasting and ceremonial centre of the medieval palace.[23] Inside, it had niches decorated with stone statues of all the medieval English kings from Edward the Confessor to Richard II, set up in the latter reign. So was the enormous hammer-beam roof weighing 660 tons of oak, the largest in Europe, carved with angels holding shields displaying the royal arms. Beneath this, where once the monarchs had held state, the central law courts of Chancery, King's Bench and Common Pleas now met, each housed in a roofless wooden enclosure erected on the stone-flagged floor. They were accordingly cold and draughty, and the voices from one competed, huge as the space was, with those from the others. When the courts were not in session, Commons committees could meet in their premises.[24] On the western side of the hall was a large open space of beaten earth and cobbles, Old Palace Yard, where horses and carriages could draw up and which gave entrance to the Houses of Lords and Commons.[25]

We do not know where or how Cromwell lodged when he initially attended the Long Parliament, or virtually anything about his life in London or Westminster outside the business transacted in and around the House of

Commons. His parliamentary record is one of official business, set in that huddle of buildings which must have become rapidly as familiar to him as any of the domestic premises he had occupied.

POLITICAL DEBUT

Cromwell had certain distinguishing characteristics among the 507 men eligible to attend the House of Commons in November 1640. For one thing, he was among the least prosperous, as his income even at Ely had never reached £500 a year, and only forty-three other MPs were below that level (one being his brother-in-law, Valentine Walton). It is yet more telling that he was very unusual in that category in not apparently being the client of an aristocrat, whose patronage would compensate for his own lack of resources. He also, however, had two aspects to his profile which counted in his favour. One was experience: he was among the 40 per cent of members who had sat in a Parliament before 1640, and having been part of both of those called previously, he knew how the system worked.[26] The other was that he was potentially very well connected, the fecundity and former importance of his family having yielded a quite unusual number of relations in this House of Commons: eleven cousins and five or six more men at a further degree of removal in the family tree.[27] There is, however, no sign whatever that this collection of people operated as an affinity; rather, they represented a pool on which Oliver might draw if common beliefs and vested interests created a context in which mutual support would be advantageous. To become an attractive ally, he would have to rely on his own abilities.

These were soon manifested. He had made little impression on the Parliament of 1628–9 and none on the Short Parliament; on the Long Parliament his impact was rapid and dramatic. In keeping with the bitter and angry national mood, that Parliament ignored the king's initial appeal for support against the Scots and set about challenging the policies and personnel of his existing government. As part of this process, it reviewed judicial cases in which prominent critics of the regime had been punished by it during the previous eleven years. One of these was that of a young Londoner from a northern family of minor gentry, called John Lilburne; he was small and excitable, with neat features, bobbed hair, a trim moustache and stylish clothes. In 1638 he had been convicted by one of the royal prerogative courts which bypassed the usual process of criminal justice, of distributing books that attacked the authority of bishops. He was publicly flogged and placed in a pillory in Old Palace Yard and had been imprisoned ever since because of his obstinate refusal to admit his offence: he thus made a very credible Puritan martyr. On the Long Parliament's fourth day of business, Cromwell presented a petition from Lilburne for his release. It was promptly referred to a committee to consider such appeals, which met in the palace in the premises of the Court of the Exchequer, and to which Oliver was now added.[28]

The big question here is how far Cromwell was operating as an individual, and how much as part of a team, faction or party. The dominant group in the Long Parliament during 1640, which led the attack on royal policy and ministers, was known at the time, informally, as 'the Junto', a term that has been taken up by historians in recent decades. Its most prominent members were the earls of Bedford, Warwick and Pembroke, Viscount Saye and Sele, John Pym, John Hampden, Oliver St John, Sir Henry Vane, Denzil Holles, Sir Arthur Hesilrig and William Strode. It is fairly clear that by late 1640 these men had become convinced that not only was it necessary to remove the existing royal ministers and advisers, and to force Charles to abandon his policies of the 1630s, but to limit royal control over the government and the Church to ensure that the king could never reintroduce such personnel and actions in the future. In doing so, they had two natural sets of allies, both motivated by religious considerations. One consisted of the Scottish Covenanters, who wanted a closer co-operation between the two kingdoms to restrain the monarch and eliminate the possibility of further war between them, and a reform of the Church of England to make it more similar to the now reformed Scottish Kirk, removing bishops, cathedrals and many ceremonies. The second natural constituency of support comprised the

English Puritans, who were enthusiastic supporters of the latter course, and most if not all of 'the Junto' could themselves be included in the category of Puritan.

It is entirely possible therefore that Cromwell was one of the lesser members of 'the Junto' and that he co-operated with its plans and undertook tasks like the defence of Lilburne at its behest. There is, however, almost no evidence of this, contemporary or retrospective, and this is one part of our general lack of any wider context for Oliver's activities in Parliament: of the meetings and conversations which took place between him and other members, of either House, or the company he kept in leisure hours.[29] It is true that both St John and Hampden were among his cousins, by marriage or blood, but it is not clear what can be presumed from that. During the first year of the Long Parliament the only member of 'the Junto' who was regarded as personally linked with Cromwell, at the time or in retrospect, was John Hampden. A fellow MP of his at that time called Sir Philip Warwick, who became a convinced political opponent, asserted in his memoirs that Hampden recommended Cromwell to his allies, saying that he 'would sit well at the mark', a reference to jousting apparently meaning that he was steady and dependable, and could be trusted to get results.[30] Another MP later termed Hampden Oliver's 'bosom friend' in the early years of the Parliament.[31] It is not clear, however, what these assertions denote.

At any rate, Cromwell rapidly became a hard-working and prominent member of the House, being named to twenty-one other committees or sub-committees in the first session of the Parliament, until the autumn of 1641, and moving nine items in debate.[32] His areas of interest, as defined by this activity, may be grouped roughly under three headings. The first consisted of the continued investigation of punishments meted out by courts and commissions acting under the royal prerogative to critics of the regime during the 1630s.[33] Two descriptions survive of him speaking in the House on behalf of the victims of these. One, which has become famous and much quoted, is in Sir Philip Warwick's memoirs. It is so vivid that it is worth giving again:

I came into the House well clad and perceived a gentleman speaking (whom I knew not) ordinarily apparelled, for it was a plain cloth suit which seemed to have been made by an ill country tailor. His linen was plain, and not very clean, and I remember a speck or two of blood upon his little band [at his throat] which was not much larger than his collar. His hat was without a hatband, his stature was of a good size, his sword stuck close to his side, his countenance swollen and reddish, his voice harsh and untuneable, and his eloquence full of fervour.

The real point that Warwick was about to make, which is less often repeated, is that this coarse-featured, untidy and grubby provincial was 'very much hearkened to', convincing even the haughty royalist Warwick himself that the government had been guilty of serious injustice.[34] Eight years after the event, another MP reminded a fellow of how Cromwell had defended another man who had attacked the English bishops and been flogged and imprisoned by the royal government as a result. This was apparently five months after his championing of Lilburne, and standing in the gallery (presumably as the chamber was full) he 'dropped tears down with his words'.[35] This plain, unsophisticated and passionately emotional manner of public speaking was that of a Puritan preacher, and it was clearly very effective, even in the sophisticated environment of the Commons. It must have been the way in which Cromwell had previously caught the attention of the Cambridge Puritans and freemen.

As effectively all the victims of royal justice whose cases were being discussed were opponents of Laudian religious policy, this activity meshed naturally with the second area of Cromwell's concern, which was the reform of the Church. One aspect of this was to move against the leaders of the Laudian movement, and he engaged in a personal act of vengeance here against those whom five years before he had termed 'the enemies of God' when on 22 December he was appointed to a committee to draw up charges against Bishop Wren. This eventually (in July) drew up articles of impeachment against the bishop, but as the Lords failed to co-operate, the prosecution foundered.[36] Another aspect of Oliver's interest in religion was to support the alterations in the structure and practices of the Church to make them more similar to the reformed Continental Protestant traditions and to the Kirk of Scotland as transformed by the Covenanters. This cause was given impetus by the presentation of the so-called 'Root and Branch Petition' on 11 December, by the nation's Puritans, for the abolition of bishops, cathedral deans and archdeacons.[37] Cromwell was subsequently named to a sub-committee of the House's grand committee on religion, on which Pym, Hampden and Valentine Walton also sat.[38]

On 9 February the House debated the petition, and the state of the Church, and one of the defenders of the customary government was a Dorset gentleman, Sir John Strangeways, who claimed that to remove bishops was to invite a general levelling of the ranks of society. Cromwell immediately attacked him, and his customary intemperance of language carried him away, to the point at which several shocked members interrupted him and demanded that he be called to the bar of the chamber to answer a formal charge of misconduct. Pym and Holles persuaded the House to allow Cromwell to explain himself informally, and it was accepted that the rules were on their side. He made clear, more temperately, why he thought Strangeways's logic ridiculous, and this was accepted, though the issue of abolition itself was deferred indefinitely at the end of the debate.[39] In May, Cromwell returned to the attack. On the 11th he supported a motion that the government's financial problems be eased by confiscating the estates of deans.[40] At the same time he was working with Vane to draft a bill for the abolition of bishops, which was then handed to Hesilrig to find a stalking-horse, of a respected MP not too closely associated with 'the Junto', to present it. On 21 May it was entrusted to a Kentish gentleman called Sir Edward Dering.[41] Both measures, however, failed, and Dering subsequently changed sides to become a supporter of the existing Church government. The majority of the Commons, let alone the Lords, were as yet unwilling to do more than restore the religious situation which had obtained before the Laudian supremacy.

Towards the end of the session, Cromwell, like 'the Junto', therefore adapted his tactics to trying to limit the powers of the Church's leaders, and so secure greater freedom and safety for Puritans. In August he proposed that bishops be removed from the House of Lords, and in September joined his Essex cousin Sir Thomas Barrington and others in arguing that the existing Church service, officially enforced on all churchmen, gave offence to many good ministers. These initiatives also failed, but on 8 September the Commons accepted another motion of Cromwell's, that all parishes should pay for sermons to be held on Sunday afternoons, and be free to allow lecturers to preach on weekdays as well: this was a notable blow for an institution which he had promoted since the mid-1630s.[42] With this and an order by the House to churchwardens to remove the altar rails and innovations in churches favoured by the Laudians – of dubious legality because the Lords did not concur – Cromwell had to be content by the time of the autumn recess.[43]

All this amounted to a clear policy, shared by Puritans in general, and by 'the Junto', to ensure that Puritans could never again be exposed to the harassment they had suffered under Laud's primacy: the Root and Branch Petition had stated explicitly that bishops, deans and archdeacons could no longer be trusted because they had proved to be such effective agents of the wrong religious party, which had been attempting to re-Catholicize the English Church and attack godly Protestantism. What is much less plain, in Cromwell's case as in that of his allies, is the form of ecclesiastical government which was intended to replace them. Sir Philip Warwick indeed later claimed that Oliver had told him, and another MP around this time, concerning religion, 'I can tell you, sirs, what I would not have, though I cannot what I would.'[44] Whether this was because he himself did not know, or because what he favoured was too radical to be publicly admitted, is left open by the statement. All that can be said of his intentions in this regard was that, like most of the House but perhaps not most Puritans at this time, Cromwell was not immediately attracted by the Scottish model, based on parish committees answering to local boards of ministers and elders called presbyteries, which enforced a common system of belief and service. In February he wrote to a friend asking for a copy of the arguments the Scots had presented for uniformity in religion between their nation and England, because he needed to consider them closely.[45]

His third broad area of interest in the first session of the Parliament comprised secular issues, and one category of these consisted of the measures favoured by 'the Junto' to limit independent royal power and enhance that of Parliaments. On 30 December he proposed that a bill for the compulsory calling of a Parliament every year, first put forward by Strode, be given a second reading.[46] This subsequently mutated into an act to ensure that no more than three years elapsed between Parliaments in the future, which passed both Houses and was accepted by the king. In May, Cromwell supported a call for a national declaration of willingness to defend the known laws and the Protestant religion, enforced in every parish on most adult males, and this, known as 'the Protestation', was adopted.[47] This was because its meaning was ambiguous enough to allow of use by both reformers and conservatives, but it would be employed with especial fervour by the former.

Some of Cromwell's energy in this area of activity, however, was vested in an issue of much more local and traditional concern to him: that of controversial schemes for fen drainage. The way to this was opened in December, when he was put onto a committee to hear complaints arising from these.[48] It was, however, by another route that he became embroiled in the most bitter such case: a bill to confirm the lands conferred on the queen as part of the royal marriage settlement. Cromwell was accepted onto this committee too, which received a petition from inhabitants of an area around Somersham, a village on the fen edge a few miles north-east of St Ives, which he would have known well from his time there. The queen's agents had enclosed land there in which these people had common rights, and then sold it to the ever-acquisitive earl of Manchester, who had vested it in his son and heir Edward, Lord Mandeville. The latter had been raised to the House of Lords in his own right by King Charles as a further reward to the old earl, for being a loyal servant; but once more the royal judgement had been at fault, as Mandeville turned against his policies and became a member of 'the Junto'. Now the aggrieved commoners asked the Commons to uphold their case against the enclosures, and Cromwell took their side.[49] He was probably convinced, as he had been at Ely, that the developments concerned actually were of dubious legality and harmful to the local people. He may in addition have been hitting back at the Montagus for the part played by the earl in humiliating him ten years before.

In doing so, of course he was running against his usual allies in 'the Junto', something highlighted by the fact that Denzil Holles represented Mandeville's interests in the dispute. Tension was ratcheted up in May when the local people began to attack the enclosures physically, and Holles presented a petition from Mandeville, asking that his rights over the disputed land be confirmed until the legal question was settled. Cromwell did not condone the violence, but accused Mandeville of provoking it and also of breaching the privileges of the Commons by making his petition. With an equivocation which would later become a hallmark of his style when dealing with legally dubious matters, he suggested but did not assert that the rioters may have possessed a legal right to assembly, if not necessarily to what they did next against the banks and fences of the enclosures. He then, equally in enduring character, resumed the attack with raised stakes: he noted that the House of Lords had responded to Mandeville by ordering the local militia to disperse the rioters if necessary, and he accused the peers of making war on the king's subjects.[50]

The chair of the committee was a Wiltshire lawyer called Edward Hyde, who was also emerging as one of the more prominent MPs and decades later recorded his impressions of Cromwell's role in the hearings. According to these, Mandeville himself had attended, and there were many witnesses on both sides. Those against the lord were uncouth and badly behaved country bumpkins, encouraged by Cromwell who treated the modest and courteous Mandeville with rudeness and violence of tone, and rounded on Hyde himself when the latter tried to impose better behaviour.[51] It is a vivid picture, and conforms to all the other evidence for Cromwell's violent temper and aggressive manner, and his tendency to polarize the world between imagined forces of good and evil. Still, Hyde himself was a skilful manipulator of truth in his memoirs, when dealing with opponents, and a tendency to distortion would be amplified by the gap of nearly thirty years between the incidents concerned and the composition of the memoir of them.[52] None of the parliamentary diarists writing at the time recorded a similarly bad impression of Cromwell's behaviour in these hearings, and he did not suffer any falling off in his appointment to bodies thereafter, nor his apparent loss of credit as a speaker. Moreover, he won the point for which he was striving, the establishment of a new committee to hear the case.[53] As in the Strangeways affair, he could find enough support in the House to face down those whom he offended with his discourteous and bellicose behaviour.

His remarkable disregard for rank, when pursuing a cause, was revealed again in a different affair, equally petty in the annals of the realm but significant to an understanding of Cromwell. It was an intervention in a dispute between two brothers from one of the wealthiest families in Wiltshire, the Thynnes, over their deceased father's estate. One, Sir James, claimed that his privileges as an MP prevented his sibling from taking legal action against him, and then petitioned the Lords for redress against his brother. For some reason this seized Cromwell's attention, and in May he accused Sir James of abusing the system of privilege. He followed this up by moving that the accused man be called to the House to explain himself. The result, in July, was a division between MPs over the case, in which some like Hyde defended Sir James and others joined the attack on him, ending eventually in a judgment that he had indeed been in the wrong.[54] The matter must have given further notice that Cromwell was a formidable advocate and opponent.

All told, the surviving evidence from the first session of the Parliament suggests that at many points – and especially those concerning the big public issues – Cromwell operated so closely in partnership with 'the Junto' as to seem almost an extension of it, but only where its views and ambitions coincided with his own. At others, he collided with members of it, and altogether he looks like a maverick pursuing his own enthusiasms and impulses. What is especially significant is his high success rate, and ability to get away with abrasive, truculent and disrespectful behaviour which flouted social and cultural niceties. Both his identity as an independent operator who happened to share most of the ideals and instincts of 'the Junto', and his capacity to recover from mistakes, are well illustrated by a well-known incident on 9 August. Clearly he had picked up on, and agreed with, a growing sense on the part of 'the Junto' and its allies in the Commons that the governor (tutor) of the heir to the throne, the prince of Wales, might not be wholly relied upon to act in their interests. This was the marquis of Hertford, who had started the Parliament as a reformer and was now slowly moving over to support of the king. Cromwell proposed that two of the leaders of 'the Junto', the earl of Bedford and Viscount Saye, be joined with the marquis in his post. He did not even get a seconder, indicating both that the House was not yet prepared to signal its distrust of Hertford and that Cromwell had taken 'the Junto' by surprise with his plan, along with everybody else.[55] Yet the incident did him no harm, as on 24 August the Commons for the first time gave him the honour of carrying a message from them to the Lords (to suggest a conference to expedite the disbanding of the English and Scottish armies).[56] An occasional gaffe could be forgiven to a member whose regularity of attendance, and willingness to discuss a variety of issues, was proven by his still increasing appointment to committees, on a host of matters ranging from the important to the trivial.[57]

A sense of Cromwell as somebody pursuing personal agendas, usually in alliance with others, is borne out by his lack of appearance in some of the other great political events of the session. The most obvious example is the prosecution by the Commons of the earl of Strafford, the king's principal adviser in secular matters by 1640 and the one who had done most to persuade him to renew the war against the Scots. The latter, and 'the Junto', regarded him as an especially dangerous man, and the king's refusal to dismiss him (and, ideally, to lock him up for a time) forced them into an all-out battle with Charles as the Commons launched a prosecution for treason against the earl to remove him by force. This went on through the spring and ended in the earl's execution on 12 May. Through all these dramatic events, Cromwell remains invisible: he voted with the majority against Strafford but played no known part in the prosecution.

THE MATURE MEMBER OF PARLIAMENT

When the Long Parliament adjourned for six weeks on 9 September, politics were calmer than they had been for over a year. Both of the warring armies had been paid off, and the Scots had withdrawn from England, without having achieved either their religious or their political objectives there. The king had assented to the abolition of Ship Money and the prerogative courts which had condemned people like Lilburne. He had also replaced most of his ministers and councillors with people who had been opposed to the policies of his personal rule and shifted leadership in the Church to them. At the time of the recess he was in Scotland, surrendering most of the royal powers over government there, and confirming the acts of the Covenanter revolution and consolidating in office those who had led it. Three factors remained which threatened continuing instability in British politics. One was the now implacable mutual dislike between Charles and 'the Junto', and the concomitant need of the latter to prevent the king from regaining control of policy-making. The second was the division among the English between those who wanted the further reform of their Church, like Cromwell, and those who wished to restore the form it had taken under Elizabeth and James: the latter were so far the majority in Parliament, and probably the nation. The third was that Charles had failed to win the trust of the Covenanter leaders in Scotland, who suspected him – probably correctly – of having encouraged unsuccessful plots to overthrow them even while he negotiated with them during his visit.

Nonetheless, it is possible that English politics would have continued to calm down, and public opinion in and out of Parliament to swing back towards Charles, had not the Irish Catholics rebelled just after the

Houses reassembled on 20 October. Alone among the kingdoms ruled by the Stuarts, Ireland had retained a Catholic majority after the Reformation, a result partly due to the feeble nature of the Protestant missionary effort, and partly because the reformed religion was imported and enforced by English newcomers intent on grabbing Irish land and offices. It was they who had been installed in power ever since, leaving the Catholics in possession of most of the island but bereft of security for their titles to their property and the practice of their religion. Almost four decades of uneasy peace fractured dramatically in late October 1641when many of the Catholics launched a rebellion intended to win for their religion and nation the same gains which the Covenanters had made in Scotland, and directly inspired by that example. The result was that they rapidly won control of most of the island, but not its capital, Dublin, and of a number of other significant towns and districts. In the process a slaughter took place of Protestant settlers which probably represents the greatest civilian massacre in the history of the British Isles, creating horror in Britain and providing moral justification for a war of reconquest and retribution.

The problem for 'the Junto' was that King Charles could not be entrusted with control of the army to be raised in England to carry out this enterprise, for fear that he would then turn it on his English opponents, to avenge his humiliations of the preceding year. The chief tactic of its members to prevent this was to convince Parliament and the nation that the monarch was unfit to exercise such control, and its principal initial instrument for this was a Grand Remonstrance published by the House of Commons to make the case that Charles had been comprehensively guilty of misgovernment since coming to the throne. This was fuelled by a strong suspicion among its supporters, amounting in some virtually to a belief, that at best the king's attitudes and policies had encouraged the Irish uprising and at worst that he was actually complicit in fomenting it, to destabilize the politics of the archipelago to his advantage. The Remonstrance blamed that uprising on a conspiracy which involved English Catholics and royal advisers, and so rendered the present royal government unfit to suppress it. It also sought to gain parliamentary control of religious policy with a view to the further reform of the Church. It deeply divided the Commons, passing by just eleven votes in the early hours of 23 November.

The result was over a month of political crisis, in which 'the Junto' ramped up the pressure on the king. Crowds of Londoners petitioned and demonstrated at Westminster for the reform of the Church and the exclusion of the bishops from the Lords, causes supported by the Commons. By the end of December both Charles and his opponents had become convinced that each was planning an armed coup against the other, and the king believed that the life of his Catholic wife was in danger, both from a coup and from parliamentary impeachment. His nerve broke, and on 4 January 1642 he led a party of armed men to Parliament to arrest Pym, Hampden, Holles, Strode, Hesilrig and Mandeville. The attempt failed, and the outrage it provoked cost him the support of the majority of the citizens of London, as well as convincing most of the Commons that his entire government needed to be replaced. At this, Charles left his capital, moving slowly up to York in the course of the spring. He was determined never to return unless with assured security, which effectively meant an army; and to prevent this, his opponents would need to raise one of their own. As his supporters left Parliament, the nation began to divide into two armed camps, and so to slide into civil war.

Through these dramatic events, Cromwell's parliamentary career continued to evolve along the same trajectory which it had shown during the spring and summer: steady support for 'the Junto', especially over issues relating to the Church, and an increasing participation in the activities and the tasks of the Commons. On the third day of the new session of Parliament he spoke in favour of a bill to eject bishops not merely from the House of Lords but all secular offices, and urged that if that measure reached the Lords, the bishops there should be barred from voting on it. He won the support of the House. Three days later he secured the renewal of a debate over whether the king should be asked to desist from a policy on which he was now embarked, of filling up the bench of bishops with new men untainted by Laudianism: Cromwell spoke with especial bitterness against one of the proposed men, the Master of Emmanuel College, Cambridge, whose godly and evangelical tone had much in common with that of Puritans. This was most probably because the individual concerned had sided with Henry Downhall in his dispute with the Puritans at St Ives: once more, Oliver had an eye on old scores.[58] In the end, the House voted seventy-one to fifty-three to confer with the Lords for joint action over the matter, and Cromwell was named first to the committee to draw up the Commons' arguments.

On 6 November he successfully moved that the favourite military man of 'the Junto', the earl of Essex, be placed in command of the militia (now the only armed force) in the Midlands and southern England, to secure this region against the presumed menace from the Catholics.[59] Essex was already the king's general there, and so Cromwell's point was that the earl should be removed from royal control and hold his office at the behest of the two Houses. Oliver was also prominent in the wrangle over the Grand Remonstrance, and years later Edward Hyde asserted that a friend of his had told him that at its end Cromwell had whispered that had the measure been rejected, he would have left England.[60] Throughout the tense period between November and January, Oliver fiercely harassed selected supporters of the king, moving variously that they should be committed to prison, prevented from naming a candidate for a by-election, or removed from the Privy Council: though in each of these cases he failed.[61]

It was after the king left the capital, however, that Oliver's prominence in Parliament really burgeoned, as moderate and royalist members left the Houses and the king's opponents redoubled efforts to control him and to suppress the Irish rebels. In the first seven months of 1642 he was appointed to thirty-four committees, made twenty-eight motions in the House, carried twenty-four messages to the Lords, managed a conference with them, and represented the Commons on other missions.[62] The pace of all this activity greatly accelerated in the summer as the king's opponents, left behind at Westminster as the royalists departed, prepared frantically for war. On 28 May alone Cromwell carried messages to the Lords to hasten instructions for their supporters in the regions closest to the king's court at York, to put the militia on a war footing, and to approve individuals to command it in Buckinghamshire and Devon. On the same day he also moved the House to get London's armourers, gunsmiths and saddlers to report weekly on for whom they were making arms; and he was named to a committee to consider outrages committed by soldiers on their way to fight in Ireland.[63] The role of messenger to the Lords was one which traditionally required tact and diplomacy, not qualities much associated with Cromwell at this time; but perhaps he was learning more of both, on the job, or perhaps his rough and passionate eloquence was expected to be as effective with the peers as it often was in the Commons.

In these seven months, Cromwell's activities display three main preoccupations. The first was his abiding one, with religion, which continued although the other two, which were new, tended now to overshadow it. In this area he was starting to become a national figure, so that in late March he was one of three MPs, with Pym and Hampden, to whom ministers in Monmouthshire, a Welsh border county, delivered a petition complaining of the dangerous number of Catholics there; and he was the one who recommended it to the House, which decided to seize their arms.[64] As usual, his savagery showed against particular individuals, especially those who had personally crossed him. In February the Commons debated the publication of a collection of actual and intended speeches by Sir Edward Dering. This was intended to explain his conversion to being a defender of the king and of bishops, but also reflected badly on certain MPs, and disclosed Cromwell's involvement in the preparation of the bill to abolish bishops. Cromwell moved that the book be publicly burned, and Dering expelled from the House and imprisoned. Once again, he seems to have acted in this matter on impulse, and without care to prepare his way, for when he proposed a fellow MP to write a reply to the book, that man immediately refused.[65]

His second enthusiasm during these months was a new one: the suppression of the Irish rebels. This was an ideal cause for a born-again Puritan, representing a holy war against the followers of a false and satanic religion, the chief enemy of his own. They had furthermore rendered themselves utterly evil in Cromwell's eyes by making a treacherous and unprovoked attack on his fellow believers, resulting in atrocities against civilians unprecedented in the known history of the British Isles (and the death rate of Protestant colonists in Ireland as a result of the rebellion, bad as it was, had been mightily swollen in the telling). Two factors intensified the zeal with which English people like Cromwell supported this struggle. One was that they regarded the Irish rebels as the principal weapon of an international Catholic conspiracy directed by the Pope and involving some of his adherents in Britain, including advisers of the king, probably his wife, and possibly Charles himself (a belief which was no less potent a component of ideology for the fact that it was wildly wrong). The second factor was that religious animosity against the rebels was enhanced by an ethnic one, that for centuries the English had regarded the native Irish as a semi-savage and intrinsically hostile race; an attitude which was not much alloyed now by the fact that many supporters of the rising were the descendants of medieval English settlers, who had been pushed from power by the Protestant newcomers, and so held to the old religion.

Accordingly, Cromwell threw himself into support for the reconquest of the island in various ways. In February he was put onto a committee to promote the sending of an army, and in March onto a joint commission of MPs and lords to carry on the same work. The minutes of that have survived, and show that he attended regularly from the start.[66] He was thereafter made a member of successive bodies to ensure that money, men and ships were collected for it, spoke in favour of measures to do so, and carried messages to the Lords urging them to expedite these.[67] When a scheme was produced in March, to finance the war from loans secured against land to be confiscated from the rebels, he eventually contributed six hundred pounds, in two instalments, from the stock of capital which had been raised by the sale of his estate in Ely. This would potentially gain him a thousand acres in the richest Irish province, of Leinster, and was an obvious gamble, based on the premise that the rebellion would indeed be crushed, and relatively swiftly. His subscription was the average one by an MP, yet these sums were usually put up by wealthy people with cash to spare, and Cromwell was risking a large proportion of a lump sum off which he and his family were currently living.[68]

That risk was increased as the effort to send aid to the Irish Protestants was disrupted by the growing political breakdown in England, as the king's enemies left behind at Westminster – who having retained the support of around three-fifths of the Commons and a third of the Lords, referred to themselves as 'Parliament' – prepared for war. Those preparations became Cromwell's main preoccupation as well, and he took to them with the same gusto that he had applied to the regaining of Ireland. He was indeed as natural a civil warrior as he was a holy warrior, having already, in the peaceful mid-1630s, divided his nation between God's enemies (who happened to be his own religious opponents) and God's friends (who happened to be his own religious allies). As soon as it had become plain that the king had left his capital, on 14 January 1642, Oliver moved in the Commons that national measures be taken for defence, and this seems to have been the genesis of what ultimately became the Militia Ordinance of 5 March. In that measure, the first major one ordered by the remnant of the Parliament at Westminster, in despite of the monarch, the trained bands who were the regular protectors of each county were placed under the leadership of men trusted by that party.[69] True to character, Cromwell also denounced individual royalists for speaking for the king and against his opponents, and sought their arrest. At first these were relatively obscure people, but he eventually elevated his attack to greater targets: on 11 June he acted as a teller for the first time in a division which concerned an important issue, namely, whether to accuse nine noblemen who had joined the king at York of promoting war against Parliament. His side won by 109 votes against 51, and he was sent to prepare the Lords to receive the proposal.[70]

He also gave increasing attention to the mechanics of military preparation: of getting the right men appointed to county posts, of discouraging activity by local royalists, and of ensuring that arms and money were collected for his cause.[71] On 5 June MPs subscribed money themselves for the defence of that cause, Cromwell lending five hundred pounds which depleted his stock of cash even further.[72] Four days later the two Houses published an order directing all good people to bring in money, silver or gold plate, weapons and horses for their defence against a king seduced by wicked men into making war on them: the value of the horses and arms was to be refunded, and the value of the money and plate repaid with interest, when Charles was brought to heel.[73] The king's response was to revive the medieval instrument of commissions of array, to empower men loyal to him to raise the militia and additional forces in each county to defend him. The reply of the party at Westminster came on 15 July, when it commissioned the earl of Essex as its commander-in-chief, to recruit an army and fight the king's followers.[74] With that, war had effectively begun.

All this means that Cromwell has a presence in the parliamentary records on almost half the days in June and early July 1642, but for a biographer it still amounts to no more than a skeleton of evidence. Once more the sources are completely lacking for the discussions which went on around all this business, and the company that he kept.[75] If there seems to have been one person with whom he can be seen co-operating tactically in the first half of the year, it is Denzil Holles, a younger son of the earl of Clare who was, as shown, a prominent member of 'the Junto'. On 28 April he persuaded Holles to move the Speaker to allow an action, and Holles then proposed that Cromwell be sent on an errand to the Lords; and both initiatives succeeded. When the Commons divided in June over whether to accuse the nine peers who had gone to the king of an affront to Parliament, Holles acted as teller alongside Oliver (again with success).[76] These may not, however, have been more than fleeting and opportunistic moments of co-operation. No more than before, moreover, is it possible to tell what Cromwell's aims and ideals were: it remains easy to say what he opposed, but not what he wanted instead. Perhaps he really was not sure himself, and just believed that if the king were freed from the influence of Catholics and Arminians or Laudians, and the power of higher churchmen was broken, so that none could ever abuse it again, then all would naturally turn out well. On 8 April the two Houses had issued a declaration promising a reformation of the Church, in government and liturgy, after an assembly of chosen clerics had been called to advise on it, and it may have been widely presumed that good results would follow naturally, once the opponents of reform were eradicated.[77]

A canny recent commentator on Cromwell's career in 1640–2 has suggested that 'it would be perfectly feasible to write the parliamentary history of that time without mentioning him at all'.[78] This is a just verdict: he was a very active, prominent and successful MP of the second rank, who cannot be credited with a leading or decisive role at any point. Most of his interventions, although persuasive at the time, ultimately led to nothing because the Commons did not persevere with the issues concerned or the Lords were unco-operative. The closest he came to changing history was by initiating the moves which led to the Militia Ordinance, but he played no further part in them and the need for such a response was so obvious that somebody would surely have suggested one if he had not. To a biographer, however, this period of Cromwell's life is crucial, giving him extensive experience in Parliament, and an accumulated trove of trust and popularity there among the king's opponents, which was to prove invaluable during the rest of his career.

INTO THE FIELD

As the summer of 1642 wore on, an increasing number of Cromwell's party at Westminster left Parliament in order to get home to their constituencies and areas of natural influence to expedite the war effort there. He was no exception, and there was a particular importance to his return to Cambridge. The town was a major river crossing, route centre and local capital, but the real danger there by July came from the university, some parts of which – perhaps the majority – were emerging as royalist. In particular, the wealth of the colleges, in cash and plate, could provide an important resource for the king, in raising an army. At the end of June, Charles responded to the actions of his enemies by calling for contributions of cash and other materials, by asking the university to lend him money at the same rate of interest that his opponents were offering. The response was apparently warm and rapid, because within three weeks he had written again, giving thanks for a large sum.[79] By the time that news of these activities reached London, it was reported (most implausibly) that twenty thousand pounds had been sent by the colleges.[80]

On 24 July, Charles upped his bid, by ordering the colleges to send him their plate, a store of treasure amassed over centuries, on the grounds that his enemies were planning to seize it. He promised to repay its value.[81] At the same time, members of the university were starting to arm themselves – probably for fear of attack by the townsmen – by ordering chests of weapons from London, though most were confiscated by the mayor on arrival.[82] News of all these developments reached the MPs left at Westminster, who responded with a string of measures in mid and late July, encouraged by Cromwell. Arms deliveries to the university were forbidden and Oliver was repaid the value of a consignment which he himself had bought and sent to defend the town, while the mayor was told to keep those he had seized and Cromwell was directed to ask permission from the county's lord lieutenant for the townsmen to start military drill.[83] Cambridgeshire was starting to divide, with some local men speaking for the king, and others – including one of those who had backed Cromwell for election at Cambridge – denouncing them to Westminster for doing so.[84] Both Houses ordered the formation of a committee of their supporters in Huntingdonshire, including Valentine Walton, to combat royalism there, as they could not trust the regular officials.[85] If effective, this would block the direct route from Cambridge to the king.

As August arrived, Charles's request for the college plate galvanized the royalists further. Walton and his friends failed to secure Huntingdonshire, as when he summoned the county militiamen very few obeyed, and the mayor and other leaders of Huntingdon left the town rather than get involved. Cromwell's own cousin Henry, son of the family patriarch Sir Oliver, raised fifty armed men who marched through Huntingdon and were reported to be ready to escort the plate up the Great North Road to the king's headquarters.[86] This was an early sign of division among the Cromwell cousins, which was to lead to Henry and one of his sons becoming royalist officers, while Sir Oliver's younger brother Sir Philip had one son who supported the king and two who opposed him.[87] In the Isle of Ely a number of parish ministers were royalist, and when the king's proclamation of the earl of Essex as a traitor arrived in Ely itself, it was published by the town crier, with a guard of honour bearing halberds, assembled by the sheriff. The guard may have been intended to deal with trouble, but the only objection raised was by a single local gentleman called William Dodson, who threatened to cut off the crier's hand. The crowd turned hostile to Dodson, who was taken aside by a deputy bailiff and a justice of the peace and advised to leave town.[88] He did, to reappear later in Cromwell's life. At Cambridge, a militia band appeared led by a gentleman called James Dowcra, whose seat was just to the east of the town, which had been ordered there by the high sheriff of the county, to keep the peace. This turned out to be code for keeping the townsmen quiet while the college plate was carted off towards the king. It was the final step in the series to secure Huntingdonshire and Cambridgeshire for the royalists – but at this moment Cromwell exploded onto the scene.

He had apparently come up to the area around the beginning of August, passing across the green and gold landscape of the opening of harvest, on his own initiative, as no order exists from the Commons for him to do so. On the other hand, both Houses would have wished his mission well, because they had an obvious interest in getting a grip on the region and keeping the plate out of Charles's hands. Cromwell had no authority over any of the militia, and so set out to raise a force of armed volunteers from the western part of Cambridgeshire. This was the portion bordering his old haunts of Huntingdon and St Ives, which he would have known best.

In particular he may be presumed to have called on his Puritan network, and obvious places at which to do so would have been Eltisley, home of his brother-in-law John Desborough, and Godmanchester, former site of a lectureship which had probably been held by the Dr Wells whom he had tried to protect. Dowcra had come into Cambridge with flags flying and drums beating, and made his base at King's College, where the plate was to be collected. It was now that Cromwell arrived with his partisans, and Dowcra shut himself into the chapel yard of the college, calling on loyal royalists to help him. None apparently did, and Dowcra and his men soon surrendered. He was sent a prisoner to Westminster, where he was released in February on promise of good behaviour, and he went home to remain placidly loyal to Cromwell's party for the rest of the war.[89] The confrontation at King's College had been one between a group of committed partisans, prepared to fight for their beliefs, and a band of men who obeyed the established power, and adapted their attitudes when the source of that power shifted.

Cromwell now seized the magazine of arms and ammunition laid up in Cambridge Castle, on the north side of the bridge, for the defence of the county.[90] This, and the arms taken from the militiamen, must have greatly increased the power of his vigilante squad, and he spread some of that to the north and east of the town to ensure that the college plate could not reach the king. Two young gentlemen returning home to East Anglia from the royal court at York, along the road between Huntingdon and Cambridge, were ambushed by some of Cromwell's musketeers, who had hidden in a ripe cornfield. They informed their captives that they had to be searched and explain their business to Cromwell himself, but were easily satisfied when the youths blandly insisted on their innocence and gave them a shilling: a genial venality could possess even Oliver's followers.[91] What actually happened about the plate will probably never be known. The House of Commons was informed on 15 August that Oliver had prevented any from reaching the king, and so deprived him of twenty thousand pounds' worth of funds. On the 22nd the House learned that Magdalene College had tried to get its consignment through the blockade but this had been captured, and ordered that it be brought to London to swell their war chest. On 1 September, however, the House was told of the arrest of some heads of colleges who had apparently conveyed their plate to Charles.[92]

A contemporary letter from the town describes the failure of Magdalene College to get its collection through but adds that other colleges were still trying.[93] A later memoir told of how a young royalist don (who was known to the author) managed to cart a lot of plate down small lanes at night and so through to the king, and a tract probably written by the don concerned also asserted that such a convoy slipped through Cromwell's cordon.[94] Later in the war three college bursars and a Huntingdonshire gentleman were denounced for having helped convey plate to the king's base.[95] The account books of three colleges record amounts of it to be sent off: conversely it is true that a lot of plate objects dating from before 1642 still survive in the university, but then it is not known how much more had existed.[96] So it looks probable that some got through to the royal headquarters, despite Cromwell's efforts.[97] The most important point that can be established is that Oliver was believed in London and Westminster, at that time, to have played a heroic role in preventing the plate from fuelling the royalist war effort.

Certainly the men left in the Houses of Parliament were happy to support him. It is possible to dramatize and glamorize his action in stopping the passage of the plate – as much as he did – by presenting it as a tremendous risk, a headstrong initiative of his own which could rebound badly on him if the king and his enemies made peace at the last minute and the illegality of Cromwell's behaviour was highlighted. By mid-August 1642, however, the chances of that happening were minimal, and what Cromwell did could have been covered by the general instructions of his party to prevent King Charles's military preparations.[98] At any rate, the Commons weighed in strongly on his side as soon as they heard of the events in the region, getting a directive drawn up to indemnify him, Walton and their friends, and ordering the arrest of officials who had opposed them.

Cambridgeshire gentry who had assisted him were sent the thanks of the House, and some in London who held county offices and were trustworthy were ordered home to reinforce the war effort there. Oliver was empowered to guard the crossings of the Cam and Ouse to stop any aid reaching the king from East Anglia.[99]

Most effective of all, his party in the capital assembled a hit squad, a body of four to five hundred armed horsemen which was despatched from London to Cambridge to give its cause there supremacy. Its members professed a belief that they were fighting a Catholic plot to destroy all they held dear. This force arrived on 29 August, and within four days had taken over the town, the university and the Isle of Ely, and arrested all the royalist leaders in the county, including three heads of colleges and Bishop Wren. Cromwell himself joined forces with this little army in its work, directing the seizure of one of the university leaders from his bed at one o'clock in the morning. The bishop's household and some of the colleges were plundered of money and plate, which were loaded onto a cart and sent to London with the prisoners.[100] The Cambridgeshire parliamentarians were left to take over the militia and settle the county as a support for their cause.[101] Cromwell seems to have returned to the capital with the horsemen and their charges, because by 6 September he was back in the Commons and appointed to another committee; his job in his constituency was, after all, done.[102]

THE CAVALRY CAPTAIN

When Cromwell made his return to Westminster, he must have been conscious that he would not remain there long, for he had already been entrusted with a command in the field army being assembled to fight the king. The commission for this from the earl of Essex is lost, but subsequent pay warrants prove it to have been as captain of a troop of 'harquebusiers' (light cavalry) in Essex's own horse regiment. The dash, speed and impact of cavalry action seem instinctually to have appealed to Oliver. The commission was probably signed in August, and the troopers were still being fitted out, and possibly still being raised, on the 29th, when a warrant was issued by the earl. It was to provide horses and equipment for three corporals, two trumpeters (who would act as messengers as well as directing the men by sounding signals), a farrier to care for the horses and a saddler to mend their harness, and scarves for all the men, so they could recognize each other in battle as there was no common uniform.[103] By 7 September there were sixty troopers enlisted, who were issued with a month's pay.[104]

A week later the parliamentary committee at Westminster that directed the war effort ordered Cromwell to muster the troop and lead it to join the main army, which was gathering at Northampton.[105] No details survive of how and where it had been recruited: whether in Cambridgeshire, Huntingdonshire, London, or all three places. There was an eyewitness description written ten years later of a meeting at Huntingdon, where Oliver declared that he sought the welfare of those present and to stand with them 'for the liberty of the gospel and the laws of the land'.[106] This could be an example of his tactics used to raise his troop, but it could have taken place in the following year. The quartermaster (adjutant) of Cromwell's unit was his brother-in-law John Desborough, and it seems likely that some of the troopers came from the same western part of Cambridgeshire as Desborough, and had been part of the force raised there to stop the college plate leaving Cambridge. More than that cannot be said, and it increases the discomfiture of the biographer that at this dramatic moment Cromwell disappears from history again: he features in no contemporary source between 13 September and 17 December.

It is possible to reconstruct a hypothetical portrait of Oliver leading his soldiers towards the Northampton rendezvous, by using contemporary evidence for how they *should* have appeared, according to the military handbooks of the age. As captain, he should have ridden at the head of the column, and we know him from portraits later in the decade as a burly man of average height with thick brown hair cut in a bob at his collar, the large bulbous nose which was a family trademark, a high colour in his face, a short and closely trimmed beard and moustache, a tight impatient mouth and a direct stare from heavy-lidded chestnut-hued eyes.[107] Behind him should have ridden the cornet carrying the troop's colours, or flag, and the rest of the men should have followed that.[108] Harquebusiers had in theory a set armament, of a metal helmet open at the front and strapped under the chin, metal back and breast plates fastened together over the torso and a gorget, or crescent-shaped piece of metal to guard the throat. The helmet was lined with leather to cushion the head, and the rest of the armour worn over a thick jacket of white or yellow leather called a buff coat, with sleeves and thigh flaps, which could stop a sword cut and prevent bruising from the plates and gorget.

Weaponry would consist of a pair of pistols and a sword for each man, in holsters and scabbard hung from belts or saddles, and in theory a carbine, or gun 2 feet 6 inches in length, slung from a strong leather strap around the trooper's neck. The pistols and carbine would fire by the wheellock or flintlock methods, whereby the trigger caused a flint or piece of iron pyrites to strike a metal wheel or pan and send sparks to ignite the gunpowder with which the weapon had been loaded, and shoot a lead ball.[109] Cromwell's troop would have needed to undergo at least some training, on recruitment or the march, to make it at all effective in action. At the minimum its members would have had to learn how to guide their horses, with words, clicks or chirps, and bridle (ideally lined with wire to stop an enemy cutting it) and reins. They would have needed to know how to get their steeds to stop, turn and rear, and to manoeuvre on muddy ground and ploughed fields. Ideally, they would have had the time and means to get their horses accustomed to the noise of drums, trumpets and shots, and the shouting of massed men, and – in optimum circumstances – the jabs of infantry weapons in simulated battles.[110]

At any rate, that was the theory; but in reality we have no idea how much training Cromwell and his troopers received, or how well they were equipped. The unit was given the standard sum paid out for the raising of a horse troop in Essex's army, which would probably not have been sufficient to cover the whole cost to mount and equip each man.[111] This is even when the expensive and cumbersome carbines are deducted, as horsemen during the war generally did without them and Cromwell's men may not have acquired them even at its start.[112] On the other hand, the payment may not have been needed for all the expense, as some of the horses and kit could have been contributed or bought directly for use of the troop by well-wishers to the cause or to specific people in the unit. Some of the troopers could have paid themselves for items or possessed them already. In addition there is a further complication: that one of the eulogies of Cromwell published after his death claimed that he raised the troop at his own expense.[113] This was clearly part of its strategy to make the point that he was already a substantial gentleman before the war (like that of his education at Lincoln's Inn). It is not true, however, as Cromwell had, as shown, been paid the usual sum for the purpose from his party's war treasury, but it may well be that he dipped into his shrinking capital fund to ensure that his men got all the equipment which the payment could not cover. All in all, we are probably justified in imagining him and his troop walking their horses towards Essex's army clad in the full rig expected – perhaps minus the carbines – and observing the due order of march directed by the manuals; but we cannot be sure of this.

Essex's army moved west from Northampton to Worcester, across the autumnal Midland countryside, as the woods began to show bright colours and the harvested fields fade to brown. The king had marched to Shrewsbury, and from there he commenced his advance on London in October with a force of roughly equal size. His enemies shifted east to block his way, and in Warwickshire they lost contact with him, before finally blundering into him at Edgehill, where the grassy limestone ridge which runs diagonally south-west across Midland England drops sharply to the broad river valley of the Warwickshire Avon. There they joined battle on the sunny, unseasonably cold afternoon of 23 October. The royal force was complete, but units of Essex's were still scattered into overnight quarters some distance off, and could not come up in time. Both armies drew up in the conventional formation of the age, with cavalry on the wings and infantry in between. The king's right wing of horsemen was commanded by his charismatic nephew Rupert, a German Protestant prince whose family had lost its territory in the Continental wars of religion and who was seeking a homeland. Both royalist wings charged first, and completely routed the parliamentarian horse units opposite, and some of the foot regiments next to them.

Essex had thus lost a third of his army at the opening of the battle, but the royalist cavalry now threw away its victory by pursuing the fleeing enemy, abandoning its own infantry and leaving most of the earl's foot units intact. Essex kept his nerve and launched his infantry against the king's, which was less well equipped, supporting the attack with a few horse and artillery units he had kept in reserve. A third of the royalist foot soldiers now broke under the impact and ran, leaving their comrades to stand their ground desperately, and the fighting to degenerate into a bloody and confused chaos which ended when darkness fell. About one and a half thousand bodies littered the field, and at the end of a freezing night the survivors on both sides were too exhausted and traumatized to renew the action. They marched off in opposite directions, Essex to regroup and the king to occupy Oxford and prepare another advance on London, through the Thames Valley.[114] Where was Cromwell amid all this? We don't know.

We can, however, make an informed guess. There is one contemporary source which mentions his presence at the battle, an account written by Nathaniel Fiennes, a son of Viscount Saye of 'the Junto', who described how one of his brothers had arrived at the action towards its end and rallied a body of the fleeing parliamentarian horse. He gathered them on the relative safety of a hill, where two more horse troops, one led by 'Captain Cromwell' (who is probably our man), eventually joined them. Hampden's brigade, which was also late in reaching the field, then arrived and they all moved down together to join Essex's main force as the action was ending. This suggests that Cromwell's was another of the bodies of horse which was quartered too far off to make it to the battle until near its end. However, in an appendix the account states that Cromwell had been one of those captains of Essex's horse regiment on the right wing of the parliamentarian army who had fought all the way through the battle and never abandoned his men. This would seem to indicate that he had been on the field from the start, and though caught up in the general rout of his wing, he had kept his troop together and brought it back to the field.[115] Which version is correct?

It is possible to swing the balance of probability by looking at later accounts of Cromwell's career written by enemies, which deal with his conduct at Edgehill. Neither of them implicates him in the disaster to the cavalry wing, which ought to have been an obvious failing with which to reproach him. Both instead state that he and his men were away from the battlefield when the action started, and that he deliberately avoided going to the aid of his comrades until it was safely over.[116] This was an obvious slur on the reputation of somebody who was late to the fight. The list of captains given at the end of one account, who were honoured for not abandoning either the field or their commands, would be compatible with one who led his troop to join the earl, though too late to affect the action, and the right wing of Essex's army was where the rest of his horse regiment was stationed. It is therefore the most probable conjecture that Cromwell's experience of the first great battle of the war was the frustrating one of arriving at the field to find the cavalry of his side in flight, and joining those horsemen whom he saw making a stand, before getting to the main body of his army as night fell.[117] It was inglorious, but still praiseworthy, and Fiennes, son of a political ally of his, made sure that he got the praise.

Fifteen years later, Cromwell returned to consider the implications of Edgehill in a speech to a Parliament, which has been much quoted in modern times. He reported that he had suggested to Hampden, who again appears as a particular friend, that Essex's horsemen were 'most of them old decayed serving men and tapsters, and such kind of fellows', while the royalist horse were 'gentlemen's sons, younger sons and persons of quality'; and that is why the latter routed the former. He therefore proposed that they 'must get men of a spirit that is likely to go on as far as gentlemen will go, or else I am sure you will be beaten still'. Cromwell claimed that he therefore undertook to find these recruits.[118] Unhappily, for present purposes, the speech was delivered in the particular circumstances of April 1657, when he was head of state and the army on which he relied was unpopular with the House of Commons and at loggerheads with it over political and religious issues. Oliver was therefore reminding the MPs that his soldiers had won the war and acknowledging that many of them were drawn from outside the traditional ruling class and suggesting that this should not matter. Its relevance to the situation in 1642, and any actual conversation which may have taken place then, is unknown.

After repairing itself, Essex's army marched to defend London, and when the king launched his attack on the capital in November, it faced him just to the west, reinforced by the well-trained and well-equipped City militia. The royalists were outnumbered, and retired to Oxford, to settle down there for the winter and start organizing the provinces to support an extended war effort. The king's enemies, based on London and Westminster, set about the same task, while Essex's soldiers quartered around the capital. Invisible to history, Cromwell and his troop must have taken part in all these events. They re-emerge in the records on 17 December, when they received half a month's pay.[119] By then the troop had grown to eighty men, an indication of good leadership, and also adequate payment by the parliamentary treasury. It was not a bad end to a year which had generated such promise for most of its run and such frustration near its end. The new enterprise of organizing the provinces for victory promised much to a provincial such as Cromwell, representing a country town, and before 1642 wore out, he must already have been preparing, with great anticipation, for this new phase of his career.

3

❖

THE CAVALRY COLONEL

The project of the rival parties in the winter of 1642–3, to harness the provinces systematically for their war effort, had two major and interlinked aspects. One was to set up new organizations to mobilize local communities and extract military resources from them. The second was to authorize local partisans to take up arms in their areas and install garrisons at fortified strongpoints. The former process was commenced at Westminster in November and December, when the first of a series of regional associations, which grouped counties under co-ordinated leadership, were established. Two of these were to be of especial concern to Cromwell. One was the East Midland Association, of Derbyshire, Leicestershire, Nottinghamshire, Rutland, Northamptonshire, Buckinghamshire, Bedfordshire and Huntingdonshire, which was placed under the command of a young Leicestershire aristocrat called Lord Grey of Groby, heir of the earl of Stamford. The other was the Eastern Association, of Norfolk, Suffolk, Essex, Hertfordshire, and Cambridgeshire and the Isle of Ely, the command of which was given to another nobleman with a matching name, Lord Grey of Warke.

The generals concerned were commissioned directly by the earl of Essex as commander-in-chief, and they were supposed to bypass the traditional county defence system of the militia, led by county lord lieutenants and their deputies, in order to recruit and maintain regular soldiers. The lieutenants were instructed to provide arms and ammunition for the latter, while themselves keeping the militia ready for action, but it was not clear how the two systems of defence and authority, the lieutenancy and the association, actually operated with respect to each other. Committees of supposedly loyal gentry were established in each county to provide for the needs of Essex's field army. To pay for these needs, more loans from supporters were solicited, but also it was now decreed that everybody in areas under the control of the party based at Westminster, who had not voluntarily contributed to its defence (or who had given token amounts), should be made to pay a sum representing a fixed proportion of their wealth. A quarter of the money raised was to be used to cover the expenses of the regional associations; and in addition, deputy lieutenants were empowered to levy rates on their counties to provide for their defence. The county committees were expected to send representatives to regional meetings to oversee the affairs of each association.[1]

The role of local commanders and garrisons in the war was to be of crucial importance, for two reasons. The first was the functional one: that they preserved the resources on which their party depended, and could disrupt those of the enemy and conquer territory. The second was a moral one: that when the military situation in general was stagnant, or adverse, successful exploits by local generals and garrison governors provided an invaluable source of news to show that their cause was still vibrant and victorious, and so blessed with divine favour. They were delivered to the public by a huge new industry of printed propaganda, embodied in newspapers, broadsides and pamphlets, which was employed by both sides, but more rapidly and on a much larger scale by the parliamentarians.[2] Local commanders often sought deliberately and systematically to send heroic accounts of their deeds to the London or Oxford presses, which would inflate their own reputations and so increase both the support that they received from the central authorities and their local prestige. It was claimed of the parliamentarian governor of Derby, Sir John Gell, that he 'kept the diurnal-makers [newspaper-writers] in pension, so that whatever was done in the neighbouring counties, against the enemy, was attributed to him'.[3]

As will be seen, Cromwell was to become a master of such manipulation of the press.

In the winter of 1642–3, however, two commanders in particular were emerging as the most charismatic and admired of the local champions of Parliament (to adopt now the slightly dubious, but long historically conventional, title which the party at Westminster claimed). One was a Kentish gentleman and MP, Sir William Waller, who raised a local army to clear the south-eastern counties of royalist strongholds, and having done so proceeded in the first three months of 1643 to strike as far westwards as the Severn Valley. His nickname in the London press was 'William the Conqueror'. The other was Sir Thomas Fairfax, heir to the main parliamentarian nobleman in Yorkshire, Ferdinando, Lord Fairfax. The seat of the family was in the rich arable land of the Ainstey, near York, but they found most of their support for the war in the independent-minded, and generally Puritan, cloth-working districts of the West Riding. There they built up a popular military base, and won victories against usually superior numbers which caused one pamphleteer to hail Sir Thomas as 'the Rider on the White Horse', after a character in the Book of Revelation.[4]

These men had established themselves as heroes before Cromwell had even begun to make a name for himself as a soldier, and for good reason. Not only did he lag behind them, and many others, in time, because of his respectable but undistinguished service in the field army, but in a hierarchical society he had no obvious pre-existing local power base. He was, after all, still only a minor gentleman, not a knight or nobleman, with no landed estate and at best patchy experience of local government, and only of its lowest rung. The reputation he had won for himself in the Commons counted for little out in the counties: but thither he was now bound, to make a command, and a military following and reputation, from scratch. If it ever occurred to him to return to the relatively safe haven of the House and stay there, there is no sign of this: instead both duty and his natural taste for action seem to have propelled him headlong into a continuing career as an army officer, this time based in the familiar setting of his home region.

THE ARMED POLICEMAN

Cromwell's commission as the colonel of a horse regiment in the new regular Eastern Association defence force was almost certainly signed by Grey of Warke in late January 1643: once more the commission itself has not survived, as part of the general problem, for a historian, that Cromwell left no personal archive. The authorities at Westminster were still calling him a captain up to 25 January, but on the 26th the parliamentarians of Norfolk were giving him his new rank.[5] He seems to have spent his last weeks in London in a welter of activity. On 6 January he played a leading part in a Commons debate over whether an act should be passed pardoning royalists for their actions thus far in the war, as part of a set of moves to make peace possible. It is a sign of how far he could break with normal friendships and alliances when they went against his beliefs that both John Hampden and Nathaniel Fiennes, who had been so useful to him in the matter of his conduct at Edgehill, acted as tellers in favour of the measure and he served as one against them. His usual savagery towards opponents had kicked in, and his side won by seven votes.[6] He was also gathering money in mid-January, presumably to launch his regiment, getting granted the voluntary contributions of parliamentarians in Cambridgeshire, and given more of what was owed to his existing troop from the central war treasury.[7]

In the third week of January that troop, quartered in Hertfordshire, performed a signal service for its cause. The new high sheriff of the county had returned from the king's court with a commission of array, to secure the shire in Charles's name. He fixed up several copies of a proclamation, calling on the parliamentarians there to lay down arms, in St Albans on market day. Unhappily for him, six of Cromwell's troopers were there and saw a copy, and promptly arrested him. He was rescued by a crowd, but later in the day, when he had retired to an inn, the troopers returned with more of their comrades, took him prisoner again and escorted him to London with some other local royalists.[8] That quashed the attempt by the king's supporters to take over Hertfordshire: it was not apparently the work of Cromwell himself, who was not recorded as being present, but the action of his men reflected well on him and was later taken as one of his accomplishments.

By 23 January, Cromwell was at Cambridge, and had set about the twin tasks of godly iconoclasm and the terrorizing of suspected royalists. His arrival precipitated the defacement of a stone screen installed by Laudians at Peterhouse College chapel and a canopy above the seats for doctors of divinity in the university church of St Mary's, presumably as both had religious imagery.[9] He immediately took the opportunity, also, to pay off old scores again, by sending some of his troopers to search the house of Robert Bernard, the lawyer who had helped bring about his humiliation at Huntingdon over a decade before. They found nothing incriminating, and indeed Bernard was now a parliamentarian who sat on the county committee for Huntingdonshire: but Cromwell's reaction to this disappointment was to write to his victim declaring that Bernard had escaped this time by being 'wary', but that 'subtlety will not save you'.[10] A different sort of reckoning probably took place around this time when Cromwell himself led his horsemen to the mansion of his uncle and godfather, Sir Oliver. The latter now obeyed the demands of his nephew's party, but his son had, as said earlier, joined the king. This made his godfather vulnerable to Oliver, who confiscated all of his family arms and plate. He did so while observing all of the courtesies due to the head of his family, removing his hat in his godfather's presence and asking for his blessing; but these niceties made the old man find the plundering of his property all the more galling.[11] The seizure of arms, horses and gold and silver objects from Catholics (whatever their allegiance) and suspected royalists was one of the activities in which Parliament expected its new regional associations to engage. It had a double value, in that whatever was taken could be used directly to equip the new soldiers being raised; which made it desirable to find as many suspects as possible.

The Eastern Association was duly inaugurated at a meeting at Bury St Edmunds, the main town of West Suffolk, on 9 February, attended by representatives from most parts of the region. Cromwell arrived for it in a coach with three other men. One of the pleasant aspects of the new organization, for him, must have been that it adopted Parliament's standard scale of pay for soldiers, in which a colonel got a handsome £2 5s 6d per day: this would provide a useful stream of income if the money came in.[12] Strategically, the association gave a new importance to Cambridge, which was designated as a major military base at the western end of the region, to shield the latter against a possible attack by the royal army around Oxford. For this purpose, at the end of February it became a gathering place for thousands of new-raised soldiers from the various counties.[13]

This concentration of force allowed a further round of reformation and coercion to be applied to the university. It was probably at this time, or a little earlier, that an episode occurred, reported in a memoir, by which Cromwell demanded of the heads of colleges what they would contribute to his party's war effort. They all refused to give anything, whereupon he summoned them to meet him and other committeemen (presumably of the county team which supplied the field army) in the university Register House the next day. There he gave a long speech urging the heads to make contributions. The Vice-Chancellor replied that to do so was contrary to the king's directives, and then Samuel Ward, still the master of Cromwell's undergraduate college of Sidney Sussex, and now very old and deaf, asked what Cromwell had been saying. When told, he muttered 'not a penny, not a farthing'. The provost of King's College stroked his beard and made a long statement in which he seemed to find merit in both parties in the war. This did not find any sympathy with Cromwell, who answered him 'I am more beholden to the other two than thee, for though they refused yet I understood what they said.' The provost made a second long speech, against civil war as a thing evil in itself, and got the further reply 'I do not understand thee yet; methinks thou dost not understand thyself.'[14] To Cromwell it was literally incomprehensible that somebody should oppose an armed conflict which he regarded as righteous.

He then turned on the university, forcing the colleges to remove the organs and other furnishings from their chapels.[15] Grey of Warke had issued a general order to the troops in his command on 23 February, to disarm not just Catholics and royalists but anybody who did not seem sufficiently supportive of the parliamentary cause. That gave the soldiers at Cambridge what they took to be justification to enter colleges and loot them, even allegedly of collections of ancient coins, along with the coats and goods of fellows. It was said afterwards that Cromwell himself led them, breaking open the college gates at night and inspecting every room inside; his men were accused of burning bookshelves for warmth and selling stolen books for a fraction of their true value.[16] Such reports caused scandal in the House of Lords, which issued an order of protection for the university on 4 March, followed three days later by one from the earl of Essex.[17] At the same time, Cromwell led the local parliamentarians in a programme of fortification of Cambridge which was expected to cost two thousand pounds. Letters asking for contributions were sent to the inhabitants of villages in the county.[18]

The pressure was lifted off the university in mid-March, not just because of the directives for its protection but because the concentration of soldiers there dispersed, leaving a substantial garrison.[19] The threat from the king's army had not materialized, and there was now an apparent need for armed force in the core territories of the Eastern Association, where the formation of the organization, and the new pressure being put on Catholics, royalists and those who wanted neutrality, was triggering unrest. One unit available was Cromwell's own new horse regiment, now raised to the full normal strength of five troops. These included his original one, now under the command of a new officer, a young Puritan called James Berry who had been a clerk in a Worcestershire iron foundry, showing how far the net was now being cast for good recruits. Cromwell's brother-in-law John Desborough got a troop of his own, and another was given to a first cousin of Oliver's from a Nottinghamshire gentry family, Edward Whalley. The family connection was even closer in the case of the fourth troop, which was captained by Cromwell's oldest surviving son, Oliver, and the fifth, which went to his nephew, Valentine Walton's son. For the time being, the regiment was largely a family business.[20] One reason why it could be raised so speedily is that money was flowing in to Cromwell from the association at regular intervals, the support system working as it was supposed to do.[21]

In the second week of March he led the new unit on its first mission, a policing operation in Norfolk and Suffolk. It rode up the smooth slopes of the chalk hills east of Cambridge, and into the sandy heaths of the Breckland, where the bracken would still have been russet after the winter, but with the gorse coming into yellow flower. Beyond that was the arable country of Norfolk's central boulder clay plateau, and the second city of the realm, Norwich, with its royal castle, cathedral and encircling walls. Grey of Warke had been through it a week or two before, arresting the mayor and some local royalists and reducing it to obedience, but Oliver still dramatically ordered the gates to be closed that night, for fear of attack. At dawn the next day, 14 March, he moved on with eighty volunteers from the city to the fishing port of Yarmouth, its small streets crammed into a narrow peninsula, its quay busy with ships, and fumes rising from the outhouses where herrings were smoked. There he picked up another group of local partisans, and the combined force, about a thousand strong, pounced upon its intended prey, the smaller port of Lowestoft, strung out along the edge of a cliff to the south.

The reason for the raid was that a suspicious number of local gentlemen had been reported as converging on Lowestoft, and it was feared that a royalist uprising was intended there. On the approach of the parliamentarian force, the townsmen barricaded their streets and stretched chains across them to stop horsemen, and mounted three large guns, presumably taken from their coastal defences, to cover the approach from inland. Cromwell summoned them to surrender, whereupon they replied that they were prepared to hand over the gentry who had arrived from outside, but not to allow the occupation of their community. Their weakness was that, like Dowcra at Cambridge, they did not actually want to fight anybody. Some of the Norfolk men crept under a chain and came up to the artillery position, threatening to open fire. At this the gunner fled, and they unchained the street and let in the horsemen, whereupon the town gave up. Eighteen prisoners were taken, including seven of the gentry who had come into the place.[22] Cromwell's men and one of the East Anglian horse troops then moved on a few miles to quarter at a nearby mansion, Somerleyton Hall, the home of a Suffolk gentleman, Sir John Wentworth, against whom suspicions had been alleged. They took away all his weapons and horses, fed the house's stock of hay and grain to their horses, and helped themselves to some of Wentworth's goods, plus £160 in gold.[23]

What was really going on here? Two of the prisoners taken in the town did turn out later to be active royalists, but a third was a Norfolk squire called Thomas Knyvett who has left ample records. They show that he certainly sympathized with the king against his opponents, but both in public and private he denied that there ever had been any conspiracy at Lowestoft and insisted that he was there to get a passage to the Continent and escape the war. A fellow prisoner confirmed this story. He was released a few months later, and Cromwell subsequently admitted that Knyvett had not been armed. By 1644 the earl of Essex was convinced that he was entirely innocent and signed a declaration to this effect, while the Suffolk parliamentarians had formally exonerated another of the captives.[24] Knyvett also pointed out that Yarmouth and Lowestoft were bitter rivals over the herring fishing grounds, and so the defensive measures taken by the latter town were a natural response to the appearance of an armed force of their traditional foes.[25] This is certainly plausible.[26] As for Wentworth, he was actually a member of the Suffolk parliamentarian administration, and remained so after the looting of his home.[27]

It looks, therefore, very probable that there was no royalist conspiracy for Cromwell to crush. The story that was sent to the House of Commons, however, was of the prevention of a very dangerous plot.[28] In the reports provided to the London press, the danger was magnified still further, and so was Cromwell's part in thwarting it. One newspaper asserted that the plotters had been armed by Catholics in the service of Spain.[29] Another told readers that Lowestoft had fallen because Cromwell himself gave it a 'hot charge'.[30] A third one attributed his victory to his skill in taking the town by surprise, and called it 'the best piece of service that hath been done a long time'.[31] His reputation in the capital thus swollen by what was probably a non-existent achievement, he could turn his regiment back westward, passing through Norwich and across the clay farmlands to the marshes at the mouth of the Ouse. There sat the port of King's Lynn, which had been reported as restless under the control of the Eastern Association. On 20 March Cromwell's men occupied it, and their presence immediately restored outward obedience. The mayor tactfully treated them to a civic feast, before they made a triumphant return to Cambridge.[32]

In late March the politicians at Westminster reinforced their war effort by passing measures which laid a weekly, heavy and uniform property tax upon their territory and ordered the seizure of the property of royalists there and the use of its profits to pay their soldiers. County committees were established to enact these ordinances, and Cromwell was put on those for Cambridgeshire and Huntingdonshire.[33] These steps were taken at the opening of the campaigning season, when Essex's field army was to attack the king again. The function of the now apparently secure territory of the Eastern Association was to act as one of the main supply bases for that army, and so once more Cambridge was the centre of a major concentration of soldiers as recruits for it gathered there.

Their presence produced a renewed ordeal for the university. On 23 March soldiers surrounded a meeting of its Senate and demanded that it confer a degree on a parliamentarian leader. When it refused, many of its members were imprisoned by the county committee on which Cromwell sat. One of the university's endowed preachers was chased across the marketplace by soldiers who allegedly mistook his academic hood and gown for a religious robe, shouting 'A Pope! A Pope!' A complaint to Lord Grey brought no response. Then the official service book, to which Puritans objected, was torn up in the university church, and soldiers raided colleges again at night, allegedly stealing food and also the books of fellows, which they sold. Students were pressured into denouncing their tutors as royalist, and college groves and orchards were cut down, and bridges broken.

Prints of the Apostles were seized and burned in the marketplace as 'popish idols'. Troops were billeted on the colleges and the old court of St John's was turned into a prison for royalists.[34] Old Samuel Ward was arrested by Cromwell's own quartermaster, though nothing could be proved against him, and he was released after two days.[35]

In early April the great concentration of soldiers came to an end, as about six thousand of them departed to join Grey of Warke in Hertfordshire and be led by him to reinforce the earl of Essex.[36] Essex had originally ordered Cromwell to conduct this force to Grey, but in the event Oliver remained behind to defend the Eastern Association.[37] To assist this work, Grey ordered every county in the association to keep two representatives at any one time residing at Cambridge to form a committee which would oversee the regional war effort.[38] Only a few weeks before, Cromwell's continued presence would hardly have seemed necessary, as the policing action of March had reduced the whole associated region to compliance, and the counties on its borders – Bedfordshire, Northamptonshire, Huntingdonshire and Lincolnshire – were firmly in parliamentarian hands. Now, however, the situation had changed.

The danger which was developing came from the north, and its origins lay in an army that had been raised during the previous autumn by the earl of Newcastle, the king's commander in Northumberland and Durham. In December the increasingly embattled Yorkshire royalists, based at York itself, had asked Newcastle to bring his eight thousand men to their aid, as his own counties were completely secured. The earl duly occupied York with his army, added the local forces to it, and began pushing back the parliamentarians and establishing a chain of garrisons southward into the Midlands. In particular, he sent one to occupy Newark, a Nottinghamshire market town with a medieval castle, situated at the superbly strategic position where the Great North Road bridged the largest river of the North Midlands, the Trent, and crossed another major highway, the Fosse Way which connected the East Midlands to the south-west of England. To compensate for their shortage of trained and experienced officers at the outbreak of the war, both sides had filled the gaps in their respective corps with Scottish veterans of the Continental wars, to which Scots had been attracted in large numbers by the relative poverty of their own land and the zeal of their faith, which caused many to wish to fight alongside fellow Protestants abroad. One of these, Sir John Henderson, was put in charge of the royalist outpost at Newark, and spent the following two months defending it and raiding neighbouring areas.

In February and March the earl of Newcastle's strength increased further. He was joined by the queen, Henrietta Maria, who returned from the European mainland with experienced officers and a trove of weapons and munitions.[39] He now felt able to reinforce Henderson with a brigade of horse led by Lord Charles Cavendish, a son of Newcastle's cousin, the earl of Devonshire, and a classic dashing royalist cavalry commander. This gave the Newark base formidable striking power, and by the end of March its troopers were pushing eastwards into Lincolnshire. That county's parliamentarians were given a balancing reinforcement, from the cavalry of their fellow partisans in Yorkshire's East Riding, much of which was shipped over the Humber estuary to join them. The resulting composite force met Cavendish's men on Ancaster Heath on 11 April, and was routed, abandoning the western half of Lincolnshire to the royalists.[40] The advance of the Newarkers encouraged in turn the king's local adherents in the East Midlands. During the second week of April some took up arms and occupied Stamford, Peterborough and Crowland, so giving them control of the area where Lincolnshire, Rutland and Northamptonshire met.[41] All this meant that the enemy was suddenly almost on the frontier of the Eastern Association.

Newcastle's army, and its outposts, had a spiritual as well as a military menace to Parliament's adherents. In the course of the autumn, the king had begun to accept help for his war effort, including recruits to his forces, from the English Roman Catholic community, which reacted against the intense hostility and suspicion manifested towards it by the parliamentarians. In the event, most English Catholics remained neutral, and a few even supported Parliament.[42] Nonetheless, Catholics also made a contribution to the king's war effort out of all proportion to their numbers, and this was especially true in the north.[43] They were therefore particularly numerous in Newcastle's northern army, 39.5 per cent of the field officers recruited in Northumberland, and 48 per cent of those from County Durham, being Catholic: of 117 Catholic royalist colonels in Britain, the earl employed 49.[44] Although they did not form a majority of his forces, such a substantial presence enabled the parliamentarian press to dub them 'the popish army', and as such an especial danger to English liberty and the Protestant religion.[45]

The first reaction of Cromwell and the controlling committee of the Eastern Association to the approach of this threat was to make the Ouse their defensive line, with Cambridge as a centre of operations behind it; and to order the levying of four thousand pounds to fortify both.[46] Holding the Ouse meant securing Huntingdon, though this was in the territory of the Midland Association, and Cromwell, the local man, proceeded to do that. In mid-April he moved there with his horse regiment and added local parliamentarians to give himself a total force of two thousand foot and ten troops of horse and dragoons, the latter being horsemen armed with short firearms who rode into combat and then dismounted to use their guns: they were especially useful in skirmishing.[47] In Huntingdon he seized more arms from local royalists and engaged in another persecution of his old enemy the recorder, Robert Bernard. The latter had secured the protection of the county magnate, Viscount Mandeville, who had succeeded his father in the title of earl of Manchester. The new earl had written to Cromwell to defend Bernard as a loyal parliamentarian, and Oliver now informed his victim that he would allow him to return to Huntingdonshire, but knew him to be a covert royalist (the implication being that he would sooner or later be exposed and punished).[48]

Even as Cromwell secured the western end of the Ouse line, the parliamentarian regiment defending Norfolk, under Sir Miles Hobart, pushed out to occupy Wisbech, the port at the mouth of the next river northwards, the Nene, and prepare to invade Lincolnshire.[49] Upstream along the

Nene lay Stamford, and then Peterborough, which was a short march from Huntingdon along the Great North Road. The royalists in both towns, weak in numbers and experience and having no fortifications, retreated before the double threat of Cromwell and Hobart.[50] That allowed Oliver to move up to occupy Peterborough in turn, on 18 April, and levy money from it to support his force, as he had in Huntingdonshire. According to detailed, if hostile, local accounts, his men proceeded to wreak the full force of Puritan ire upon its cathedral, a Norman abbey church with a long spine studded with towers and spires, and an arcaded and turreted entrance. They smashed the great western window, with its scenes of church history, tore up the service books and seats and pulled down the pulpit and font. Cromwell did not lead them in this work, but when a bystander begged him to stop them, he allegedly replied that they did good service.

His men went on to cut down the bell ropes and make them into tackle to reach the carvings on the ceiling and break them off with poleaxes. The communion rails were burned and the stonework over the altar was broken up. All the tombs, including those of Queen Catherine of Aragon and Mary, Queen of Scots, were defaced. The organs were carried out to the marketplace and jigs played on them while soldiers danced clad in looted clerical copes and surplices. Documents were stolen from the charter house and books from the library. Finally, the brass, tin, iron, tapestries and velvet cloths, and some of the books, were sold off in the town by the looters: iconoclasm had a material as well as a spiritual dividend. One of the books was bought by a cavalryman serving in the troop of Oliver's son, who returned it to the cathedral, so sounding a faint note of kindness and appreciation amid all this destruction.[51]

Of the places occupied by royalists along the southern fringe of Lincolnshire, after the victory of the Newarkers a couple of weeks before, only Crowland remained; but there they were prepared to fight. This was because Crowland was a natural fortress, sited on a gravel peninsula jutting into the Fens north-east of Peterborough which was flanked by water and marsh on two sides. It was a small town focused on the ruins of another great abbey, one aisle of which had been retained as the parish church, crowned by a massive peaked medieval tower, which formed a natural landmark, lookout point and military base. Fortifications on the neck of the peninsula would render it virtually impregnable. That, of course, presented a good argument for making an attack before these could be finished, and so on 25 April Cromwell and Hobart converged on the town with reinforcements from the Lincolnshire parliamentarians, led by a local gentleman, Sir Anthony Irby. The defenders had already deterred a previous attack by a local force – and incurred much odium – by tying parliamentarian prisoners to the outside of the defences.

The new attackers now launched themselves at the royalists from three sides, but the assault was called off because a storm of wind and rain made operations impossible. For three days a blockade was maintained of the town and on 28 April a fresh attack was prepared. The defenders, however, now reckoned themselves to be outmatched. They had some musketeers, but many of their men had only the scythes and knives with which they harvested fenland vegetation, and they were probably much outnumbered. They slipped away in small boats, leaving the town, and their captives, to the enemy. It does not seem that any casualties had been suffered on either side throughout the whole business.[52] There is no indication that Cromwell commanded the force which reduced Crowland: it was a composite one of different local detachments, he had no formal authority in Lincolnshire, and he was socially outranked by Hobart and Irby. The enterprise looks like team-work, and indeed a letter written by a local parliamentarian describes it firmly as Hobart's victory.[53] Yet when the achievement was reported in the London press, most of the accounts celebrated Cromwell as its hero just as had happened after the capture of Lowestoft. One reported that he had taken the town after a day's fighting, and the other that 'the heroic and valiant Colonel Cromwell' had driven out the royalists.[54] This time the discrepancy was too much for some at least of his fellow commanders, who bitterly noted it.[55]

Cromwell and his own men now returned southward, and en route launched a raid into Northamptonshire where they sacked the houses of local royalists who had hitherto been spared by that county's parliamentarians. The enterprise would have been useful in supplying money, arms and fresh horses, but as such confiscations of property from presumed enemies were routine at this period, this particular enterprise must have been unusually savage to merit the notice it got in the main royalist newspaper.[56] Some at least of Cromwell's soldiers were returned to Cambridge and billeted in Pembroke College, where they apparently found the beds comfortable, as they allegedly made off with them.[57] New horses were bought for the regiment in the association, from as far away as Hertfordshire, where the county committee paid for six. Even there, some of Cromwell's junior officers were seizing them, and equipment, from suspected royalists on their own initiative, including among their victims a wildly indignant man who had lent money to support Parliament.[58] When stories of such cases reached the Lords and Commons at Westminster, its members first indemnified the actions concerned, by formally authorizing Cromwell, Desborough, Whalley and any county committeemen or officials who aided them, to seize horses, arms, cattle, goods and money from suspected persons at will. A week later, however, they recognized that horses were being taken from loyal supporters of their own party, and ordered that no more could be confiscated without proper records being kept, and the consent of county officials obtained.[59]

The spring had been a good one for Oliver, as he and his men had accomplished a number of actions to subdue and defend their region, which had been given glowing notices in the press, and presumably in Parliament as well. Those notices had been exaggerated, and there is no need to credit him with being in command of the defence of the Eastern Association, or of having any grand strategic vision of his own for this: the measures taken for it were collective efforts. Nonetheless, he had acquitted himself well. In doing so, however, he still remained a minor local figure, on a level with many others in the parliamentarian war effort. Nine months after the war had started, he was hardly as yet a warrior at all, having functioned more as an enforcer and bully-boy. If it is accepted that he arrived too late for the battle of Edgehill, neither he nor any of his men had actually engaged in any fighting, and in none of the actions in which they had taken part had anybody definitely been killed, on either side. All that was about to change.

FIRST BLOOD

The main campaigning season of 1643 had opened well for the earl of Essex, as he had reduced Reading and forced the king's main army back on Oxford, where it was paralyzed largely for lack of arms and ammunition. The queen, guarded by Newcastle's soldiers at York, had plenty of those, but was separated from him by the Midlands, where their enemies held most of the county towns. At one point the royal couple discussed a plan for Charles to abandon Oxford and move his military base to Peterborough, where he was closer to Henrietta Maria and could harness the resources of the East Midlands and East Anglia.[60] Fortunately for Cromwell, this was not adopted, and a simpler strategy agreed whereby the king stayed on the defensive at Oxford while his wife conveyed the supplies to him across the Midlands, joining him herself with the main consignment. The logic of this was equally apparent to Parliament, as was the remedy: for its adherents in the Midlands and the north to unite their forces and at least block her way or at best overwhelm the Catholic queen and the earl of Newcastle's popish army together. To that end, in April the Commons ordered the parliamentarians of Leicestershire, Derbyshire and Lincolnshire to join together at Nottingham, a county town which guarded the next major crossing of the Trent above royalist Newark, and was strongly held for Parliament.[61] Cromwell was sucked into this concentration of troops at the opening of May, when the earl of Essex ordered him to join his soldiers around Cambridge and Huntingdon to the contingent going to Nottingham from Leicestershire, which was commanded by the general of the Midland Association, Lord Grey of Groby.[62]

There were two problems in responding to this order. One was that the way north was blocked by the Newark royalists, who were also pinning down the Lincolnshire parliamentarians. The other problem was Grey of Groby himself, who was a classic dim-witted posh boy: young, genial, weak-willed and hesitant. Grey protested that he dared not leave Leicester for fear that it would be captured behind him by the very active local royalists. He therefore declined to join forces with Cromwell at Stamford, as had been expected. On 3 May a furious Oliver denounced him to the Lincolnshire parliamentarians for sacrificing the common good to local interests, and proposed a new rendezvous deeper into Lincolnshire, over the gentle watershed from the Nene Valley in that of the River Witham, which flowed north towards Lincoln. The place he proposed was Grantham, an open market town on the Great North Road a short journey beyond Stamford. There he proposed to meet Grey along with the Lincolnshire and Derbyshire contingents, and the Norfolk regiment which had served alongside him at Crowland, and form a body strong enough to sweep on unopposed to Nottingham. The Lincolnshire men, receiving this letter, forwarded it to the House of Commons, which ordered them, and Grey, to follow Cromwell's plan.[63]

It was now early summer, and as Cromwell rode up the Great North Road again, the evenings would have been lengthening, the cuckoos calling and the landscape passing into a medley of brilliant greens from grass and foliage, and of white blossoms, as the hawthorn and cow parsley came into flower. On crossing Huntingdonshire, he gave the local royalists another pillaging, and his reputation for severity in the enemy press was enhanced by a story that was almost certainly an invented atrocity tale. It was asserted that when he entered the house of one parish minister, the man's son had told him that he himself might one day be in need of mercy. Oliver's alleged response was to have the young man's tongue bored through with a hot iron.[64] Even given Cromwell's volcanic temper, this sounds preposterous; but it is significant in that it indicates the figure that he was starting to cut in his opponents' imagination. On 9 May he entered Lincolnshire, and found nobody there yet from Leicester, Derby or Norfolk. Of all the forces ordered to meet him, there was just the Lincolnshire contingent, led by the man who had taken over command of the defence of that county against the royalists, Lieutenant-General John Hotham.[65]

Hotham was rich, arrogant, conceited, duplicitous and fundamentally inept.[66] His father, Sir John, was the governor of Hull, and became a national figure, and parliamentarian hero, at the very beginning of the war, when he denied King Charles entry into the town and access to the huge magazine of arms stored there. The war effort in Yorkshire had subsequently been handicapped by the feud that both Hothams had carried on with the Fairfaxes, whom they loathed because of their Puritanism and their populism, and with whom they had regularly failed to co-operate. By contrast, they had good relations with some of the Lincolnshire gentry, into whom the younger John had married, and he had led the cavalry detachment from Hull which had gone to their aid in the spring. He also, however, had good relations with the royalist earl of Newcastle, who should have been his greatest enemy but with whom he kept up a correspondence in secret, in which he professed friendship for the king's cause and admiration for the earl.[67] This seems to have sprung from three motives. One was insurance, in case the royalists won the war. Another was that by playing the earl along, Hotham sought to dissuade him from attacking Hull and its outlying garrisons in Yorkshire's East Riding. The third was that the Hothams seem genuinely to have hoped for a compromise peace as the ideal conclusion to the war, which would secure the position of Parliament as a part of government but rule out any further reform of the Church or state. They had always stopped short of actual betrayal of their own side, but their affable relationship with the enemy did inhibit them in prosecuting the war with vigour.[68] It is hard to imagine a parliamentarian officer less suited to working with Oliver Cromwell than the one who met him now.

On 13 May their combined force rode to within sight of Newark and challenged the royalists inside to battle, Cromwell probably hoping thereby to provoke one and Hotham to deter one. There was no response, and they rode back to Grantham, quartering their men in the town and nearby villages. As they did so, Sir John Henderson and Lord Charles Cavendish slipped out of Newark with their horsemen and dragoons, linked up with more local royalist soldiers, and fell upon their enemies, taking two or three of the Lincolnshire troops by surprise in their quarters west of Grantham and killing or capturing them all. This, however, gave the alarm to their fellows, and allowed time for Cromwell and Hotham to gather the rest of their men and set out to meet the enemy. The two forces came in sight of each other near the village of Belton, a couple of miles west of Grantham, as dusk was falling, and stood facing each other as the dragoons exchanged shots. As the royalists did not attack, Hotham and Cromwell agreed to do so themselves; and so Oliver went at last into his first real action.

If he did so according to the textbooks – which the language of his own account suggests that he did – then there was a set procedure to be followed. The attacking horsemen would load, and wind up or cock, their pistols, tie their swords to their wrists for easy use, and advance in their troops, so close together that the knees of the riders touched. The troops would be in diamond- or wedge-shaped formations, drawn up in lines. The riders would trot their steeds forward with bodies upright in the saddle and legs close and straight by its sides, feet turned inwards to make the legs grip better. Each would have a pistol ready in one hand, resting on a thigh, and the other hand holding the reins under the pommel of the saddle. To avoid tiring the horses, and to maximize impact, the riders would maintain their gentle speed until within a hundred paces of the enemy, and then launch into a full-scale charge. On coming up to the foe, each would fire his pistol at a chosen man in front, and often then hurl it into the face of that enemy or another. If time allowed, the second pistol could be drawn and fired; otherwise the sword was grasped. The horsemen receiving an attack would often each have his right knee locked behind the left one of the man next to him: this was the ideal formation for attackers as well, but would often not be practicable at the charge. They too would expect to fire at close range at the oncoming riders and their horses. When the attacking force crashed into the defending one, the latter might break at once under the impact. If numerous, confident and well-trained enough, they would halt the attack, and the two bodies would then fire, hack and push at each other until one gave way. Once one did begin to break up, it was doomed, and at that point those who could would turn their mounts and flee, pursued by the victors. Rallying broken horse soldiers for another fight was almost impossible, as the horses would be exhausted and the troops depleted, scattered and mixed together, so that the formations in which they fought could not be reformed.[69]

Cromwell's own account of what happened next was given in a famous letter to Hobart, once more the commander of the Norfolk contingent expected at the rendezvous; a copy of which was promptly published in a London pamphlet. Oliver began by emphasizing the comparative weakness of the parliamentarians, with just twelve horse troops, some of poor quality and incomplete, facing a hostile force carrying more than twenty-one troop colours (flags) of horse and three or four of dragoons. He then described how with the help of God (whose favour was mentioned repeatedly) his party had gone in at the trot and then the charge and routed the enemy as soon as it hit them. His soldiers then chased the fleeing royalists, 'and we had the execution of them two or three miles', killing or mortally wounding almost a hundred, capturing forty-five and releasing their own comrades who had been taken prisoner earlier. In short, it had been an immediate, complete and major local victory.[70]

Virtually all historians subsequently have taken Cromwell's account at face value. The greatest of those to write on the Civil War under Queen Victoria, Samuel Rawson Gardiner, actually declared that the whole future of the war was decided in this skirmish, as it showed for the first time that Parliament – or rather Cromwell – could field cavalry capable of defeating the formidable royalist horsemen.[71] Two scholars have suggested that Cromwell's account seems to exaggerate the comparative weakness of his own side, and one has suggested that the size that he attributes to the enemy force exceeds that of the total garrison of Newark at that time.[72] It was indeed very rare for any report of a victory during the war to admit that the victors had enjoyed superior numbers, as to emphasize the opposite was the surest way of demonstrating the favour of God. In extenuation of Cromwell's account, it may be argued that he was facing horsemen gathered from a second royalist garrison as well as Newark, and that royalist troops were often weaker than parliamentarian ones, because commanders preferred commissioning more to filling up the old; so a larger number of colours did not necessarily mean a proportionately larger number of men. It is more noteworthy that some of the other parliamentarian reports contradict Cromwell with respect to the greater numbers, though there is no consistency between them.[73]

There is, however, a lot more that is odd about Cromwell's account than that. Sir John Henderson and Charles Cavendish were both experienced and aggressive commanders, whose normal mode of response to contact with an enemy was attack, and who were already on the offensive; yet on sighting Cromwell and his fellows at Belton they stood still and hesitated until they were charged themselves. This strongly suggests that they believed themselves to be facing a stronger foe. Furthermore, Cromwell casually mentions that he and Hotham had marched to Lincoln after the action; but this was a retreat, falling back on the county's main parliamentarian base instead of holding their position at Grantham where they were awaiting the other commanders. After such a notable victory as he describes, they should have consolidated their position, or raided up to the walls of Newark, or moved on to meet the others further west. Finally, it is actually not clear from his letter who was in command during the action. While giving God the praise for the success, Oliver always speaks of 'we' when describing decisions, which would suit a joint command. In Lincolnshire, however, the supreme authority was Hotham's, whom Cromwell never mentions.

Actually, the problem is even more complicated than that, because Cromwell provided two accounts of the action, the one which has been cited, and always is, and another one nineteen months later, which reveals it to have been a much messier affair.[74] It has gone almost unnoticed by historians.[75] In this Cromwell declared that he and Hotham had agreed to attack, and he duly charged the enemy's left wing and routed it, chasing it two miles. On returning he found that the royalist right wing was still intact, because Hotham had not moved at all. In his defence, Hotham replied that he had attacked as agreed, but been beaten off. What neither added was what happened when Cromwell returned; whether the two commanders then attacked again together, and broke the remaining troops, or allowed the royalists to withdraw. The latter is more likely, as neither man mentioned any subsequent second victory, and with darkness falling and Cromwell's men and horses tired, it seems unlikely that any further action should have been possible. Cromwell's glorious victory therefore turns into a drawn fight, and his famous letter into a face-saving device.

It is interesting that a royalist diarist entered into his private notes that in the fight Cavendish had taken forty-three prisoners and lost forty-two of his own side as captives, including a peer, which may be closer to the true scale of the result.[76] In his second statement, Cromwell also admitted having done exactly what the royalist horse had done at Edgehill – and according to his admirers from Gardiner onward, he never did – which was to chase after a body of fleeing enemy whom he had just routed, abandoning the field and the rest of the army of which he was a part. Nonetheless, his face-saving letter worked, and the parliamentarian press duly reported the event as an outright and splendid victory of the sort that he had set out to represent: the royalist press employed the same trick on the opposite side.[77] Within two weeks, the Commons had paid Cromwell an implied compliment, and also faced military realities, by moving Huntingdonshire and its resources from the Midland to the Eastern Association, so acknowledging that its defence – which Oliver had conducted – depended wholly upon the latter.[78] It also remains true that by winning his part of the engagement, against whatever actual odds, he had pulled off something remarkable. Henderson, Cavendish and Hotham were all experienced soldiers who had seen service in Continental wars. Cromwell was the only rookie among them, but he was also the only one to achieve a striking success. It did testify eloquently to his quality, and augur well for the future, after all.

Strategically, the fight at Belton changed nothing. It did not win any new territory for Parliament, or open a new corridor through Lincolnshire for its troops, or weaken the Newark royalists, and the proposed great meeting of local forces at Grantham was abandoned. Instead, in late May, Cromwell and Hotham, and their men, passed west from Lincoln to Nottingham, and there the meeting sought at Grantham actually happened, on Parliament's insistence. The vapid Grey of Groby turned up from Leicester and the dour and self-seeking Sir John Gell, whose alleged manipulation of the London press has already been cited, came from Derby. The Nottinghamshire soldiers were already concentrated at their county town, and the combined strength of all these detachments amounted to a proper army, reputed to be five or six thousand men.[79] While its leaders were arguing over where and whether to meet, in early May the queen had sent her first convoy of arms and munitions across to Oxford; it is possible that the royalists were weak at Belton because some of the Newark horse had been escorting it.[80] Nonetheless, she herself was still at York with most of her supplies. The combined force at Nottingham now resolved to march to reinforce the Fairfaxes, who had just won another striking victory over Newcastle's men at Wakefield – and attempt to crush the earl and the queen.

Instead it was Newcastle who took the initiative, as June opened, by sending a large force to Newark to pin down that at Nottingham. This turned out to be the advance guard for Henrietta Maria and her main convoy making for the king, which arrived at Newark on 16 June. The strategy of Cromwell and his companions therefore altered to one of waiting for the queen's little army – which was almost the size of theirs – to resume its march south, and then intercept and defeat it. The Fairfaxes were left to carry on fighting the earl of Newcastle in Yorkshire, furious that their fellow partisans at Nottingham had not come sooner and trapped Henrietta Maria in York. In the last week of June Cromwell and his fellows gave up the wait and divided into three bodies, to be stationed at Nottingham, Derby and Leicester to cover the possible routes that the queen might take south. Cromwell remained at Nottingham. When Henrietta Maria did move at the opening of July, however, she did so with such speed and strength that she cut through the parliamentarian cordon with ease.[81] As she was preparing to march, on 30 June, Newcastle destroyed the Fairfaxes' army on Adwalton Moor, and rapidly completed the conquest of the West Riding of Yorkshire. His dreaded 'popish army' was now free to march into the Midlands. It is possible that the disunity of the parliamentarians at Nottingham, and the lack of strong overall leadership there (which should have been Grey of Groby's role) contributed to this compound disaster, but there is no real proof of that. Nor is there any that Cromwell was more eager to attack the queen or more forward in taking measures to do so than his fellow officers.[82]

Nevertheless, there is no reason to doubt that he must have felt anxiety and frustration during those weeks waiting in and around that town on the Trent, with its sandstone cliffs and caves, its hulking medieval castle and the broad slow river flowing by. Midsummer drew on, and as the swifts screamed in the sky above the town at dawn and evening, and in the valley around the foliage became a thick uniform green, the elder came into creamy flower, foxgloves bloomed purple and glow worms made small points of emerald fire in the grass after nightfall, he would have had four especial reasons for discomfort. The first was the mounting bad news from Parliament's forces elsewhere. Its army in the south-west, under Grey of Groby's father the earl of Stamford, had been annihilated by the Cornish royalists, who had broken through into Devon and Somerset and commenced the conquest of the West Country. Essex's field force had ground to a halt in Oxfordshire and remained there stricken by pay failure and disease which wasted away its strength, including that of its Eastern Association contingent under Grey of Warke. A raid from Oxford led by Prince Rupert had left Cromwell's friend and cousin John Hampden mortally wounded, and eventually Essex had given up and pulled back his remaining men to the lower Thames and London area.

The second problem was one consequence of the removal of local forces from such a broad swathe of parliamentarian territory to produce the concentration at Nottingham: as Grey of Groby had feared, this had freed the royalists in their home patches to prosper. In Cromwell's, once more Cavendish was raiding across Lincolnshire as far as Peterborough, Stamford and the Fens, allegedly driving away over a thousand horses as well as many cattle from the summer pastures of the latter. Once again, also, his dominance of the county encouraged others among the king's partisans in the region to declare themselves and take over more of it. In particular, a magnate who had hitherto remained neutral, the earl of Kingston (i.e. Kingston upon Hull, alias Hull), was commissioned as the royalist general in Lincolnshire, Norfolk, Cambridgeshire, Huntingdonshire and Rutland, and established himself in a base at Gainsborough, the only place on the Trent below Newark where the river could be passed before entering the wide waters of the Humber estuary.[83] Once more Parliament had lost control of the western half of Lincolnshire, and Cromwell was cut off from his home base.

This development fed into the third problem, which was that the removal of the forces at Nottingham from their home territory had snapped the fragile supply lines which provided their pay. In Cromwell's case, the Lincolnshire royalists were now in the way, so although the Eastern Association had money ready for him, it could not get through.[84] At Nottingham, all of the gathered soldiers were put on free quarter, a system whereby they were supposed to pay for their food, drink and lodging, and the needs of their horses if they had those, with tickets stating the full value of what they consumed. The local suppliers were then supposed to take these to the pay base of the units concerned, in the case of Cromwell's, at Cambridge, and receive the money owed, which would then be deducted from the next payment made to the troop or regiment. The chances that ordinary people from Nottingham and its area would make the journey to Cambridge in wartime were slim, and there was no guarantee that enough money would be waiting there for them anyway. In practice therefore, even if the system was properly observed, the tickets would take many months, or even years, to be redeemed.

Gell and Hotham allowed their men to ignore the system altogether, and take whatever they wanted from the local population without issuing any tickets, which was effectively plundering.[85] Cromwell tried a more honourable course, of borrowing money from citizens of Nottingham to keep his men paid, which he then expected the deputy lieutenants of the counties in which they had been raised to repay: his force included units from all across the Eastern Association which had been sent for the defence of its frontiers.[86] He also used his own credit to raise money, as a conscientious officer was expected to do, and turned to his family for help: his mother responded by writing to a friend who was looking after some of her funds. This was a Cambridge merchant, and one of the Puritan group who was identified as having got Cromwell elected to represent the town in Parliament. She asked for fifty pounds of her cash reserve to send to her son, and her utter dedication to his cause shines through her request: 'the almighty prosper the work and our precious friends engaged in his service against the unchristian and malicious enemies of his Church and people'.[87] More generally, all the commanders at Nottingham initially hoped that still greater numbers would join them from parliamentarian bases further afield, such as in Northamptonshire, Warwickshire and Cheshire, and so give them the overwhelming force with which to attack the queen at Newark. Cromwell urged the Eastern Association to despatch more soldiers to him, who could also escort the money he needed across enemy territory.[88] No response, however, could be made before the gathering at Nottingham broke up. The committee to co-ordinate the Eastern Association, based at Cambridge, could describe Cromwell to the mayor of Colchester as 'our only bulwark next to God', but this still could not produce a swift enough reaction.[89]

The fourth worry which Cromwell and the other commanders at Nottingham had to cope with in June was the bad effect that their inactivity was having on the increasingly desperate politicians at Westminster and on general opinion in the capital. By the second half of June, it was rumoured there that their failure to defeat the queen was the product of disloyalty. A scapegoat was needed to extenuate their failure to accomplish anything, and exonerate most of them; and the perfect one was at hand, in

John Hotham. His frequent communications with the royalists (which he cloaked as negotiations for exchange of prisoners) were arousing suspicion, and, in his accustomed style, he had made himself obnoxious to his fellow officers. The Nottinghamshire men had found his acid wit abrasive and been shocked by the way in which his soldiers took supplies. He had allegedly challenged Lord Grey to a duel, allowed his men to fire on Cromwell's, and treated Cromwell himself with scorn: apart from their natural incompatibility, Belton had probably left bad feeling. In mid-June, Cromwell and Grey's wife sent a letter to the earl of Essex accusing Hotham of a range of misbehaviour. Essex responded by ordering Sir John Meldrum, an old Scot of proven loyalty with extensive military experience, to go to Nottingham and assume overall command there. With him, he sent an order for Hotham's arrest, to answer the charges.[90]

By 21 June, Meldrum had arrived, and Hotham had been seized in his bed at midnight by musketeers and hauled to a cell in Nottingham Castle. The House of Commons endorsed these proceedings. The job of escorting Hotham to London, however, was entrusted to Grey of Groby, and so the prisoner promptly escaped. He made for his base at Lincoln, from which on 24 June he sent a furious letter to the House of Commons, expressing especial bitterness that the charges against him had been made by some of Cromwell's men, whom he called sectaries who wished to destroy the Church of England. He added that the only valour they had shown hitherto had been in defacing churches; which would have been more or less true had it not been for Belton, and shows how deeply more orthodox parliamentarians disliked radical Puritans of the kind with whom Cromwell was associated. The House summoned Hotham to make his case in person. Had he acquiesced even now, he would probably have saved his father's position and quite possibly his own, being at worst dismissed from his command. Instead, and in character, he made the wild and fatal gamble of writing to the queen and the earl of Newcastle, offering to surrender Hull and Lincoln to them and implicating his father in the deal. When he went on to Hull, however, some townspeople and officers there, who were firmly loyal to

Parliament and already disliked him and his father, grew suspicious. They staged a coup which resulted in the arrest of both Hothams and their shipment to London by sea, to face charges of treachery as well as incompetence and bad conduct.

The fall of the Hothams – in which Cromwell had played a key role – had three beneficial effects on Parliament's cause. First, it removed a pair of lacklustre commanders and potential traitors from a key pair of districts. Second, it enabled the blame for the wasted time and opportunity at Nottingham to be laid firmly on Hotham junior, and took the heat off Cromwell and the others. Third, when the Fairfaxes arrived at Hull, as refugees from the ruin of their army on Adwalton Moor, they found a power vacuum there which the House of Commons promptly filled by installing Lord Fairfax as governor in place of Sir John.[91] Having come to the town as defeated refugees, therefore, this very different father and son found themselves handed a new power base, large, wealthy and well fortified, from which to rebuild the parliamentarian war effort in Yorkshire.

For Cromwell, the expedition to Nottingham had been a prosperous one, as he had fought and won his first action, and destroyed his first adversary upon his own side. It was also almost certainly during the course of it, moreover, that he first met a fiery Nottinghamshire gentleman called Henry Ireton, in his early thirties with an intent gaze and bushy, curly, light brown hair accompanied by the usual moustache and triangular beard, who would be of great importance to him. For Cromwell's cause, however, the expedition had, as emphasized, been an appalling failure, as the queen had got through to her husband with her entire cargo of arms and munitions, and the useless concentration of parliamentarian soldiers in the North Midlands had exposed their home territories to royalist attack. The consequences manifested rapidly. On 13 July the royal couple met with their forces on the former battlefield of Edgehill, and simultaneously the western royalist army, reinforced by some of the king's cavalry, smashed the army of Sir William Waller in Wiltshire. Parliament was now left with no large field force anywhere except that of Essex, which was depleted and on the defensive.

Left to range unchecked, the king's followers overran most of Wiltshire, Somerset and Gloucestershire, and on 23 July Prince Rupert stormed Bristol, capital of the West Country and England's second largest port. The western royalist army then turned south to conquer most of Dorset, and then to reduce the main towns of Devon, while Charles himself prepared to besiege Gloucester. In desperation, Parliament had opened talks with the Scottish Covenanters to seek aid from them, but even this initiative had one immediate apparent ill effect, in that Lord Grey of Warke, the general of the Eastern Association, refused to serve on the deputation sent to the Scots. He was deprived of his offices, and so the association was left leaderless for the time being.

This would not matter, however, if its local commanders, like Cromwell, worked together and with the co-ordinating committee at Cambridge, to defend its territory. Cambridge itself was now strongly fortified, with lines of banks and ditches accompanied by breastworks and bulwarks, and an outlying fort.[92] As long as royalist soldiers were roving the Nene Valley, however, the association could not be safe, as the Great North Road and lesser routes gave easy entry into it from there across Huntingdonshire. In mid-July Cromwell had led his men south from Nottingham to join the earl of Essex's field army, which had moved up to the Northamptonshire–Buckinghamshire border in another doomed attempt to try to intercept the queen.[93] After her escape, he was sent by the earl to secure the Nene Valley again with his horse regiment and some infantry. He found Peterborough held by the two foot regiments which Norfolk provided for the protection of the association, led by Sir Miles Hobart, who had been with him at Crowland in the spring, and sent by Sir John Palgrave. The local royalists, however, were in Stamford, a short way up the Nene and the Great North Road, and the three colonels now formed a partnership to clear them out, like that which had regained Crowland.[94]

The advance on Stamford was in heavy rain, but a bloodless success. The royalists numbered only around five hundred and were facing three to four thousand enemies with over a dozen field guns, in an unfortified town; so they pulled out before the attack began. They did so, however, only a short distance, to a mansion just outside the town, Burghley House, which had been built by Queen Elizabeth's most trusted minister, Lord Burghley, as his main country residence. This they occupied as an improvised stronghold. It was ill suited to that, being no fortress but a huge cream-coloured stately home with four straight external walls, full of windows on the upper two floors and with doorways opening on the ground level. Cromwell and his fellows launched an assault on it at 2 a.m. on 24 July, to use the cover of darkness, and opened up on it with their artillery. The men inside endured the bombardment and beat off the Norfolk musketeers; but by the afternoon they decided that their position was hopeless. They were granted the harshest terms which convention allowed to a surrendering force, no more than their lives, and most of them were sent off as prisoners to Cambridge or London. The house was thoroughly looted, even though its owner, the earl of Exeter, was a boy living in London, whose lately deceased father had been a parliamentarian. The victors then heard that royalist sympathizers at Stamford had rung the town's church bells to summon help, and around four hundred 'clubmen', country people armed with clubs and farm implements, were heading towards Burghley in response. The fact that they had been summoned by the bells seems to suggest that these sorry individuals did not believe they were fighting for the king's cause, but to defend their home district against invaders, as none of the parliamentarians were local men. Cromwell sent part of his horse regiment and some dragoons to deal with them, led by Desborough, young Walton and the William Dodson who had opposed the king's proclamation at Ely almost a year before. These routed the locals and killed around fifty of them, completing the victory.[95]

It is possible that Cromwell led the joint force to Stamford and Burghley, though he had no formal right to do so, and the fighting at the house was conducted by foot soldiers from the two knights' regiments. Cromwell himself was quoted as recognizing the key role of Palgrave's men in one local report, and the only member of the expedition to send an independent account did not identify any one leader for it, but always used a plural.[96]

No account of the action survives directly from Oliver, to show how he viewed his role. In those sent to parts of the association, and to the London press, however, the same trick was worked as after the attacks on Lowestoft and Crowland, and Cromwell was given credit for the whole success. For the first time he was made the hero of a pamphlet, entitled *Colonell Cromwells Proceedings against the Cavaliers*, and the newspapers which noticed the victory took the same line.[97] Nonetheless, what happened at Burghley was overshadowed by another parliamentarian success at the other end of Lincolnshire, which was soon to suck Cromwell into a much bigger and more desperate mission.

That was the work of the man who had succeeded John Hotham in command of the parliamentarian forces in Lincolnshire, based at Lincoln itself: Francis, Lord Willoughby of Parham, who was the more active of Parliament's two lords lieutenant for the county. He was another young aristocrat – in his late twenties – who unhappily combined the intelligence of Grey of Groby with the tactical sense of John Hotham. In mid-July he decided to make his mark as a leader by launching a surprise attack on the new royalist base which the earl of Kingston had established, but not yet fortified, at Gainsborough. Willoughby came on it at night and had an easy victory, taking Kingston and most of his men prisoner. The captive earl was sent off down the Trent towards Hull in a pinnace, whereupon royalists fired on it from the bank and forced its surrender. Unhappily, one of the cannon shots sliced Kingston in two, leaving parliamentarians with an eye to divine providence to recall that the dead earl had during his previous period of neutrality allegedly declared that if he ever took a side in the war he should be cut in half.[98] For a moment, Willoughby's action looked like a brilliant coup, especially welcome in a month of so many defeats for Parliament, and that is how it was presented in the parliamentarian press.[99] Rapidly, however, he proved to have put himself into a trap, as he and his own men at Gainsborough were surrounded and besieged in turn by fresh royalist forces led by Lord Charles Cavendish. The House of Commons ordered all the soldiers that the Eastern Association could spare to be sent to Willoughby's relief, paid with an extra three thousand pounds to be levied on the associated counties.[100] Cromwell duly set out.

He took with him his horse regiment, two troops from Norfolk and about a hundred dragoons, and his way lay northward through the land of Kesteven, which comprised the south-western part of Lincolnshire. At that season it would have been one of sprawling fields of ripe wheat and barley, rough green pastures, copses of trees carpeted with ferns and fungi, swift brown and white butterflies, and great gentle hillsides unrolling to disclose more vistas of field and wood. If the weather were warm, those vistas would have been bluish with haze; if showery, towards evening the shadowed valleys and copse-patched hillsides would have been landscapes of jade and violet. At Grantham, Cromwell's men were joined by all of the parliamentarian horse based at Nottingham, including Henry Ireton, plus two companies of foot soldiers from there. They moved together over the watershed into the Trent Valley, and at the village of North Scarle found Sir John Meldrum with all of the Lincolnshire parliamentarian horse and dragoons. The old Scot was legally the overall commander in this region, with the commission given to him by the earl of Essex in June. It was he who had summoned in the Nottinghamshire men, and he who now assumed leadership of the combined force of 1,700, as it rested and slept through the evening and then mobilized at two o'clock in the morning of 28 July, to complete the advance on Gainsborough.

As their enemy approached, the royalists threw a screen of horsemen out to skirmish. Meldrum and his fellows made the accepted move in response and sent their dragoons ahead to clear the way. These were, as has been said, essentially mounted infantry, riding lighter and poorer horses than the cavalry, as they were not expected to charge on them, and having no armour or pistols. Instead they rode up to a battlefield, dismounted, and left one man in every ten to hold the horses while the rest went forward on foot, often using the cover of hedges and ditches, and fired the muskets or carbines they carried to soften up an enemy force and drive back or rout its advance guard.[101] On this occasion, the move failed, as the royalist horsemen charged the dragoons and put them to flight, so that Meldrum and Cromwell, disgusted, had to bring up their main body to the attack, whereupon their opponents retired. Following them, the parliamentarians became aware that the enemy had drawn off from the siege, but that a large body of their horse was drawn up on the summit of a high hill to the right, the lower slopes of which were pockmarked by the burrows of a rabbit warren.

For what followed next, as for the initial action just described, we are reliant mainly on three detailed letters from Cromwell himself, but these are broadly corroborated by the co-signatories of one of them and by Meldrum's despatch to the House of Commons and by the royalist newspaper.[102] Despite the forbidding terrain, the parliamentarians decided to attack, and the Lincolnshire horsemen led the way up the slope, with the Nottinghamshire and Norfolk men in the centre and Cromwell's regiment at the rear. Once at the top, they fanned out into battle order, Cromwell leading the right wing, and found the main body of the enemy advancing to attack them, whereupon they hastily picked up speed to avoid being hit by a charge while stationary. The two masses of cavalry crashed together and came to a complete halt, the two sides firing, hacking and pushing at each other. Eventually it was the royalists who broke and fled, streaming away on either side of their own reserve, a block of horsemen consisting of Lord Charles Cavendish's own regiment, which held its ground. The victorious parliamentarians galloped after them, likewise passing on either side of Cavendish's men, save for two or three of the Lincolnshire troops, which held back to face this remaining enemy.

Cromwell was in the rear of the pursuit of the fugitives, and it was now that he showed his quality as a leader, and above all his remarkable ability to learn. After his experience at Belton, he did not continue to follow the defeated and fleeing royalist main body, but retained an awareness that a division of his opponents was still undefeated and on the field. He and one of his captains, his cousin Edward Whalley, managed to halt three or four troops of his regiment and turn them round to return to the summit of the hill. There they saw that Cavendish had led his regiment against the Lincolnshire troops and shattered and driven them off. At this moment, when the victorious royalists were disordered and unsuspecting, Cromwell's troops slammed into their rear. No horsemen could cope with an attack under those circumstances, and Cavendish's broke and were pushed pell-mell down the hillside in front. Under these circumstances, most could outrun their pursuers, but these did not, because a bog lay at the foot of the slope, in which many of the fugitives got mired. One was Cavendish himself, who was cut in the head by one of Cromwell's troopers, and fell off his horse. Once he was on the ground, the commander of Oliver's own horse troop, the former clerk James Berry, ran him through with a sword and gave him his death wound. Cromwell had turned what would have been a drawn battle into a glorious victory, in which the main enemy commander in Lincolnshire had been killed.

That at any rate was his own story, and there is no reason to disbelieve it. This said, two aspects of it, both characteristic of his way of representing events, do bear further comment. One is the complete absence of mention of his commanding officer, Meldrum. It must have been Sir John who decided to attack the hill, led the vanguard up it and commanded the attack on the main royalist body and pursuit of it. Yet neither he nor any other chief officers present appear in Cromwell's account, which only refers to Cromwell himself and his own captains, directed and favoured by God. It would be possible to take this silence as an implied rebuke to Meldrum for haring off after the fugitive enemy and leaving Cavendish's regiment intact, were it not for the fact that all Cromwell's accounts of military actions at this stage of his career, and all those which he or his supporters sent to Parliament or the London press, airbrushed out colleagues in the same way.[103] The other abiding characteristic which features in his account of the battle is its savagery, which was rare, though not unique, among commanders on both sides in this war. The joy he took in 'doing execution' on the fleeing royalists at Belton may be recalled, and the pamphlet published in his name upon the actions at Burghley similarly exulted in the slaughter of the wretched clubmen. Now, he recounted the killing of Cavendish, when lying wounded on the ground, with relish, using a phrase for it, that Berry thrust him 'under the short ribs' which echoed that employed for the despatching of ungodly enemies by Israelites in the Old Testament. As a prisoner, Lord Charles would have been a valuable prize, who might be exchanged for the release of a prominent parliamentarian captured by the royalists, but – overtly at least – Cromwell never seems to have considered that, or felt that his death needed justification. Although a fellow Englishman, and fellow member of the Church of England, Cavendish was given the same status as a Biblical Midianite or Amalekite: one of 'God's enemies' indeed.

At any rate, when Meldrum and Cromwell and their men reunited in Gainsborough later that summer morning, with a grateful Willoughby, and began unloading fresh supplies of ammunition for the garrison, they must have been elated. Then a report came in of a small body of royalists, with field guns, to the north of Gainsborough. Cromwell borrowed some infantry from Willoughby, and led out his horsemen again with them to attack this new enemy. They duly drove back some royalist cavalry, in the process climbing another of the hills which bordered the town – and then had an appalling shock. In the valley in front they saw a succession of full-strength foot regiments marching towards them, and realized that they were facing Newcastle's entire field army. The earl had flung a bridge of boats over the Trent below Gainsborough and taken his men over it to the attack. Cavendish's tactics now became plain: he had orders to retreat out of harm's way until the earl arrived, so that they could crush the parliamentarian relief party together. Instead he had, fatally, only withdrawn to the top of the nearest hill, trusting in his own strength, that of his position, or Newcastle's arrival at an earlier hour.[104] At any rate, the parliamentarians had just been taken by surprise, by a much stronger enemy: they and the 'popish army' of the north were face to face at last, but under the worst possible circumstances for them. The whole achievement of the morning was unravelling.

Willoughby's foot soldiers fled back to the town, and Cromwell's horsemen commenced a rapid retreat southward, joined by Meldrum and the other cavalry. Newcastle's own superb horse regiments were now hot on their heels, and Cromwell, Whalley and one of the Lincolnshire colonels had to gather a rear guard and fight a series of holding actions at gates between fields, where the narrow passages allowed a few to fend off many, to allow their main body to get clear. It was another excellent feat of arms, but, inevitably, merely one of damage limitation. After a long while, the pursuit slackened, and the parliamentarians escaped to Lincoln. From there Cromwell and his own original force rode south at full speed to Huntingdon and then Cambridge. Along the way he fired off the succession of letters, already quoted, to the House of Commons and to local commanders and committeemen in the Eastern Association, which now represented another brilliant exercise in damage limitation. On the one hand they portrayed the battle at Gainsborough as a wonderful victory, while on the other they admitted that Willoughby and his infantry were once again besieged in the town, this time by a much more powerful enemy. They accordingly appealed for urgent fresh supplies of money and men to make possible a second relief force.

In one sense the result was a huge success. The Commons completely accepted Cromwell's view of events and immediately ordered the measures he had requested, the levying of three thousand pounds and two thousand men from the Eastern Association.[105] Moreover, this was the first moment at which the House began to view Oliver as a talented soldier, and potential leading commander, and in the short term as the man to assume the defence of the Eastern Association. It had just awarded him his first formal office inside it, by directing that he be made military governor of the Isle of Ely, that natural fortress in the Fens, surrounded by marsh and water meadow, which could protect Cambridge from the north and Norfolk and Suffolk from the west.[106] The newspapers published reports on the events at Gainsborough which repeated his own in proclaiming a great victory: one declared that the town had been saved 'by the magnanimity and courage of Colonel Cromwell'.[107] It was all, however, in vain. An excellent insight into the state of affairs in the Eastern Association at this time is provided by the papers of Cromwell's cousin Sir Thomas Barrington, a leading Essex gentleman, Puritan and local parliamentarian leader. He and his colleagues on the county committee and deputy lieutenancy (who led local military defence) found themselves hit simultaneously by demands from Parliament for men, cash, horses and other supplies to rebuild the armies of Essex and Waller, to raise a new mobile cavalry force to protect London, and now to give Cromwell the power to fight Newcastle. They might have had the resources to obey one of those, but not more, and could not do anything in a hurry. When a foot company was ordered to Cambridge it refused to go, because some of the soldiers wanted to go home to fetch in the harvest, some wanted more pay, and some wanted to get any pay. When money was collected, it was found that there were too few men willing to serve, and no horses left available in the county to mount new cavalry. When a company did set out for Cambridge, it soon mutinied, returned and refused to march again, and the Essex foot already at that town went home when they found they would be asked to serve in Lincolnshire.[108] Fresh recruits sent from Norwich to Cromwell's own horse regiment deserted and fled home taking their horses and weapons with them.[109] Two weeks after Cromwell had sent out his appeal and the Commons had reinforced it, absolutely nothing had been accomplished.

In that time the parliamentarian position in Lincolnshire, and on the northern border of the association, had collapsed. Willoughby, abandoned inside Gainsborough by those who were claiming to have saved him, experienced the rare nightmare, for a local commander, of being attacked by a field army with a proper siege train. Newcastle's one included mortars, a form of artillery so successful that they have not changed much since: short, fat, squat tubs of metal which were set at an angle of forty-five degrees to fire metal canisters packed with explosives up into the air. These had lighted fuses attached, of rope or tow soaked in saltpetre mixed with alcohol or water and protected by wooden tubes, and were intended to fall inside the fortifications of a stronghold and explode on impact or soon after, blowing everything and everyone around each to smithereens.[110] As they left the defences completely intact, mortars were weapons of terror, to kill, wound and demoralize the besieged garrison. As such, they could have little effect on soldiers brave and determined enough to tough things out, providing there were not too many of them. Willoughby, however, was not the sort of commander to produce such defenders, and once the shells began raining down on the town, and setting it alight, his men mutinied. He was forced to surrender after three days and retire with his garrison to join Meldrum at Lincoln, leaving all weapons, ammunition and colours behind. Immediately, however, Newcastle marched upon that city, and the two parliamentarians abandoned it in turn, with the rest of their field artillery. Most of Willoughby's soldiers had now deserted, and he fled to the only town left in the county which still held to his cause, Boston, a port at its south-eastern corner where the Lincolnshire fens met the North Sea. There the corporation informed him that unless Parliament could reinforce him, it would invite in Newcastle's royalists.[111]

Willoughby was suddenly experiencing the domino effect of defeat, and the sensation of being a supporter of a lost cause. High, dry and frantic at Cambridge, to the south, Cromwell must have felt the same, as men melted away there. East Anglia lay open to Newcastle's army, and that is exactly where the king now wanted it to go. From his post at the siege of Gloucester, he asked the queen, left in control of the royal headquarters at Oxford, to order the earl to attack Norfolk and Suffolk, and Huntingdonshire, bypassing the well-fortified Cambridge and inaccessible Ely.[112] On 13 August a perfect bridgehead was provided into the former counties when the port of King's Lynn, at the north-western end of Norfolk, declared for Charles. It had long been a centre for local royalists, and those now seized control. The only parliamentarian garrison between the earl of Newcastle and the town was a weak one at Wisbech, and then there were none between Lynn and Norwich. The port was itself a useful one, and it was set at the mouth of the Ouse, which meant that the main line of defence for the Eastern Association, established along this river in the spring, had just been breached. As Willoughby had fallen back on Boston, most of the Norfolk men had abandoned Stamford, and Cromwell told those who remained to strengthen Boston. This left the Nene Valley open to the enemy again; so that the way was clear for a royalist advance on Huntingdon as well.[113] One parliamentarian newspaper reported that it had been decided to evacuate Cambridge in the case of a royalist advance and carry all the artillery and ammunition to the Isle of Ely, to strengthen that as a last refuge in the region.[114]

The Eastern Association was saved by Sir Thomas Fairfax, with the unwitting help of Queen Henrietta Maria. Seeing the danger to East Anglia, Fairfax gathered all the forces at his new base of Hull, and struck deep into Yorkshire, coming up on the east side of the earl of Newcastle's base at York to threaten it. Had the Hothams still been in charge of Hull, this would never have happened, and so by taking the action which had precipitated their fall, Cromwell had unwittingly made possible his own preservation. The Yorkshire gentry appealed to Newcastle for aid; and at the same time, the queen decided not to send the earl her husband's order to him to advance, but to leave it to him to decide whether to do so or not. As a general, Newcastle always tended to caution, and this was reinforced by the veteran soldier he had employed to command his army under him, almost inevitably an old Scot, called James King. The two took counsel and decided to withdraw their field force from the Midlands, pick up more recruits in Yorkshire, and lay siege to Hull itself. To take the town would at once give the entire huge county to King Charles, equip him with a major port on the east coast, avenge his exclusion from it in 1642, snuff out a troublesome and strategic enemy base, and inflict a further tremendous blow on parliamentarian morale. By contrast, to march on south with Fairfax loose in their rear would risk the loss of the summer's gains in Yorkshire and also the cutting of Newcastle's increasingly extended supply lines. As a result, Lincolnshire was organized not as a launch pad for a royalist offensive but as a southern defence for Newcastle's territory, with a frontier drawn through a chain of castles and market towns captured or occupied two-thirds of the way down the county. King's Lynn was simply abandoned to its fate.[115] For the foreseeable future, the pressure was off the association, and it, and Cromwell, could recover and make preparations for a counter-attack. This was exactly what Parliament was about to enable them to do.

THE EARL OF MANCHESTER'S ARMY

In the face of the spate of defeats and losses during the summer, the politicians at Westminster took a number of remedial actions. The most important were the decisions not to sue for peace (narrowly taken) and to ask for help from the Scots, as described. It was generally assumed that any such help would carry the price tag of reforming the Church of England to make it more like the Scottish Kirk, an objective sought by the Covenanters ever since their victory in 1640. As a signal of willingness now to pay that price, Parliament had in June ordered the convention of the long-promised assembly of clergy (and some lords and MPs) to reform the Church. It was fixed for 1 July, in the gorgeous Gothic setting of Henry VII's chapel at the end of Westminster Abbey, and was instructed explicitly to propose ways to make the Anglican Church more Scottish. On the other hand, the ordinance convening it made clear that unlike the Scottish Kirk's national assembly, it had no independent power to act, but could only advise Parliament on such matters as the latter directed it to consider. On 19 July the commissioners to treat with the Scots were sent on their way. Parliament also ordered the raising of a mobile cavalry force, 6,600 strong, to protect London, East Anglia and the south-east, and created a huge reserve to defend London itself, of over 20,000 men, by placing all the militia of the area under a single committee. It imposed a new weekly tax or 'assessment', in proportion to wealth, on its territory, and a sales tax on many commodities, while to fill up its armies, the conscription of recruits was now imposed.[116]

For Cromwell, the most significant of these measures were those designed for the overhaul of the Eastern Association in the face of the apparent threat now posed to it by Newcastle's army. On the last day of

July the Commons had received a petition from parliamentarians in Norfolk, pointing out that the strategic position of the association had completely altered. When it was established in the winter, it was secure territory, and so the organization had been designed to act as a supply mechanism for Essex's field army and a policing agency to keep its counties quiet and compliant. Now it had a frontier directly on enemy-held land and a powerful army apparently poised to invade it. The petition accordingly asked for permission for the association to raise a field force of its own, numbering 8,000 foot and dragoons and 2,000 horse, which would be capable of taking on Newcastle and supported by the weekly assessment. The House forwarded this to the central committee for the association, at Cambridge, asking how this could be done without leaving Essex's army unpaid. The reply from the committee, which would have included Cromwell, clearly came rapidly, because on 9 August the Commons agreed to the raising of a total army of 20,000, including a field force with 10,000 foot and dragoons, by compulsory enlistment. The support system for this was to be managed by a central committee of a hundred men, taking turns to serve in shifts of two weeks at a time with a quorum of seven, and meeting at Cambridge or some other frontier town. The ordinance for this was passed by both Houses the next day, and they subsequently agreed that the soldiers would be paid by an assessment levied parallel to that used to support Essex's army, and of the same amount. This promised to yield £22,520 every month.[117]

There was absolutely no chance that Cromwell would be appointed to command the new field force: that honour had to be reserved for an aristocrat, and the one chosen was simply the most important in the region who was also a fervent partisan: Edward Montagu, the new earl of Manchester, who was nominated by Parliament to be commissioned by Essex as Serjeant-Major-General of the Eastern Association on 10 August.[118] His credentials as a parliamentarian hero had been established early on, when he was the only member of the House of Lords whom King Charles had marked down for arrest when he made his attempt on Pym and the other four members of the Commons in January 1642, and since then he had risen ever higher in prominence in the House, succeeding his father to the earldom in November 1642. When attendance in the Lords fell to ten people during August, Montagu held to his post there and acted as their Speaker. He was just over the age of forty, and had absolutely no experience of military affairs, but a personality which promised solid and sensible leadership: committed, responsible, cautious, industrious, and with a plodding tenacity for getting jobs done. He was certainly a good organizer and administrator, and had some abilities, or at least aspirations, as a mediator and conciliator; though he could at times be touchy and irascible himself.[119] As a leading parliamentarian zealot, he had everything to lose personally from a royalist victory, and as the natural boss of Huntingdonshire, a vested interest in pushing the enemy away from the association. His portrait shows an anxious-looking man with dark, melancholy eyes and a moustache and chin-strap of beard so neat that they seem to be painted onto his face.[120]

Cromwell's feelings on hearing of his appointment are of course unknown. He may have harboured a lingering resentment of the manner in which the earl's family had supplanted his own in local power, and a keener one of the part played by the earl's father in his own humiliation at Huntingdon. He had clashed with the earl of Manchester himself, then Viscount Mandeville, two years before in the parliamentary committee which had discussed the Somersham enclosures. On the other hand, the earl was both a fervent leader of Oliver's own cause, and a prominent Puritan, of acknowledged personal piety, so in ideological terms somebody whom he could follow.

The distraction of the earl of Newcastle by the siege of Hull granted Manchester the ideal circumstances in which to raise his new army: a lengthy period of undisturbed activity, while in control of almost the whole mass of his territory, with the lingering threat from the earl, and the presence of the royalist garrison at King's Lynn, to spur on partisans to the work and convince taxpayers and local officials that it needed to be done. Between mid-August and late September the bulk of the new force was recruited. It was intended that there would be four horse regiments, and at least three were in service by the end of September. Cromwell's was the only one with a previous existence, and incorporated wholesale as the largest, most cohesive and most experienced body of cavalry which the association already possessed. The other two were new-raised. One was Manchester's own, with a personal bodyguard for him of troopers in scarlet coats and breeches. The other was given to an experienced Dutch soldier, Bartholomew Vermuyden, who was also made quartermaster-general of the new army, with overall responsibility for billeting. Manchester also raised a regiment of dragoons.[121] The mechanism for conscripting the new foot and horse soldiers was for the county committees to specify the total of men required from each parish and to order its constables to choose them, give them clothing and shoes suitable for service, and escort them to a rendezvous. Those who refused to go had to pay a ten-pound fine, or enlist in the militia, or face prison, while constables who failed to make their quotas were fined in turn or themselves drafted. There was a natural tendency to pick men of whom the parish knew little or wished to be rid. The county committees could demand a horse, or the price of one, from each person already registered to provide one for the militia, and empower the constables to requisition the rest. If there was still a shortfall, the remainder could be purchased.[122]

To raise and equip so many men in little more than a month was a tremendous achievement, and a sign of reviving morale in the association now Newcastle was off its back and there was determined new leadership. The earl of Manchester reached Cambridge four days after receiving his commission, and moved on immediately to meet Cromwell at Huntingdon and concert measures.[123] The recruiting drive naturally produced serious strains, not least because Parliament did not pass the ordinance for the taxation to pay the new army until the end of the time in which it was raised. The earl and the central committee at Cambridge discovered with horror that the officials in Essex sent the men, but did not give them weapons, flags, drums, clothing or footwear, so they were effectively useless, and half deserted on the way: the earl pronounced them 'more dreadful to me than

any enemy'. It is entirely possible that things were not much better elsewhere. Nonetheless, amid a barrage of orders, pleas and invectives, the
county officials and the association's commanders and central committeemen kept on working together to repair the deficiencies, and slowly
began to do so.[124]

Even as the new army expanded, so did Cromwell's own regiment: by
autumn the unit which had been five troops strong in the spring had
doubled in size: a sixth troop was added in April and a seventh in June, and
then four more in August and September.[125] Horses to mount them were
commandeered in Northamptonshire and Cambridgeshire. As the suspected
and actual royalists in those counties had by now been pillaged of their
steeds, people of impeccable record lost theirs instead, being handed tickets
stating the assumed value of the animals, to be redeemed from the association.[126] It was growing into probably the largest horse regiment in the entire
English Civil War. Two impulses in Cromwell seem to have propelled this
process. The first was to develop a mobile strike force, directly under his
control, to defend the association as the danger to it grew through the
summer. The second was to dominate the cavalry wing of Manchester's new
army by leading not only the most experienced and reputable unit in it, but
by far the biggest. The manner in which the expansion occurred seems
mostly ad hoc. Henry Ireton, the Nottinghamshire parliamentarian and
Puritan, had led his troop to be part of that county's contingent which
joined Cromwell and Meldrum for the relief of Gainsborough. After
retreating from there with Oliver, he transferred to his command, apparently with his men, and was duly rewarded with promotion to sergeant-
major and the post of Cromwell's deputy in governing the Isle of Ely;
another of Oliver's protégés, William Dodson, was left there with Ireton as
lieutenant-colonel of the foot regiment which made up the garrison, perhaps
to balance him.[127] Another new troop was funded by the young women and
men of Norwich, who had offered to pay for the raising of another foot
company for the association as the royalist threat to the latter increased
in the summer. The central committee asked for a horse unit instead,

probably persuaded by Cromwell who promptly helped himself to it. It was nicknamed 'the Maidens' Troop'.[128]

There is most information on the recruitment of the one captained by Ralph Margery, in Suffolk in August and September. Cromwell wrote to local parliamentarian officials there to give Margery warrants to seize more horses from local royalists to mount his men, if they thought this practicable. The result was an outcry against the new captain for taking the steeds from men with good political records. An embarrassed Cromwell wrote back with the announcement that he would not seek to defend Margery, followed by a defence of him. He suggested that the man must have followed Parliament's own definition of what constituted royalism, but if it turned out that he had not, then the local parliamentarian leaders needed to choose his victims instead. He then went on to propose that Margery and his troopers be sent to join Cromwell's regiment at once, with arms, and that if they then gave good service that would justify all they had done, anyway. Finally, he offered to return a horse taken by Margery from one parliamentarian gentleman, the seizure of which had given particular local offence, or else pay the value of it. Oliver was here employing his scatter-gun effect, of firing a succession of different responses at a problem and hoping that one would take care of it.

This correspondence was to provide posterity with some of Cromwell's subsequently most celebrated and admired headline statements, when he declared that 'a few honest men are better than numbers' and (most particularly) 'I had rather have a plain russet-coated captain that knows what he fights for, and loves what he knows, than that which you call a gentleman and is nothing else. I honour a gentleman that is so indeed.'[129] 'Russet', in this context, was a kind of homespun woollen twill, the cloth of a yeoman. Modernity, starting with the Victorians, has cited these to praise Cromwell both for a high regard for moral character and for a dedication to meritocracy and democracy, holding personal virtues to outweigh high birth. In large part, such attitudes can be sustained – after all, he himself had *been* such a russet-coated man, ten years before – but it is worth looking closely at what he meant at that time.

As he himself left no archive, we usually have only his side of a correspondence, and so lack much of the context of his replies. In this case, there
seem to have been three reasons for his comments. First, and most obvi-
ously, he wanted reliable and committed partisans, who would fight steadily
and inspire their men when the opposed lines of cavalry crashed together in
a close-order fight, and put up with failed pay and hard service in between.
The experience of working with the likes of Grey of Groby, Hotham and
Willoughby would have sharpened his sense of the failings of those
appointed largely because of the standing of their families. Moreover, at the
time at which he made these remarks, he had to reckon with a horse troop
just sent from Suffolk under a Captain Johnson, which was well paid and
yet so unruly that he feared its men might cut his throat: their proximity
clearly enhanced his wish for recruits and officers who were soberly behaved
and properly disciplined; in short, 'honest'.

In addition, however, he may have had two other motivations for his
comments. One was that as he was himself from the lower end of the gentry
class, he lacked the social weight which would count when commanding
officers higher in the social order. To build a loyal military following would
be easier if he had subordinates with whom he would not find such a difficulty. The other factor which may have counted in his declarations was one
that has already been noted in the context in which they occurred: the
controversy stirred up by Cromwell's existing captain, Margery, when
seizing horses for his new troopers from gentry whom he had apparently
decided arbitrarily to count as royalists. One of the elements in the situation
which would undoubtedly have intensified resentment was that members of
the local elite were being roughly and despotically despoiled by somebody
who was not their social superior or natural leader; and Cromwell felt
obliged to defend his captain. As so often in his career, it is hard to disen-
tangle high, and appealing, principle from opportunism and self-interest.

When Cromwell spoke of 'honesty' in people, now and later, his use of
the term also had hints of a religious connotation: that they were unequivocal
Puritans. Such a stance was, however, already becoming less straightforward

than it had been hitherto, because of the calling of the Westminster Assembly, and so the formal commencement of religious reform. This development forced the parliamentarians to face up to an issue which had hitherto been ducked – the future form of the Church – and by September the Westminster Assembly was already starting to divide into factions that were termed 'presbyterians' and 'independents'.[130] Broadly, the former favoured a Church roughly on the Scottish Covenanter model, in which the authority of the bishops was replaced by that of a hierarchy of parish and provincial bodies, mixing clergy and laity, which culminated in a national assembly. This system would act to impose a strict discipline on the population, including a definition of orthodoxy and a prescribed order of service. The latter preferred to decentralize authority to the parishes, and allow more latitude to variety in details of belief and practice, within a broadly defined framework of reformed Protestantism under the overall control of the secular state embodied in Parliament. Their more radical representatives would also tolerate, at least for a time, the ability of ministers to attract congregations which operated outside the traditional parish system, and were voluntarily assembled bodies of fellow believers attracted to particular preachers. Such 'gathered churches' were already appearing in and around London because of the collapse of ecclesiastical discipline, and members of the more orthodox parliamentarian majority were bestowing on them the term 'Anabaptists'. This had hitherto been applied to extreme Protestants on the Continent who denied the need for national Churches altogether and wanted Christianity to be constituted entirely of voluntary congregations attracted by individual leaders, who represented between them a multiplicity of sects with differing views concerning doctrine and worship. For over a hundred years, these had functioned as the favourite bogeys of most European Protestants, of all the main denominations, and suffered often vicious persecution as a result: all English monarchs from Henry VIII to James I had burned them alive when they were detected in their dominions.

From the first appearance of this division in the parliamentarian ranks, Cromwell and his regiment were associated with the independents, and some observers charged him and his men with still more radical beliefs. In mid-September, writing to his cousin Oliver St John, he had to defend his troopers against the charge of being Anabaptists, insisting that they were 'honest, sober Christians', a sweeping claim which ducked the question of what they actually were, on the Puritan spectrum. A few weeks later he repeated this tactic when writing to another cousin, Sir Thomas Barrington in Essex, complaining that his men were insulted as Anabaptists, but were 'honest men, such as fear God'.[131] One of his subordinates, almost certainly Dodson, commented with horror that Cromwell's deputy at Ely, Henry Ireton, made the Isle 'a little Amsterdam' (referencing the remarkable toleration of different forms of religion which was permitted in that Dutch city), where soldiers preached from church pulpits and congregations formed in private houses: he claimed that whole families of religious radicals were immigrating there from London to establish them.[132]

It is easy at the present day to characterize Cromwell's religious attitudes as genuinely impartial and inclusive, avoiding partisan labels and being prepared to employ and promote zealous parliamentarians from across the spectrum of Puritan belief. This may, however, need qualification in two different ways: that at this stage he was in too much need of supporters and recruits to be choosy about their attitudes; and that to allow independents to hold, articulate and practise their beliefs was in itself to support independency as a religious stance. There can be little doubt that to do this chimed with some of Cromwell's own deepest convictions and instincts: ever since his conversion to Puritanism he had shown a consistent sympathy for Puritans who suffered punishment for their beliefs and a concomitant determination to remove the national hierarchy of leading churchmen who had inflicted such punishment. It also, however, had a potential practical benefit, as well as the potential risk of being smeared, or at least having his men smeared, with Anabaptism. It seems to have been his membership of a powerful local Puritan network which secured Cromwell a place in Parliament and so launched his public career. Now, his support for religious independency promised to give him a new network of clients, in Manchester's army and outside, which transcended a regional base: the recruitment of Ireton was an early testimony to that. Presbyterianism, while according less with his own beliefs, also had less to offer politically as it was embraced by most of the parliamentarian gentry and so would have given him less prominence and value as a patron and ally.

One of the reasons why Cromwell was concerned for the reputation of his men in the autumn of 1643 was that he was caught up in the general crisis of subsistence which beset much of Manchester's growing army because of the lag between the ordinance for its recruitment and that for its financial support. Hitherto, his regiment had been unusually well paid, partly because of his energy in soliciting the money due to it from the association, and partly because his foray into Norfolk and Suffolk had introduced him to the local officials there, who gathered and sent funds, and won their esteem. Both factors were reinforced by his membership of the co-ordinating committee of the association and his ability to join it frequently because it met in his own home territory at Cambridge. Now his position was weakened. For one thing his new superior the earl of Manchester had more political and social clout, and so could take precedence over him in securing resources: Cromwell complained bitterly to St John that the earl's own new horse regiment was well paid but still – he asserted – mutinous and untrustworthy.[133] For another, some of the East Anglian officials thought that Cromwell's men had received too much preferential treatment already, so that those of Norfolk now pointed out that they had already sent him a total of £827 that year, plus sums given to him when he was actually in their county, which was quite enough for one unit of just eight troops (to that date). With the rest of Manchester's swelling army now consuming hundreds of pounds more, they were not in a mood to pamper that one regiment any further.[134] Cromwell was left sure of no source of revenue except the rents from royalist estates in Huntingdonshire, and with no large fortune of his own on which to fall back, in the manner of an aristocratic officer, was reduced to writing letters to friends in London and the association begging them to get funds despatched to him. He expressed pride in the discipline of his men, because they had not plundered the local population to replace failing pay, but he feared he could not keep them effective as a force (and keep increasing their numbers) without more cash to cover the costs of their food, lodging, replacement clothing and the needs of their horses.[135]

Ramshackle, raw and underpaid as his new army was, the earl of Manchester launched it into action within a month of the decision to form it, and at the obvious target, the only enemy fortress within the current bounds of the association: the isolated garrison at rebellious King's Lynn. Within a week of the port's declaration for the king, Parliament had sent a horse troop and ships to blockade it by land and sea, and for lack of any help, the royalists inside could only sit and wait for the inevitable siege.[136] In commencing his operations, Manchester immediately made Cromwell his effective lieutenant in charge of all the cavalry, although he had no formal commission to be this, as the most experienced, senior and respected horse officer in the association. This informal position seems to have been a trial run to see how their relationship, and Cromwell's abilities in the role, would work out. There was a moment of crisis when the earl of Essex ordered Oliver to join his army instead, with all his horsemen, for the expedition to save Gloucester from the king's besieging army which Essex was about to lead. Manchester stood firm against this, and the order was rescinded.[137] Instead, as the siege of King's Lynn properly commenced in the first days of September, Cromwell and the army's cavalry units were stationed to the west of the town, to range between it and Lincolnshire, give warning of any relieving force, and repel one if possible.[138]

The Norfolk Marshland west of King's Lynn is a flat country of creeks, cottages and orchards which at that season would have been glowing with ripe apples. Oliver called at the siege of the town itself, directing part of the bombardment of it, and (according to one parliamentarian journalist) causing the screams of women and children to rise from the interior as shots landed inside. Then he led the horse regiments into Lincolnshire.[139] Behind him Manchester wore down the resistance inside Lynn. The town was protected on one side by the Ouse estuary, and on most of the others by creeks and marshes, which made breaching the land defences difficult. The earl therefore decided to use his overwhelming numbers of foot soldiers by launching them against the land-ward walls with ladders and across the estuary in boats. On realizing what was coming, the garrison offered to negotiate, and got generous terms on 19 September, the royalists being allowed to go home unmolested and the towns-people to enjoy their traditional privileges – providing that they paid a huge sum to make up the shortage of pay for Manchester's infantry.[140]

This success was a boost to parliamentarian morale across the nation, enabling London journalists to claim that it offset the recent loss of Exeter to the royalists. It was accompanied by two even greater pieces of good news. In early September the earl of Essex had marched his army to the relief of Gloucester, without Cromwell but with some of the impressive London militia. He had driven the royal army away from the city and so saved it as a major parliamentarian base, but his march back to London was blocked by the king at Newbury on the 20th. The earl stood cannily on the defensive on high ground full of enclosed fields which maximized his strength in infantry. The royalist attack suffered heavy losses, including some important commanders and politicians, and the king retreated, enabling Essex to make a triumphant return to the capital. Five days later Parliament finalized a treaty with the Scots, entitled the Solemn League and Covenant. It obliged the Covenanters to send a large army to Parliament's aid in the following year, tipping the balance of forces in England in the latter's favour. In return, Parliament promised to pay the Scottish army, sending £100,000 in advance to help raise it, and to reform the Church of England to make it as similar to the Scottish Kirk as possible, without a clear obligation to make it exactly the same. It was confidently expected that within three months the invading Scots would have conquered so much northern royalist territory that taxes imposed upon that and the seizure of royalist estates would cover the subsequent cost of their force in England.[141]

The tide seemed suddenly to be turning in favour of Parliament's cause, and Manchester and his army received a bounty in return for their part in bringing this about. The Houses decreed that the earl was to be made governor of King's Lynn and endorsed his wish to appoint Cromwell's brother-in-law and friend, Valentine Walton, as his deputy there. The ordinance for the new tax on the association, of £22,520 per month, was completed, with Cromwell given a seat on the committees named to raise it in Cambridgeshire and Huntingdonshire. It was explicitly ordered that his enlarged regiment should be supported by all the counties of the association in unison. Manchester was then awarded a share of all the other parliamentarian sources of revenue in those counties. At the same time, Lincolnshire was added to the association, and Manchester empowered to appoint governors for garrisons in the south-east of that county, giving him the ability both to defend the core of the association more effectively and to launch an attack on the area which the earl of Newcastle had conquered in August. This did raise the question of what to do about the existing commander in the county, Lord Willoughby, and the Lords decided to ask the earl of Essex to give him a place in the main field army. This foundered, however, on the problem that Willoughby could not persuade his remaining soldiers to march to join it until they had been paid the money already owed to them, which was now forty weeks in arrears. Essex noted acidly the care now taken to pay Cromwell's troopers, which contrasted glaringly with the way in which the Lincolnshire men had been abandoned. No solution was found to this problem, and so Willoughby remained in his native county and the question of the clash of authority between him and Manchester remained unresolved.[142]

Manchester certainly wasted no time in exerting his authority over the shire thus added to his command, and in doing so sent Cromwell on a new mission. All this while, the earl of Newcastle's army had continued to besiege the Fairfaxes in Hull, though unable to make progress because the garrison was strong and could be supplied and reinforced by sea, while to the landward side drainage dykes were opened to flood the area in front of the defences. Nonetheless, the royalists kept up the pressure, and in the course of September a project was floated to evacuate the cavalry cooped up in the town, where it could do no good, across the Humber to Lincolnshire, where it could reinforce Manchester's army to the point at which it could take the offensive against Newcastle's. As King's Lynn surrendered, therefore, Cromwell led a party north along the Lincolnshire coast, travelling fast through the cooling days and lengthening nights, to reach the Humber coast and travel by boat across the estuary to the besieged town to plan this operation. It was a dangerous journey, as Parliament still had no stronghold in the county except Boston, in the extreme south-east, and under Newcastle's orders a royalist fort had been built on the Humber opposite Hull.[143] On the 22 September Oliver reached the beleaguered town, and probably for the first time in his life came face to face with Lord Fairfax and his son Sir Thomas. In the latter, he would have seen a man in his early thirties, with a long lean face, blade-like nose, thick eyebrows, a moustache and a tuft of beard, and dark expressive eyes, framed between waves of dark hair falling to his shoulders. It was agreed that Sir Thomas would bring most of the cavalry in the town over into Lincolnshire within a few days, having them put into small boats, four or five men and horses at a time, both to avoid detection and because the besieging royalists had burnt the larger vessels that had been available.[144]

This operation was duly carried out successfully, Fairfax landing twenty-one troops of horse and dragoons at a rendezvous point where Cromwell and Willoughby waited with their own men to cover the disembarkations. They all then had a hair-raising ride southwards across Lincolnshire while the governor of Newark, Sir John Henderson, reinforced from Newcastle's army, led a strong force of royalist horse and foot to intercept them. He took by surprise the parties they had sent out to scout to the west and routed or captured them. Cromwell and Fairfax themselves were almost caught on the edge of the Lincolnshire fenland, but fled across it in good order along the causeways to the safety of Boston. Cromwell blamed Willoughby for the disaster to their outposts, while Fairfax, by contrast, credited the lord's local cavalry with having saved them when the enemy attacked.[145] Then they waited in this small medieval port, dominated by its lantern-headed parish church tower, the tallest in England, for Manchester to bring up infantry from King's Lynn.

The earl arrived at the end of September, still fulminating about money. The windfall from King's Lynn had contented his foot soldiers for the time being, but more was now needed for the whole army and the new taxation had yet to kick in. Cromwell shared his mood, commenting that he had wept to arrive at Boston and find no cash there awaiting his men. Nonetheless, their army was much better equipped than it had been a month before, cartloads of arms, ammunition and coats having been sent to it not only from the association but from London.[146] It was also a full-scale field force, the combined horsemen of Cromwell, Fairfax and Willoughby being variously estimated by parliamentarian observers and journalists at between forty and sixty-two troops, or between two and five thousand men.[147] The foot were also put at between two and five thousand strong.[148] A strategy was agreed both to reconquer Lincolnshire and to raise the siege of Hull, which consisted of attacking a royalist fortress in the county and thereby drawing out its royalists, and their supporters at Newark, to come to its aid. This done, the royalist force could be destroyed in the field, so laying the rest of Lincolnshire open to penetration and forcing Newcastle to abandon his attempt on Hull and rush to secure his southern frontier.[149]

The objective selected was one of the closest royalist garrisons to Boston, so giving the attackers the advantages of speed and short supply lines: a small but robust castle at Bolingbroke where the chalk hills of northern Lincolnshire met the fen country of the shire, known as Holland. It was a polygonal circuit of greenstone walls within a broad and deep moat, once a residence of the medieval dukes of Lancaster: Henry of Bolingbroke, who became King Henry IV, had been born there. It sat on the top of the chalk scarp, looking down onto the marshlands below and backwards across the rolling, grassy hills, locally called Wolds, a summer land of sheep, skylarks, blue flowers and blue butterflies, now fading and raked by winds as the autumn progressed. On 10 October Manchester's army advanced across the Holland fens, and he sent a foot detachment to surround the castle while he spread his cavalry through the villages to the north and west, with its commanders in the town of Horncastle, to keep watch for an approaching relief force. That was his first mistake. Parliamentarian scouting had often been slack: at all of the actions in which Cromwell had hitherto been involved – Belton, Gainsborough and during the recent retreat to Boston – his side had either initially or eventually been taken by surprise, even when, as at Belton, it had deliberately tried to provoke the enemy to attack. So it happened now, as Henderson mustered the composite force with which he had recently chased Cromwell and Fairfax, and set out at once, faster than Manchester was expecting. That evening he came down on the earl's cavalry outposts and caught them unprepared, driving them into a mixture of retreat and rout. All night Manchester rode up and down the six miles he had unwisely put between his foot and horse divisions, rallying and gathering the latter. Some units had to cut or bluff their way through the royalists in order to reach their own lines, but by morning most were safely back with the main army, which the earl mustered on Bolingbroke Hill.

At a council of war held there, Cromwell advised against seeking battle, as his men and horses were too tired after the night-time retreat. The decision went against him, to advance towards the enemy, and Manchester ordered his cavalry units half a mile ahead of the foot to locate the latter. That was his second error, repeating the first by opening too wide a gap between his cavalry and infantry. At noon the march began, and the parliamentarian horsemen soon located Henderson's in a mass ahead of them. The royalists could see Manchester's infantry in the distance, and realized that they had a chance to charge and destroy his horse units before the foot could arrive to support them. Accordingly, they advanced to the attack, and the two forces met in the large open fields belonging to the village of Winceby, long stripped of their crops and so good terrain for riders.

There are no good records for the strength of either side, and each, as usual, claimed afterwards to have been outnumbered. The royalists had a more varied military toolkit, with some foot as well as dragoons and their main body of horse. Their precipitate decision to attack resulted in their advancing in more confusion than usual, but both sides threw out a dragoon screen in front, the members of which dismounted and fired a volley at each other. The parliamentarian horse were advancing themselves, not wishing to be hit while static by a charge, and like the royalist horse were in two bodies, one behind the other, Cromwell leading the association horsemen in the van, singing psalms, and Fairfax bringing on his north-erners in the rear. When the enemy dragoons loosed off their shots, Cromwell led his men down on them at full speed, expecting to strike them before they had a chance to reload; but their foes were abler than he had thought, and fired a second volley at close range. Cromwell's charger was killed underneath them and he was thrown to the ground. At this moment the front body of royalist horse charged between the dragoons and hit Cromwell's men while they were disordered from the volley. This was a textbook action, performed just when it should have been after the dragoons had done their work; and it ought to have been the end of Oliver. As he dragged himself to his feet, he was knocked down again by a royalist gentleman, Sir Ingram Hopton, who moved in to finish him off. Rocked by shot and then by the impact of the oncoming cavalry, and seeing their leader fall, his troopers should have broken and he should have died as Cavendish had done, and the battle been lost.

This did not happen. Instead Cromwell's men rallied to save him, and it was Hopton who fell at their hands, enabling one of them to help Oliver onto a new steed. The two bodies of horsemen collapsed into a disorderly melée, and the strength of the counter-attack by Cromwell's force pushed the royalist front line back onto the second one. The parliamentarian right wing was then forced back in turn, but at that moment Fairfax brought up the second division of their cavalry, in a hammer blow against the other flank of the enemy. A Yorkshire regiment there, loaned by Newcastle, broke under-neath this and fled, sweeping away the rest of their fellows in their panic, and the other half of Henderson's horsemen, realizing that their comrades were abandoning them, crumpled in turn, and turned their mounts to run. The dismounted dragoons and the foot soldiers were left to the mercy of the victors, who also chased the defeated royalist riders for miles and killed or captured as many of them as possible. The country lanes were left strewn with bodies.

It was a total, and major, victory. The earl of Manchester reported around three hundred royalist corpses on the battlefield and many more in the country beyond, and eight hundred prisoners: he said he had lost only twenty men. There were also about a thousand captured horses, though a lot of these were of such poor quality that the victors sold them off to the country people at knock-down prices.[150] This may have been a factor in the royalist defeat, and one royalist commander noted ruefully the superiority of the parliamentarians' weapons, which may also have counted.[151] His side had made not a single tactical mistake, save perhaps to sacrifice order to speed in their attack; and yet they had lost. Manchester had made the errors, but his men had won, and his overall strategy proved resoundingly successful.

In the earl's own despatch, Cromwell was praised for playing his part well, but Fairfax was credited with the victory.[152] Nonetheless, Oliver's publicity machine – whoever was running it – was still in action, and one of the pamphlet accounts published of the battle in London harped on the marvel of his narrow escape from death and implied that it had been his men who had broken the enemy. Fairfax was not mentioned.[153] All this, however, was fine-tuning of a glory in which everybody in the combined force shared. Most of the royalist horse had escaped, and even some of the foot and dragoons, but they were widely scattered, and demoralized, and Lincolnshire now lay open to the victors. Henderson was dismissed from his command at Newark. The battle confirmed a general sense that Parliament's fortunes had turned the corner towards recovery, and it also secured its immediate strategic objective of relieving Hull. As their enemies fled the field, Manchester's army heard a distant thunder of artillery to the north, marking a major sally by Lord Fairfax's men from the town which routed a section of the besiegers and captured their guns. This blow, and then the news of Winceby, persuaded the earl of Newcastle to raise the siege and retreat to York.[154]

As he did so, Manchester advanced on Lincoln, the garrison of which had been depleted by men sent to Winceby. His first attack was beaten off, but after that the defenders were ready to accept good terms, and got them on 20 October, being allowed to march away if they left their weapons behind.[155] The earl was ready to grant such lenience because the scales of war had apparently tipped again. Just as Cromwell's success at Belton had been alloyed by the discovery that only half the action had been won, and that at Gainsborough ruined by the immediate appearance of the earl of Newcastle, so now the greater victory at Winceby seemed for a moment to be negated. News had arrived that units of the king's own army, which had returned to its Oxford base, had thrust deep into the south-east Midlands. The Eastern Association's army was therefore in the position of a man who has punched an opponent on the jaw and sent him reeling, only to feel a blow in the kidney from another assailant. King Charles's soldiers had occupied the town of Newport Pagnell, which stood in a strong position where the old Roman road between London and the West Midlands, Watling Street, crossed the River Ouse. From there, having thus turned the line of the river, they were raiding across Bedfordshire as far as Hertfordshire, where they threatened the northern side of London, while a strong party had seized Huntingdon.[156] The association lay wide open to them on its south-west flank, and the king commissioned his nephew Prince Rupert, increasingly regarded as his best general, as the royal lieutenant-general in all the counties within its bounds, plus those which provided the way into it.[157] Invasion seemed imminent, and Manchester now sent Cromwell towards Huntingdon with much of his army, at full speed, while he prepared to follow with the rest.

This time the crisis then evaporated as swiftly as it had developed. Anxious to re-establish his dominance, the earl of Essex ordered Manchester to pull back his men, and sent part of his own field army from the London area to tackle the problem, reinforced by some of the city's militia. The royalist raiders fell back before it, and those in Newport Pagnell, outnumbered, not yet secured by fortifications, and allegedly misunderstanding orders, evacuated the town on 27 October. It was immediately filled with Essex's men and turned into one of the strongest parliamentarian fortresses in the nation, and the line of the Ouse was made safe again. Nevertheless, Manchester's campaign had lost its momentum, and three different reasons can be proposed for this. The first was simply that the season was now so late. The darkness was creeping towards the afternoon, the leaves and the first frosts falling, and a damp chill rising from the ground, and it was time for field armies to get into winter quarters. Something of the condition of Manchester's horse soldiers by now can be learned from a line written home on 20 October by Nathaniel Rich, an ardent Puritan who had led a troop from Essex to join the earl's own regiment: 'the winter is already come, and our lying in the field hath lost us more men than have been taken away either by sword or bullet'. The new money had still not arrived, or was not arriving in sufficient quantities, and Rich's attempts to tide his men over by paying them from his own income had been ended when somebody stole his whole stock of cash as he and his troop slept in a meadow outside Lincoln. They could take food and lodging awhile with the unpopular system of free quarter, but this did not provide the means to mend weapons and saddles, and replace horses' shoes.[158]

It is also evident that the earl of Manchester was starting to manifest his consistent style as a general: ponderous, cautious, uncharismatic and blinkered. He could lead well enough when he had a fixed and obvious short-term target, and clear and positive orders, but once that objective was achieved he tended to flounder. A third reason for the halting of his army's momentum was that there was no longer any royalist threat to the association, while the remaining enemy fortresses in Lincolnshire proved hard nuts to crack. The earl of Newcastle had withdrawn his southern line of defence to northern Derbyshire and Nottinghamshire, where he strengthened his grip with a set of new garrisons before going north to meet the new and powerful prospective challenge from the Scots.[159] Newark and the other outlying garrisons were left to fend for themselves. As described, those in Lincolnshire fought hard, Bolingbroke Castle itself not surrendering until November, and Gainsborough having to be taken by storm in December:

territory lost in three weeks in the summer needed three months to be recovered. Manchester left this work to Willoughby and to Fairfax, who was now joined in the task by the old Scot Sir John Meldrum. The earl's main army was quartered across Lincolnshire, Huntingdonshire and Cambridgeshire to protect the association, while his cavalry raided the Newark area for livestock and wool (which was used to renew their worn clothing). Manchester himself settled a parliamentarian administration in Lincolnshire and then ranged the associated counties ordering further levies of men.[160] The Fairfaxes tried to persuade him to join them in attacking Newcastle's army, but he declined the invitation.[161]

Cromwell spent most of this period with his cavalry in their Lincolnshire quarters, before departing near the end of the year to pursue his political ends at Westminster. He was using the process of reorganization and recuperation to extend his own clientage in the region. After the fall of Lincoln he settled Ireton in his new post at Ely, with Dodson. The earl of Manchester exercised his new power to appoint garrison commanders by giving first Boston and then Lincoln to a local parliamentarian, Edward King, whose recommendations were his piety and zeal for the cause, and his vehement hostility to Willoughby. He would be a potent ally in any struggle with the lord to settle the question of authority in the county. Cromwell's own animosity towards Willoughby, for losing most of Lincolnshire in August, would have recommended King to him, but he now took care to install one of his own friends and clients to keep an eye on the new governor. This was the celebrated radical John Lilburne, whose release Cromwell had secured as a result of his maiden speech in the Long Parliament, and who had since followed a roller-coaster career as a soldier, getting captured and charged with treason by the royalists and then released as part of an exchange of prisoners. When this happened, Oliver invited him to join Manchester's army, which Lilburne did in October, to find that Cromwell had got him a commission as major in King's garrison regiment at Boston.

Lilburne rapidly proved his value in that post, by arbitrating in a clash which manifested the growing tension in the parliamentarian ranks over the prospective religious settlement. Some of King's own officers joined with certain townspeople and some of Cromwell's troopers to hold a private religious meeting at Boston. This seems to have been a classic example of the kind of gathering that independents and sectaries favoured for worship and which mainstream Puritans, let alone royalists, regarded as abhorrent and traditionally illegal, although there is no indication of what actually happened at this one. King reacted in orthodox fashion, by arresting those who had attended. Hearing of this, Lilburne, whose own sympathies lay firmly with independency, tried to pacify the governor, and rode across the Holland fens to Sleaford, where Cromwell was quartered, to enlist his help. This Oliver promptly gave, and King was pleased enough – at least according to Lilburne – with the latter's service in his new role, and impressed enough by Cromwell's reputation, to release his captives. Cromwell then rewarded King by encouraging the earl of Manchester to enlarge the man's commission to include Lincoln. Peace was thus restored for the time being, and Oliver's role as a local power broker and patron of radicals enhanced.[162] At Ely he gave full support to Ireton in encouraging independency, and he allegedly tried to promote a petition among his own officers to ask Parliament to grant some kind of tolerance of divergent religious beliefs among its supporters: effectively, to promote the independents' cause. According to this account he could not secure support from all, and the measure was dropped.[163]

Cromwell could end the year with much satisfaction. He had not been the saviour of East Anglia and the parliamentarian East Midlands during the summer, although he had tried to put himself forward for the role: as shown, he would have been virtually helpless had Newcastle's army actually attacked. He had not established a defensible perimeter for the Eastern Association: also as shown, the strategy to do so had been a collective one, and so had the achievement of security for the region, after the frontier with the enemy had been pushed back and forth a few times over. He had not proved the superiority of Parliament's cavalry over the king's, after a long period in which the royalist horsemen had always been superior:

Charles's followers had always been vulnerable to defeat in local actions, and Cromwell's military successes had not yet risen above those.

What he had done in the course of the year was to establish himself as the leading horse commander in the Eastern Association, and the most active soldier within it in defending its territory against threats from the Midlands and north, usually by waging war beyond its boundaries. He had also raised a very large, effective and loyal regiment and extended a more general if as yet informal and ad hoc authority over the other horse units in Manchester's new army. He had begun to build himself a network of clients in that army and in the region, with a special reputation as a protector and supporter of religious independents. He had also acquired considerable and consistent acclaim in the parliamentarian press, in a fashion which at times bordered on the mendacious. None of this had made him, as yet, more significant than many other local parliamentarian leaders or given him any national weight as a soldier. Even at the local level, indeed, he had not yet presided over a single decisive victory: at Crowland, the achievement was shared; at Belton, it was only partial; at Gainsborough it had immediately been reversed; and credit for the undoubted major success at Winceby had neither been earned by nor accorded to him. He had, however, made a very good beginning, establishing himself both as an able military man and a rising one.

4

❖

THE LIEUTENANT-GENERAL

On 20 January 1644, Parliament rewarded the earl of Manchester and his army for its good initial service by raising the property tax on the Eastern Association, which was designed to support it, by 50 per cent. This would supply a tremendous £33,780 per month, for four months, which would be sent to a single association treasury under the earl's direct control. As a symbolic gesture of self-sacrifice, to prevent the tax burden on the region from rising still higher, all officers in the Eastern Association army from the rank of captain upward, including Manchester and Cromwell, were to be paid only half the salaries owed to them for the rest of the war, and claim the balance after it. Likewise, captains were henceforth to pay themselves for all losses of horses and arms by their men other than in battle, and if they took free quarter, soldiers were then to get only a third of their wages, to provide the means to pay off what was owed to the people from whom they had taken food and services. It was a classic deal whereby extra funding was provided in exchange for efficiency gains, with a built-in incentive to officers both to ensure that their men were responsible and well behaved, and to win the war.[1] It was also, of course, a tremendous vote of confidence in the earl and his men, providing them with the chance at last to build a still larger and more effective field force.

Two days later, Manchester's power was strengthened further, when the House of Commons ordered the earl of Essex to award him explicitly the same authority over Lincolnshire as over the rest of the association, firmly subordinating Willoughby and his horsemen to Manchester's command. The earl was also given the power to purge Cambridge University of unreliable dons and appoint committees in each county to replace suspected clergy.[2] On that same date, 22 January, Cromwell got his share of the reward package, by being commissioned as the earl's lieutenant-general, formally recognizing his existing position as second-in-command of the army, and especially as leader of the horse. Like every other higher officer he would only receive half the pay for the job as long as the war lasted, but that was topped up because he continued to be paid separately both as colonel and captain of horse.[3] On 16 February both he and Manchester received a further honour by being added to the brand-new body, the Committee of Both Kingdoms, established by Parliament to direct the joint war effort that it was now making with its new Scottish allies.[4] It had nineteen other English members, several of whom, like the earl and Oliver, were expected to be away from it in the field for most of the year, and on the receiving end of its orders rather than sharing in the formulation of those. Both of them indeed left London before the first meeting.[5] Nonetheless, membership was a striking sign of Cromwell's rising status as a soldier as well as a politician. The turn of the year had gone superbly for him.

REMAKING THE ARMY

Oliver was certainly in the House of Commons at the time when these measures were passed, and it must be presumed that he played a significant part in arguing for them. In December one member had noted that the House was now split between three factions. One consisted of those who wanted resources to be prioritized for the expected Scottish army, and was led by Sir Henry Vane and other men whose own northern property was currently in the hands of the royalists and could rapidly be freed by the Scots. A second lobbied for effort to be put instead into building up the army under Sir William Waller, and was made up largely of West Country members whose estates might be freed by that force. The third, which in size matched the other two together, consisted of supporters of the main field force under Essex, who argued that this ought still to take precedence.[6]

It may be surmised that the success of Manchester's army in making the gains that it did was due to the fact that it was detached from this tripartite rivalry and could draw on support from all three interests; after all, the assessment being increased to pay it was entirely from its own region and did not compete with that for Essex's men, which the taxpayers of the association had to continue to provide as well. The reputation of the army for piety and immediate military success no doubt also counted in its favour, and so must a petitioning campaign in praise of Manchester as a commander, organized across the Eastern Association.[7] Certainly Essex himself was seen to engage in gestures of solidarity with Manchester and his officers at this time: on the day after the ordinance was agreed to increase the assessment in the Eastern Association, he invited Manchester and Cromwell to his London mansion, along with friends of his own. From there they went together to hear a famous preacher at a nearby church and then to join a feast provided for most of Parliament by the Merchant Taylors' Company at their hall.[8]

It seems that the establishment of the Committee of Both Kingdoms was pushed through by people like Viscount Saye, Oliver St John and Sir Henry Vane, who were allies of Cromwell before and after and so would presumably have pressed for his inclusion in it. Likewise, it may be presumed that Cromwell supported its establishment, especially as he was named to the Commons committee instructed to set it up; but clearer evidence of his involvement seems missing.[9] The plainest glimpse of his activity in Parliament during this winter concerns the achievement by the earl of Manchester of absolute military authority over Lincolnshire. Cromwell himself proposed this in the House of Commons and then supported it, and indulged his own dislike of Lord Willoughby, by launching a bitter attack on the latter's competence upon 22 January. As part of it he accused Willoughby of having surrendered Gainsborough when Cromwell was near it with a relief force; a claim which was, as must be plain from the account of events given previously, an outright lie. He was opposed on this point by a friend of the lord, but this speaker then conceded the issue of the command by announcing that Willoughby now wanted to retire anyway; and so Cromwell's motion was carried.[10]

This resolution contrasted with the response of the Lords, who had instead formally thanked both Manchester and Willoughby for their services and decided to ask the earl of Essex to mediate between them. In character, Willoughby himself then reacted to his removal by behaving both impulsively and stupidly, and challenging Manchester to a duel. News of this was leaked by Manchester to the Commons, which warned the Lords of the matter on 1 February, and they arrested Willoughby and set up a committee to consider what should be done. This reported after five days that the lord had intended to insult the earl as he passed through the cloisters of Westminster Abbey after attending the Westminster Assembly of churchmen, and that Willoughby held that he had been provoked to such drastic action by 'Colonel Cromwell's business'. Upon further investigation, it was learned that what Willoughby meant by this was that Cromwell had made wounding comments about the lord and his officers (which was, as seen, true), and that these had been accompanied by a campaign by Manchester's officers in Lincolnshire, led by Edward King, to get signatures to a declaration denouncing Willoughby. In response, Manchester denied any knowledge of that declaration, and announced, piously and evasively, that credit for the victories in Lincolnshire should only be given to God.

The committee duly concluded on 7 February that the earl was blame-less in the matter and ordered Willoughby to make peace with him. This was apparently done, and Willoughby returned to Lincolnshire and resumed command of his soldiers there, this time serving under Meldrum in local operations. He continued to complain to the Lords, however, of fresh slanders spread against him by King all through the spring, and King admitted the existence of the declaration he had tried to promote against Willoughby. Cromwell, for his part, continued to feed information to the

Commons against the lord and in support of the colonel. The case rumbled on into May, King claiming that he had only acted under Manchester's orders and that Willoughby and his officers were generally regarded in Lincolnshire as responsible for the loss of most of the county in the previous August. The Lords tried to fine and imprison him in response, whereupon the Commons took up his case in June and complained that this unilateral action by the other House was a breach of its privileges. The matter was resolved with King's release and return to duty, but Manchester had now come to regard him as a divisive figure in Lincolnshire, who was quarrelling with the parliamentarian county committee and had outlived his use: so he subsequently dismissed him from his offices.[11] The whole affair provides a good insight into the campaign of defamation which had been mounted against Willoughby by Cromwell and King, with or without Manchester's connivance. At any rate, the main objective, to gain the county unequivocally for the earl's command, had been achieved. It is possible that the timing of Oliver's commission as lieutenant-general, signed on the same day, was a reward for his vital part in the victory.

Once the political work was over, and the money and power secured, the former could be collected and the latter exercised. Some 95 per cent of that four months' worth of new taxation eventually came in, and the counties of the association were now totally subservient to Manchester, who appointed their treasurers, sent auditors to examine their accounts and agents to galvanize their committees, and could replace negligent local administrators. He used these powers tactfully, instructing his central treasury to inform county treasurers of how their money was being spent and ordering his cavalry captains to work with local committees to commandeer horses. Defaulters on taxes were strictly punished, and the money was collected from the refractory by armed force. Manchester further drove on support for the war effort by sending preachers into his counties to encourage it and started the replacement of existing parish ministers.[12] He himself led the purging of the university, swiftly and brutally.[13]

It was announced at the opening of March that his field force would be increased to 10,000 foot, 3,000 horse and 2,000 dragoons, and that any officers found to be dissolute in their lifestyles would be cashiered and replaced by sober and pious men. 'This brave army is our violets and primroses, the first fruits of the spring,' crowed one London newspaper.[14] A captain was sent to London to buy new weapons for it, and spent £6,665 on them.[15] To supply the extra horses and replace lost mounts, the central committee gave several thousand pounds more to a lieutenant to act as its main agent in buying them from civilians, and extra sums to individual officers to do so directly.[16] The new resources were given to a horse division which had suffered badly from underfunding through the winter: at the opening of February a captain in Vermuyden's regiment complained that it had been sent only £2,000 of £9,000 due to it, and that its troopers were now going barefoot and underclad in continuing cold weather, and their steeds unshod and some dying of exposure.[17] Now the great refurbishment began. Not only were existing units re-equipped and recruited but it is in this spring that certain evidence exists for the fourth horse regiment which had been planned since the previous summer.[18] By April Manchester's army was the largest, and probably the best armed, mounted and clad, in Parliament's service.[19]

The officer corps of the Eastern Association army was not a stable and compact entity recruited from the associated counties alone. The new horse regiment was commanded by the younger son of a Northamptonshire squire, George Fleetwood, with Thomas Harrison, the son of a prosperous Staffordshire butcher, as its major. Both men were avid young Puritans who supported religious independency, and had gone from being London law students to join Essex's army when the war broke out. In the winter of 1643–4 they had transferred to Manchester's, probably attracted by its reputation for piety and its prospects of good pay, and especially by Cromwell's growing fame or notoriety as a patron of soldiers with their views.[20] Cromwell's own regiment shared in the general overhaul, and just as before, as the number of horsemen in the army increased, so he expanded his unit still further to preserve its overall dominance. It now reached an extraordinary total of fourteen troops, more than twice the size of most cavalry regiments. Three of its captains were Londoners.[21] Oliver's cousin Edward Whalley remained in direct charge of it, having been promoted to lieutenant-colonel as it underwent its last expansion in the autumn.[22] Turnover among the rank and file of Manchester's horse division was considerable, because of the hardness of service: of the eighty-three men in one troop in September 1643, only forty-two remained by April, though the unit itself had been recruited back to full strength.[23]

One new recruit to the army was to give Cromwell especial vexation: a Scottish veteran called Laurence Crawford who had transferred from the war against the Irish rebels to Parliament's service during the winter. He was the son of a laird with a small castle near Glasgow, and though now only in his early thirties had over a decade of experience in the German wars before going to Ireland as a colonel.[24] Crawford reported to the House of Commons in December, and clearly impressed it, because he was duly recommended to Manchester, who showered him with commissions on 1 February. Crawford was made serjeant-major-general of the whole army and commissary-general of its horse. The latter office was second-in-command to Cromwell in managing the cavalry, but this was really an insurance policy in case Oliver was killed or incapacitated, because Crawford's real job was to command the infantry, so giving them a leader apparently as impressive as Cromwell was in charge of the horse soldiers. In addition, the Scotsman's great experience of warfare was honoured by making him president of the army's council of war, which advised the earl on strategy.[25] This, and their matching duties, made it highly desirable that he and Cromwell got on; but the odds were stacked against that from the start.

The reason for this lay in the religious tensions swelling within the parliamentarian ranks, as the tectonic plates within English Puritanism lurched further apart under the pressure of the need to reform the Church. Until the end of 1643, the rival factions forming within the Westminster Assembly had managed to play down their differences, at least to the world at large, but on New Year's Day five leading independents in it broke cover by publishing a manifesto. This represented them as moderates offering a middle way between a rigid and repressive presbyterianism and the anarchy promised by the sects (those commonly termed Anabaptists) who wanted to disestablish the Church altogether. What they now proposed was a national religious structure regulated by the state and composed of a federation of congregations served by individual ministers, who would be allowed to differ in minor matters over their attitudes to doctrine and ecclesiastical government. By characterizing doctrinaire presbyterianism as an extreme position, they were of course being very provocative to its adherents, who made up most of the assembly, as well as to Parliament's new Scottish allies. After this the poles around which those who wished to reform the English Church could rally were increasingly well defined, and polarization duly began to set in, even while both presbyterians and independents remained a very broad spectrum of opinion.[26]

The raising of the religious temperature inevitably affected Manchester's army faster and more severely than the others, simply because of the efforts to which the earl and Cromwell had gone to attract godly recruits, especially to the officer corps. When the earl left Westminster on 19 February to rejoin his men, one of the Scottish delegation of divines resident in the English capital gleefully told a friend at home that Manchester was now determined to weed out sectaries from them.[27] The earl had an eager agent for this work in Crawford, a classic intolerant Scottish presbyterian, who within two weeks had suspended a lieutenant in Cromwell's regiment from duty, and denounced him to Manchester as an Anabaptist. His grounds were that the man had refused to swear a legal oath, probably that of loyalty to the Anglo-Scottish alliance prescribed by the Solemn League and Covenant. Refusal of any oaths was a scruple associated with sectaries, who often interpreted Scripture to hold that Christ had forbidden swearing of any kind. Immediately the accused officer appealed to Cromwell, who – whatever his feelings concerning the man and his religious views, though both may have been warm – had suffered a double slight to his authority. First, Crawford had interfered in the horse division of the army, of which

Cromwell was the usual commander, and indeed in Cromwell's own unit of it; and second, the Scotsman's initiative was a direct challenge to Oliver's growing position as a patron and protector of religious radicals.

It was not technically illegal, as Crawford was formally Cromwell's second-in-command over the horse, and claimed that the lieutenant had disobeyed his orders at a time when Oliver was away and the Scot was in charge of his men.[28] Nonetheless his action was a blow to Cromwell's authority and his reputation as a protector of his clients. The result was a letter to Crawford which rejected a cajoling or comradely tone for one of icy courtesy and barely restrained fury, and which deployed once more Oliver's classic 'scatter gun' effect of argument. On the one hand he questioned whether his officer actually was an Anabaptist; on the other, he asserted that even if the man was one, and blatant about his beliefs, his faithful service and devotion to the common cause should excuse him. Cromwell then went on to point to the de facto tolerance of diverse religious opinions during the war, across England, cast doubt on whether legal authority currently existed to end it, and accused Crawford of acting without precedent in trying to sack a soldier simply because of his beliefs concerning religion.[29] Oliver was effectively declaring Manchester's promised campaign to weed out heresy from his army dead at the start, at least in the cavalry. It seems that Crawford buckled under his pressure, and that their mutual commander the earl was too busy (as Cromwell claimed) or too tactful to intervene. A lieutenant with the same name was promoted by Oliver to captain four months later.[30]

In the same period, the fissure which had opened between the two generals divided Colonel Edward King from the man whom Cromwell had installed as his major (with the additional duty of reporting to Oliver on King), John Lilburne. Lilburne claimed afterwards that it had been King's presbyterian chaplains who had ruined their good working relationship by convincing him that Lilburne was a dangerous radical. The partnership between the two officers was breaking down by March 1644, and collapsed in May when Lilburne resigned his commission. Cromwell, ever the good patron, promptly had his friend appointed as lieutenant-colonel of Manchester's dragoon regiment. Lilburne then formed an alliance with other discontented officers in King's regiments, and with the colonel's enemies on the Lincolnshire county community, to get King sacked. Only Manchester could do this, however, and the earl too had presbyterian chaplains, who protected King; and the colonel now felt able to harass and imprison men in the areas he governed, whether soldiers, ministers or lay civilians, for not conforming to the official ceremonies of the Church or for meeting for worship outside it. By now, if not long before, Cromwell had abandoned his support for King, and this would have made it the easier for Manchester eventually to lose patience with him and dismiss him in August, as described.[31] Thus far, Cromwell had reacted to the growing religious tensions within the Eastern Association army with the same determination and ruthlessness as he showed in war, defending the independent interest and even extending this to possible sectaries, with resolution and success. As a result, as that army gathered for the campaigning season of 1644, it was at once larger than ever before, better equipped and paid than ever before, and more seriously divided than ever before.

THE SLOW SPRING

During the first three months of 1644 the army remained in winter quarters. In early January Cromwell was at Ely, where it seems that his wife and younger children were now living; which makes sense, as the combination of the surrounding fens and fortification made it one of the most secure parliamentarian fortresses in the region, and one under Oliver's control as governor and Ireton's direct and reliable care.[32] During his visit, Cromwell supressed the choral services in the cathedral, which Puritans found offensive, driving out the congregation from one when the choirmaster ignored an initial order to desist. He does not seem to have let his soldiers attack the church fabric as he had done at Peterborough, but used the threat of doing so as a means of keeping the clergy cowed.[33] One parliamentarian newspaper put him in the Newark area at this time instead, and credited him with surprising two royalist horse troops quartered in villages outside the town. From the first, the stories went, the captain alone escaped, running from his bed in an inn with his breeches in his hand; while in the second case the troopers were attending a wedding, and their lieutenant tried to hide under the marriage bed.[34] It may have happened. If so, the Newarkers took a dramatic revenge in mid-January, when they surprised three of the best troops in Cromwell's own regiment and destroyed them, taking 120 prisoners.[35] The shattered units were rebuilt in the spring, and Cromwell escaped all censure because he had gone to attend Parliament; but the incident demonstrated that his soldiers were not invincible.

Meanwhile the war was developing, despite the rigours of the season. The king's equivalent strategy to Parliament's alliance with the Scots was to make a truce with the Irish rebels so that he could recall the army which had been fighting them in his name. In the autumn and early winter units of this began to land, at Bristol and Chester, and formed the nucleus of two new local armies. One was given to Sir Ralph Hopton, and ordered to invade the south-east and threaten London from the south: by December it had secured most of Hampshire and put a detachment into Sussex. The second was ordered to conquer Cheshire and Lancashire, where Parliament had strong outposts, and so cover Newcastle's rear as he turned to face the Scots. By January this had overrun most of Cheshire and was besieging the last parliamentarian stronghold in the county, at Nantwich. Parliament retaliated effectively. It ordered Essex to remove his men from Newport Pagnell so that some could be lent to Sir William Waller to repel Hopton: Manchester was directed to take over the defence of the town and its district instead.[36] Waller then did the job, shattering Hopton's army in a series of attacks and capturing its Sussex outpost.

Still more dramatic news came from the north. As Parliament had sent Waller to destroy the new royalist army in the south-east, so it despatched Sir Thomas Fairfax to deal with that in Cheshire, joining his own horsemen to local forces in the north-west. He did this, surprising his enemy outside Nantwich and winning a complete victory to add to his roll-call of successes. Even as he did so, the Scottish allies of Parliament launched their invasion of England, much earlier in the year and in much greater strength than had been expected. Twenty-two thousand marched into Northumberland in late January, delivering Parliament the largest army which had yet been at its disposal, outnumbering anything the king could field. Nonetheless, its initial effects were muted, because Newcastle (now promoted by the king to the title of marquis) marched to face it, and although his men were far fewer in total, he had more cavalry, of excellent quality, and his foot were also superior in experience and ability to the Scottish equivalents, too many of whom were inexperienced.

The Scots were commanded by Alexander Leslie, earl of Leven, a canny and experienced general who had defeated Charles I resoundingly in 1640. He and Newcastle adopted the same tactics, of manoeuvring around each other seeking terrain on which their own strengths would be maximized and those of their opponents negated. Each time one found it, and offered battle, the other would decline the contest, and the result was a stalemate which lasted all through February and March, disappointing Parliament's hopes that the Scots would simply steamroller their way through the north.[37] It was Newcastle's rear which was his weakness, now that Fairfax's victory at Nantwich had re-established the parliamentarian strength across the Pennines; and Parliament now launched a strike against his great outpost at Newark which would expose his southern flank still more. It empowered Meldrum to gather an army from the parliamentarian garrisons and local troops of the East Midlands, and lay siege to the royalist fortress. This was duly accomplished, the resulting composite force including Willoughby, King and Lilburne, all on dreadful terms with each other. By March, Newark was in desperate straits.

While these stirring events were happening, Manchester's army was preparing for action. From mid-February it was under the command of the new Committee of Both Kingdoms, which was now expected to co-ordinate the joint strategy of its own forces and that of its Scottish allies across the nation. Such a coherent war plan was clearly a good idea, but the committee did not seem to know what to do with Manchester's men. First it decided – as Manchester and his officers themselves wanted – to send them to besiege Newark, but then resolved that this could be done by Meldrum with local soldiers, including those in Manchester's Lincolnshire garrisons. The rest of the earl's forces were now ordered instead to concentrate in Bedfordshire and prepare to launch raids on the royal field army itself in its winter quarters. These would pin it down while Waller finished off Hopton in the south.[38] Cromwell and Crawford duly gathered a large body of their soldiers there at the end of February, and their first operation was to attack a local royalist garrison, ten miles west of Newport Pagnell, called Hillesden House.

This was an obvious target, for a number of reasons. One was simply that it was the nearest body of enemy soldiers. Another was that it was strategically positioned, in the hills south of Buckingham where it could turn the line of the Ouse and be a launch pad for strikes into Bedfordshire and where it also guarded the approach to Oxfordshire. Finally, it was a soft target, for the place was not yet properly fortified, the vital ring of earthworks around it, which could stop cannon shot and assaulting soldiers, being less than half complete. Manchester's two subordinate generals wielded a sledgehammer to crack this nut, bringing 1,800 men on 4 March to attack the 150 inside. The garrison made a fight of it, but those left alive eventually did surrender as the odds made extended resistance hopeless.[39] The house's fall opened the way for Cromwell's cavalry to raid across northern Oxfordshire, plundering the countryside to weaken the king's resources and diminish his reputation. Oliver allegedly led 1,500 of them to drive off cattle from under the very walls of Oxford. More of his men helped to escort a large convoy of munitions across the Midlands to the isolated and blockaded parliamentarian stronghold at Gloucester, so that its men could attack the surrounding royalist territory.[40]

Despite these achievements, March 1644 must have been a terrible month for Cromwell. One reason for this was personal: that the concentration of soldiers in garrisons could be an invitation to disease, and in the second week of the month his oldest surviving son, Oliver, died suddenly at Newport Pagnell. His killer was smallpox, the same virus which had carried off his elder brother Robert, five years before, and the blow to Oliver senior can only be imagined.[41] The second stroke of fortune affected the whole of his army. It had failed totally to pin down the king's one, for Charles sent units both to reinforce Hopton and to keep Cromwell at bay, and instead Manchester's men became immobilized themselves, around Newport Pagnell and Bedford. Then terrible news arrived from the North Midlands. Earlier in the spring, the king had sent his formidable nephew Rupert to Shropshire, to start building a new army there around the last of the veteran regiments returning from Ireland. On 21 March the prince launched this force upon Meldrum's force around Newark and enforced its complete surrender, so that it had to give up all its weapons and equipment and march away. As it had been formed by bleeding local parliamentarian garrisons of men, those left in the Lincolnshire strongholds felt themselves too weak to resist any attack and evacuated all in the shire except Boston. All of the gains of the previous year, including Gainsborough, Lincoln, Bolingbroke Castle and Crowland, were abandoned or captured in a few days of panic.[42] Manchester's army had gained a house but lost a county.

The feelings of its members could at best have only partially improved as better tidings arrived soon after from other regions. Rupert did not invade the Eastern Association, even though it lay open to him, but retired to Shrewsbury while the king decided where he was most needed next. Then on 29 March, Waller and his reinforcements from Essex's army faced Hopton and his reinforcements from the king at Cheriton in Hampshire. The royalists repeated their mistake at Newbury, by allowing themselves to be drawn into an unco-ordinated and piecemeal set of attacks onto ground which favoured the enemy, and they were repulsed with heavy losses. The threat to the south-east was ended for good, and much of Hampshire regained. The king subsequently dismissed Hopton from his command and absorbed his army into the main royal one. Within two weeks even better news came from the north.

During March the Committee of Both Kingdoms had repeatedly ordered the Fairfaxes to invade Yorkshire, and so menace Newcastle's rear while he continued to face the Scots.[43] On 11 April Sir Thomas attacked the royalist force which the marquis had left to hold the county, at its base in the town of Selby. Fairfax's soldiers were always good at street fighting, and he won another stunning victory.[44] The Yorkshire royalist strength was now crippled, and Newcastle's men open to being assaulted on both sides. Immediately the marquis abandoned the north-east and force-marched most of his army back down the Great North Road to its vital strategic base at York. There he threw his infantry into the city to save it from the Fairfaxes and sent his cavalry to safety in the East Midlands. The Scots followed him with almost equal haste and joined the Fairfaxes, the joint force then camping outside York and keeping Newcastle and his foot soldiers trapped inside.[45] All this was wonderful for parliamentarian morale; but each success underlined the point that the army of the Eastern Association, the largest, most favoured and best paid in Parliament's service, seemed to be doing nothing.

It was certainly vulnerable to criticism. At London, most informed people blamed Meldrum himself for the disaster at Newark, and others attributed it to the misconduct of the religious independents in his army or of Willoughby (whose military career now ended at last); but some to the failure of Cromwell, now dubbed 'the great independent', to march to its aid.[46] Manchester and his subordinates therefore embarked upon a propaganda offensive. First the earl and the Eastern Association's central committee issued a pamphlet listing all the victories obtained by the association's soldiers over the past year, to show how much they enjoyed divine favour and how valuable they were to Parliament's cause. The association's central treasury paid for two thousand copies to be printed, and read in parish churches.[47] Next, the earl's chaplains commenced a series of despatches informing the Westminster Assembly of the day-to-day actions of the army and demonstrating how active and effective it was; which were then published.[48] All this would only be consequential, of course, if the army actually did do anything effective, and here it was still crippled by the contradictory orders of the Committee of Both Kingdoms at Westminster, which in one week directed it to join Essex and Waller to attack the king, and in the next bade it block another strike upon the East Midlands by Prince Rupert.[49] It did not help matters that Rupert himself was stalled in Shropshire by an equally indecisive king, and could suddenly head in any direction.[50] As a result, the bulk of Manchester's forces still dawdled in Bedfordshire through mid-April, as the hawthorn hedges turned emerald green and the blackthorn pure white, primroses coated the banks of the brooks pale yellow, and bluebells began to carpet woodlands with azure; and the days lengthened and the traditional campaigning season opened. There was even a real danger that its whole financial basis would be stripped away, as the taxation on which it depended was about to expire, and Parliament might not think that worth renewing. An expeditionary force sent north from it in early April reduced Crowland again, and so opened the way into Lincolnshire, but nothing more could be done in that direction for the time being.[51]

The turning point came in late April when the Committee of Both Kingdoms suggested that the earl of Manchester restore the situation in Lincolnshire while also leaving the ultimate choice of what to do with his soldiers up to him.[52] Regaining a county which was part of his association was the kind of mission that the earl understood, and to be in the East Midlands would enable him both to protect the rest of his territory and to keep an eye on Prince Rupert. On 20 April his main army left Bedford, and then moved up the Great North Road to Stamford, reaching that in full strength, at nine to ten thousand, and with regular pay coming in.[53] Cromwell went ahead with 2,000 horse to clear the way to Lincoln, the local royalists, outnumbered, retreating before him. They concentrated their strength to hold Lincoln itself, and Manchester's army closed in on it upon 3 May, Cromwell's cavalry positioning itself to the west to prevent an attempt by Newcastle's horsemen quartered in Nottinghamshire to come to the city's relief. The royalists were too thinly spread and badly outnumbered to defend the full circuit of walls effectively, and the parliamentarian foot got over them easily with scaling ladders equipped with hooks. The royalists shut themselves into the cathedral close, and further action was stalled for three days by pouring rain; but in the dark and early hours of the 6th, Manchester's infantry set their ladders against the close's walls as well and stormed it, killing or capturing the whole garrison.[54]

It was, at last, a major victory for the Eastern Association forces, reclaiming the whole shire for Parliament as the remaining royalists in it fled; and a pamphlet was promptly published to spread and celebrate the news.[55] The achievement was also lucrative, as some of the men who stormed the close were said to have taken £100 to £150 each in loot, and £1,200 was extorted from the city to reward the regiments which had taken it. So many weapons were captured that they could be used to arm new-raised foot units.[56] Good news then arrived from Westminster: the heavy taxation of the Eastern Association, needed to sustain the army, had been renewed for another four months. It was said that the capture of Lincoln had assisted this result.[57]

As soon as the city fell, Manchester threw a bridge across the River Trent at Gainsborough, made by lashing boats together and laying planks across them, to establish direct contact with the armies of Leven and the Fairfaxes, encamped outside York. Within a week they were all co-operating, as Manchester sent Cromwell and his cavalry to join two thousand horsemen sent by the allies outside York, to blockade Newark and bar the way to any attempts to aid the besieged marquis of Newcastle from the East Midlands. Together they made a reassuringly huge mounted force, up to six thousand strong.[58] What none of them knew was that they had already made a decisive impact on royalist grand strategy, which had been hanging on Manchester's movements. In late April, King Charles had instructed Rupert that if the earl came south and united his men with those of Essex and Waller, the prince was to bring his to reinforce the royal army; but if Manchester turned north instead, towards Leven and the Fairfaxes, Rupert should go north himself, and invade Lancashire. There he was to rescue the local royalists, who were in danger of annihilation in the wake of Fairfax's victory at Nantwich; and then he was to relieve York if that was still besieged.[59] As soon as Lincoln had fallen and Manchester bridged the Trent, the prince mobilized, and took the road towards Lancashire with all his soldiers.[60] Although neither of them realized it, he was now on a collision course with Cromwell.

TRIUMPH IN THE NORTH

Almost a year after his frustrating midsummer hanging around the Trent Valley, Cromwell found himself back in that lush landscape. The hawthorns had come into their creamy white blossom, which was now in its foaming plenitude and releasing an almost stagnantly sweet scent. Green grass and corn were rising and thickening, and the foliage of trees settling into a more uniform and similar green; and once more he was waiting in the valley, watching the movements of an enemy for the moment to pounce, in combination with a disparate set of allies. Once again, also, the plan was to be frustrated.

This was because one potential foe – Rupert – did not arrive, and the – other – Newcastle's cavalry regiments – moved away. As Rupert's army invaded Lancashire, so Newcastle's horse, led by a clever, dissipated and ambitious young aristocrat called George Goring, who could handle mounted soldiers superbly, shifted north too, into Derbyshire and Yorkshire's West Riding. This put both into a position to menace the besiegers of York from the west, and so Cromwell's shielding cavalry army had to ride into the West Riding too to block them.[61] This would open a yet wider gap between Manchester's foot, still at Lincoln, and his cavalry divisions, which invited remedy. The earl's orders, decided by the House of Commons and forwarded by Parliament through the Committee of Both Kingdoms, were to ensure that Rupert did not interfere with the siege of York.[62] From Lincoln he could clearly no longer do this, with the whole prospective theatre of war moved north: but the strategic situation also provided a rather obvious remedy.

It was actually suggested by the allies outside York, who in late May sent Sir Thomas Fairfax and a Scottish nobleman to the earl of Manchester to invite him to bring up the whole of his army to join them.[63] The situation at York had reached stalemate, as the earl of Newcastle was still bottled up in the city with the best of his foot, but his enemies could not properly surround it. It had a circuit of medieval walls three and a half miles round, with outworks and new external forts, and another river called the Ouse ran through the centre of it, with the only existing bridges inside the walls.[64] The Scots and the northern parliamentarians could camp on either side, but, if stationed thickly enough to beat off attacks, not blockade it well enough to prevent food from coming in for the citizens and the royalist soldiers. As a result, the marquis could simply wait for his opponents to get tired and go away. If the Eastern Association infantry arrived, however, it would enable a tight cordon to be put round York, and then the place would start to starve and its surrender, and the loss of the king's main base in the north, become only a matter of time. Furthermore, the move would concentrate an enormous mass of soldiers outside the city which could deal with any attempted relief of it. Manchester's instructions to hold off Prince Rupert would be faithfully observed in a changed context, and his foot division would be able to maintain better contact with his horse in the West Riding. The earl was convinced, and on 25 May began his march from Lincoln.[65]

Progress was delayed because the weather had continued unseasonably wet, and the ground was so sodden that the earl's heavy artillery could not move over it.[66] In London, criticism of him as a torpid and uninspiring commander mounted, the Venetian ambassador remarking that 'whether from reluctance to go far from the Associated Counties, or for lack of courage, he has always shown himself very slow in carrying out his orders'.[67] In leaving its home territory, his army was going beyond the reach of its regular pay lines, and had to live off free quarter: immediately the money failed for the infantry, while Cromwell's horsemen, further off, were already running short of provisions.[68] It now became all the more important that both horse and foot be supplied with sufficient food, and so henceforth the army's agents toured Yorkshire, buying supplies in markets and requisitioning them where money was not available. More were bought in East Anglia and shipped up the Ouse. Locals who could not supply food were ordered to give money in lieu of it, with which it might be bought elsewhere, thus effectively laying an illegal tax on the county.[69] By 3 June, all of the Eastern Association infantry had reached York, and filled the gap in the siege lines, making a bridge of boats across the Ouse to maintain contact with their allies.[70]

Cromwell and his horsemen were now ranging the West Riding between Sheffield and Wakefield, a rolling green country given to mining and cloth-making, with the high and barren Pennines on the western horizon. Goring's cavalry had now crossed those out of reach, to join Rupert in Lancashire; and Cromwell's job was to seal the passes through the hills to stop them coming back. Two small royalist garrisons in local mansions were forced to surrender and the contents of the houses looted, so doing something to remedy the lack of pay. In late June, Oliver and the horse units moved further north, to Ripon, to watch and block the passes to the west.[71] The leaves thickened to a uniform dark green, the meadow grass rolled in the wind like a green sea of pollen heads, and still the enemy did not come. Back at York, the earl of Newcastle realized that he was in trouble as soon as Manchester's foot soldiers arrived, and offered to surrender the city if he and his army were allowed to march away from it. The allies wanted finally to destroy his power as well as to capture his base, and so insisted that his men surrender their weapons with the city and disperse, but the marquis refused.

So the blockade was maintained and a bombardment began, thousands of local people being conscripted to dig the siege works. On 16 June Manchester's men sprung a mine under the city wall – a charge of gunpowder left in a chamber tunnelled underneath it – and brought part of it down. However, Crawford, who had overseen the operation, deliberately neglected to inform his Scottish and northern allies of it, so that his soldiers could have the full credit for taking the city. Unsupported by other attacks, they were trapped and surrounded just inside the wall, and routed with around three hundred losses. The incident left Manchester and his army humiliated and embarrassed, and their allies resentful.[72]

There were other reasons for resentment between them, as the huge concentration of soldiers in Yorkshire had brought together representatives of the whole spectrum of opinion regarding religious reform, including the two extremes. The Scots, and the independents in Manchester's army, soon realized how much they differed over the matter, and became mutually hostile.[73] Crawford claimed that Cromwell, Whalley and Lilburne framed a petition to Manchester to remove all officers from his army who opposed the independents' plan for the Church, and threatened those who refused to sign. An English presbyterian officer in the army asserted that Cromwell and Whalley had offered him promotion to colonel if he supported their cause.[74]

Meanwhile, Prince Rupert was wreaking havoc in Lancashire. Three days after entering the county his army stormed Bolton and destroyed the local parliamentarian army inside it. It then laid siege to Liverpool, and took that by assault on 11 June, so bringing most of the shire under royalist control. Rupert then spent the middle part of the month recruiting locally, an enterprise which went well because he seemed to guarantee his soldiers victory, so preserving their lives, and his habit of taking towns by storm awarded them great windfalls of loot. Many of them carried precious bales of cloth away from Bolton, and though much of the wealth of Liverpool was brought away by sea before it fell, what remained was comprehensively plundered.[75] This swelling of his army, and the arrival of Goring's thousands of horsemen to join it, made the prince too strong for the allies outside York to send one of their three armies to defeat him, as the Committee of Both Kingdoms had wanted when he first entered Lancashire. Instead they despatched two thousand men under Meldrum to reinforce Manchester, the main parliamentarian stronghold left in the county, and waited for Rupert to come to them.[76]

This he now had to do. While he was pursuing his career of conquest in the north, things were going badly for his royal uncle in the south. In May, Parliament had persuaded Essex and Waller to sink their rivalry and launch a direct, pincer-like attack on the king's own army at its base at Oxford in late May. If Charles had been reinforced by Rupert and his western army, he could have matched their numbers, but the former had been sent north and the latter was bogged down in a siege of the Dorset seaport of Lyme. Facing a near-certainty of being trapped as Newcastle had been in York, he left most of his infantry to hold Oxford, and fled into the West Midlands with most of his cavalry, his enemies marching in pursuit.[77] From there, in early to mid-June, he bombarded Rupert with a series of orders that instructed the prince to relieve York with all speed, and defeat the armies before it so that they could not subsequently renew the siege; and then to return south immediately to save the king. He did give his nephew some discretion in declining the risk of relieving York, and permission to rejoin him at once instead; but made clear that to achieve both objectives in succession would be the preferable course.[78] At the same time, Rupert was warned that five thousand more Scots were crossing the Tweed, and that he needed to get to York before they did, and reinforced his opponents.[79] Rupert was thus given a succession of difficult tasks to perform in utmost haste.

He set about them with exemplary skill, moving his army north to reach Clitheroe on 24 June so that he could pick up reinforcements from the Cumbrian royalists and then cross the Pennine pass through Skipton. His regiments filed along the dales beneath the bare peaks, their skirts of moorland flowering white with cotton grass. As the slopes became gentler, they crossed into Nidderdale on 30 June, passing under the grey mass of Knaresborough Castle, another former fortress of the dukes of Lancaster, now held for the king by Sir Richard Hutton. From there they had a short and direct route to York.[80] Rupert's choice of that pass took Cromwell and his cavalry by surprise, as they had watched those further south, and they retreated to join their comrades outside the city. At first the allies there hoped to give the prince battle while keeping it besieged, but they realized that he had come in such strength that they needed both to concentrate their forces, and find more.[81] Meldrum and his men were urgently recalled from Manchester, and Parliament's small local army in the West Midlands was called up to join the allies.[82] In the interim, Manchester, Fairfax and Leven decided to unite all their men between Prince Rupert and York. On 30 June Cromwell and the retreating allied horse accordingly occupied the most promising battleground in the prince's path, a few miles from the city. It was a large tract of land grown with scrub grass, gorse bushes and bracken, with clumps of hawthorn and patches of bog, in which the wet weather had left standing water. Despite the latter, it was level, capacious and open enough to enable a very large composite army to deploy easily, and was crossed by cobbled tracks, made for livestock, along which its men could march to their positions.[83] There Cromwell and his companions waited for their comrades to join them. The place was known by various local names, but history was eventually to settle upon that of Marston Moor.

On the next day, the first of July, the rest of the three armies around York came up to join the cavalry, abandoning the siege lines with such haste – propelled by fear that Rupert would strike before they had got into battle order – that they left behind some of their artillery and ammunition, and plenty of spare clothing. When they had all assembled, they made up the largest crowd ever gathered together in one place on English soil in the whole of the seventeenth century – probably around twenty-eight thousand men.[84] The battle which they were preparing to fight might have been the biggest in English history.[85] Scouts reported a body of royalist horse advancing directly upon them, which seemed to indicate that the allied expectation had been correct, but no enemy then appeared. Instead, towards evening, came the news that Rupert had completely outmanoeuvred his foes. The body of horse had been a decoy, a single troop sent as a blind while the prince moved all the rest of his army north-east to Boroughbridge and crossed the River Ouse there. He had then marched swiftly down the other side of the river, sweeping up all the cattle of the villages along the way as provisions for the people of York. On arrival outside the city an advance guard had driven off the men whom Manchester had left behind to watch his bridge of boats, and so captured the crossing. The allies were left on Marston Moor with nobody to fight, while Rupert had both accomplished his objective of relieving the city and joined his army to that of Newcastle inside it. As he controlled the crossings of the river, the initiative now rested squarely with him.[86]

That evening, dejection hung over the huge composite army on the moor, and its generals called a meeting of senior officers to decide on a response. The English were mostly for finding a way to attack Rupert at once, but the Scots prevailed in urging a more cautious strategy. This was to move the entire force south-west through Tadcaster to meet the reinforcements – about five thousand men – coming up from Lancashire and the West Midlands. Then they would halt south of the River Wharfe, which flows through Tadcaster, to block Rupert's direct line of march back to the Midlands. One of the king's letters to his nephew had been intercepted, and the allies knew that the prince's instructions were to get his men back to rescue the royal army as soon as York had been relieved. By putting themselves directly in his way, his opponents hoped to bring his force to battle and destroy it as they had just failed to do on the moor that day. It was also planned to send men over the Ouse by another bridge of boats, to the south of York, so that they could raid the East Riding and interrupt the flow of supplies to Rupert's and Newcastle's armies and starve the prince into moving, preferably straight at them and into their trap. The foot soldiers were billeted for the night in the nearby villages, especially Long Marston. The supply system for the three armies had started to break down, and the men had for a week been issued with a single bread roll a day each, and nothing else, including beer to wash down the food safely. They now rapidly drank the village wells dry and were then forced to suck water out of the puddles on the tracks and fields around. The horse soldiers were left to sleep beside their horses on the damp moor.[87]

Prince Rupert, however, was making his own plans, which were not those expected by his adversaries. He had not gone into York itself, but sent an advance party to contact the earl of Newcastle while he and the bulk of his army camped to the north-east. The marquis returned a reply to him which may have had a decisive and fatal effect on his strategy. This informed Rupert that their enemies were now fleeing from him, and did not appear to wish to fight. He then placed himself and his men at the prince's disposal.[88] This may have persuaded Rupert that the allies were demoralized and vulnerable, and that it was possible to shatter their armies as well as relieve the city before returning south, for which his uncle had hoped. He therefore took Newcastle at his word, and peremptorily commanded him to have all his infantry ready to march at dawn, to join Rupert's men in an attack on the retreating enemy. The prince claimed to have an unequivocal order from the king to fight at once.[89] Newcastle afterwards insisted that he had tried to persuade the prince to leave their opponents alone for the time being, as the allied generals were quarrelling and would break up and go their separate ways, while five thousand reinforcements would join the royalists very soon.[90] He was wrong again: the allies did not intend to divide, but to fight Rupert, and the reinforcements marching to them were both closer than those coming to the royalists, and much more numerous.[91] If Newcastle gave the advice, at any rate, the prince now rejected it.

Dawn in late midsummer comes around four o'clock, and so the north-eastern sky at that hour on 2 July 1644 would have been turning aquamarine, with the first pink shades, as Rupert's army mobilized and prepared to cross the Ouse. The allies started to move at the same time, concerned lest Rupert march straight through York and ahead of them to Tadcaster and away to the south before they had broken camp.[92] The Scottish foot went first, and the rest followed, while the horse, including Cromwell's, withdrew to a long ridge which stretched between the villages of Tockwith and Long Marston to the south of the moor. This was the highest ground to break the flat expanses of the plain of York, and allowed the cavalry to mass there, covering the rear of the armies, with a good view towards the city and a slope in their favour in case of attack from it. It was a strong position, and the generals remained there too. To their surprise, around nine o'clock, the moor behind them began to fill up with royalist regiments, and they realized that Rupert had come out to fight. A 'hot alarm' was sent to the soldiers on the march to call them back with all speed, and they did return, though the rest of the morning was needed for them to do so. All this time, Cromwell and the cavalry remained on the ridge, facing the enemy in battle order.[93]

Rupert had expected to be pursuing a fleeing enemy.[94] Instead he found himself staring at thousands of hostile horsemen, massed ready to fight him at the top of an upward slope twelve hundred yards long which represented the strongest position in the area. He probably had no idea of how far the rest of the allied army was beyond them, and how ready it was for battle; and also could not have had any precise sense of its size, either absolutely or relative to his own force, except that he knew it was large. The wind was also from the front, which would blow the powder smoke of his musketeers and artillery back into their faces when they fired.[95] He drew up his regiments for battle, on the edge of the moor closest to the enemy, but there he stuck.[96] All his instincts were to take the offensive, which had served him well throughout his short but glorious military career in England. However, as he later recorded, on this occasion he felt unable to attack a difficult position, against unknown odds, without his full possible strength; and that he lacked because although Newcastle arrived on the moor as the prince's army did, his infantry from York did not. They had delayed in order to secure the equipment which their enemies had abandoned in the siege lines, and to receive pay. It was said that the marquis further dissuaded Rupert from attacking until they came up to strengthen him.[97] Presumably at the prince's behest, a party of his soldiers – a regiment and some horse – probed forward to occupy ground at the western end of the ridge, on the left flank of their enemies, and was promptly attacked and driven off.[98] After this the royalists stood and waited on the moor.

Gradually the rest of the allied armies made their way back, and by early afternoon were all on the ridge. The foot soldiers found themselves crammed together in fields of wet green corn, mostly rye, which took up much of the ground, and which was now flattened by them: the villagers of Long Marston would have no harvest that year. Showers fell, keeping the men damp and making it difficult for them to maintain the burning cords needed to fire the matchlock muskets which were their main firearm.[99] The earl of Leven had overall command of the whole composite force, being both the most experienced general and the one with the largest army, and he now worked with Manchester and Lord Fairfax to get all their men into a final battle order, in the customary pattern, which Rupert had also adopted, of foot in the centre and horse on the wings.[100] Sir Thomas Fairfax was given the post of honour of a cavalry leader, in charge of the right wing, with his own Yorkshire regiments and some of the Scottish horse. Next to them were positioned most of the huge mass of Scottish infantry, and beyond them, to the left, and the west, most of the Eastern Association infantry under Crawford. Cromwell was given charge of the left wing of horse, rounding off the allied position.

Our man has been largely lost to sight in the past few pages, in which much more has been heard about people like Prince Rupert; this reflects the nature of the records. Now, however, he comes back into focus. Cromwell, with Manchester, would have been responsible for the ordering of his cavalry wing, and put it into three lines. The front two consisted of the whole of the Eastern Association horse division, and the third one was made up of three regiments of the Scottish cavalry, under David Leslie who was the best of Leven's subordinate officers. Somewhere on the front line was another Scottish regiment, Hugh Fraser's dragoons, who would be first into action if battle began. The probable total of mounted men under Cromwell's command was four to five thousand.[101]

As soon as the allied army was formed up, the great guns on both sides began to bombard each other's positions, and the cannonade continued for the rest of the afternoon. There was general agreement that it had remarkably little effect, though the royalist horse on the right wing withdrew a little in the face of it.[102] Later in the afternoon, Newcastle's seasoned infantry at last arrived from York, though lacking a quarter of their expected strength, which had been left to hold the city. The royalist commanders conferred, and could not agree on whether to attack the enemy or not. To do so meant directing their men to push uphill against a well-prepared army with wind and sun in their faces. The folds of the ridge, and perhaps the position of some of the opposing units on or beyond its crest, meant that the royalists below could not make a clear appraisal of its numbers, but it was certainly enormous.[103] It is not surprising that in the end Rupert decided in favour of caution, to hold his position for the rest of the day and review the situation in the morning. As evening approached, he concluded that as his enemies had not attacked all afternoon, they had no inclination to do so, and started to stand down his army. He ordered provisions to be brought to it from York, and told the earl of Newcastle that he could take a rest, so that the marquis retired to his coach. Rupert himself went to eat, sitting on the ground at a distance from his men, while many of his troopers on the right wing dismounted and lay down to doze beside their horses; they had, after all, been awake since before daybreak.[104]

Sitting on his warhorse at the front of the massed cavalry gathered at the left end of the allied lines, Cromwell would have had an excellent view of the royalists on the moor below. During the course of the day the 'pioneers' of the army, the despised labourers in it who did the hard work of digging defences and clearing ground, had removed the obstructions – bushes and hummocks – from the terrain on which his horsemen had formed up, and on the downward slope in front, giving him perfect conditions in which to deliver a charge.[105] The royalist position was that which Rupert had occupied in the morning, when he was still considering an immediate attack on the ridge, and so was dangerously close to the enemy: this favoured whichever side decided to take the offensive first, as those attacked would have the minimal amount of time in which to prepare a response. The main remaining obstacle was a ditch running between the opposed armies along the edge of the moor, from east to west. Towards its eastern end it became quite a significant obstacle, with a bank and hedges, but to the west, in front of Cromwell's horsemen and Crawford's infantry, it was shallow and intermittent. To slow an attack on his position, Rupert had lined it with musketeers for much of its length, and on his right wing, facing Cromwell, stationed two foot regiments behind the ditch and in front of where his right wing of horse came up to the rest of his infantry, to provide covering fire. Five hundred more musketeers were placed at points within his front line of horse, to shoot up approaching horsemen, slowing their pace and breaking their ranks.[106]

To Leven and the other allied generals, from their vantage point on the high ground, it must have been obvious that even with the addition of the northern foot, the royalist army was significantly smaller than theirs; but it was still the largest that the king's supporters were to put into the field during the whole of the war.[107] To the English and Scots crowded onto the ridge, it was also an especially obnoxious one. Rupert had attracted much odium in the parliamentarian press, both for his German upbringing and the ruthlessness with which he waged war, and there were hints in some pamphlets that he had dealings with devils.[108] The core of his marching army was formed of regiments returned from the Irish war, which parliamentarian propaganda tended to elide with the Irish Catholic rebels themselves. As for Newcastle's men, most of what had long been reviled as his 'popish army' was now gathered there. Cromwell would have seen below him on the green moor a series of broken ribbons of colour. Directly in front, Rupert's cavalry squadrons were formed up in two dense lines, with a much smaller body detached to the left of them (from Oliver's viewpoint): the westering sun, when it shone between the showers, would have gleamed on helmets and breastplates, and bright pennants flapped in the wind overhead.[109] To the right of the enemy horsemen, the lines of royalist infantry began, with larger banners waving among them and the different regiments distinguished by their own hues of coat, usually blue, green, red, yellow and white. This great linear expanse of variegated colour stretched on to the right until it passed out of sight behind the allied infantry crowded at Cromwell's side, the total battlefront being about two and a half miles in length. Up on the ridge, the sense which would have impressed itself most forcibly on a newcomer to the allied position would probably have been smell: for almost twelve hours, thousands of horses, and unwashed men, would have sweated and relieved themselves on the same stretch of ground, joined for the latter half of that time by the rest of the near thirty thousand soldiers packed along the summit and slope to their right. The resulting stench would have been augmented by the acrid powder smoke drifting from the artillery, as its bombardment continued to echo along the line. The thunder of this would have blended with the voices of the allied soldiers as they sang psalms to while away the time and think themselves into the role of Old Testament warriors preparing to smite the ungodly, amid the reek of perspiration, urine, dung and sulphur.[110]

In early evening, Leven and his fellow generals decided that they had waited long enough and agreed to attack. There is no record of why they chose that particular moment, but the logic of it is apparent. They had, after all, been seeking battle ever since Rupert had approached the area, and had only deferred it so far that day because they held such advantages of ground that it was preferable that the enemy try assaulting them. By evening, it had become clear that the royalists were not going to oblige, and it may have been apparent from the vantage point on the ridge that they were going off guard, food supplies arriving and some of the troopers dismounting.[111] At this season, the end of midsummer, there were three hours of daylight left at seven o'clock, enough to finish the job. At any rate, around that time Leven ordered an immediate general advance, at top speed, down the slope in front and into the enemy.[112] All the allied soldiers had been told to put pieces of white paper, or white handkerchiefs, in their hats, to distinguish them from their foes, and to shout 'God with us!'[113]

Only around 250 yards separated the opposed forces, which could be covered in a few minutes, even on foot. Crawford's Eastern Association infantry came down the hill in three brigades at a 'running trot' and easily drove away the royalist musketeers in the ditch, and its own musketeers then exploded into fire as they neared the enemy foot regiments.[114] The ears of the men shooting, in such massed numbers, would have suffered painfully from the sheer intensity of noise, and many would probably have been left deaf for some time after the battle. What impressed observers most at the time was the quantity of black smoke created by the discharge of so much gunpowder, which soon concealed that part of the field in a fog in which the flashes of further volleys could be seen; the murk thickened when the royalist muskets began to reply. The powder smoke would have got into eyes and noses, scorching them, and onto tongues; and the parching effect of that would have been compounded subsequently by another feature of powder smoke deposits in the mouth, when, inevitably, swallowed: that they are a powerful laxative.[115] The impact of the lead shot on human bodies, especially at the short range involved in this case, would have been horrific, as the metal was soft enough to spread on impact, so that a ball half an inch across could produce an exit wound up to 6 inches wide.[116] The Eastern Association infantry swiftly stove in and outflanked the royalist foot regiments opposite, preventing them from doing anything to support the horse division next to them as Cromwell attacked it.

Before he could do that, it was necessary for Fraser's dragoons to clear the royalist musketeers out of the ditch in his way, but with the element of surprise they did that immediately.[117] This episode did allow time for the royalist cavalry to remount and form up, but we hear nothing of the musket units which Rupert had intended to stand between the squadrons and soften up an attack with their shot: perhaps they had stood down when the provisions were brought up from York, or perhaps they could not make their weapons ready in time, or perhaps the royalist horsemen surged forward to meet the oncoming enemy and blocked their fire. We can never know. As soon as the way across the ditch was clear, Cromwell led his front line down the slope and onto the level ground of Marston Moor, picking up speed with the momentum of the descent and finally going into the full charge in close order. The rest of his cavalry division followed. The noise, of sixteen to twenty thousand hooves of heavily laden running horses, would have been thunderous, and the ground would have shaken. Then would have come the great crash, as the front lines of the opposed wings came together, and the shooting and hacking and the shouting and screaming began. There was a long, hard and confused struggle, in part of which the royalists counter-attacked and charged Cromwell's regiment in flank and rear.[118] At the end of it the incredible happened: Prince Rupert's men broke, irrevocably, and fled headlong for York, abandoning the battle altogether. These were some of the finest cavalry in the world, victors in every action they had fought hitherto, but now they had been beaten. How had this occurred?

Three possible explanations were offered in the immediate or long-term aftermath of the battle. One was provided by royalists, but not until the 1660s. It held that Rupert had prepared a strong defensive position on his right wing, but that it had been thrown away by the man he had put in command of it: John, Lord Byron.[119] The latter had charged Cromwell's force when he was fired upon at the opening of the attack, crossing the ditch (in one account called 'the morass') instead of waiting for the enemy to come to him, and so disordering his men and making them vulnerable to a massive counterstrike by the enemy. If true, this account would explain why the royalist musketeers Rupert had installed between the horse squadrons were so ineffectual, if Byron's men surged forward and blocked their fire. There are, however, two problems with it. One is that it does not tally with the parliamentarian accounts of the action, which agree that their horse division crossed the ditch and attacked their enemy beyond it at maximum speed, seizing the opportunity of surprise without a preliminary bombardment. The other is that none of the royalist accounts blamed Byron, or mentioned any rash initiative on his part, until Rupert decided to make a scapegoat of him decades later, by which time Byron was dead and so could not defend himself.[120] Such an action by him may have occurred, but there is no good evidence for it, and weighty considerations against believing in it.

The second explanation for the collapse of the royalist wing is that Cromwell and the Eastern Association horse simply outfought it, which is of course the one offered by members of their army after the action.[121] The third is that the Scottish third line of the allied division struck the vital blow, by taking their enemies in the flank or rear after they had brought the Eastern Association men to a standstill.[122] This was naturally argued by the Scots, and they produced one key piece of evidence in their favour: that early in the action Cromwell himself suffered a slight wound in the neck and had to retire from the fray for a short time to have it dressed. He undoubtedly was wounded, as English sources favourable to him confirm this.[123] It is not certain how this happened: the most detailed account held that he was burned in the neck by the accidental discharge of the pistol of a trooper behind him: but this was asserted by an enemy, and the circumstances of the injury may have been more honourable and glamorous.[124] Nor can we ever know with certainty whether the injury did force him to retire from the fray, and if so for how long. Subsequently one of his political allies argued that the Scots could not possibly have decided the action because their men were mounted on 'little light Scottish nags' incapable of taking on the larger royalist war horses in the close-order hacking and shoving which broke a cavalry line.[125] This was probably true, but if the Scottish riders had attacked the enemy in the flank or rear, which is what their partisans argued, then the discrepancy would count for much less.

In the last analysis, we shall probably never know what happened. Both the English and the Scottish claims for the success are credible, and it remains possible, if unlikely, that Byron did wreck Rupert's carefully prepared defensive position with a rash advance. One factor, however, almost certainly counted decisively in the result: the discrepancy in numbers between the two sides. As said, the total strength of the allied horse and dragoon division must have stood at somewhere between four and six thousand. By contrast Rupert's favourite engineer, who later made a plan of the royalist dispositions which was presumably based on one drawn up at the time, put the strength of the royalist wing at just 2,600 horse plus 500 musketeers (who, as said, seem to have played no part). That is a significant difference, even if the royalist figures do not include officers. As neither the equipment nor the morale of Cromwell's troopers was inferior to that of Rupert's, it is hardly surprising that in the end the latter gave way. The matter may be as simple as that.[126]

After routing their enemies, a detachment of the allied horse continued the pursuit of the prince's horsemen. Rupert himself had to flee from it, and according to his enemies only escaped by hiding in a bean field.[127] As Newcastle was embroiled in the struggle in the centre of the battle, the combined royalist army was left without any overall leadership.[128] The bulk of the victorious allied cavalry then overran and captured Rupert's artillery train,[129] and halted, as dreadful news began to arrive from the eastern side of the field. A succession of tattered horsemen from Fairfax's command on the right wing of the allies appeared, including Sir Thomas himself, bleeding from a sword cut across his face and having lost his own horse to a musket shot. He had stripped the white token from his helmet, which identified him as a parliamentarian, in order to get through the enemy lines to safety. He and his men had faced much worse terrain when attacking the royalist wing opposed to them than Cromwell had, and their superiority in numbers was not as great, and their opponents had been given the time to co-ordinate their horse units with musketeers in a very effective defensive formation. As a result, Fairfax and some of his leading troops had broken through the royalist lines, but most of their force had been halted behind them, and then shattered by a counter-charge by Newcastle's cavalry with George Goring in command. In the centre, the allied infantry offensive had been stopped and then thrown back by the veteran northern foot soldiers, and when Goring's troopers swept away the allied horse from the east of the battle line, the Scottish and northern foot regiments on that side mostly fled as well. A few Scottish infantry units stood like islands, as the second wave of northern horse broke around them, and the discrepancy in numbers now weighed in again, as the royalists made every attack count, but were now out of any reserves to continue the pressure on their battered enemies.[130] Nonetheless, up to half of the huge allied army was now on the run, and all three of its generals had given up the day as lost. Leven and Lord Fairfax had fled clear away from the field, and even Manchester had apparently abandoned his own victorious soldiers and ridden off.[131]

Those soldiers now faced a stark choice. The army of the Eastern Association was still substantially intact, as were the Scottish horse and dragoon units with them. They could save themselves by abandoning their fellows and retiring in good order from the field, westward, to link up with the reinforcements coming up from that direction, and retreat into the Midlands to protect the association and await orders. The royalists would then have rescued their dominance in the north and defeated the Scottish challenge, restoring the national situation to the balanced one of the opening of the year. Alternatively, Cromwell and his companions could adopt the more risky, and heroic, strategy of turning on the remainder of the battlefield and attempting to defeat the victorious enemy there, so duplicating their achievement on the western flank and winning the battle, and perhaps tipping the balance of the entire war, outright. It is clear that such a decision required the agreement of all the commanders concerned: Cromwell, Crawford, as leader of the association foot, and David Leslie, as the man in charge of the Scottish regiments. There seems to have been no argument or hesitation among them: buoyed up by their dramatic success against Rupert's famous cavalry, and so probably filled with a sense of divine favour, they decided on a combined offensive to the east, to try to win the battle outright.[132]

It is clear what happened next, but as in the case of the victory over Rupert's horse, not exactly how it happened. It seems that Crawford attacked the royalist foot regiments while Cromwell and Leslie swept round the rear of those with their horse and assaulted Goring's cavalry. The latter were exhausted, caught on the bad ground which had impeded Fairfax's men earlier, and depleted because troops had gone in pursuit of fugitives, been damaged by the resistance of the Scottish foot regiments, or been held up plundering the allied baggage train, which represented the jackpot of loot for victorious soldiers on a battlefield. It seems certain that they were also significantly outnumbered, and with all these considerations in play it is no surprise that they were easily routed, and chased to York under a rising full moon. Many of the royalist foot must have broken and run at this point or tried to surrender, but many also stood their ground, especially Newcastle's northerners.[133] These now became prey to the Eastern Association horse and foot and their Scottish companions, who as said before had particular reason to regard them with loathing. The Eastern Association men, and especially Cromwell's cavalry, had long taken pleasure in killing, evident in the reports of their actions – including Oliver's own letters – at Belton, Gainsborough and near Burghley. Now they could do it on a tremendous scale, until the last resistance was extinguished. Around eleven o'clock this had been done, and Manchester's army formed up so that the earl himself – who was now back on the moonlit field – could ride down its ranks and thank his men personally.[134] They had won a stunning victory.

When dawn broke over the moor, it was covered in naked bodies, because during the night the common soldiery among the victors had assiduously stripped their fallen enemies of their clothing, the best items of which could be used to kit themselves out afresh, and the rest of which could be sold. Any personal possessions suffered the same fate. Many of the men thus despoiled were still 'groaning and gasping their last'. The country people were conscripted again, to bury the corpses in pits dug into the moor, and reported that they had interred a total of 4,150. A large number of the stripped corpses had the smooth white skins of gentlemen.[135] One of them was a Lancashire squire, whose wife came to search for his body. Their family later told a story, which may be true, of how Cromwell had urged her to desist, lest she be abused by some of the allied soldiers still looking for loot on the field.[136] Many of those who got away would have been wounded, and died later, so it seems likely that between a third and a half of the royalist infantry perished altogether. There were one and a half thousand prisoners, and they and the dead were stripped of their weapons so that a huge cache of military equipment fell into the hands of the victors. The share of Manchester's army was 10 cannon, 4,500 muskets, 40 barrels of gunpowder, 3 tons of musket shot and 800 pikes, the long spears carried by a third of the infantry in most armies.[137] The earl of Newcastle had got away to York, but his coach fell into the hands of the allies, and contained his cabinet of correspondence, which included the letters proving the treason of the Hothams, who since their arrest a year before had languished in the Tower of London, for lack of solid evidence against them.[138] That was now secured.

In York that morning, Rupert reckoned up the survivors of his army and found that most of the horse, both his own and that of Newcastle, under Goring, had escaped and rallied, but very few of his foot were left. To avoid being trapped in the city, he led this whole force north with all speed, covering twenty miles before nightfall and heading for Lancashire via Swaledale, far to the north of his route into Yorkshire the previous week, and so safer from pursuit. The marquis of Newcastle, his spirit broken by the loss of his own infantry, quit the city for the coast and sailed into exile in Germany with some of his senior officers. The remnant of his once proud northern army was left to hold York against the now absolutely inevitable resumption of the siege.[139] The victorious allies had first the task of rounding up the thousands of their fellows who had run from the battle, including, embarrassingly, their generals Leven and Fairfax. They waited two days on the field to complete this work and for the reinforcements from Manchester and the Midlands to come up. Then Cromwell, Leslie and Sir Thomas Fairfax were despatched with most of the cavalry and dragoons to pursue Prince Rupert's retreating force and try to destroy it before it crossed the hills. The foot soldiers closed in once more upon the hapless city.[140]

During these days, also, the news of the battle began to be communicated to London and Westminster, through both formal and informal means. The generals, once reassembled, wrote despatches to Parliament and the Committee of Both Kingdoms, representing the victory as a joint effort aided by divine sponsorship, in which all components of the allied army had played their part.[141] Privately, they also tried to give the impression of collective success: Lord Fairfax papered over the lamentable performance of his own army by writing to a friend that it had initially been disrupted, but had rallied and won a great victory, with the aid of Manchester's men, especially Cromwell.[142] Inevitably, that created an appetite among those hearing the good tidings for details which explained how a triumph on this scale had been achieved, and as these were provided, cracks began to appear in the impression of unity. Thomas Harrison, the fiery major of Fleetwood's horse regiment under Cromwell's command, appeared in the capital and spread the story 'that Cromwell alone, with his unspeakably valorous regiments, had done all that service'.[143] Then, however, a Scottish captain arrived at Westminster with letters from his army and the waggon loads of captured royalist flags, reported to the two Houses, and, while giving credit to Cromwell and his men, naturally played up the part of his own countrymen as partnering them throughout. His narrative was subsequently published.[144]

Two more letters rapidly reached the Commons, one from an Englishman accompanying the allied army, which gave equal credit to Cromwell and Leslie, with help from Sir Thomas Fairfax, and one from Manchester's chief of scouts, which made the earl's army the agent of victory; the second was also printed.[145] One of Manchester's chaplains then published a tract which likewise attributed everything to the men of the Eastern Association, though he then issued an apology that commended Leslie's regiments as well.[146] Both these publications gave full prominence to Cromwell and Crawford, but also tactfully implied that Manchester himself remained in overall control of his army. The Scottish representatives in London were exasperated by this eulogizing of the Eastern Association army, believing firmly in Leslie's vital role in co-operating with Cromwell and seeing that this downplaying of it both denigrated the importance of their nation's services to the alliance and favoured the independent faction in the arguments over the reform of the Church.[147] Journalists made their own choices among the hardening partisan interpretations of the battle.[148] Most newspapers stressed that the victory resulted from a partnership between Cromwell, Crawford and Leslie, with Sir Thomas Fairfax showing personal courage.[149] A few took the line advocated by Harrison, of glorifying Cromwell and the Eastern Association army (while not naming the Scotsman Crawford as leader of its foot soldiers).[150] One tract eulogized Oliver as 'crowned chief victor of the day'.[151] Conversely, one newspaper, *The Weekly Account*, credited the three generals with the result and did not mention Cromwell at all.[152]

We have a very good insight into Oliver's own attitude to the battle, provided in a now famous private letter which he sent to a friend immediately afterwards.[153] It was addressed to his brother-in-law and ally Valentine Walton, to break the news of the death of his son, of the same name, in the battle. This was Cromwell's nephew, who commanded one of the original troops in his regiment, and whose leg had been broken by a cannon shot, almost certainly when charging Rupert's artillery train immediately after routing his horse wing. The shattered leg was amputated, and the youth died as a result of the operation. In one sense, the letter is a work of great shrewdness and compassion. It began by announcing the terrific news of the victory, and then went on to break that of Walton's personal loss, reminding him that Oliver himself had lost two eldest sons, one only recently, so would know his pain. He then consoled his friend by representing his son as a hero and a saint, whose death in God's cause had assured him of an immediate place in heaven.

There are other aspects of it which are equally revealing of Cromwell, and perhaps in less comfortable ways. One is his habitual bloodthirstiness. He both dehumanized and demonized the defeated royalists, rejoicing that 'God made them as stubble to our swords', and characterized them (once more) as 'God's enemies'. He emphasized that the only regret of Walton's poor, mutilated, dying son was that he could no longer kill them. It should be made clear that such an attitude to adversaries in this war was not either necessary or universal among Cromwell's party. Sir William Waller, who was as devout a Puritan as Oliver, and whose men could be as destructive to cathedrals, had summed up the conflict in the previous year as 'this war without an enemy'.[154] Another revealing feature of the letter is that it shows how Cromwell himself regarded the victory as the achievement of his cavalry alone. He portrayed it to his friend as the result of a series of charges by them, referring dismissively to 'a few Scots in the rear'. This was to ignore the vital work of the Scottish dragoons in clearing the ditch in front of him, while whatever their specific contribution to the breaking of Rupert's horsemen, the three regiments under Leslie certainly added significant weight to his numbers. Most of the other accounts acknowledged the way in which Leslie partnered him throughout the battle. The letter proves that Cromwell was not aloof from the attempts of subordinates like Harrison to scoop the credit for the victory for his cavalry, but shared and promoted them.

It also reveals a political motive for doing so, which the Scots in London had swiftly recognized. Cromwell described the result of the battle as 'the Lord's blessing upon the godly party principally'. So what did he mean by 'the godly party'? It could not have been the general parliamentarian-Covenanter alliance, or he would neither have dismissed the Scots so contemptuously nor needed the qualifier 'principally' for a result which clearly favoured the whole alliance. He must have meant his own faction of the parliamentarians, the religious independents, whose cause he had promoted so zealously during the weeks before the battle, as described, and was to pursue with more zeal and intolerance thereafter. His ingrained tendency to regard his particular religious movement, grouping or network at any one time – which was always on the more radical and extremist side of a current spectrum – as that favoured by the Almighty, was now acting to widen the divisions within the ranks of those fighting the king.

Cromwell's pursuit of Rupert was a complete failure, as the prince had a two-day start and moved at frantic speed. By the time that the allied force reached the pass that he had taken over the Pennines, Rupert was already through it and had left a rear guard of musketeers there which could easily hold the narrow valley against horsemen. Cromwell and Fairfax led their troopers back to join the main allied army before York, which was having more success.[155] Most of the former defenders of the city were now lying in pits on Marston Moor, and the remnant was not sufficient to hold such a long perimeter against a co-ordinated attack and had absolutely no hope of relief. On 16 July it surrendered, on being granted very generous terms, under which the garrison could march away with its weapons and possessions, and any civilians who wished to leave could do so with all their goods. The allies were anxious to end the siege at last, and could afford to be lenient because of the huge trove of arms, ammunition and booty already gained from the battle.[156]

In June one of the Scottish representatives in London, writing to a friend at home, commented that if the allied army before York could both defeat Prince Rupert's army and destroy the city, then the war would be won. In his view, such an achievement, by the Anglo-Scottish army, would be a dramatic vindication of the alliance between the two national parties and an assurance that the Scots would have a powerful influence on the reform of the Church of England, so bonding together the two nations in peace and security thereafter. The achievement had now been secured, and Cromwell was in a position to claim much of the credit for it, and in doing so to help ensure that all the Scotsman's hopes for the consequences would be thwarted.

THE SOUR AUTUMN

The green fields were now gold, and the wet early summer had been succeeded by a drought.[157] The conditions were therefore perfect for further campaigning, and the obvious question was how the allies who had taken York were now to be employed. Each side in the war had started the spring with five armies, but the king had lost one almost immediately when Hopton's had been crippled at Cheriton. Now Marston Moor had cost him two more, Rupert's and Newcastle's. For much of June it had seemed as if Parliament's southern commanders would finish off the rest, as having driven Charles out of his Oxford base, Waller and Essex divided their forces. Waller continued to pursue the king into the West Midlands, hoping to catch and destroy the remnant of his field army with him, while Essex marched into the West Country, to annihilate the royalist one there and reconquer the region. The earl began well, relieving Lyme and capturing Weymouth and Taunton, while the western royalists, led by Rupert's younger brother Maurice, retreated before him. In the Midlands, however, the king gave Waller the slip, doubling back towards Oxford to collect the foot soldiers he had left there and so restoring his own army to its full strength. On 30 June Waller attacked it at Cropredy Bridge, up the River Cherwell from Oxford, and was beaten off. His army then disintegrated, from lack of pay and morale, leaving Charles suddenly free to pursue Essex into the West and rescue that region from him. Parliament could only hope that the earl would be able to defeat him there single-handed.

The Fairfaxes had settled into York to make it their new military base and repair their own army after its mauling at Marston Moor. The Scots and the earl of Manchester decided that the effort of feeding their two great forces together was now too much, and decided to separate, the former moving into the West Riding and the latter into South Yorkshire. Moreover, cramped billets in temporary huts in the siege lines outside York had caused disease to break out seriously among their soldiers, and to quarter them apart from each other, in fresh country, promised to ameliorate that problem as well.[158] Back in the capital, the Committee of Both Kingdoms remained in awe of Rupert, who had stopped in Lancashire to recruit, and feared that he would succeed in raising a new body of foot which would join the cavalry he had rescued from Marston Moor to give him a powerful strike force again. It therefore ordered Leven, Fairfax and Manchester to lead their armies over the hills against him.[159] In fact there was no need. The men of Lancashire were no longer inclined to fight for Rupert, when most of those who had joined him in the previous month had not returned. On 25 July he gave up and moved south to Chester to make a fresh attempt to find new soldiers there and in North Wales, abandoning the north altogether.[160]

Accordingly, on 30 July the allies resolved finally to separate.[161] The Fairfaxes set about the task of reducing the Yorkshire castles still in royalist hands, while the Scots moved north to besiege Newcastle, the king's main port on the east coast of England and the source of London's supply of coal for winter fires, which royalist control had cut off. Its fall would also secure the Scots' lines of communication with their homeland and give them a useful bargaining counter when dealing with the English Parliament. The earl of Manchester and his leading officers, including Cromwell, resolved to return to Lincoln, in their own association, to fill up their army again and restore proper pay to it; and to await further orders. This should have represented a move which bestowed further security and prosperity to it, and them, and prepared it for further glories. Instead, as it marched south in easy stages, it was already beset by a series of events and developments, some of which were to lower its morale in general, and all of which were to affect Cromwell in particular.

The first was that after the surrender of York, some of the Eastern Association cavalry broke the terms of surrender and plundered the goods which royalists removing from the city were taking with them. This was a major breach of honour, reflecting badly on Manchester's whole army, and as a measure of damage limitation the earl immediately published a proclamation ordering the looters to return them on pain of death. He also established a court martial to try offenders, presided over by Cromwell, both because of his exalted rank and because he commanded the horsemen who had committed the misconduct. He opened it with a speech which condemned the latter as an insult to God, and the court spent several days on its work. Nonetheless, Cromwell's behaviour in it remained controversial, Crawford (who also sat in the court) claiming that Oliver had pushed himself into the presiding role to protect his own men and then argued that one lieutenant deserved to be reprieved purely because of his godliness: once again, Oliver was perceived to elevate his role as patron of religious independents above other considerations.[162]

The same factor also seems to have played a part in the next affair, that of Tickhill Castle. This was yet another former stronghold of the medieval dukes of Lancaster, situated just south of Doncaster, a town which the earl of Manchester made his army's headquarters in late July. It had a royalist garrison and, to prevent this from raiding his soldiers' billets, Cromwell sent the dragoon regiment to occupy the village at the castle gates and stop the defenders from getting out. It was commanded by the radical and turbulent John Lilburne, friend and client of Cromwell. He immediately discovered that the soldiers inside the fortress were unpaid and disliked their officers, and so were willing to surrender if they could go home safely. This was agreed on 25 July, and on the next day Manchester, Cromwell and Crawford all arrived to take possession of the fortress: this was duly cried up to Parliament and the public as another achievement of their army.[163] The problem was that the surrender had come about because Lilburne had directly exceeded his orders, which had only been to coop up the defenders of the castle.

For the details of the wrangling that resulted, we have only his version of events, supported in outline by Cromwell and others of their party. According to this, on receiving the overture from the garrison, Lilburne rode at once to Doncaster, where he found the earl of Manchester with Cromwell and his other chief officers. The earl refused to believe that the castle would be surrendered that easily, and did not want to be distracted by a comparatively small stronghold like Tickhill, so forbade Lilburne to negotiate. Manchester was supported in this decision by the presbyterians around him, Crawford and his chaplains, who disliked Lilburne both as a hothead and troublemaker, and as a religious independent. Preparing to return, thwarted, to his regiment, Lilburne was however advised by a senior officer, who may have been Cromwell himself, to proceed anyway. This was enough for the bumptious lieutenant-colonel, who agreed terms with the royalists and returned to base with them. Manchester's reaction was explosive. He was already probably feeling sensitive about his authority following his conduct in the recent battle, and this flagrant indifference to it caused him to speak of hanging Lilburne for insubordination. Cromwell, however, intervened to calm the earl down and persuade him to accept the situation, so rescuing his friend once again. A festering mutual resentment, however, remained between Manchester and Lilburne, which may have also affected relations between the former and Cromwell.[164]

The third uncomfortable matter which affected the army, and Oliver, at this time, consisted of the paralysis of strategy that set in during August. The earl of Manchester and his commanders made clear to the Committee of Both Kingdoms that they wished their next target to be Newark, so long a menace to their association and the equivalent hub garrison for the king in the north-east Midlands to York in Yorkshire and Newcastle in the far north-east. The committee, however, disagreed, backed by Parliament, and believed in doing so that it was taking the broader and wiser view, ordering them instead to march across to Chester and finish off the remnants of Rupert's army. Once more it was placing a high estimation on the prince's ability to rebuild his strength by fresh recruitment in an area – North Wales and its March – which had already supplied thousands of soldiers to the king's cause. If Rupert did raise and equip a new body of foot there, to add to his still formidable cavalry, then he could strike at will at the Scots, the Fairfaxes or Manchester, now that they had separated and become vulnerable.[165]

The earl of Manchester and his officers were horrified by this command, and having reached Lincoln they sent a collective protest to the committee, arguing that if attacked, Rupert would simply retire behind the formidable defences of Chester, and the River Dee on which it stood and on which he held all the crossings. Manchester's army would be held at the river, with its supply routes from the association severed by the numerous powerful royalist garrisons of the North Midlands. Weeks of wrangling ended in a half-hearted compromise whereby the earl agreed to send a strong party to join local parliamentarians in attacking Rupert; the earl could then lead the rest of his army where he wished.[166] In fact, once again the committee had overestimated the prince's ability to attract new followers after the shattering blow dealt to his reputation on Marston Moor. His new levies deserted as fast as they arrived, and in any case arms and ammunition could not be found for them. On 20 August, Rupert gave up the job and marched for Bristol, to make a fresh attempt to raise men there.[167] By the end of the month both the Committee of Both Kingdoms and Manchester realized that there was no longer any reason for the earl to send any of his men to Cheshire. Meanwhile, most of his army had done nothing for about five weeks.[168]

Unhappily for Cromwell, this had not been true of all of it, because on starting his march from Doncaster to Lincoln, the earl of Manchester had detached a strong body of infantry and his siege train. These were given to Crawford, with orders to clear southern Yorkshire, northern Nottinghamshire and Derbyshire of royalist fortresses. This he accomplished with remarkable efficiency in the course of August. His achievements were given full prominence in the press, and so Cromwell had to endure the spectacle of his biggest rival winning glory while he himself sat idle.[169] He had led his cavalry to quarter around Newark and blockade it, in preparation for the expected siege. Immediately the nimble Newarkers had pounced on three of its troops and badly mauled them; Oliver himself came to inspect the damage on the next day. As the prospects of a siege receded, his horsemen were deployed instead to the east of the town, to protect the main body of the army at Lincoln from more raids launched by the royalists inside.[170] During the remainder of August, Cromwell virtually fades out of sight, a sad fate for somebody who in the previous month had been a national hero of his cause. His frustration boiled over in a letter to Valentine Walton at the beginning of September, in which he expressed his longing for effective service if only Manchester and the infantry 'set me loose'. He added darkly that there were some in the army 'much slow to action'.[171]

Mixed up in this bitterness, and running through the problems described earlier, was the increasingly serious division in that army over the future nature of the Church. During the summer the national print war between advocates of a presbyterian and an independent model had continued to hot up, and in August the Scottish clerical representatives in London urged Parliament to hasten the work of reimposing uniformity on English religion and halting the (to them) disturbing multiplication of different opinions concerning it.[172] One of the Scottish churchmen in the capital noted that the independents there increasingly regarded Oliver as their leader, and therefore cried up his reputation, while most of the House of Commons had no strong feelings about ecclesiastical government and were inclined to tolerate the beliefs of anybody who advanced the war effort, until it was won.[173] Cromwell may have believed that the performance of his horsemen at Marston Moor had represented a divine mandate for independency, or at least was inclined to represent it as such. According to both Crawford and Manchester, in the months following the battle, he launched a purge of officers who would not support the toleration of diverse religious opinions, from the horse regiments of the Eastern Association army. Crawford also reported that Cromwell had incited independents in the infantry not to obey Crawford himself.[174]

The earl of Manchester later admitted that he had turned against Oliver in the course of the autumn because he had come to suspect his intentions and dislike how he used his power in the army. The earl believed that his lieutenant-general had crossed a vital line, into a full-blown partisanship for independency, and intolerance for those who wanted a rigid presbyterian system, while Manchester himself held to a genuine impartiality between the positions for the sake of unity among his soldiers. He claimed that Cromwell had spoken against the Westminster Assembly, as persecutors, and said that he would now be willing to fight the Scots because they exerted their influence in the same cause. In his view of things, Oliver was trying to turn their army into a force which could if necessary coerce Parliament into a settlement that allowed greater liberty to diverse opinions under the broad Puritan umbrella. Manchester admitted that as a result he had withdrawn his previous support and favour from Cromwell.[175] A dismayed ally of Manchester in the Commons wrote to the earl in September urging him to treat Oliver with more respect.[176] This growing breach made long-term co-operation between them impossible, so that it was only a matter of time now before one or the other lost his command. Cromwell provided his view of the situation in a letter to Walton, though in terms which evaded the real issues, at least as far as people like Manchester and Crawford were concerned. He protested that he and his men were slandered 'by false tongues, to God' when they desired only 'the glory of God, the honour and liberty of the Parliament, without seeking our own interests'. He rejected accusations against them of being partisan and divisive as jealousy provoked by their godliness and good discipline.[177] If this was how he dealt with Manchester's concerns, then theirs was truly a dialogue of the deaf.

The MP who advised the earl to treat Cromwell better also urged him to intervene personally to get his cavalry supplied, and here lay another major cause for discontent on Oliver's part. On marching towards Lincoln at the beginning of August, the earl of Manchester had informed the Committee of Both Kingdoms that his army had been on half pay for the past three months, as none of the money due in taxation for the past four had arrived. The committee could only write to the officials of the association and urge them to do something about the problem. On arrival at Lincoln, the earl found none of the promised recruits there, and told the committee that the horse regiments in particular had hardly been paid for a quarter of a year. Cromwell himself had been paid in the course of the year only just over a third of what was due to him. Meanwhile the epidemic which had broken out in the army before York was continuing to spread, so that a third of its soldiers were ill.[178] Underlying this situation was a major systemic problem: that even the heavy taxation imposed on the Eastern Association since January was not enough to maintain the number of men in its army at the rates of pay promised to them. The situation was worsened by the creation of new foot regiments, each with its own complement of officers, instead of filling up existing units. By September, the army was only two-thirds of the size of that which had marched to York.[179]

The corn harvest was over, and the bright golden fields faded to sandy yellow, and then to yellowish grey. Yellows and browns were starting to appear among the leaves, and after sunset on fine evenings there would have been a new chill in the air, and a scent of woodsmoke. The fighting season was passing, and Cromwell and his underpaid and unused horsemen were still languishing between Lincoln and Newark. Then, in early September, came the news which changed everything: the king, joining his own field army to that of Prince Maurice, had trapped that of the earl of Essex in Cornwall, at Lostwithiel, and destroyed it. Most of Essex's cavalry had escaped by night, but the foot had surrendered and been stripped of weapons, plus the supply and artillery trains. Had Charles lost this campaign, most of the West Country would have slipped from his control and he would have had difficulty in carrying the war into another year.

Now most of the West was restored to him, and he had destroyed both of Parliament's southern armies, Essex's and Waller's, leaving London open to attack. Parliament therefore gave the obvious and essential command: with the Scots tied down before Newcastle and the Fairfaxes pinning down the remaining northern royalists in their castles, the earl of Manchester's army was the only one available, and had to march immediately to face the king, at least to pen him back into the West, and at best to defeat him. It was ordered to join the remnants of Waller's men at Dorchester, while fresh equipment for Essex's defeated infantry, who were allowed to return eastward under their terms of surrender, was to be despatched to meet it at Portsmouth. Once rearmed, it could reinforce Manchester and Waller.[180]

Manchester reacted with the speed and determination which he always brought to clear orders and obvious, practicable objectives, and ordered his soldiers to march at once. They moved at a remarkable pace: on 9 September they were in Huntingdonshire, on the 10th in Cambridgeshire, and on the 11th in Hertfordshire.[181] There they rested, spread across a swathe of villages and market towns and subsisting on free quarter for lack of any ready pay.[182] The earl of Manchester had ordered the horse regiments to go on ahead, and immediately, to the newly established parliamentarian garrison at Abingdon in Oxfordshire, as the Committee of Both Kingdoms had required. However, he received a letter from Cromwell's protégé Henry Ireton, who was back on active service with the army, protesting that the troopers could not march until they received some money, and that they were now too weak in numbers to make it through the narrow wooded defiles of the Chiltern Hills unless dragoons went with them to clear away enemy musketeers. Ireton painted a picture of horse officers who had lent all their own money to their men, and borrowed more, to keep the steeds shod; but that many horses were still being led riderless for lack of shoes. Another letter informed the earl that the local townspeople were refusing to supply his soldiers with food on credit.[183]

When he received these complaints, the earl of Manchester was in London, which he had reached on 11 September to present the troubles of his army to the Committee of Both Kingdoms and seek remedies.[184] Those troubles were threefold, the first being the material shortages just described. The second was that the earl flatly disagreed with the strategy being advocated by the committee, because he thought that the strength of the royal field army was now such that even combined with Waller's soldiers, the Eastern Association army would not be able to defeat it. If it fought and was broken, then Charles could advance on London without hindrance. The earl therefore urged that the parliamentarian forces be allowed to regroup closer to the capital so that they could meet the enemy with greater strength and closer support systems.[185] The third problem he brought was the religious dispute in his army. On the march into the Home Counties, according to Crawford, Cromwell had repeatedly pressurized Manchester to get rid of the Scotsman, and the earl, in exasperation and desperation, had responded by dragging both of his subordinate generals to the capital in the hope that the authorities there would talk some sense into them and get them to co-operate.[186] Manchester was to be disappointed on all three counts. Only promises of money and equipment were provided, the committee refused to change its strategy – though Manchester was allowed to decide his own route and time when marching into the west – and the earl was asked to make further efforts to reconcile Cromwell and Crawford himself.[187]

Cromwell, on the other hand, did well out of the visit, having his own seat on the Committee of Both Kingdoms, where he was at last sworn in alongside Manchester, and his own power base in Parliament, which he also attended.[188] On 13 September he made his re-entry into the Commons, and was formally thanked by the House for his services, especially at Marston Moor, 'where God made him a special instrument'.[189] This formula left open the possibility that others had also contributed to the victory, but it highlighted him as a hero of the occasion. He immediately made use of the favour shown to him to plead his cause, allegedly suggesting to his friend and relative Oliver St John a motion whereby a parliamentary committee was to be appointed to confer with the Scottish commissioners and leading members of the Westminster Assembly about the divisions in the assembly over the form of the Church. It was to try to reconcile them, but if this proved impossible, to find 'some way, how far tender consciences, who cannot in all things submit to the common rule which shall be established, may be borne with according to the Word and as may stand with the public peace'. This was agreed by the Commons, and so the first step taken towards recognizing some form of independency within the settlement: it was a major victory for Cromwell and his allies.[190] Buoyed up by this, he was obdurate when some of the Scottish commissioners and others tried to get him to sink his differences with Crawford, Oliver declaring that his horse colonels would resign unless the Scotsman was sacked. Manchester and his chaplains defended Crawford as blameless and a good soldier, and so the rift between Cromwell and the earl widened. It was said that Oliver was now trying to get Manchester dismissed from his command as well.[191]

On 22 September, Manchester began leading his army westward, making for Reading. He was in a bitter mood, and conscious that members of the Committee for Both Kingdoms had begun to suggest that he was deliberately delaying his progress.[192] The committee had ordered him to send a party to Banbury, at the northern end of Oxfordshire, to watch Prince Rupert, who had moved up onto the western edge of the Midlands, and protect the Eastern Association. Perhaps glad to be rid of him, the earl sent Cromwell, with his horse regiment and some dragoons and foot, up to 1,500 men in all, which also, however, depleted the main army further.[193] Oliver's allies in the London press were boosting his profile again, and one paper, *Mercurius Civicus*, now declared that Rupert himself had given him the admiring nickname 'Ironside' after Marston Moor, because of the resilience of his cavalry during the battle.[194] It does not appear in any royalist source, and seems to be a pure journalistic invention, but was now to descend the centuries, in the plural, as a popular name for his horsemen.

In riding to Banbury, Oliver was taking his place in a military configuration which was to shape the succeeding campaign. In the early autumn local parliamentarian forces had laid siege to three major royalist fortresses which guarded the eastern perimeter of the king's main base at Oxford: the

Within the image, the labels read:

Robert Earle of Essex his Exellence etc: Generall of the Army

Alexander Lesley his Exellence Generall of the Scotch Army etc:

His Exellence Sr Thomas Fairfax Captain Generall of the Army etc:

Edward Earle of Manchester etc: Major Generall of the Association etc

Philip Skepon Esqr Major Generall of the Army etc:

Oliuer Cromwell Esqr Leiuten Generall of the Horse etc

Sr Wil: Waller Maj: Generall of Surry Sussex & Hampshire etc

Sr Wm Brereton Maj: Generall of Chesire Staforsh & Lankashire

Edw: Massey Esqr Major Generall of the Western Counties

Rich: Browne Esqr Major generall of Oxon Berksh: & Buckingham

1. This may be the earliest portrait of Cromwell (bottom row, second from left), a crude but still distinctively individual woodcut on a broadsheet published in August 1646. It was a catalogue of Parliament's victories in the Great Civil War then concluding, in a manner which emphasized the achievements of the more aristocratic and conservative generals, such as the earls of Essex and Manchester, and downplayed Cromwell's.

2. Cromwell's home town of Huntingdon would have been perfectly familiar to him in this painting of one corner of it from the end of the eighteenth century: the medieval parish church and houses, and the sprawling Ouse with its animal and human activity, are not changed from his time.

3. A view of Ely, painted around 1800, again shows virtually no change from the sight which would have greeted the young Cromwell from that angle. The medieval cathedral still rides on its hill above the Ouse, like a great vessel, and dominates the landscape physically, politically and religiously.

4. The grammar school in Huntingdon, in which Cromwell was taught by Thomas Beard: part of a former medieval hospital, and now the Cromwell Museum.

5. A nineteenth-century print of a contemporary miniature of Cromwell's mother, a person generally respected for her piety, modesty and common sense, and consistently supportive of her son without interfering in his career.

6. Sir Oliver was the leader of the dynasty of which our Cromwell led a junior branch. His portrait displays the prominent nose which was a family trait, and his wealth – which Sir Oliver was to dissipate – is suggested by the elegance of his dress.

7. A miniature, painted from life, of Cromwell's wife Elizabeth at the time of her husband's period as head of state. Her modesty, unpretentiousness and seclusion from politics were as valuable to him as her devotion, and theirs was an enduringly happy marriage.

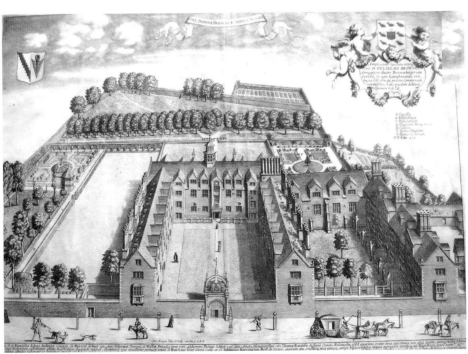

8. Cromwell's Cambridge college of Sidney Sussex, drawn near the end of the seventeenth century, with its original central court unchanged from his time there near its beginning.

Ten HISTORICAL PRINTS
representing the
MARRIAGE, WARS,
SUFFERINGS & DEATH,
of the Royal Martyr:
KING CHARLES the 1st.
Printed & Sold at ye White Horse
without Newgate. London.

9. This is a highly imaginative eighteenth-century depiction of the wedding of King Charles with his French queen, Henrietta Maria. It does however sum up the dual aspect of the union: usually happy and fertile royal marriage, but also a political liability, in that the wife whom the king deeply loved was a fervent member of the Roman Catholic faith feared and hated by most of the British.

10. This Victorian history painting depicts the entry of Cromwell into the House of Commons when first elected to Parliament in 1628. It conveys well the crowded and informal, and simple, seating arrangements in the chamber. He would probably not have stood out as much, in sober black clothing and linen collar, as he is made to do here.

11. Another Victorian artist recreates the dramatic scene, which Cromwell would almost certainly have witnessed, which closed the 1628–9 Parliament, when members resisted the king's dissolution of it and held down the Speaker to pass some final motions. It incidentally provides a nice view of the end of the chamber as it was at the time (and until the nineteenth century).

12. The Victorian painter Ford Madox Brown achieved this splendid painting of Cromwell imagined at the nadir of his fortunes in the 1630s, as a working tenant farmer at St Ives. The Ouse Valley landscape is authentic, as is the crowding of incidental rustic detail, and our man's air of depression and introspection may well be also.

13. Another nineteenth-century reconstruction of a dramatic moment in parliamentary history for which Cromwell would almost certainly have been present, Charles I's attempted arrest of the Five Members in January 1642. Again, it gives a good sense of the layout of the House of Commons, although there would have been more benches and people.

14. Sometimes Victorian history painting erred on the side of drama. This famous representation of Cromwell's cavalry action at Marston Moor conveys its frenetic action and the armaments well, but to enhance its protagonist's heroic credentials it loses the co-ordinated discipline of a close-order attack, and gives Cromwell a wound in the arm, rather than the neck.

15. Some Victorian history paintings are so fine that they can readily be forgiven inaccuracies. Augustus Egg's famous scene of Cromwell kneeling in prayer on the night before the battle of Naseby puts him and his men in nineteenth-century military tents, when he would have been quartered in a house or cottage (and the moon was not full); but it is so atmospheric that it remains a beautiful work of art.

16. Sir Thomas Fairfax became Cromwell's most reliable military and political ally in Parliament's war effort, and his immediate commander in the last year of the war. This contemporary engraving captures his dash, flair and energy, and also his blade-like nose and long, dark, thick and waving hair.

17. Henry Ireton was another of Cromwell's most loyal and reliable allies, though this time a junior one and client: he was his deputy in governing Ely and commanding the New Model Army cavalry, and eventually became his son-in-law. This portrait, painted years later, displays his stubbornness, courage and dedication, bonded by a firm Puritan faith which matched Oliver's.

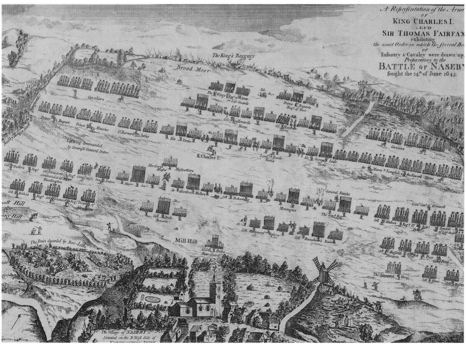

18. Robert Streater's famous plan of the battle of Naseby, first published in 1647, is an admirable guide to the layout of the armies there, though it may increase the actual size of the royal army.

19. A Victorian history painting of the battle of Naseby seems to capture the alleged moment when a Scottish noble caught the bridle of King Charles's horse and so prevented him from leading in the royalist reserve and possibly turning the action in his favour.

20. A nineteenth-century illustration of the storming of Basing House by Cromwell's men in October 1645 embodies well the sheer chaos and violence of the event, which ended in the destruction of the house and the deaths of many defenders.

town and castle of Banbury, which lay near the top of the Cherwell Valley north of Oxford; Donnington Castle, sited where the River Kennet pushed through the chalk hills of western Berkshire; and Basing House, the mansion of the marquis of Winchester, which lay at the north-east corner of Hampshire, and blocked the main route from London to Winchester and Salisbury. To take these would restrict Charles's winter quarters severely, and deal a proportionate blow to his reputation. As yet the three sieges were incidental to the course of the war, but they were about to become crucial. This was because the king, by now advanced into east Somerset and west Dorset on his way towards London, had become aware of the massing of enemy forces in front of the capital, and decided to adapt his immediate objective to the relief of the three garrisons, after which he would review future possibilities. One being discussed was an invasion of the Eastern Association, where the royal army might take up winter quarters.[195]

Meanwhile, the earl of Manchester had ground to a halt at Reading, convinced that the soldiers still with him were too few to face the oncoming royal army without reinforcements. The Committee for Both Kingdoms became almost apoplectic in its continued orders to him to keep marching and fight the king, backed by resolutions of the House of Commons. At one point, on 7 October, it actually ordered Cromwell not to wait for orders from his general, but to go immediately to reinforce Waller, taking all the Eastern Association horse except five hundred left outside Banbury and five hundred to protect Manchester's infantry. Parliament ordered new body armour and pistols for his horse regiment to equip it for action. Oliver duly set out for Reading, ostensibly to collect the rest of the cavalry and start his westward march. The earl's feelings, and those of his entire army including the men under Cromwell, could not have been improved by the news that the Newark royalists had taken Crowland again, making it a garrison for the third time and threatening the borders of Cambridgeshire and Norfolk while the association's protecting force was far away.

As Manchester argued with the committee and Cromwell came up to him, the king continued to advance, Waller falling back before him and sometimes harried by the royal cavalry, until by mid-October the royal army had reached the borders of Hampshire. The earl's strategy now had to be adopted by default, all plans for a westward march by the Eastern Association army cancelled, and a concentration of parliamentarian forces made at Basingstoke, near the besieged royalist stronghold of Basing. Waller's horsemen retreated there, with Essex's cavalry, and Essex himself arrived with his freshly armed foot soldiers. A strong party of militia infantry came from London, and more soldiers from local contingents. Manchester's army, including Cromwell, was first of all at the grand rendezvous. It was the largest concentration of its own soldiers that Parliament was to make during the war.[196]

The king's advance was a huge gamble, based on two false assumptions. The first was that Rupert would reinforce him before he made contact with the enemy, with four to five thousand veterans consisting of the prince's own cavalry, that which had once been Newcastle's and was now called 'the Northern Horse', and a force coming out of Wales. The second was that his enemies would not combine their own armies before he had relieved Donnington Castle and Basing House. He was reinforced in his boldness by the high morale of his soldiers and their eagerness for battle, the fruits of their victory over Essex. Although they still consisted of his original field army combined with the western one under Prince Maurice, action and hard marching had worn them down to 5,500 foot and 4,000 horse. On 22 October he reached Donnington, its besiegers having retreated before him, and depleted his numbers still further by sending three horse regiments to relieve Banbury, which left him with eight thousand men in all. Prudence really should have dictated that he now retired to safety at Oxford, but he chose instead to settle near Donnington, to await the return of the party sent to Banbury and the arrival of Rupert's.

To the south of Donnington lay the main town of western Berkshire, Newbury, and that and the villages around provided snug accommodation for his men. In case of emergency there was a natural stronghold between Newbury and Donnington. It consisted of a long triangle of land defined by the River Kennet, on which the town stood, and its tributary the Lambourn, just beyond which the castle was sited, and which joined the Kennet eastward, and downstream of, both Donnington and Newbury. The peninsula concerned was large enough to accommodate the whole royal army and yet compact enough to be defensible, with the two rivers, swollen by the autumn rains, providing moats around three sides. The fourth side was open to attack, but faced west, away from the direction from which the enemy would arrive. The problem, which does not seem to have occurred to Charles and his advisers, is that what might in the right circumstances be a natural fortress could in the wrong ones turn into a death trap.[197]

NEWBURY

Incredibly, and by sheer luck, Manchester's strategy – enforced on his political masters by his failure to enact theirs with sufficient speed – had worked. He led 4,500 foot, 3,000 horse and 120 dragoons to the rendezvous at Basingstoke.[198] Had he taken this force rapidly into the West in September as Parliament and the Committee of Both Kingdoms had ordered, he would have faced a royal army which had, as said, around 5,500 foot and 4,000 horse, plus more dragoons. To balance the odds, he would have joined with Sir William Waller's party in Dorset, which would have added up to 3,000 more horse and dragoons to his strength.[199] Manchester would therefore have been able to fight Charles with superiority in cavalry but inferiority in infantry (and it was that which really worried him in his replies to the committee). The result of any battle between them would therefore have been largely down to the terrain, and the other circumstances under which it was joined, and whether the king could or would have picked up further soldiers from his local garrisons.[200] In other words, as the earl had protested, it would have been a gamble.

Now, however, King Charles had brought his army right up to his enemies, on the fringe of their own quarters, and weakened it further on the way. He had no prospect of rapid reinforcement, and had not moved fast enough to attack Parliament's generals before they could unite all their forces. That union had been made, within striking distance of the king and his soldiers, enabling Manchester and his fellow commanders to move against him immediately with a numerical superiority of at least two to one, extending across all the arms of war.[201] If they used this advantage to destroy the royal army – which combined Charles's original field force with Maurice's western one – then the king would have no significant body of soldiers left in the field, and the war would be as good as won. The amazing victory at Marston Moor would be matched by one in the south, and all the frustrations of the autumn set at naught. It must truly have seemed a providential turn of events.

Autumn, however, was almost gone, and the campaigning season was definitely over. Darkness was backing up into the afternoon, and cold and damp gnawing more deeply. The land between Basingstoke and Aldermaston, into which the huge parliamentarian force was moving, was that of the Hampshire and Berkshire Barrens, a district of relatively poor soils, with many heaths and woods. The former were already in their faded yellow and red winter hues, while in the latter the stands of birch and silver birch were clad in golden leaves, and those of oak in duller gold. The ashes and hazels were yellow and the dark green of the holly was starting to show against the ruddy brown of the woodland floors. The weather was horribly wet, and mud became the element in which the soldiery had to walk, ride, rest and – too often – sleep.[202] A journal has survived of the marches of one of Manchester's foot regiments, which he had given to his young cousin Edward Montagu to command. On the night of 21 October the men slept beneath the trees of a gentleman's park, and for three of the succeeding five nights there is the forlorn entry 'lay in the field'.[203] Once more the assembly of a large army provided an enormous problem of keeping it fed and clothed.[204] No sooner was the whole force together than soldiers began to run from it, towards the comfort of nearby London.[205] The job of finishing off the king had to be accomplished swiftly.

On 22 October the united force began its advance, moving north over the River Kennet and then westward, and three days later it was within four miles of Newbury. Great bodies of royalist horse were in sight to the west. At that point the earl of Essex had to abandon the action, stricken by a worsening bowel infection and becoming feverish, and was carried away to Reading on a feather bed. On the following day the parliamentarians advanced to within two miles of Newbury and began to skirmish with the enemy. News reached the assembled force that the Scots had taken Newcastle by storm, giving the allied cause its first really big success since Marston Moor and ensuring Londoners a supply of coal for warmth in the coming winter. Many regiments sank spontaneously to their knees in prayers of gratitude.[206] The commanders, including Cromwell, then reached the top of the hill above the confluence of the rivers Kennet and Lambourn, just to the east of Newbury, from which they could finally view the royalist position; and they did not like what they saw.

Finally realizing that no reinforcements were approaching, but that a tremendous enemy attack was, the king had positioned all his soldiers in the triangle of land between the rivers. His defence of it was strengthened near the eastern end by a large mansion, Shaw House, which sat on his side of the Lambourn near its meeting with the Kennet and had ancient earthworks in its grounds that made defences for infantry. The only bridge across the Kennet northward into the royalist position was at Newbury itself, which was strongly manned. The only one across the Lambourn southward into the position was blocked by Donnington Castle, a small but towering rectangular medieval fortress on the high ground just above the crossing. It was towering no longer, because the guns of the besiegers had beaten much of it into ruin, but this hardly mattered, because the defenders had expertly constructed a tight double perimeter of new fortifications around it. Made of thickly packed earth and stone and so hard to breach, low and sloping to deflect cannonballs, and with deep ditches and five huge bastions to provide flanking fire, these were both largely impervious to bombardment and virtually impossible to storm.[207] The only weak point in the king's position was the open country to the west, in the widening space between the rivers, and that had the village of Speen, and woods, fields and enclosures, to impede entry, and could only be reached by a long flanking march round from the north.

To prevent quarrelling and resentment, overall leadership and direction of the combined army had been vested by the Committee of Both Kingdoms in a council of war, consisting of the three generals, Essex, Waller and Manchester, Waller's horse commander Sir Arthur Hesilrig, Cromwell, and two civilian representatives of the committee, one English and one Scottish. In case of disagreement, decisions would be taken by majority vote. Essex was now out of action, but all the other members were present, and at the debate on the hill above the rivers, the council was reinforced by all the next tier of officers, including Crawford. Eventually a majority resolved on a daring and demanding battle plan. The earl of Manchester was to remain on the eastern side of the royalist position, with all his infantry, under Crawford, and 1,500 horse. The other commanders would take the remaining two-thirds of the soldiers: Essex's rearmed foot, the London regiments, and all the rest of the cavalry, under Cromwell, Waller, Hesilrig and Essex's general of horse, a capable and reliable Scottish veteran called Sir William Balfour. These would march through the night to the north of Donnington and the Lambourn, cross that little river by the next bridge upstream from Donnington, and assault the royal army from the west, on its open side, the following day, 27 October. As battle was joined there, Manchester would launch his men against the eastern side of the enemy position, across the rivers, in a diversionary attack which would prevent reinforcements being rushed to the other front. The king's men would therefore be rolled up from the west and annihilated, and Charles himself captured, in the narrowing fork of the rivers. The massive numerical superiority of the parliamentarians permitted such a division, and removed much of the risk of trying to co-ordinate an action over such a wide area while the royalists had the advantage of operating on interior lines.[208]

The fourteen-mile march west into the chalk hills by the great body of soldiery which included Cromwell, went smoothly, though the royalists noticed it and those on the now threatened western side hurriedly started to dig a breastwork to defend their position.[209] The parliamentarians paused to rest during the night, crossed the Lambourn as planned, easily driving off a defending party at the bridge, and then swung south and east during the morning. Their troubles started then, because the countryside which they had to traverse to reach Speen, and the enemy's defensive line, was even more broken, by woods, fields, hedges, ditches and patches of heath, than they had expected. They could not make contact with the enemy until the middle of the afternoon, with only a couple of hours remaining until nightfall. Then they deployed in traditional fashion, with the horse on the wings and the foot in the centre; and it was the job of the foot soldiers to capture the village of Speen itself, and break the enemy line, before the horse could go forward on either side and press home the attack.[210]

The infantry assaulted the village with ferocious determination. The defenders were from Prince Maurice's western army, and had the advantage of the hastily improvised earthwork in front of them and a few field guns. On the other hand, they must have been significantly outnumbered, and the fact that they had been placed in what was supposed to be the rear of the royalist army indicates that they were not regarded as the best units; and yet it was they who now bore the brunt of the major assault. This being so, they probably did well to resist it for an hour before they broke and fled back through the village. This released the cavalry on both wings, and Balfour led the earl of Essex's horse on the right, taking them and some musketeers unopposed down the slope towards the Kennet, and then eastward through the meadows along its banks. The king had stationed himself, with his reserve of foot and most of his horse, in a huge field which lay along the centre of the ridge between the rivers. Balfour's troopers swung north uphill and broke into it, taking the royalists there completely by surprise and routing some of them. The king was almost captured, with his young son, the prince of Wales, but a furious counter-attack broke Balfour's men and drove them all the way back to Speen.

Cromwell was on the left wing, with his horse and that of Sir William Waller. The latter was also there, with his own cavalry commander Hesilrig, and it seems that, as the highest-ranking general, he took charge: as will be shown below, Cromwell was subordinated to somebody else. At Marston Moor the conditions for a successful advance had been ideal: a clear view of the enemy and with it a certainty of favourable numerical odds; a downward slope in front and virtually no obstacles; the element of surprise, and nothing to disrupt the developing assault. Now none of those factors were present. The ground certainly sloped gently downward ahead, but along a narrow lane between enclosures which prevented the regiments from deploying properly. Afterwards, when explaining why the parliamentarians did not make better progress, Cromwell specified that they were filing along this track towards the large open field crowded with enemies, and feared being destroyed while trying to get into order.[211] They were also bombarded relentlessly by the royal artillery, stationed just beneath Donnington Castle on the higher ridge to the north.[212]

The royalist foot soldiers who had retreated from Speen were now lining a long hedge which marked the western boundary of the field where the king and the bulk of his horsemen were stationed. To get round it and them, Cromwell and his companions had to approach the field at its north-western end. Their slow progress, and the bombardment from Donnington, had given ample warning of their approach, and Cromwell's fears proved all too prescient. The parliamentarian horsemen were hit by a charge of most of the king's cavalry, led by George Goring, the commander who had routed the right wing of the allied army at Marston Moor. It caught them as they were in disarray crossing a hedge and a ditch and drove them back, and then did so again when they attempted a counter-attack. The victorious royalist horsemen were not checked until they ran into the main body of parliamentarian infantry around Speen. One trooper got behind Waller and was preparing to kill him when one of Sir William's bodyguards struck the man down instead.[213] Where Cromwell was in this melee, none of the sources say, though Manchester later believed that one reason for the poor performance of his men was that he was not in charge of them.[214] As the royalist horsemen retreated, the daylight finally failed and the action broke off. It was a bruising reminder that Oliver's cavalry were only victorious under favourable conditions.

Meanwhile, at the eastern end of the battlefield, Manchester had played his required part, although not with the perfect synchronization which had been planned. In the morning he made a probing attack which was presumably intended to distract attention from the main body approaching from the west. It was thrown back, and he duly made his main effort in late afternoon, although not for some time after the battle had started at Speen. It does not seem as if this made any difference, because the king did not detach any men from the eastern end of his position to reinforce the western end. If Manchester's job was to keep some of the best of the king's infantry pinned down, he accomplished it, although his own assault was in strength and a serious enterprise, which was defeated after intense fighting. The whole battle lasted about three hours and ended under a rising full moon, with a few hundred killed on either side.

Newbury had not been lucky for King Charles. Over a year before he had attacked Essex's army in the hills to the south of the town, and been beaten off with heavy losses. Now he had fought on the ridge to the north, and it was he who had beaten off his attackers; but he had still not defeated them. They were now preparing to eat and sleep, two-thirds of them around Speen and the rest under Manchester back on the hilltop to the east. They would certainly renew the attack in the morning, and it seemed quite likely that their numbers would eventually wear down the king's men and result in his surrender. An alternative strategy was now called for, and had been in place since the morning, when the royal artillery and baggage trains had been taken across Donnington Bridge and lodged safely on the slope just under the castle walls. They were now withdrawn into the castle itself, along with the wounded from the battle, and the whole army was evacuated northward over the bridge by ten o'clock. The king, his son and a guard of three hundred horsemen then galloped over the hills north-east to Bath to join Rupert. The rest of the royal forces marched at full pelt north-eastward over the open chalk terrain, carrying on all through the night until by morning they were nearing the Thames at Wallingford. That was a walled town dominated by a huge medieval royal castle and held by a royalist garrison, which provided safe passage over the river, and out of danger. The bright moonlight lit the way on the forced march, and though at this season it probably meant frost, that would have hardened the mud and speeded up progress. It was the exhausted parliamentarians in the fields around Newbury who would have suffered from the cold. Those on the western side of the battlefield, like Cromwell, could hear the enemy on the move, but decided that they were redeploying around the castle, and that the struggle would be renewed there in the morning.[215] It was left to Manchester to send out his small party of horse to harass the retiring royalists, and that was easily repelled.[216]

Near the end of the long night, the parliamentarians on the western side realized that their foes had vanished, and a hurried council of war produced a decision to send Cromwell, Waller and Hesilrig to pursue them with almost all the cavalry. This body of horse – around seven thousand – was probably the largest ever mustered together for action in the course of the war.[217] It was, however, far too late, its quarry having too much of a start on it, and accomplished nothing. The effort of the hard ride was just another piece of difficult duty for cavalry which had already been on the move, and mostly sleeping rough, for a week, and fought a hard battle.[218] It did, however, allow admirers of Cromwell in the London press, who were unable to find anything glowing to say about his conduct on the previous day, to eulogize him as the heroic leader of the pursuit: *Mercurius Civicus* used its new nickname for him, of 'Ironside'.[219] Meanwhile, the commanders left behind at Newbury were spinning the story of the battle for the Committee of Both Kingdoms and Parliament, as a great victory resulting in the total defeat and rout of the royal army. This was immediately accepted, and a national day of thanksgiving ordered by Parliament, as was the case following only its most glorious achievements.[220] That representation would be the more credible, however, if the battle were immediately followed by the capture of Donnington Castle with all the guns, baggage and wounded royalists held inside. This did not happen, as the fortifications remained just as effective, and an attack by Manchester's foot soldiers was beaten off; however, the governor informed the king that he would not be able to hold out for more than a week of renewed siege.[221]

Baulked of their prey, the council which commanded the combined army left the castle blockaded and wrote to the Committee for Both Kingdoms for siege guns heavy enough to smash its defences. They also asked for food and money to keep their men in the field, and moved most of them north over the hills into the Thames Basin, quartering them under cover in the villages at the bottom of White Horse Vale.[222] It was now the first week of November, and the calendar at the time meant that the season would be ten days more advanced than it is now. Nonetheless, to disperse to winter quarters would risk losing all the fruits of their success at Newbury, especially as the king was still in the field. In White Horse Vale, facing north towards Oxford, they could block another attempt to relieve Donnington or make a further strike at the royalists. The latter was what the Committee of Both Kingdoms, backed by Parliament, now ordered: a general and immediate advance into the royalist heartland around Oxford, to disperse both what was presumed to be the beaten royal army and the reinforcements expected to be brought to it by Prince Rupert.[223] The council leading the army, however, concluded unanimously that by this time of year the roads were too bad to enable it to move at the speed required. Quite possibly also its commanders were uneasily aware that the royal army had in fact got away intact, and that it might already have been joined by Rupert's large force, making it much more formidable. The shortage of food was causing more of their own men to desert, and so their numbers were falling: Crawford and some others of Manchester's foot officers complained to the earl that their men were now 'like ghosts'. The ruling council therefore persuaded the committee and Parliament to cancel its order and allow them to retreat to Newbury and press home the sieges of Donnington Castle and Basing House.[224]

In fact, the king and Prince Rupert had indeed united their forces by 2 November, and two days later added infantry from the Oxford garrison, while the relief party sent to Banbury had returned after driving off its besiegers. Rupert was officially declared commander of this composite army, numbering ten to fifteen thousand men, and he promptly led it, with Charles, to relieve Donnington, and – if opportunity provided – crush the enemies whom the king had fought at Newbury. It marched back to Wallingford on 7 November, and the next day crossed the Thames and then White Horse Vale, and paused for the night about six miles from Donnington, on the northern slopes of the great rolling chalk hills, the Berkshire Downs, which lay between the vale and Newbury. The soldiers slept in the open fields, without food, to keep the army moving at maximum speed.[225] On the face of things, as the parliamentarian generals had been expecting that such a relief attempt might be made, they should both have kept their army in its path, north of Newbury, and put out patrols to give early warning of the appearance of the enemy. They had already chosen a battlefield, a heathland between the castle and the downs to the north, if the king came from that direction.

In the event, they did not learn of his advance until late on the evening of 8 November, when their own soldiers were almost all on the wrong side of the Kennet, the foot being mostly in Newbury itself and the horse quartered in the villages to the south of the town. The positioning of the cavalry was said to be due to its need for forage: by this time of year the grass had stopped growing, and so horses were dependent on stored hay and oats. The countryside east and north of Newbury had apparently been eaten bare of these commodities earlier in the preceding manoeuvres. As for the bad scouting, the commanders admitted that there had simply been a failure of intelligence. Their council of war agreed that it was now too late to get between the king and the castle, and that their infantry should muster in Newbury early the next morning and the cavalry on a large common to the south of it.[226]

Once again, the royalists moved faster than their opponents had expected, marching before daybreak and reaching the castle at midday.[227] The parliamentarian cavalry, on the other hand, and especially the Eastern Association regiments, was much slower to gather than expected, and by the time it was assembled together, south of Newbury, its enemies were already at Donnington. Its tardiness was blamed upon its now miserable condition, hundreds of horses dead and the survivors weakened, and their riders deserting. The king's army crossed Donnington Bridge again and reoccupied the huge field where much of it had been posted during the recent battle. Now, however, it drew up facing south, towards Newbury, and put itself into order to fight again. Cromwell's troopers on the common would have had a good view of their waiting enemy, even as they had at Marston Moor. Once more they were looking at the great broken ribbons of colour stretched across the landscape in front of them, along the southern slope of the ridge between the rivers. This time, however, the circumstances were very different. Instead of a showery midsummer day, clearing towards evening, this was a wet and windy winter one, the bright leaves coming down fast from the trees in the valley. They were not clearly outnumbering their opponents. Nor could they readily get at the latter, because between them lay the River Kennet, which could only be crossed at the bottleneck of Newbury, crammed with their own infantry. To attack the king's position, they needed to file through the town and then try to fan out and deploy for action with the rest of their army, at the foot of the ridge on which the royal soldiers were drawn up. They would have to perform that deployment under the noses of fully prepared enemies with the slope in their favour, made up of veteran regiments who in total now probably equalled the strength of the parliamentarians. Their attempts to do so would also be disrupted by the royal artillery, which was once again set up in front of the castle. The likelihood of being charged and broken up while trying to get into battle order was overwhelming.

Conversely, it would be equally suicidal for the royalists to launch an attack on the parliamentarian position, if their enemies decided not to move. That action would make the Newbury bottleneck work against them instead of in their favour, as they had to fight their way through a hedge filled with musketeers and then into a town which had been fortified and was defended by several thousand infantry. If they managed that feat, at certain heavy cost, they would then have themselves to issue from the town on the far side and deploy afresh for battle in the face of a huge force of fresh cavalry with a slope in its favour. The situation was one of natural military stalemate, and it is not surprising that councils of war were called by the commanders on both sides and took a decision to stay put. There was some skirmishing in the course of the afternoon, as two parties of parliamentarian horse drew out towards the royalist position, and two royalist horse regiments then chased them back behind their defences. At nightfall the king's men withdrew across the Lambourn to the area round the castle again, colours flying proudly and drums and trumpets sounding, and most settled down to sleep in the cold and sodden fields.

On the following morning, 10 November, the king retrieved his artillery and baggage from the castle, left it fully resupplied, and accompanied his army as it marched slowly westward towards the safety of his own territory. Prince Rupert kept it in battle order, ready to turn round and fight at any moment, and for a time drew it up on a heath to await an attack. Once again, he was challenging his enemies, and as the parliamentarians thronged out of Newbury at last, onto the ridge between the rivers which had been the royalist position, an enlarged council of war was called by their commanders in a cottage there, with colonels present as well as generals. This meeting was much recalled afterwards, because the opportunity thus offered to engage the royal army was not only the best of the whole campaign but likely to be the last. Attack on the previous day would have almost certainly resulted in defeat. Now the odds seemed much more even, but no better than that, because of the strength and high quality of the royalist force, and its obvious preparedness for battle. This was not an easy decision to make, and opinion was divided and heated, but in the end the majority decided in favour of caution, and the royal army was allowed to continue its retreat. A party of parliamentarian horse tried to shadow it but was routed by an ambush left by Rupert behind a barn. The royalists settled westward up the Kennet and deeper in the chalk hills, around Marlborough, took on supplies, and waited to see what the parliamentarians would do next.

The one hope that Parliament's soldiers now had of salvaging any concrete gain from the wreckage of the campaign was to reduce Basing House, which had remained under siege while all this drama had been going on around Newbury. The composite army therefore moved east towards Basing, but found itself leaking deserters and sick men steadily as it went and its members faced yet more service in winter conditions. The weather was getting worse. The infantry lacked firewood, food or shelter, all the villages having been stripped bare of the first two in October, and the cavalry would in any case be largely useless for siege operations – a point which Manchester's chaplain alleged was made by Cromwell and Waller to the earl as they rattled eastwards in his coach. Manchester, Waller, Balfour and Essex's foot general informed the Committee of Both Kingdoms that the horses were now so worn out with being ridden in bad weather that they would be ruined if more was expected of them. They also predicted that if their hungry foot soldiers were expected to sleep in the thickets around Basing while trying to starve out the house, the rest would desert. The committee told it to go into winter quarters, but as far west as possible to put pressure on royalist territory and prevent the relief of Basing. A council of war was called on 19 November, and decided to ignore both parts of that suggestion, and depend instead on the committee's final gracious acknowledgement that the commanders on the spot needed ultimately to decide what to do. It was resolved to save the remaining men and horses by putting them into snug accommodation for the winter immediately, in the Thames Valley between Reading and London. This was securely inside Parliament's territory; and Cromwell was one of those who signed the decision. The siege of Basing House was left to a small body of foot, which fled when a royalist relief force approached on the 22nd, and resupplied the garrison. With that, the king could disperse his own army for the winter, at last.[228]

The largest field force which Parliament had yet assembled in this war had achieved absolutely nothing. The sieges of Banbury, Donnington and Basing had all failed, and the king's winter quarters remained almost as extensive as before, enabling him to prepare the more effectively for another year of fighting. The much-vaunted victory at Newbury had turned out to be illusory, as the army allegedly defeated there had returned strengthened within two weeks and twice challenged and humiliated their adversaries. Altogether, a combined panel of Parliament's most senior commanders had accomplished less than for most of the time they had managed to achieve individually. As Cromwell headed for London after seeing his men into their billets, he must have known, as his fellow generals must have done, that they now had a lot of explaining to do.

5

❖

BORROWED TIME

The mood in the capital to which the generals returned in November 1644 had a new hostility towards them. Until now, newspapers and pamphlets could on the whole be relied upon to cry up parliamentarian successes and minimize defeats; and as Cromwell knew better than most, the accomplishments of individual commanders could be eulogized beyond what seems now to have been their objective desserts. Now the opposite effect obtained, centred above all on the events of 9–10 November, when the royal army had twice challenged Parliament's commanders to battle and they had twice refused. There was a strong (and false) impression that those commanders had still heavily outnumbered their enemies, by at least two to one, which made their conduct seem even more pusillanimous, or even disloyal.[1] *Mercurius Civicus* spoke of their 'improvidence and imprudence'.[2] *The Parliament Scout* noted that some attributed the failure to the absence of the earl of Essex, others 'that our generals are godly but not worldly men, others speak of plot and betrayal, others God's judgement for our being too worldly'.[3] *A Perfect Diurnall* talked darkly about a forthcoming punishment of mistakes.[4] *The Scottish Dove* belied its name, declaring that God's anger had clearly been aroused by the presence of traitors or wrongdoers in the parliamentarian ranks, who needed to be rooted out.[5] In his private journal, a London merchant and landowner called Thomas Juxon, who was fervent both as Puritan and parliamentarian, wrote that 'God seems not to favour the great officers' and that 'our great army is now shamefully beaten and cudgelled out of the field'.[6]

Faced with this suspicion and hostility, the returning generals had two immediate options: to form a united front and persuade public opinion of the necessity for their actions, or to blame each other and hope that somebody else would become the scapegoat. Depending on the outcome of either tactic, there were three possible scenarios for the fighting season in 1645: that the existing system of military leadership would be vindicated and maintained; that one or two generals would be replaced and the rest retained; or that a clean sweep would be made of the lot. Cromwell's future was prospectively in this melting pot, along with those of the rest.

FURORE

The policy initially adopted by the military leaders was to try to allay the anger in the capital by taking collective responsibility for the campaign and explaining plausibly why the decisions taken had been rational and wise. This was entrusted to Sir Arthur Hesilrig, who duly appeared in the House of Commons on 14 November, rather theatrically still attired in his battlefield dress of a leather buff coat, sword and pistols. He explained the decisions taken at Newbury as the product of a prudent weighing of odds in the prevailing circumstances; and got nowhere. The Commons remained unpersuaded and unappeased, and the demands for better explanations continued.[7] It did not help their feelings when the commander of the troops which had been driven from the siege of Basing House when the army retired to winter quarters wrote complaining that he had been betrayed and abandoned.[8] On the 22nd, Cromwell and Waller arrived in the Commons, to be greeted with an unwonted coldness and to be observed as looking unusually subdued as a result. The following day the House formally ordered them to prepare a justification of their actions on the campaign.[9] From what followed, it is clear that this was the tipping moment, as the two men decided that the fastest and most effective way of allaying the anger of Parliament and the public was to offer them a scapegoat.

They chose the earl of Manchester, Cromwell's own immediate superior, as the fall guy, and the reasons for this may readily be surmised. Oliver's rank as the earl's lieutenant put him in a privileged position to deliver information concerning his commander's shortcomings. As said, his own relations with Manchester had deteriorated to the point at which it seemed unlikely that they could work together much longer, while Waller may well have blamed the earl for not marching rapidly into the west to reinforce him in September, and so leaving him to make his humiliating retreat before the king. Moreover, Manchester was vulnerable. He had already gained a reputation as a torpid and over-cautious commander by the early summer, and had come close to being disowned or bypassed by the Committee of Both Kingdoms for his failure to obey its orders to take rapid action in the autumn. At the battle in October, he was handily isolated on the eastern side of the terrain, enabling Waller, Cromwell and Hesilrig to unite in blaming him for their lack of decisive success in the west. He had certainly (as was now to be shown) argued strongly for avoidance of battle when the king offered it in November. The facade of solidarity was already cracking in the army, and Manchester being isolated and set up for attack, as letters were being sent from officers to London, claiming that on 10 November Cromwell, Waller, Hesilrig and Essex's officers had all wanted to give battle to the royalists, but had been overruled by the rest of the council of war. The earl was really the perfect choice, and it must be imagined that Cromwell was encouraged and supported in it by frantic discussions conducted with his own friends and allies in Parliament and the armies before he delivered his blow. Moreover, Oliver was the perfect person to deal it. He had a savage streak in his nature which enjoyed inflicting death, injury or humiliation on those against whom he had taken, and he had already played a crucial part in bringing down Hotham and Willoughby, two other inadequate upper-class commanders. In Willoughby's case in particular, he had destroyed a general's reputation by delivering a set of falsehoods to the Commons. Manchester's fall was designed to be a larger version of that lord's.

The blow was dealt on 25 November, when Cromwell and Waller made their reports. Nobody subsequently commented on Waller's speech, so it must be surmised that it was relatively brief and supportive of Cromwell. The latter spoke for a long time, and caused a sensation. His delivery was, like many of his orations, extremely emotional, laced with tears. It was also deadly in its aim and intention, because it charged Manchester not merely with incompetence but with a consistent and deliberate design to sabotage Parliament's war effort by preventing decisive victory. He did so by telling a string of lies and distorted truths. First he accused the earl of frustrating his army's wish to besiege Newark after Marston Moor, when the records of the Committee of Both Kingdoms show that Manchester had sought exactly this. Then he alleged that his commander had single-handedly frustrated the design to march his army to attack Prince Rupert at Chester, when the same records prove that the earl was supported by his officers in objecting to this and eventually agreeing to a compromise plan. That was prevented by Essex's defeat, and now Cromwell portrayed Manchester as delaying his army's progress to rescue the military situation in the south from the beginning. In fact he had marched at top speed to protect London, and only slowed down there because of his very real fear that the strategy being forced upon him was too dangerous. Cromwell accused his superior of halting his army in Hertfordshire in September for no reason, when he knew that Manchester was struggling to resolve the religious divisions in it, and its lack of pay and equipment, before heading for battle.

The volley of accusation went on. Oliver naturally made full play with the earl's genuine resistance to his orders to make for Dorset and engage the king there with Waller. He then told stories of Manchester's foot-dragging and obstruction all through the Newbury campaign. He accused him of preventing decisive victory in the battle by sending in his crucial diversionary attack far too late, though, as said, there is no sign that the king was able to divert any soldiers from that wing to reinforce the other. Thereafter, Manchester was charged with preventing the pursuit of the fleeing royalist army after the battle, and then an advance into the Oxford area to prevent it from reuniting, and then the interception of the royal army on its return to relieve Donnington. The decision not to attack it when Rupert offered the chance was laid firmly at his door, as was that to abandon the siege of Basing House and give up the whole campaign. Oliver's version of events included a ringing and emotive account of an exchange in the council held in the cottage on the morning of 10 November. It claimed that when Cromwell and others argued for an immediate attack to win a decisive victory, Manchester had replied 'if we beat the king ninety-nine times he would be king still, and his posterity, and we subjects still, but if he beat us but once we should be hanged'. The clear implication was that the earl did not think it worthwhile fighting at all.[10]

Cromwell also excused the performance of his own horsemen in the battle as the result of the terrain, as described, and candidly acknowledged that he and most of his men favoured independency, and some might be Anabaptists, but that they had been accepted only as good and faithful soldiers who fought well.[11] He promised that they would peacefully accept a presbyterian settlement, if one were imposed.[12] The whole thing worked, as Oliver's speeches to the House often did. It provoked a long debate, which kept MPs sitting far into the afternoon,[13] but was generally received, as the newspaper reports cited below demonstrate, with satisfaction and approval. One journal writer who heard of it at second hand spoke of Cromwell's 'clearness and ingenuity'.[14] It must have helped that he was clearly supported not just by Waller, but also, now, by the latter's lieutenant Hesilrig.[15] It was the sort of thing that most of the Commons wanted to hear: that the failure of the campaign had not been due to the will of God, or collective and sequential misjudgements, but because of one bad apple in the barrel of commanders.

Formally, the House's response was to refer the relations made by both Cromwell and Waller to a committee with a remit to consider a remodelling of the parliamentarian armies, chaired by an MP called Zouch Tate. It had powers to cross-examine Cromwell, Waller and Hesilrig, and send for papers from the Committee of Both Kingdoms. Two days before, the committee itself had been ordered by the House to consider ways of combining the existing armies into a single body as large as possible.[16] Press responses were mixed. Some accepted that Cromwell was now fully vindicated and exonerated, reporting the satisfaction he had given the Commons: these tended, of course, to be papers already approving of him.[17] Others disapproved of the rift that Oliver had just opened in the parliamentarian leadership and declined to report his speech: these included one which favoured independency.[18] Manchester had suspected that Cromwell might turn on him, and his countess had reputedly made a last-minute attempt to head this off, inviting Cromwell and his civilian ally Sir Henry Vane to supper on the previous night and telling Oliver that her husband 'did exceedingly honour and respect him etc'. He was said to have replied, dourly, 'I wish I could see it'.[19] Cromwell may have expected that the earl's reaction to the subsequent attack on him by his most important and famous subordinate officer would be as choleric as most of Manchester's responses to slights or obstructions, but even he may have been surprised by its strength. On 26 November the earl asked the House of Lords to permit him to defend himself, and two days later he delivered his response, which like Cromwell's speech was long and detailed.[20]

There were three aspects to it. The first was a dignified and thorough rebuttal of Cromwell's accusations, pointing out the inaccuracies and injustices of those concerning his behaviour between July and October as has been done above. He covered his part in the decisions taken on the Newbury campaign by saying, again correctly, that in every case they had been the product of a majority of votes on the army's council of war, of which his was only one. Likewise, his actions when sending in the attacks on the eastern end of the royalist position during the battle were all taken on the advice of his senior officers, who were named and all prepared to testify to this fact. He was also right in pointing out how poorly Cromwell's own cavalry had performed both at the battle and on the morning of 9 November. When discussing the crucial meeting of the council of war in the cottage on the following morning, he insisted that it had been Hesilrig, and not he himself, who had uttered the words beginning 'if we beat the king ninety-nine times . . .' and that though Manchester had supported him, neither had been referring to the war in general. Instead they meant that if they defeated the king north of Donnington that day, he could shelter the remnant of his force behind his powerful local garrisons (as he had done two weeks before), whereas if their army was destroyed, then there was nothing to stop the victorious monarch immediately advancing upon London.

Thus far, the earl of Manchester was largely in the right in objective terms, and had been sober and restrained, but there were two other elements in his defence which were to explode the political situation instead of stabilizing it. The first was that he admitted that he had come sincerely to believe that God did not intend either side to gain an outright victory in the war, and that a negotiated peace was to be the divinely ordained outcome. He did not say when he had reached this conclusion – it was most probably after the defeat of Essex at Lostwithiel, following that of Waller and balancing the great victory at Marston Moor – but he had articulated it in the debate on 10 November if not before. In this situation, he believed that the main strategic imperative was to keep Parliament's main armies intact, and thus never to fight unless at an advantage, so as to retain a strong position from which to bargain for good terms. This was a dramatic admission, and coupled with the earl's emphasis on his own inexperience as a general, and reliance on the advice of his more experienced subordinate officers and of councils of war, must have given an abiding impression of a timid and torpid commander. Moreover, his stance was not of a kind likely to reassure many religious independents, whose vision of a future church structure was most unlikely to be acceptable to the royalists and would almost certainly be one of the main casualties of a negotiated peace.

What really made his presentation political dynamite, however, was that he did not merely set out to counter Cromwell's accusations, or to accuse him in turn of specific failures of military performance, but to return the compliment and attempt to destroy his reputation altogether, politically as well as militarily. He accused him of trying to undermine Manchester's authority in the Eastern Association army during the Newbury campaign by telling the men that the earl was responsible for their continuing long service in autumnal conditions and that Cromwell would have led them home long before. More generally, the earl appealed to conservative and moderate opinion by representing his lieutenant-general as a dangerous radical. He described Cromwell's pressure on him to dismiss all opponents of independency, above all Crawford, from their army, and went further to claim that Oliver had spoken of being willing to fight the Scots to prevent an intolerant presbyterian settlement, and use his soldiers to prevent a treaty with the king that established one; and had expressed contempt for the Westminster Assembly. Yet more incendiary was the earl's insistence that Oliver had inveighed against the power and privileges of the nobility and expressed his desire to overturn it. All this was to play to the very worst prejudices of those who feared the socially transgressive potential of religious radicals. Whereas most of Cromwell's accusations against Manchester can be checked against contemporary records (and found wanting), the most serious of those made against him by the earl in return – the invective against nobles and the willingness to fight his own allies to protect independency – cannot be independently verified. Both are extensions of attitudes which Cromwell certainly held: his fierce advocacy of independency and his irritation with inept aristocratic commanders such as Grey of Groby and Willoughby, which must have been compounded by Essex's defeat at Lostwithiel and Oliver's growing estrangement from Manchester himself. Cromwell was also noted, all his life, for intemperate outbursts, from the time when one ruined his youthful political career at Huntingdon. How much the earl exaggerated, however, it seems that nobody can say. What is clear is that he was accusing Oliver of treason as effectively as Oliver had accused him: a commotion over the conduct of a campaign had turned into a political vendetta.

His fellow peers mostly heard the earl of Manchester with apparent sympathy, and formally referred his account to a committee of six, which carefully mixed men who were not currently likely to favour independency with those who were.[21] It also asked the earl for a written version of his speech, which he duly delivered on 2 December. The House pronounced itself satisfied, and sent a copy to the House of Commons, which provoked another long speech from Cromwell, in which he tried to escalate the dispute to a new level by suggesting that by appearing to accept Manchester's accusations against him the Lords had breached the legal privileges of MPs. A majority were inclined to agree with him, and it was resolved to set up a conference over the matter between the Houses. This was held on the 4th, and the two rival charges, Cromwell's against Manchester and Manchester's against Cromwell, were read out. Three days later, the Commons set up a committee of lawyers to decide whether the Lords' behaviour over the earl's accusations did indeed constitute a breach of privilege. The row was now starting to tear Parliament apart, horizontally as well as vertically.[22] As these resolutions show, Oliver had succeeded in rallying considerable support in the Commons, among those who had sympathy with independency, those who were sensitive about their own House's powers and privileges, and those who were simply convinced by his speeches.

There were, however, powerful forces building up against him and in favour of Manchester. A majority of the Lords, as described, had rallied to a fellow peer. The Scots by now identified the independents as the greatest barrier to their abiding dream, which had brought them into the war: to establish a presbyterian Church in England equivalent to that in Scotland, which would ensure religious uniformity and harmony between the two nations. They now took up Manchester's cause as their own, persuaded by his speech. One of their clerical representatives in London wrote that it was time to break the power of independency by removing Cromwell from the army.[23] It was rumoured that they had declared they would not fight for Parliament again until this was done. The earl of Essex, who still enjoyed a great reputation among parliamentarians and led a strong faction in both Houses of Parliament, also threw his weight behind his fellow aristocrat. He had long favoured a negotiated peace, on good terms, and was now prepared to ally with the Scots, and offer them a Church of England roughly on their model, to get one. He supported Manchester in the Lords, and it seemed inevitable that the presbyterian majority in the Westminster Assembly would also be favourable to the earl.[24]

A striking apparent insight into the forces moving against Cromwell, but also the limitation of their powers, is provided by a retrospective account left in the memoirs of a leading parliamentarian MP, lawyer and politician called Bulstrode Whitelocke. Long afterwards, he recollected that late one night at this time the earl of Essex had invited him, and another prominent lawyer and MP, John Maynard, to his mansion. There the two men found a gathering which combined the earl's leading supporters in the Commons with the Scots commissioners. They sat down and the Scottish Lord Chancellor, the earl of Loudoun, said that Cromwell had to be removed, as a bitter foe of both the Scots and Essex. He sought the lawyers' advice on how to do so, and Whitelocke claims they answered that Cromwell was a very able man with a large following in the Commons, and that it would be necessary to have solid proof of his misconduct – such as that he had deliberately tried to set English and Scots against each other – if any move against him stood a chance of success. They added that they were not aware of any such evidence. Essex's greatest supporters in the Commons, Cromwell's former ally Denzil Holles, and Sir Philip Stapleton, both thought that it could be found and a majority formed against Cromwell. The Scots were, however, persuaded that an open attack on him by their two groups in conjunction would be unwise unless undeniable proof of Cromwell's misbehaviour could be obtained. The meeting broke up at 2 a.m., and Whitelocke believed that Oliver had a spy in it, because he was subsequently notably more gracious to the two lawyers.[25]

The controversy therefore remained thus far formally one between Cromwell and Manchester, and both mustered their supporters and witnesses, as manifested in subsequent written depositions. Cromwell's view of his opponent was endorsed by several officers in the Eastern Association army who were under his command in the horse division, most or all of whom shared his enthusiasm for independency; but also by Waller and

Hesilrig and some of their officers, and the commander of the siege of Basing.[26] There were also dirtier tactics used by sympathizers: a libel against the record of both Manchester and Essex was scattered around London.[27] Manchester was supported by some presbyterians in his army: Crawford, one of the earl's chaplains, and an anonymous officer who had known Cromwell since the opening of the war in East Anglia and was almost certainly William Dodson.[28] The first and the last of those robustly enlarged on Manchester's portrait of Oliver as a dangerous and unscrupulous radical. Essex's officers stood aloof from the fray. Everybody understood that although some of those engaged, like Waller and Hesilrig, may have chosen sides for tactical and fortuitous reasons, this was more than a spat between two generals. It was a dispute which fed off deep divisions between parliamentarians, linked to their instincts and beliefs concerning the proper conduct of the war, the nature of the religious settlement to follow it, and even the proper location of power within society.

It also mapped at points onto an emerging partisan landscape within Parliament.[29] For the first two years of the conflict, there had been tension, and at times dispute, in both Houses between those whose preferred that an end to the fighting would be in a negotiated compromise, and those who wanted utterly to defeat the king and his followers. The latter tended naturally enough to be prepared to prolong the war further and make greater sacrifices in it, and wanted an eventual settlement which was less like that of the pre-war religious and political establishment. Most members were not firmly identified with either group, and support swung between them and individuals migrated between them according to changing circumstances. Cromwell of course was always firmly identified with the people who wanted outright victory and far-reaching reform. During the winter of 1644–5 these existing ideological and human groupings developed further, and acquired the nicknames of Presbyterians and Independents, transferred to them from the now opposed factions in the Westminster Assembly. The essential distinction between them remained that which had divided them before, but with some changes of policy and personnel. Those who would be happy with a negotiated peace, made as soon as possible, now allied firmly with the Scots, making a tightly controlled presbyterian Church close to the Scottish model a part of the intended deal. Essex and his allies and followers became a major component of this grouping, nicknamed Presbyterians. The Independents were those who took up the cause of winning the war outright and imposing a more radically novel settlement on king and nation, which would include a looser system of church organization, discipline and doctrinal orthodoxy. The labels did not necessarily reflect personal religious belief: there were, for example, plenty of individuals who were personally happy with a presbyterian Church but felt that religious independents should be given some latitude because of the importance of their contribution to the war effort. As before, most parliamentarian MPs and some peers cannot be allocated confidently to either group. Nonetheless, something like a rough, hazy and unstable partisan division was in place, and the emotions, instincts and reasons which were causing people to give support to either Cromwell or Manchester were often the same as those which had created it. This made the mudslinging between the two men all the more dangerous, especially as it was on the verge of causing a feud between the two Houses themselves. At the very time at which Parliament needed dispassionately and forensically to decide on the lessons of the Newbury campaign, and the measures required to wage war better in 1645, it was in danger of tearing itself apart.

NEW MODELLING

The whole context of parliamentarian politics and the terms of debate were famously changed forever on 9 December, when a dramatically far-reaching and – to most observers – unexpected measure was introduced to the Commons. This was what became known as the Self-Denying Ordinance, a draft piece of legislation that would bar all members of either House from holding military or civil offices conferred by Parliament, for the duration of the war. At a stroke, this would sweep Cromwell, Manchester, Waller,

Hesilrig, Essex and a list of lesser commanders out of the army, terminating their quarrels and making way for a new set of generals, commanding a new, consolidated, field army. It is clear from the context that it was intended to be a cross-party initiative. The proposal for it seems to have emanated from the Commons committee set up to consider the future form of the field army, to which Cromwell's complaint against Manchester had been referred. It was the chair of this committee, Zouch Tate, a fervent presbyterian, who brought in the proposal as part of a report from the committee. He clearly did so with considerable trepidation: Whitelocke, who was there, commented that he carried in the document 'like a boil on his thumb'.[30] The plan was then supported by Sir Henry Vane, a leading Independent (in both the religious and political sense) and usually an ally of Cromwell, and then by Oliver himself, as part of a long debate in a very full House, more than two hundred MPs being present. The committee chosen to draft the ordinance mixed men from different groups, but a majority on it seem to have been Independents.[31]

Cromwell may have spoken more than once in the debate. It was said afterwards that he argued that unless the war were prosecuted effectively then the English people would say that MPs and Lords were keeping it going to profit from the offices they held in the machinery to fight it. He apparently proposed that the inquiry into the shortcomings of the campaign be dropped, and effort put instead into reshaping a consolidated army with new leaders, generously declaring that he had also made mistakes as a commander. He credited Parliament's soldiers with fighting for a common cause and not for particular generals. His intervention was regarded as very important, and his words noted more than those of any other contributor to the discussion. They represented, indeed, a key component of the process by which the measure became accepted, being the first recognition, by one of the contestants in the quarrel which had broken out over the conduct of the war, that the dispute was too damaging to be pursued further and needed to be replaced by a radical remedy to the question of leadership. As ever, we are woefully lacking in any reliable record of the manner in which the idea for it was developed, and how early Cromwell's engagement with it was, and how much he had to be persuaded into becoming an advocate.[32] It seems reasonable to conclude that he would not have done so had he not come to believe both that his feud with Manchester was dangerous to the parliamentarian cause and that its outcome had become uncertain enough to endanger himself; or at least that his friends and supporters had developed these beliefs. There are no grounds at all for thinking that at the moment when the ordinance was proposed he was not aware that its enactment would almost certainly end his military career along with that of most of the other leading generals. It was clearly a sacrifice he was prepared to make, and we can never know how much considerations of altruism (of serving and saving the cause) or calculation (of rescuing himself from a potentially dangerous situation) played in his willingness to do so.[33] The proposal for the measure was given widespread support in the press, and public opinion in London also seemed largely favourable.[34]

Thereafter, Oliver was engaged in four different areas of activity in Parliament and the capital, most of which ran through the rest of the winter and into the very beginning of spring. The first was to support the progress of the Self-Denying Ordinance and the measures which accompanied it and for a time took the place of it. Given his expressed views and loyalties, it must be presumed that he did this, though his own role is invisible. Between 11 and 19 December the ordinance passed through all its stages in the Commons, often with lengthy and heated debate. A proposal to exempt the earl of Essex from it was defeated by just seven votes, the earl's supporters Holles and Stapleton acting as tellers for the minority and Vane and another prominent Independent acting for the majority: Cromwell's support for the latter can be taken for granted. Another proposal, to deny office to anybody who did not take the oath of the Solemn League and Covenant and promise to submit to any form of church government that Parliament imposed – which would have worked against some of the religious radicals whom Cromwell favoured – was also defeated.[35] On

7 January, however, the Lords rejected the whole ordinance on the grounds that to lead men to defend the realm was one of the fundamental purposes of an aristocracy.[36]

The Commons, their pride affronted, made an appeal to the Lords to change their minds, and when this failed, began to circumvent the noblemen by reconstructing the main field army with the presupposition that the ordinance would be in effect. On 11 January they decided that the army would have 6,000 horse in ten regiments, 1,000 dragoons in ten companies, and 14,400 foot in twelve regiments: this was a force of a size likely to outnumber anything the king could put into the field. Two days later they imposed the system of taxation needed to support a force of that size, the Eastern Association paying about half of the total. They also allocated funds to pay the Scottish army to advance south, giving an overwhelming numerical superiority when facing the royalist forces; in February these were secured against an extra property tax on the whole of parliamentarian territory, to be levied for four months. On 21 January the House voted to make Sir Thomas Fairfax, the military commander who had won the most victories among those not sitting in either division of Parliament, the leader of the new army. It did so by a comfortable majority, with a vote which this time opened along clearly partisan lines: Cromwell and Vane, both Independents, were tellers in favour of Fairfax, opposed by Essex's men Holles and Stapleton, who were both emerging as leading Presbyterians. As a sop, the House directed Tate's committee to find some mark of honour and recompense to award the displaced Essex. The latter's experienced and respected foot commander, Philip Skippon, was appointed to lead the infantry in the new army, and the House also named the foot and horse colonels, again holding to the rule of appointing neither MPs nor peers. Of Cromwell's existing horse officers, Fleetwood, Whalley and Vermuyden were all given regiments. A week later, Cromwell and Waller were both put onto a committee to frame instructions for the remodelled army.[37]

Tantalizingly, the post of general of horse in the new army was left vacant. Essex's commander, Balfour, was dismissed, with the Commons directing that he should receive a suitable reward, but nobody was put into his place, apparently because there was no obvious candidate among the officers who was not apparently disqualified, like Cromwell, by a place in Parliament. The MPs seem to have decided to wait to see who would emerge. Everything now depended on whether the Lords would throw out the whole plan as they had the Self-Denying Ordinance. They debated it for the rest of the month, and sent up their amendments on 5 February, one of which was sent to discussion by a committee which included Cromwell. Debates over the requirements of the peers took up the next few days. A key one was that the lesser officers chosen by Fairfax should be approved by Parliament, and here once again the Commons divided along party lines, Cromwell and another Independent, Sir John Evelyn, acting as tellers for the votes against it and Holles and another Presbyterian, and Essex supporter, acting for its supporters. This time Cromwell's side lost, by almost twenty votes, and he suffered another blow when the Commons agreed with the Lords' requirement that all officers of the new army take the oath of the Solemn League and Covenant, and refusers be barred from any further post in Parliament's service.

Oliver must have known that some of the more radical and scrupulous of the independents would jib at that. Not only did some sectaries scruple to take oaths, as said, but the terms of this one bound takers both to defend the king's authority and to maintain a national Church and bring it into the closest possible conformity with that of Scotland, all undertakings about which some parliamentarians were starting to have doubts. However, the House also agreed to reject the Lords' proposal that the soldiers would have to promise to accept any form of church government that Parliament imposed. On 13 February Cromwell and his allies returned to the attack, and a division in which he was once more paired with Evelyn as teller, against two Presbyterians, got agreement to strike out the clause purging army officers who refused the Solemn League and Covenant. Three days later, however, this was changed to a compromise with the Lords that subscription to the document was still needed to be admitted to a place in the army, especially as an officer. Such a concession was needed to get the Lords to agree to the ordinance for the new army and so set about creating the latter: people like Cromwell may have hoped that there was enough ambiguity in the terms of the League and Covenant to get it past the consciences of most officers. The day after that, the Commons set up a committee to consider how best to recruit what was becoming known as the New Model Army, and to get it ready to fight; and Oliver was made a member.[38]

The second of the four areas of activity in which Cromwell was engaged was his struggle with Manchester. The chance that the Self-Denying Ordinance would fail made it imperative that an alternative plan be followed to get rid of incompetent generals; and also both Cromwell and Manchester had names to clear from the mud-slinging in which both had engaged. Therefore, the inquiry into the failure of the Newbury campaign shuddered back into life just when it might have seemed as if the wholesale removal of the leading existing commanders ought to have rendered it unnecessary. On 26 December 1644 the Commons ordered a report into Cromwell's conduct when the king came to relieve Donnington Castle, and a week later required one on Manchester's conduct. On 10 January 1645 they humiliated both Manchester and Essex by peremptorily reprimanding them for not putting their soldiers into the winter quarters (closer to those of the royalists) specified by the Committee of Both Kingdoms. Soon after, they directed Manchester to submit to another of the committee's orders, and on the 15th gave another direction for a report on the evidence submitted by Cromwell and Manchester.[39]

On 20 January, with the Lords still refusing to pass the Self-Denying Ordinance, the Commons raised the stakes in the quarrel by declaring that the action of the upper House in appointing a committee to hear Manchester's charge against Cromwell was a breach of privilege, as Cromwell had wanted. A fresh initiative was launched to gather evidence to determine the truth of the charges that the two men had brought against each other. As a further act of aggression and intimidation, Tate's committee was ordered to discover the printer of the defence of Manchester written by his chaplain, with a view to punishing him. Manchester promptly demanded a hearing, and the House insultingly left it to the committee to decide whether to give him one. On 12 February it went after the earl again, directing the committee to inform him of the charges against him.[40] The third of Cromwell's areas of activity this winter was finally to settle scores with an older and more clearly culpable parliamentarian opponent than Manchester. As soon as the autumn campaign finally ended, and all witnesses were available to return to London, the trials of Sir John Hotham and his son, who had been locked in the Tower for one and a half years, finally opened. The letters that the younger man had sent to the marquis of Newcastle, captured at Marston Moor, now served as the conclusive evidence for the prosecution, but as much more as possible was heaped up by it. Cromwell gladly appeared as one of its witnesses, citing the failure of the defendant to rout the opposing royalist wing at Belton as an act of deliberate perfidy; which it may have been, though final proof is lacking. Both Hothams were condemned to death, but the elder asked for a stay of execution, and both Houses allowed this on Christmas Eve. The Commons, however, only did so by ten votes, and while Holles and Stapleton acted as tellers for the victorious majority, Cromwell, implacable as ever towards enemies, was one of those for the minority who wanted severity. He got his way six days later, when the Lords asked that Sir John's life be spared altogether because of his previous services. This time Cromwell and another Independent acted as tellers for the large majority which voted for death, Stapleton again being one of those opposed; and Hotham duly followed his son to face the headsman's axe.[41]

Cromwell's fourth area of activity between December 1644 and early February 1645 was to carry on his career as an MP and committeeman in general. He took up the teller's staff for other motions than those mentioned already.[42] Another major parliamentary initiative of the winter was to open and conduct peace talks with the king, a necessary measure to satisfy those in Parliament who wanted to end the war by treating. On 16 December Oliver was made one of the commissioners to hear the king's reply to Parliament's overture, and three days later was a teller in a vote to frame an answer. The division concerned showed that there was no consistent partisan frontier yet running through the Commons, for Oliver was paired with Hesilrig in favour of a motion that the MPs would reply 'in time' to the royal offer to discuss peace terms in detail. They were defeated, and Cromwell's usual ally Vane was a teller for the victorious majority.[43] Oliver was also serving on a range of parliamentary committees again.[44] Outside Parliament he was able to attend the Committee of Both Kingdoms regularly for the first time since its establishment, being present for most of its meetings and getting put onto its sub-committee for the reshaping of the army. He also carried messages from it to the Commons.[45]

As an MP he also played his part in the continuing quest for a religious settlement, on which the collective mind of Parliament had been concentrated anew in early January by two further developments. One was a pointed letter from the representatives of the Kirk of Scotland, asking what progress had been made in the matter, on which the alliance between the two nations depended. The other was the action of the Westminster Assembly in handing Parliament the problem of how the independent and presbyterian models for the Church of England could be reconciled. On 14 January the Commons resolved that it was possible – in theory – for many different congregations to exist underneath a national presbyterian umbrella. Nine days later it decided that the Church should be divided into fixed congregations for public worship, each representing a certain number of dwellings and served by a minister who was part of the national system: in other words, equivalents to the traditional parishes. Representatives of a number of these were to meet together in a regional presbytery, and above these would come provincial organizations, *classes*, and national synods. The whole Church would be subject to state power.[46] This was a system broadly equivalent to Scottish presbyterianism, but with state control, and the decisions still ducked the issues of where power ultimately lay in it, or how far the state would control it, or what would happen to congregations who did not want to be part of it.

In theory, the Self-Denying Ordinance would have allowed MPs to make themselves eligible for reappointment to high military office in

Parliament's army by resigning their seats: something that peers were of course not able to do as their nobility was inherited. There is not the slightest indication that either Cromwell or anybody else contemplated this course. To remain in Parliament not only ensured a place at the centre of power, which was not subject to the fortunes of war, but a role in the settlement of the nation after the war was won. There seems every likelihood, therefore, that Cromwell himself regarded the existence he was carrying on at Westminster and London in the first two months of 1645 as the pattern of his life in the foreseeable future: as a zealous and influential regular member of the Commons and the Committee of Both Kingdoms. It was going to take an extraordinary sequence of events to disrupt that; but such a sequence was not long in commencing.

THE INTERIM CAMPAIGN: THE WEST COUNTRY

The trail which was to lead Cromwell back to active military service began on 15 January, when the Commons decided to send a huge raiding party of six thousand horse and dragoons into the West Country, to disrupt royalist preparations for the campaigning season there. Sir William Waller was chosen to command it, because he knew the region and had done well there before, and as a final mark of honour to, and confidence in, him before he laid down his command and his men were reallocated to the New Model Army. He was, moreover, a general who had proved many times his ability to cover distances rapidly and catch enemies off guard, and could be a formidable strategist and tactician (though these talents too often seemed to abandon him on an actual battlefield). On the 29th, the House ordered him to join his troopers and commence his advance.[47] Instead he stuck on the Surrey–Hampshire border, as only seven to eight hundred of the soldiers allocated to him from what had been Manchester's and Essex's armies had turned up.[48]

Waller's mission acquired a new urgency and focus on 9 February, when local royalists recaptured the important Dorset port of Weymouth, which the earl of Essex had taken in the previous summer. They surprised it with the help of some of the citizens, in what became known as the Crabchurch Conspiracy, but the achievement turned out to be only partial. The parliamentarian garrison retreated into the twin town of Melcombe, on the far side of the harbour, and there held out under siege.[49] On the 12th, Waller was therefore ordered urgently to march to its relief, and to secure Parliament's other ports on the Dorset coast, Poole, Wareham and Lyme, if he were too late.[50] Sir William's problems were, however, continuing. He had no pay or supplies for his men, and no foot soldiers to accompany his cavalry and enable him to fight an enemy well supplied with both. On informing the Committee of Both Kingdoms of all this, he announced lugubriously and melodramatically, 'I have discharged my conscience, and now if I perish, I perish!'[51]

Despite this declaration, he still did not set out, because he had run up against the instability among Parliament's soldiers caused by their prospective incorporation into the New Model. In January some of Manchester's infantry had started a petition to have him continued as their general, and when their colonel cautiously suspended two of the officers for promoting it, and sent them to London to face the earl himself, Manchester had restored them to their commands.[52] In Waller's case, most of his men for the expedition would be drawn from Manchester's and Essex's armies, and did not know him. Their resulting unease and resentment were enhanced by the prospect of more hard service without assured pay, and with the likelihood of once more sleeping rough in weather that, this early in the year, was likely to be both cold and wet. It was especially strong in Cromwell's own huge horse regiment, around a thousand strong, which was to be a major component of Sir William's force.[53] As a leader, Oliver had two special and consistent talents. One served him especially well in Parliament, and it was his ability to make effective and persuasive speeches. The other was his success in instilling a profound personal loyalty into the soldiers who served directly under him. This was partly because of his concern for their physical welfare, their pay and the demands made of them and their horses on campaign. It must also have been because of the religious bond between him and many of them, in his protection and encouragement of independency. This bond between colonel and men much aided the good discipline of the latter, and their good performance under favourable conditions of battle. It was said that when a rumour had reached his troopers in January that they were going to be placed under the command of a Scot in the remodelling of the armies, they had immediately mutinied.[54] Now they, as well as some of the horsemen from Essex's army, mutinied again, refusing to obey Waller and embark on what seemed to them a foolhardy expedition with inadequate resources.[55] They received sympathy from newspapers which favoured independency, and emphasized their normal high quality, loyalty and discipline.[56]

On 26 February, therefore, the Commons decided both to rescue the situation and pay Cromwell a final gesture of honour and trust, parallel to that granted to Waller, by ordering him to lead his regiment himself under Sir William's command on the campaign. To remedy the material needs of his troopers, he was granted a thousand pounds.[57] Oliver attended the Committee of Both Kingdoms for the last time on the following day, ensuring that care was taken to get the money paid over, and then set out to join his men.[58] He did so with the two great advantages that Waller had lacked: he was known to and trusted by his regiment, and came with a chest of cash which would strengthen their faith in him still further. Conspiracy theorists might suggest that he had clandestinely encouraged his men in their behaviour towards Sir William, to secure just such a result; but apart from the (expected) utter lack of evidence for this, nobody suggested it at the time, and it would have been extraordinarily dangerous for him to have attempted anything of the sort. On 4 March the Commons ordered him and Waller to march for the West at once, with whatever men they had managed to gather already.[59] A week later they had advanced across Hampshire with around four thousand troopers in all.[60] All this dawdling had actually saved them a job, because in the meantime the parliamentarians in Melcombe, reinforced both by land and by sea, had sallied out, driven off their attackers and recaptured Weymouth.[61]

Their first action was the easiest, most successful and most newsworthy: to eliminate the royalist home guard for Wiltshire, being the horse regiment led by its high sheriff, Sir James Long. This was the sort of job at which Waller excelled: to trap and crush an outnumbered, unsuspecting enemy commanded by a genteel incompetent. He did it perfectly. The royalists were quartered in villages of the clay lowlands just to the west of the huge chalk wasteland of Salisbury Plain. Waller made a forced march from Andover along the high road to Amesbury, resting there in the evening. At midnight he sent part of his force, including Cromwell, to ride through the rest of the dark hours in an arc across the open sheep country of the south-west corner of the plain. By dawn on 13 March they were to the west and north of their prey, and attacked, driving the panicked royalists south and east, and so straight into the rest of Waller's men who were ready for them. Of four hundred of Long's men, only thirty escaped, the rest being killed, or captured with Long.[62] This was exactly the kind of easy, complete, victory of which Parliament and its supporters wanted to hear. From there Sir William and Cromwell moved south through the chalk hills into Dorset, where they united with the local parliamentarian forces on the 19th to make up an army near to the six thousand which Parliament wanted.[63]

This is where things started to go wrong. To protect the royalist West Country against exactly the kind of havoc that the parliamentarians intended to wreak there, the king had returned to it what remained of the regional army which had been led in 1644 by Prince Maurice. This he had now put under George Goring, with whom he had also sent some of his best horse regiments from the royal field army. That gave Goring a striking force roughly equal to that which he now faced, and he was at least Waller's equal in a cavalry warfare of raids, feints and forced marches. Moreover, he disposed of a large force of infantry, which Waller – despite frantic appeals for one – lacked, enabling him to conduct combined operations suited to a variety of terrain. The landscape of western Dorset and eastern Somerset, which was the zone in which the rival forces met, was a patchwork of woods, narrow roads between banks, and small enclosures, badly suited to mounted warfare and favouring the defence: in Waller's own words, 'every field was a fortification, and every lane as disputable as a pass'. He began to view fighting Goring as 'my hopeless employment in the West'.[64] His men faced this formidable new enemy worn out after their long marches across Wiltshire, and starting to run short of money and supplies.[65] In the last week of March, Goring commenced an expert harrying of his opponents, pouncing on and routing all of the parliamentarian detachments, including Cromwell's, west of Dorchester; and then refusing battle when his enemies combined again and offered it in a position favourable to themselves.[66]

Waller had found Cromwell an able and congenial lieutenant, thinking him blunt, but not proud or arrogant, and obedient, intelligent, and inclined to let others speak first in discussions of strategy rather than push forward with his own opinions.[67] This does seem a fair summary of his character in general, and Oliver also had the strongest possible motive, after his treatment of Manchester, to show himself to be an effective and compliant subordinate. They should have made an excellent team, the very experienced, energetic and often talented general and the charismatic, committed and gifted cavalry commander. As it was, by the opening of April they were facing the wrong opponent, in the wrong place, with the wrong resources. In the first week of that month Waller and Cromwell gave up and retreated to Salisbury, and there they stuck, their activities fading out of the newspapers.[68] At first the Committee of Both Kingdoms ordered Sir William to advance westwards again, but he did not, and on the 17th it directed him to march his men back to Reading, turn them over for integration into the New Model Army, and go on to London to resign his commission.[69] It was an anticlimactic end to the campaign, and a gravely disappointing one to Sir William's career as a parliamentarian general. Cromwell went with him, apparently expecting to do the same, and therefore almost certainly with the same bitter feelings regarding his own time as a soldier.

THE INTERIM CAMPAIGN: THE MIDLANDS

When Cromwell had ridden out from London on his spring campaign, there would have been yellow catkins on the hazels, grey buds on the willows and black buds on the ashes, but the trees in general would still have been leafless and the grass withered and bleached on the sheep runs. Now as he returned, spring was almost gone, with fresh grass in the fields and emerald leaves showing in sprays against the grey trunks of the woods, while flowers of half a dozen kinds had opened on the field banks and the floors of copses. The landscape of military leadership had been as dramatically transformed.[70] In March there had been another struggle between Lords and Commons, this time over the list of officers which Sir Thomas Fairfax had submitted for their approval, to be commissioned into the New Model Army. The lower House had altered only a few names, but the upper one changed around a third, over half of them being from Manchester's former army and many representing religious independents. This was a clear attempt to produce a less radical and potentially more tractable force, and the Commons rallied against it, inspired both by sympathy for independency and for soldiers with good records, and by a sense of collective pride. They coerced the peers by persuading the corporation of London to make the loan needed to launch the New Model conditional on the acceptance of Fairfax's list. That then got through the Lords by one, proxy, vote wielded by Viscount Saye, both Essex and Manchester backing the defeated minority.

The New Model was now on the way, more or less in the image that Fairfax had wanted for it, and that made further resistance by the Lords to the Self-Denying Ordinance pointless. It was therefore revived by the Commons and passed by both Houses on 3 April, directing that by 13 May all members of either one who had been appointed to a military or civil office by them since 1640 had to resign. It went through, however, without any clause which forbade either House to appoint or reappoint any of its members to such offices in the future, so that if Fairfax and his new corps made a mess of things, some of the old generals might return. It therefore also left a chink of hope for a future military command for Oliver.[71] For the time being, however, the old order was passing, and before Cromwell neared London most of the existing commanders, including Essex and Manchester, had handed in their commissions. The Commons spurred on Manchester to do so, and reminded him of the animosity of most of its members, by making a final declaration that he should answer the charges against him as a general.[72] Several of the Scottish officers who had served Parliament and might have continued to do so preferred now to transfer to the forces of their own nation: one of them was Cromwell's enemy Crawford, and Oliver must have been glad to see him disappear.[73] Their removal reduced the influence of presbyterianism in the New Model further, and more changes allowed one more of the cavalry officers who had served under Cromwell, a noted religious independent, Nathaniel Rich, to become a colonel. Oliver's shadow hung over the horse division of the new army, as six of the eleven regiments which now comprised it had been formed out of men he had commanded for the Eastern Association. Most of his own enormous regiment, on delivery to Fairfax, was divided into two of standard size, one being put under Cromwell's lieutenant-colonel and cousin Edward Whalley and the other honoured by being made Fairfax's own, though another leading officer in Cromwell's old regiment, his brother-in-law John Desborough, was put in effective command.[74]

On 21 April Waller and Cromwell reported to Fairfax's headquarters at Windsor to announce delivery of their men, debrief, and move on to London and civilian life. This is exactly what Sir William did, but Oliver, allegedly to his complete surprise, was offered another job.[75] The king was still at Oxford, preparing to set out from there on his summer campaign, but most of his field army was either in the west with Goring or with Rupert and Maurice in the Welsh Marches, reimposing royalist authority there. The Committee of Both Kingdoms decided that Cromwell should move on immediately with the cavalry force he had commanded under Waller, including both the new units just formed out of his old regiment. His assignment was to prevent the king from joining the bulk of his soldiers, and trap him in Oxford.[76] It was a vital duty, and represented just the kind of rapid, mobile warfare at which Cromwell excelled, and at which Fairfax knew he excelled after their service together in the previous two years. It was also a providential opportunity to end his military career with a resounding success instead of an anticlimax; or perhaps even to extend it.

As soon as he received these instructions, Oliver called his horsemen to a rendezvous at Watlington, a village sitting at the foot of the steep chalk scarp of the Chiltern Hills, upon the plain of the River Thames. It was easily reached from their quarters around Reading, and from it he marched at once towards Oxford, using intelligence given by the parliamentarian garrison at Abingdon, a major thorn in the side of the king's winter quarters, aided by four friendly Oxford University students. He quartered north of the city for the night, and in the morning was attacked by a smaller party of royalist horse, which he drove back, claiming to have captured two hundred men and four hundred horses, and killed some troopers. Having thus cleared the way, he pounced on a nearby royalist outpost in a mansion called Bletchingdon House, threatening the governor with a massacre if he did not surrender at once. The unfortunate man had women guests in the house, and only two hundred soldiers, and was taken by surprise and without hope of relief; and the place does not seem to have been strongly fortified. As a result, near midnight he agreed to hand over the house and the weapons and ammunition in it and march away, bagging Cromwell a second easy and newsworthy victory, and over two hundred muskets. On the following day, 25 April, he sent a triumphant account of his success to the Committee of Both Kingdoms, meticulously attributing all the credit to God.[77] When the former governor reached Oxford, the king had him court-martialled and shot for dereliction of duty.[78]

Later that same day, Cromwell led his men westwards across the Thames Valley to block the king's escape from the city towards his field army, and once more excellent intelligence directed him towards easy prey: three hundred royalist foot soldiers who were marching between local garrisons. He caught them at the little town of Bampton an hour before midnight, and offered them the choice between surrender and death, accepting their submission at dawn. He then sent a party to beat up a royalist horse detachment on the march to the west, and settled at Faringdon, a safe distance south-west of Oxford, where he could still block King Charles's way out. He wrote again to the committee, announcing yet more achievements and asking for money for his men, as they had to take free quarter.[79] Parliament and the press were delighted, and the Commons duly sent formal thanks for his 'great services to the state'.[80] The easy victories, however, had now run out. Faringdon contained a great house which had been made another of the king's garrisons, and Cromwell summoned it with the same blood-curdling threats which had broken the nerve of the hapless governor at Bletchingdon. Faringdon Castle, as this mansion was called, was another tough nut like Donnington, set within powerful earthworks with projecting bastions, and commanded by a hard-bitten veteran. He invited Oliver to send in his men to get killed, and this is exactly what happened. Cromwell despatched a large body of foot soldiers loaned from the Abingdon garrison to storm the defences at 3 a.m. on 30 April, and they were driven back with serious losses. He was reduced to thanking the governor for the kindness of allowing the survivors subsequently to carry away the corpses of their comrades.[81]

The unfortunate infantry from Abingdon were commanded by Richard Browne, a solid and capable man who was the governor of that town and Parliament's major-general in the region. He and they had been sent by the Committee of Both Kingdoms to give Cromwell a foot division, and the committee directed Fairfax to send more New Model soldiers to join him.[82] Trapped in Oxford, the king had sent appeals to Goring and Rupert to rescue him, and both were on their way with powerful bodies of men.[83] The plan of the committee was to make Cromwell and Browne strong enough to repel them, and keep Charles cooped up. The flaw in it was that Goring was moving much too fast and was upon Cromwell and Browne with three thousand horsemen before the reinforcements could set out, while Rupert and Maurice were approaching the west of Oxford with another powerful force. Goring reached Faringdon on 3 May, and exactly what happened there must remain in doubt, because the partisan accounts differ. Royalists asserted that he fell successively on the soldiers of Cromwell and Browne, and those sent by Fairfax to aid them, and routed both with heavy losses.[84] Parliamentarians insisted that Oliver drew up his men to fight him and Goring declined battle, though some admitted to the loss of a scouting party, and that the royalists beat up some of the quarters in which Cromwell lodged his troopers.[85] What is certain is that Cromwell and Browne retreated eastwards to the comparative safety of Abingdon, leaving Goring in control of Faringdon and the king free to march. The royalist cavalry general had thwarted Cromwell's mission in the Oxford area as effectively as he had Oliver's one in the West Country a month before. Only peripheral damage had been inflicted on the royalist war machine, which had been balanced in large part by the loss at Faringdon Castle. The king's departure on campaign had been delayed by at most one to two weeks, which was not a factor in the fortunes of war to come.

Charles left Oxford on 7 May and combined the men he took with him with those brought by Goring and Rupert, to make up a formidable army of eleven and a half thousand men. Halfway across the Cotswold Hills Goring peeled off with his three thousand to protect the West Country again, while the king and Rupert turned north to relieve the major royalist port of Chester, which was under siege. They picked up more soldiers from garrisons on the way. By 15 May the royal army was in Worcestershire, clearing away the enemy garrisons there with ten thousand men.[86] Meanwhile parliamentarian leaders generated a spray of suggestions for a strategy to cope with it. The one besieging Chester begged the Committee of Both Kingdoms to join to his men the Scottish army in the north, Lord Fairfax's in Yorkshire, and Cromwell and Browne's one, to form a composite force large enough to take on the king.[87] Parliament itself agreed that the Scots had to march south to face the royal army.[88] Cromwell himself informed the Commons that he and Browne were going to follow the king in his rear and do their utmost to hinder him.[89] As Oliver's commission as a general was due to expire in the following week, under the terms of the Self-Denying Ordinance, and as he and his men currently had a critically important role to play, it was imperative to grant him an extension of it.

On 10 May both Houses rushed one through, until 19 June.[90] A few other, local, commanders, such as Lord Fairfax, were granted the same privilege, given the gravity of the situation.[91]

Cromwell's strike force consisted of the horse regiments with which he had raided around Oxford, plus four of the New Model Army's foot regiments, sent by Sir Thomas Fairfax, and Browne's men and some from Midland garrisons. Together they totalled six to eight thousand, not enough to match the royal army alone but capable of making up a body able to do so if united with the Scots and more local parliamentarian commanders. They accordingly marched up into the Midlands, crossing the limestone hills which divide Oxfordshire from Warwickshire to quarter in various parts of the latter county and wait for opportunities and allies. They did not come.[92] The parliamentarians besieging Chester gave up that job and retreated in the face of the king's continued advance, appealing for help.[93] Lord Fairfax and the other northern parliamentarians did not feel strong enough to face the royal army without the Scots. The Scots, meanwhile, having moved down from Newcastle into Yorkshire, instead of joining him and heading on south as asked, went in the wrong direction, across the Pennines into Westmoreland.

They were prodigal in reasons and excuses. The Scots claimed to have heard that Charles intended to invade the north via Lancashire, to reconquer the region and attack Scotland, and so were moving into his path. They claimed to lack pay and food for their men, and carriages and draught horses for their baggage and equipment, and they could not move without those. They claimed that the New Model Army was now getting paid every fortnight a larger sum than they had received from Parliament in six months.[94] In reality, two considerations seem to have prevailed with the Scots more than any others. The first was that they were watching their own backs. In the previous autumn a civil war had broken out in Scotland, produced by a royalist rebellion in the Highlands led by the marquis of Montrose. The latter had notched up a succession of brilliant victories, and though he had not yet broken into the Lowlands, it seemed increasingly possible that he would, and that the Scots in England would have to return home to fight him. So they had an incentive to stay close to the border. The second probable motivation was that they had a keen respect for, and fear of, the main royal field army, and after their experience at Marston Moor did not want to face a situation in which they had to take it on alone or in combination only with Lord Fairfax's men, who had failed them there.

This was, in fact, exactly the fate which Prince Rupert, as direct commander of the royal army under the king, intended for them. His master plan for the 1645 campaign had been to reconquer the north, sweeping up there before the New Model was ready, relieving the remaining royalist strongholds and annihilating or chasing off the local parliamentarians and the Scots, while they were separated and vulnerable, and then turning south again, reinforced by northerners, to face the New Model.[95] The response which Parliament now intended was to halt the royal army in the North Midlands with an allied one made up of the Scots and the soldiers of Lord Fairfax and Cromwell and Browne. That would fight a replay of Marston Moor, and if it would be smaller than the composite force which had won that battle, the royal army was also now less than that which Rupert had led there. Instead, now, the Scottish retreat had left the component parts of the intended allied force far apart from each other, each too weak to tackle the king by itself and vulnerable to annihilation by him. Charles and Rupert could now rampage as they wished. The bitter truth of that must have sunk into Oliver as he was forced to dawdle in Warwickshire while the woods, fields and heaths of that county turned fully green around him.[96] He lacked any money for his men, so that they had to take free quarter again, and feed their horses on the sown grass now sprouting in the meadows, on which the farmers depended for their hay.[97]

Parliament, and its executive, the Committee of Both Kingdoms, now had to play its trump card, the New Model Army. In the first half of May, when it trusted to its putative allied army to stop the king, it had sent Sir Thomas Fairfax and most of that army into the West Country, to relieve Taunton. This town, taken by Essex in the previous summer, sat in the centre of the royalist territory of the region and presented a major threat to it. The response by the king's followers was to try to reduce it as fast as possible, an enterprise which would, if successful, release a reinforced western royalist army to march east and distract Parliament or join the king and give him a composite field force at least the size of the New Model. Accordingly, Parliament needed to keep Taunton in its own hands, and Sir Thomas Fairfax duly marched into Dorset and sent a relief party which saved the town in the nick of time.[98] In mid-May Parliament and its committee seemingly decided on a new strategy to trap and destroy the king's army, by making his capital, Oxford, play the role that York had done in the previous summer. They ordered Sir Thomas to take the main body of the New Model to lay siege to the city, apparently to force the king to return to save it.[99] He could then be brought to battle outside it and defeated exactly as Rupert had been outside York.

The committee now set to work to enact this scheme, and Cromwell found himself being moved as a piece in it, at the committee members' behest; an experience which could not have been improved by the irony that one result of the Self-Denying Ordinance had been to enable former generals such as Essex and Manchester – now with no love for Oliver – to take up their seats on it and join the business of ordering him around. The first plan was to send him and his cavalry to reinforce the Scottish army, both strengthening it significantly in an arm in which it was always weak and adding to the moral pressure on it to come south. The combined force was expected to shadow the royal army and fight it if it could be caught at a disadvantage.[100] That was scuppered when the Scots made it plain to their English allies that Cromwell was now so obnoxious to them that they would not fight alongside him.[101] His orders were therefore changed, to hand over most of his horsemen and dragoons – 2,500 men in all – to one of the colonels serving under him, the Dutch professional Bartholomew Vermuyden. The latter was much more acceptable to the Scots, and would lead his party north to join them instead of Cromwell: if Vermuyden performed well on this mission, it seemed likely that he would be appointed

to the vacant post of lieutenant-general of the horse in the New Model. Oliver was directed instead to come south with Browne and unite their remaining soldiers with the New Model Army, under Sir Thomas Fairfax, for the siege of Oxford. He and Vermuyden parted at Coventry, and Cromwell marched to Fairfax with a thousand horsemen and the foot regiments.[102] On 21 May the New Model Army laid siege to Oxford.[103] The implications of the change of plan were probably clear to Oliver, with the clock ticking against the extension of his military career. Sent north to the Scots, he would almost certainly have needed a further extension to carry out the expected service. As one among Fairfax's subordinates, in a static and possibly lengthy siege – for Oxford was even stronger, better supplied and well defended than York had been – he would probably just wait uselessly until his time expired, and then return to London a civilian.

The king and his military advisers, unwittingly, came to his rescue, for on hearing of the arrival of the New Model before Oxford they neither pursued their northern design nor returned to fight for the city. Instead they compromised by deciding to draw off the New Model from the siege by attacking a major parliamentarian stronghold in the Midlands; and having thus distracted Fairfax's army, carry on north and pursue their original purpose there. They chose Leicester, a prosperous county town which had never been under threat before and so had not been properly fortified, trusting instead to its medieval stone walls. On 31 May Rupert's siege train smashed holes in these, and the town was taken by storm and comprehensively sacked.[104] The royalists gained control of the county with it, and their local adherents spilled over to reoccupy parts of Rutland and come close once more to the borders of the Eastern Association, which lay wide open to the king should he now choose to march in. The blow to parliamentarian morale was tremendous, equivalent to that of the surrender at Lostwithiel the year before, and there was a huge outcry in Parliament and London against the strategy which had produced it.

Even before Leicester fell, as the king was advancing east through the Midlands, Parliament had realized the potential threat that he now posed

to the Eastern Association and decided to send Cromwell to deal with it. Oliver's instructions were to take four horse troops to the Isle of Ely and ensure that it was properly fortified, to put a powerful regional redoubt in Charles's path. A thousand pounds were assigned from the excise in the association, a sales tax imposed on many products, to pay for this work, which was to take up the remainder of the period for which his military service was extended.[105] The implication was that when that expired, the final moment for his retirement would have come. In a sense he was going home, and in another had come full circle, preparing to end his career as a soldier in the district where it had started, almost three years before.

6

❖

THE GLORIOUS YEAR

Cromwell reached Cambridgeshire at the end of May, when the summer pastures of the Fens around Ely were starting to roll with grass pollen heads and the meres were coated with opening water lilies. He travelled in his own coach, as a sign of his importance, attended by the horse troops. As it rattled into Cambridge its arrival provoked an incident which illustrated the deep divisions in the town, as in all England: one onlooker commented that a dung cart would be a better vehicle for Oliver, and was promptly reported to a magistrate by two 'godly men'.[1] Cromwell set to work at his new assignment, roaming between Ely, Cambridge and Huntingdon and finding that, because of the long security of the area, the fortifications were indeed neglected and undermanned. He and the central committee of the Eastern Association wrote to the deputy lieutenants of its counties to mobilize their local soldiers to be ready to guard them, and the Committee of Both Kingdoms empowered him to dispose of them as he saw fit. They began to gather around him at Huntingdon, reputedly three thousand strong.[2]

Then the miracle occurred, in a rapid sequence of events. First, infuriated by the loss of Leicester, the elected government of London, the common council, petitioned Parliament on 4 June for a change of strategy. It requested the Houses to increase the size of the New Model Army, give Sir Thomas Fairfax freedom to lead it wherever he decided in order best to defeat the king and regain Leicester, and to continue Cromwell in service as commander of the Eastern Association.[3] As soon as this arrived, the Committee of Both Kingdoms was given complete freedom by Parliament to respond, and it obliged by giving Fairfax in turn the requested freedom of action, and recalling Vermuyden and his men to rejoin him. It then ordered the Eastern Association to allow Cromwell to dispose of its forces as he wished, and on 9 June told him to take all the horse and dragoons he had with him and all the musketeers for whom he could find horses, and ride to join the New Model Army.[4] Fairfax had been smarting to be allowed to go after the king, and his army was behind him in this.[5] As soon as the new orders from the committee arrived, they moved north-east into the Great Ouse Valley, carrying on down it for two days to get between the king and the Eastern Association, and await the return of Vermuyden's force.[6] Vermuyden was now approaching them, but was himself an unhappy man. As before, Londoners wanted a scapegoat for a military disaster, and many of them had blamed him for the fall of Leicester, holding that he should have intervened to prevent that, as the nearest parliamentarian commander to it.[7] Perhaps also he had personal reasons for wanting to leave England. At any rate, at this critical juncture Vermuyden resigned his commission and prepared to go abroad, and the man who had for a time seemed the best qualified one to command the New Model Army's horse division vanished from the scene.[8]

On 8 June, the day before Vermuyden delivered up his commission, Fairfax called a council of war, of all his senior officers, at his headquarters in the village of Sherington, among the summer meadows beside the Ouse. His cavalry outposts were starting to clash with those of the king, and it seemed likely now that a battle was imminent. The army still had nobody in overall charge of its large and complex horse division, somebody was urgently needed, and there was no sufficiently trusted and experienced commander eligible and available under the terms of the Self-Denying Ordinance. In these circumstances the council decided unanimously to write to Parliament asking it to appoint Cromwell to the position for such limited period of time as it chose. The letter was entrusted to the fiery Thomas Harrison, a religious independent and the major to Fleetwood's horse regiment, who had served under Oliver all the previous year and caused such offence to Scots and presbyterians by coming to London after Marston Moor and giving all credit for the victory to Cromwell's cavalry. All present at the council signed it.[9] It reached Westminster on the 10th, and the Commons decided rapidly to dispense with Oliver's attendance as a temporary measure, but without a set time limit, to act as lieutenant-general of horse in the New Model Army. The Lords did no more than agree to debate the matter; but the Commons' resolution was taken by Harrison as sufficient warrant for Oliver to act.[10] On the following day he galloped back with it, and Fairfax wrote at once to Cromwell to inform him, and to summon him immediately with all the horse and dragoons he could bring.[11] Back in London, the Lords silently acquiesced and no journalists questioned the move, while some enthusiastically hailed it.[12] Oliver had suddenly made the jump to commanding the horse division in Parliament's main, consolidated, field army, and done so under a commander who enthusiastically valued and supported him. If he were to retain the position for more than a month or two, however, he had rapidly to prove his worth in it.

NASEBY

At the time of his appointment, many people might have thought that Cromwell's tenure of his new position could indeed be brief, as he was joining what looked increasingly like a discredited army. The reputation of the royal one had soared after its storming of Leicester, while after all the care which had gone into its creation, the New Model had achieved nothing in its first two months except the relief of Taunton; and the detachment sent to effect that had ended up trapped inside the town, which was immediately put under siege again by Goring and the western royalist forces. Fairfax's men had ceased to be paid properly from London or supplied with sufficient provisions by the local parliamentarian administrators, and they were struggling to find food and having to take free quarter. They were also increasingly deserting, many being conscripts who had been impressed in the spring to supply the large shortfall of soldiers needed to bring the New Model up to its desired strength. Fairfax's secretary wrote defiantly and grumpily on 12 June that 'I am confident the Lord will go along with this despised army'.[13] Parliament did its best to remedy the situation, empowering Sir Thomas to seize men for soldiers from the counties along his route of march, and to commandeer horses without payment as soon as he entered territory currently held by the royalists. A month's pay was ordered for his men.

Parliament also urged the Scottish army to march south again, although with all available money going to the New Model it could only invite the Scots to take free quarter as they moved. This would hardly make them any more popular with English locals, and Parliament made desperate attempts to get extra taxation collected, and loans raised, to pay them. This time the earl of Leven obliged the appeals of his allies. It is likely he was persuaded that with the king apparently stuck in the Midlands there was no longer a likelihood of his army coming north, and that there was now a real chance of joining the New Model to bring Charles to battle, and so having the necessary strength. By the second week of June he was marching rapidly through Yorkshire. Meanwhile, Fairfax was striving to bring in reinforcements from the parliamentarian garrisons and local forces in the East Midlands, which with those of Vermuyden and Cromwell might swell the New Model to the greatest possible extent for a showdown with the king.[14] On 12 June he felt ready to start moving straight towards Charles, though heavy rain was making progress slow.[15]

For the previous two weeks, Charles himself, and his advisers, had been trying to agree a plan of action, because after their resounding success at Leicester they had become paralyzed by disagreements over strategy. Rupert still wanted to go north, fast, whereas other councillors urged that Oxford be relieved and the New Model Army defeated outside it, instead. The king failed to decide between them, and his army wandered around Warwickshire, Leicestershire and Northamptonshire while the arguments continued. When it was learned that the New Model had abandoned the siege of Oxford and was heading in the king's direction, Prince Rupert advised a retreat westwards to link up with reinforcements, above all Goring's three thousand horsemen, recalled from the west, and another detachment of 2,700 horse and foot returning from a Welsh campaign. His opponents called for an immediate attack on the New Model while the morale of the king's victorious men was still high and the opposing army was still freshly formed and unused to working together. As Fairfax advanced, the disputes continued, and the king still dithered.[16]

As soon as Cromwell received Sir Thomas's letter, he hurried west to join the New Model, through a brimming green countryside studded with the creamy saucers of elderflowers and the paler, shyer blooms of wild roses. He had taken all the mounted soldiers he had with him, which numbered between six and eight hundred. On the morning of 12 June he and his troopers found Fairfax to the north-west of Northampton, at the village of Guilsborough, holding a council of war. Oliver's appearance provoked great rejoicing, and the council decided to call the whole army together and advance on the king at once. Until the previous night, the royalist infantry had been encamped in makeshift huts on a high hill five miles away, and their cavalry flung out in a screen between that and the approaching enemy. Just before dawn that morning, Fairfax, riding out on a reconnaissance through a wet night, saw a glow on the hill and realized that the king's foot soldiers were burning their huts and preparing to march; which they proved to be doing north-east.[17]

This was indeed where the king was going, as on the previous night, having realized that the enemy was so close, he and his advisers had resolved to make for Newark with all speed. There they intended to draw more foot soldiers out of the town and its complex of outlying garrisons, to plug the holes left in the royal infantry by casualties sustained in the taking of Leicester and desertions by men anxious to get their loot from it home. Charles's foot were indeed now dangerously reduced. By evening they were quartered in and around the small town of Market Harborough, which

Rupert made his headquarters, while Charles was accommodated in a fine house just to the west. The horse units were spread out behind to the south, the rear guard being in the village of Naseby, which stood on a ridge providing good views in each direction.[18] Meanwhile drums and trumpets had called the New Model together and most of it marched six miles to the east of the royal army, preparing to swing round upon it. Cromwell now being in charge of the horse, it must have been he who sent out units to shadow and harass the royalists, including one under his protégé Ireton, which attacked those stationed at Naseby in the evening and took them completely by surprise, capturing a number of them.[19]

The king and his advisers had thought that the New Model was moving wide of them to protect the Eastern Association, and now realized that it was both dangerously close and intending to attack. An emergency council of war was called at once, to meet at Rupert's quarters in the middle of the night.[20] As the Julian calendar, on which England depended at the time, was by then ten days out of true alignment with the sun, the date, 13–14 June, was actually Midsummer Eve and Midsummer Day, the climax of the summer solstice and one of the shortest nights of the year. Had the sky been clear as the royalist advisers gathered, it would have been briefly covered with the season's constellations: Antares red-gold in the south, Capella sparking in a succession of rainbow colours in the north, and the summer triangle of Lyra, Vega and Altair burning ice-blue over-head. Even had it been overcast, the leaves of trees would still have stood out against the midnight blue of the northern horizon. When the council met, Rupert urged an avoidance of battle, and rapid retreat to safety and reinforcement, while some of the king's civilian councillors argued for immediate engagement of the New Model. Charles decided in favour of the latter.[21] All his life he was inclined – usually disastrously – to bold and dramatic courses of action, to resolve difficult situations once and for all. They all retired for a few hours of sleep, and at seven o'clock in the morning of 14 June the king's soldiers formed up and marched south to attack their pursuing enemies.[22]

It is possible to reconstruct the actions of the king and his advisers so vividly because the records allow. By contrast we do not know how Cromwell, Fairfax and their fellow senior officers spent that night, save that they probably got a longer sleep, in requisitioned beds in cottages and farmhouses. In the morning their army marched towards Naseby, to follow the king, sending more bodies of horse to harass his men and try to slow them down and bring them to battle. Instead, climbing one of the many ridges of the Northamptonshire uplands – which one of them aptly described as 'a place of little hills and vales' – they sighted their quarry coming towards them.[23] Both forces halted on separate ridges, a valley between them, in battle formation. That valley, however, was choked with undergrowth, and stretches of bog and standing water left by the recent rain, so that for either to launch an attack across it would have been suicidal. The New Model therefore moved west along the ridge, looking for a better way across, and Rupert led the royal army in the same direction parallel to it. Both found what they wanted after half a mile, just north of Naseby.[24]

The two armies were still on parallel ridges with a broad and shallow valley between them, but that was now drier, and so allowed of a rapid crossing. The ridge on which the New Model stood was mainly taken up with the large open fields which served the villagers of Naseby. The one on which most of the army stood was down to grass, which provided ideal cavalry terrain. Another was under corn, which could be trampled like that on the ridge above Marston Moor, and again then made for good fighting terrain. The only difficulty in the position was at its eastern end, where the ridge was steeper and narrower, and the slope in front rendered more hazardous by gorse bushes and a rabbit warren. This would cramp regiments formed up there and make it difficult for them to advance, but also power-fully favoured them if they stood on the defensive. The whole position was a mile across, and the midsummer morning sun was shining upon it.[25]

Neither army had a good sense of the other's numbers, or left a wholly reliable estimate of its own, but it is clear in retrospect that the king was outnumbered, perhaps seriously. Calculations at the time and in recent years have put the royal soldiers at anything between seven and twelve thousand men, and the New Model between twelve and seventeen thousand, with the discrepancy significant in both the foot and the horse divisions.[26] Around ten o'clock both of them deployed fully in battle order, Fairfax ordering the infantry and Cromwell the cavalry.[27] On the left flank of the army Cromwell placed five horse regiments and some of the troops he had just brought from the Eastern Association, under the overall control of Ireton whom he had now promoted to the office of Commissary-General, the second-in-command of the horse division of the army. To strengthen Ireton's position, Oliver made a further deployment. His command included the New Model's dragoon regiment, which had been given to a former London chandler and stoker, a fervently godly man called John Okey, who had previously served under Sir Arthur Hesilrig. Oliver found Okey in a meadow half a mile behind the rest of the army, distributing ammunition to his men, and ordered him to get them mounted and lead them immediately to cover Ireton's flank. There, stretching across the valley in front, and to the left hand, was a thick hedge at right angles to the two armies, which marked a parish boundary. Behind it was a small enclosure, in which Okey's men could put their horses while they loaded their guns and spread out along the hedge, which would give them cover as they poured fire into royalist cavalry moving past in front to attack Ireton's men.[28] It was an excellent use of ground.

Cromwell himself took charge of the opposite, right wing, the traditional post of honour for a cavalry general, with the nine foot regiments, under the immediate command of Philip Skippon, strung out according to custom between him and Ireton. Oliver arranged the right-wing horse units in three lines. The front one consisted of five bodies, many of the men in which had come from his own former regiment, and the line was commanded by its former lieutenant-colonel, his kinsman Edward Whalley. There were three bodies in the second line, and two in the rear, one of those consisting of the new troopers he had just brought from the Eastern Association. As the army was getting into position, another cavalry detachment arrived in the nick of time from Lincolnshire, being its local home guard, some of which would have been veterans who had once served under Willoughby. Cromwell divided this into two, to cover his right flank, one at the extreme end of the front line and the second at the extreme end of the rear one. Each unit was spaced to cover a gap between those in the line in front, according to custom, so that the whole division made a chequer-board pattern, and presented a solid mass to an enemy while leaving each individual body of horse room to manoeuvre before closing with the enemy.[29] Some of the New Model's soldiers distinguished themselves from their opponents by putting pieces of white paper or linen in their hats, while the royalists stuck bean stalks in theirs, obtained from a field along their route of march. Mostly, however, the two armies relied for recognition on their battle cries: 'God our strength' for the New Model and 'Queen Mary' for the king's men.[30]

The manner in which Fairfax and Cromwell ordered their army suggests strongly that they expected to be attacked first and were preparing the best possible defensive position. This supposition was entirely correct, because after his experience at Marston Moor, and trading on the hope that the New Model would indeed be a newly constructed and fragile entity, Prince Rupert had decided to launch the royal soldiers into the swiftest and hardest possible all-out assault on their opponents. The division entrusted with the task of breaking Cromwell's position consisted mainly of the Northern Horse, the former cavalry division of Newcastle's army. These were very experienced and capable men, who had achieved great things in the north, including the smashing of Fairfax's wing at Marston Moor. To reinforce them they had a body of the equally famed and formidable Newark horse. They were, however, faced with a nightmarish task. They needed to attack their objective up a steep slope, across the ground disordered by gorse and rabbit holes. Their chances of encountering their enemy in good order and with men and horses in the first flush of energy were thus badly reduced. Moreover, they were seriously outnumbered by Cromwell's horsemen, possibly by odds of two to one, and whereas their opponents were formed into a few large regiments, they were made up of the remnants of twenty to twenty-five, all now very weak, which would have reduced cohesion further.[31]

Cromwell watched the northerners struggling up the slope towards him, and unleashed Whalley's front line upon theirs at the moment when it would seem to strike with maximum impact. The two sides came together in close order, pistols crackling and swords swinging, and the royalists resisted bravely for a time until numbers told – perhaps with the arrival of Cromwell's second line – and they fell back to the rear of their infantry, and joined their horse reserve. The first and second of Cromwell's lines now formed one powerful body, while the rest of his wing made their way down through the gorse and warren to outflank the royalist horsemen for a concerted attack by the whole division, in which the king's troopers were finally routed and chased off.[32] One observer compared Cromwell's horsemen to 'a torrent driving all before them'.[33] Four bodies of them pursued the fleeing royalist horsemen to keep them on the run, moving in close order, while the rest remained on the field for further service.[34]

Once more, as at Marston Moor, Cromwell's cavalry wing had carried all before it; but just as at that earlier battle, bad things were happening elsewhere on the field. On the opposite side, the royalist right wing of horse, led by Rupert himself, had attacked as the left wing had done, and had easier work.[35] The slope up which it had to ride was gentler, it was traversing the pasture of the fallow field, and it seems both to have been slightly larger than the other wing and faced slightly fewer opponents. Okey's dragoons, firing from the flanking hedge, wounded many of the horsemen as they surged forward but failed to halt them; and they slammed into Ireton's wing and wrecked it. Accounts differ as to whether they drove all of its units off the field or only some, but they broke through it and dispersed it, and Ireton was wounded and captured. In the centre of the field the king's infantry, despite its inferiority in numbers, attacked with such ferocity that it drove the first line of the New Model foot back onto the second. Skippon, trying to rally his men, was badly injured by a shot through his side. Within a short space of time, Cromwell was the only one of Fairfax's three subordinate generals left both unhurt and in action.

Everywhere, however, the numerical weakness of the royalists told against them. Their victorious horsemen on their right wing lacked the extra units to attack the flank of the New Model's infantry, their full power being needed to drive Ireton's troopers off the field. In the centre the progress of the royal foot soldiers was halted as soon as the first line of their opponents was steadied against the second, and they were fighting a larger force. In this situation, they suddenly found themselves bereft of cavalry support. On their left their horsemen had been driven off, and on their right, they had vanished over the ridge, keeping Ireton's men on the run. Cromwell's wing, by contrast, possessed both the additional strength and the leadership to turn most of its bodies of horse upon the left flank and rear of the king's infantry. In front that was counter-attacked by the consolidated mass of the New Model foot regiments and Okey's dragoons mounted and charged into its now exposed right flank, while some of Ireton's horse regiments were now rallying and returning. It was effectively surrounded, and began to surrender unit by unit. By the time that the victorious royalist troopers of the right wing returned to the field, the battle was lost. They joined the king back on the ridge from which they had launched their attack, and retreated towards Leicester, abandoning the remnants of the infantry, and the artillery and baggage train. Most of the cavalry, from both wings, got away, but all the rest of the royal army, the core of the king's war effort, had been destroyed, in just two hours.[36]

Although the broad outline of these events has always been clear, there remain some puzzles. One is what exactly Cromwell did during the battle, and how he co-operated with Fairfax. It must be presumed that he directed most if not all of the movements of his cavalry wing, but none of the accounts show him in action doing this, and he does not seem to have led a charge himself: for the first time he appears to have held back from the hand-to-hand fighting and overseen and orchestrated operations instead. By contrast, there are pen-portraits of Fairfax in action, both directing the battle and engaging in personal combat against royalist units. One account states that he charged with Cromwell's wing and lost his helmet in the fighting, and that both men then took some cavalry over to the left wing to restore the situation there after Ireton's defeat.[37] Another agreed that Fairfax lost his helmet, and rode around his army bareheaded.[38] Another had him leading an attack on a foot regiment, and fighting his way into the core of it, causing its collapse.[39]

Another unresolved question is whether Prince Rupert, who was responsible for the royalist battle plan, had intended anything more sophisticated than an attack all along the line in the hope that the enemy would break.[40] More than a quarter of a century later, a defence of his record blamed the defeat on the commander of the Northern Horse, Sir Marmaduke Langdale, claiming that he should have stood on the defensive until Rupert returned from chasing off Ireton's cavalry and joined him in facing Cromwell. Instead, it was asserted, Langdale had attacked at once and across appalling ground against impossible odds.[41] Nobody, however, alleged this earlier, even in the bitter recriminations among royalist commanders which followed the disaster. It looks as if Rupert was, long afterward, setting up Langdale to play the part of scapegoat in which Byron was being cast in explaining the defeat at Marston Moor; and by that time Langdale, like Byron, was conveniently dead. Another puzzle is why the royalist reserves were so ineffectual. The battle plan for the king's army provided for a force to be held back at the rear and deployed wherever there was decisive need for reinforcement in the course of the action. It consisted of Rupert's own foot regiment of eight hundred men and the king's horse guards, numbering five hundred, in addition to Charles's foot guards, probably a few hundred more.[42] These could have played a vital role, and had they been launched upon Cromwell's men, in particular, when they were forcing back Langdale's, the outcome of the battle might have been different. Nothing, however, is heard of this, and Rupert's foot soldiers and the king's foot guards were surrounded and overwhelmed with the rest of the royal infantry, while the horse guards ran with the king.

Instead, there was a story put about that King Charles himself had been leading his own guards to charge Cromwell's troopers and restore the royalist position on the left, but was diverted because a Scottish earl, afraid that his monarch was endangering his life, seized the king's bridle and dragged his horse aside, throwing the whole company into fatal confusion. The source who quoted this tale, the king's secretary Sir Edward Walker, himself however could not vouch for the truth of it, and had the designated reserves played their part, there should have been no need for Charles to try impulsively to lead in his guards himself in a panic measure. Somehow there was a lack of co-ordinated leadership in the royal army which left nobody delegated to lead the force held back to await a crisis, when the moment of that crisis came.[43]

The king's army, plainly enough, should never have fought at Naseby: Rupert had been correct about that, and the need for reinforcements. Had Goring's three thousand horsemen, and the seven hundred from Wales, and the two thousand foot coming from Wales with them, been with Charles, he could have fought the New Model Army with a fair chance of success. Had Goring's troopers alone been with Langdale on the left wing at Naseby instead of far away in the west, then Cromwell's wing would have been outnumbered, by a first-class body of cavalry. On top of this fundamental weakness in numbers, however, the king's soldiers operated a battle plan which was faulty both in conception and execution. It made the left wing incapable of performing the role allotted to it, and provided a reserve which never seems to have been deployed. Rupert's wing, and the royal foot soldiers in the centre, performed superbly, punching far above their weight, but this could not offset the basic flaws in their position. Nonetheless, it must also be said that the untried New Model Army also functioned very well, and in some cases magnificently. Ireton's wing, which contained some of the best of the Eastern Association horse such as Fleetwood's regiment, may have crumbled, but the foot units rallied well after the initial shock of the enemy attack. Above all, Cromwell's cavalry wing played its part to perfection, using its undoubted superiority in numbers to best effect. Its operation of a flawless set of manoeuvres must, as historical tradition has long held, owe a lot to Cromwell himself. Finally, everybody agreed that

Fairfax had been a model commander-in-chief, ordering and encouraging his army with exemplary skill and charisma.

Having destroyed the foot division of the king's field force, Cromwell now led his cavalry in an attempt to inflict further damage on the fleeing royalist horsemen, and at best to capture the king himself, Rupert and other senior officers. He forbade his men to dismount and plunder, on pain of death, which disgruntled many of the troopers because it denied them the jackpot of loot after a successful battle: the enemy baggage train.[44] That was left to the New Model foot soldiers, who not only made very rich profits (as the royalist baggage included much of the plunder from Leicester) but committed the worst atrocities of the war upon the female camp-followers of the king's men, killing over a hundred and disfiguring many more by cutting off their noses and slicing open their cheeks.[45] The pursuing cavalry did not take any notable prisoners, but it killed or captured many stragglers, until two miles from Leicester the royalist horsemen drew together and formed a compact mass to face and halt their tormenters, and cover the retreat of their commanders into the town.[46] The ledger of victory was becoming clear. The slaughter had been much less than at Marston Moor because of a greater willingness of the defeated infantry to surrender and of the victors to accept this. There were six to seven hundred royalist dead on the field (and one to two hundred parliamentarians), and around three hundred more killed on the flight to Leicester, but four to five thousand prisoners: probably between a third and a half of the king's army. The New Model also got a haul of five to eight thousand weapons, including the entire royal train of siege and field artillery.[47] One final factor completed the bliss of the New Model soldiery: they found a huge haul of bread and cheese in the royalist train, their own supplies having failed.[48]

The next objective of the army was clear, as it had been included in the instructions from Parliament and the Committee of Both Kingdoms when it was sent after the king: to retake Leicester, and so wipe out the shame of the loss of it two weeks before. On 17 June the army summoned the town to surrender, preparing to turn on it the same royal siege guns which had blasted holes in its walls before. The royalist governor, abandoned by the king and Rupert, who had fled on westward with their cavalry, immediately asked for terms. On the next day he marched out with his men, leaving the New Model their two thousand weapons and five hundred horses. As this happened, the joy of the occasion was completed by the arrival of a convoy of cash from London, through what was now safe parliamentarian territory, which allowed the army to be mustered and paid for the first time in months.[49]

The unity of the New Model Army meant that the victory at Naseby was not followed by a contest for the credit, between different factions of the victors, of the sort which had succeeded Marston Moor. Virtually all of the accounts sent to Parliament or published as tracts in the subsequent week applauded Cromwell and Fairfax together, sometimes adding the wounded Skippon or speaking generally in praise of all the commanders.[50] One pamphlet account took the opportunity to trumpet the manner in which Cromwell's role had vindicated him from all previous aspersions: 'see, sir, how God honours those who honour him, [de]spite the malice of enemies'.[51] This time, moreover, Cromwell chose to characterize the battle himself, in a formal letter sent to the House of Commons on the following day. It had all the hallmarks of his previous accounts of his military actions. There was a strong implication that the royalists had outnumbered the New Model, which enabled him to enlarge on the manner in which the result manifested the glory and favour of God Almighty, whom Oliver treated, as usual, as the true author of victory. He tended, again as usual, to use the plural form, 'we', throughout, which both modestly subsumed his own role in a collective one but also spared him the need to praise fellow commanders; though this time he did briefly acknowledge Fairfax's good performance.[52]

Fairfax's own despatch to the Commons, sent with an officer instructed to provide a full verbal account of the battle, affords an interesting contrast. There is much less of God in it, even while he did request the prescription of a day of thanksgiving throughout Parliament's territory which would formally express gratitude to the Almighty (and also bring home the magnitude of the achievement to every parish). Instead Sir Thomas devoted space to praising various of his officers, including the wounded Skippon and Ireton, for the courage and resolution they had shown.[53] He also avoided attempting to make any political or religious capital out of the victory; and this again contrasts markedly with Cromwell who now took Naseby as an encouragement to advance the cause of independency, even as he had taken Marston Moor to be. Sir Thomas informed the Commons that 'he who ventures his life for the liberty of his country, I wish he trust God for the liberty of his conscience, and you for the liberty he fights for'. It was delicately ambiguous, hinting that Parliament should allow freedom to a wide latitude to differing religious opinions upon the Puritan spectrum, while seeming to leave the matter up to God. What was hardly ambiguous in the statement was its reminder that men with that wide range of opinions were fighting loyally for Parliament's cause.[54]

The Commons certainly did not take collective offence at it, concentrating instead on the very obvious fact that almost immediately after Cromwell had been appointed to take charge of the New Model's cavalry, that cavalry had been the major force in winning the decisive victory over the king's own army which had eluded Parliament for three years. On 16 June, on hearing the news of Naseby, the House decided after a long debate that Oliver should be continued in that command as long as Parliament saw fit; but once more the Lords, still resentful of his attack on one of their number, and more religiously conservative, jibbed. The most that they would offer, after two days of argument, was that Cromwell be continued for a further three months, and the Commons did not make a fight of the matter. After all, their decision to appoint him as lieutenant-general a week before had not been given the Lords' concurrence, whereas now it would be confirmed; and it would always be possible to grant him further extensions. The Commons also ordered that ten thousand pounds be allocated to provide for all the needs of his troopers, with six hundred saddles and twelve hundred pistols sent to them immediately. A week later, they added a thousand horses and a further large consignment of saddles, pistols and body armour to the list.[55]

Oliver's feelings on receiving this news are not recorded. He must have felt as if God had indeed been good to him, in plucking him in one week from the verge of retirement to a new and glorious command in which he had already achieved sensational results. A possible indefinite future as a general had now been opened up for him. On the other hand, the Almighty remained capricious, giving his new position an insecurity which no other officer of the New Model had to endure, and which ensured that he would be removed as soon as he ceased to shine in it.

RETURN TO THE WEST[56]

It is clear enough that Cromwell's religion was one of the key aspects of his personal make-up and also of his national reputation. In view of this, we know strangely little about it for most of the Civil War, the records saying virtually nothing about the services he attended, the clergymen whom he favoured, or his conversations about the subject. This is also true for the men serving alongside and under him; and it is dangerous, however tempting, to imagine either the personal or communal religious life of him and them at this time.[57] There is an account provided of the religious complexion of the army and of Cromwell's place in it, by a prominent presbyterian minister called Richard Baxter. He apparently had a history with Cromwell already, in that he had known some of the men in Oliver's own horse regiment, and allegedly been invited to serve it as chaplain; and refused the position, because he had disapproved of the independency to which he already saw it as inclining.[58] Baxter's memories were recorded decades later, and the accuracy of their details cannot be confirmed from any corroborating evidence.[59] Nonetheless, the abiding impression left on him by his time in the New Model Army is still significant.

According to his account, Baxter visited the army at Leicester in order to see old friends now in it, as he was living nearby at Coventry. He rapidly realized that many of its soldiers, of all ranks, shared his own wish for a conservative church settlement, but that it was dominated and led by independents (whom Baxter called sectaries) favoured by Cromwell. Those were concentrated in Fairfax's and Whalley's horse regiments (formed out of Cromwell's own) and Nathaniel Rich's, and among the new officers in the rest of the New Model. They regarded the king as a tyrant and enemy and the nobility as oppressors, were determined to abolish the bishops and seek a wide freedom of religious belief, and were very hostile to the Scots. When Baxter arrived, Cromwell greeted him coldly and rebuked him for his original refusal to serve his regiment, but Whalley was friendly to him, and he and one of his more orthodox officers invited the minister to join their regiment as chaplain instead: Baxter thought that Whalley himself was inclined to presbyterianism but put his beliefs behind his loyalty to Cromwell. Baxter accepted the post, in which he argued hard against any who wanted to separate from the national Church, and the doctrines and discipline it prescribed; but he achieved little and was excluded from officer's meetings. He claimed to have been especially horrified – and hated – by the troop led by Whalley's major, Christopher Bethell, in which many men cried up the belief that humans could find salvation through their own free will (against the mainstream Puritan doctrine that God had predestined individuals to salvation or damnation, ultimately derived from the Continental reformer John Calvin). They also disputed the authorized translation of the Bible and condemned all formal ministry and the power of magistrates over religion. That made them the classic kind of sectary demonized by the orthodox, Anabaptists.[60]

At any rate, the newly recruited and unhappy Baxter was soon marching south and west with the remainder of the army. Midsummer was passing, and the campaigning season reaching its zenith, with three warm or mild months still to run; and in 1645, in contrast to 1644, not a day of them was to be wasted, and a great victory was to be properly followed up. After a few days' rest at Leicester, the New Model, including Cromwell, headed through the South Midlands towards the upper Thames Valley, with a subsequent choice of route before it. It could carry on southward, and then swing west, to relieve Taunton which was being slowly starved towards surrender by Goring and the western royalist army – the king's last one – with part of the New Model still trapped inside the town after relieving it. Alternatively, it could move on west through Gloucester to attack the king again, as he had retreated to South Wales with his cavalry in an attempt to raise a new body of foot soldiers and rebuild his own army. By 26 June the New Model was crossing the Thames at Lechlade, far west of Oxford, and the next day got to the top of White Horse Vale. A royalist garrison occupied the parish church of the little hilltop town of Highworth, which made easy prey, as the New Model's siege artillery rapidly pounded it into surrender: the huge crater left by one cannonball is still visible to the left of the main door. On the 29th the army rested at Marlborough, up amid the chalk hills, and there its course was determined.[61]

On the 26th the Commons had decided to recommend that Fairfax relieve Taunton, because the Scottish army had now expressed its willingness to close in on the king. The MPs had also ordered that four thousand men be drafted to fill up the New Model, and that Sir Thomas be empowered to seize more along his way. These he needed, because his foot soldiers were already reduced to around seven to eight thousand. The rigours of service accounted for much of this, but also the tendency of the soldiers to desert in order to get their loot home, a factor which affected Cromwell's horsemen even more badly.[62] After the arrival of the money from London, the army was generally able to pay for its quarters on the march, but some of the horse units did not, and they ate up the growing grass in fields again, leaving the owners bereft of their hay crop.[63] Fairfax and his officers chose to accept the advice to relieve Taunton, and moved on deeper into Wiltshire at the opening of July. The army held a rendezvous at the prehistoric monument of Stonehenge, and then marched on in a column towards Dorset, over the vast chalk saucer of Salisbury Plain, an expanse of open pasture and heathland, at the opening of a heatwave.[64] It was the season in this land of blue and yellow flowers and small blue butterflies. The toiling

271

soldiers would also probably have seen droves of the most notable inhabitants of the plain at the time: the largest flightless birds to have survived in Britain into modern times, the yellowish-brown and be-whiskered bustards, big and tasty as turkeys (which is why they did not survive much longer). The minds of the commanders were, however, by this time fixed on a different species of local life: the Clubmen.

These were associations of country people, led by their parish officials, ministers and lesser gentry, who had taken up arms to protect their property against plundering soldiers on both sides. Their immediate concern was to control the behaviour of rival local garrisons, keeping them from fighting and ensuring that the money levied to support them was done so in a regular and orderly fashion. They also, however, intended to deal with invading soldiers from elsewhere, and had a wider concern to induce king and Parliament to make peace. They had appeared in various parts of southern England and the Welsh Marches since the beginning of the year, but were especially strong and well organized in Wiltshire, Dorset and Somerset.[65] There were three reasons why they concerned Fairfax and Cromwell. One was the sheer size of their potential numbers, running into many thousands. Even if their training and equipment were inferior enough to make them a less formidable prospect than their manpower suggested, the second reason now weighed in: that they could be especially damaging if they cut the lengthening supply lines between the New Model and London as the army marched further west. The third reason was that in their newly weakened position, the royalists, from the king downwards to his local commanders, were making special efforts to woo the Clubmen, expressing sympathy for both their situation and their ideals.[66]

The first contact of the New Model's soldiers with the movement came on 1 July when some of them visited Salisbury and found the townspeople identifying with it, wearing white ribbons in their hats as a sign of neutrality and treating their visitors coldly. On the next day, Parliament's local commander in the west, Edward Massey, met Fairfax and Cromwell with his soldiers and reported that he had just fought his way through a Clubman force. Two days later, the army sweated its way into Dorchester, to be met by the governor of Weymouth who warned that the local Clubmen were preventing the county's parliamentarian garrisons from collecting money or food. News then arrived that the garrison of Lyme had got into a fight with some Clubmen. On entering Dorset the New Model took two of their captains prisoner and released them on a promise to disarm and go home. Now, however, one of the Clubmen leaders arrived with a petition for peace to Parliament and asked for a pass to take it to Westminster: Fairfax, Cromwell and their fellows disliked this but thought it wise to comply. Then four more Clubmen leaders came in with the same request, and on behalf of his army Sir Thomas replied that he would prevent plunder but could not work for a ceasefire with the royalists. He wrote to the Committee of Both Kingdoms appealing for more money to keep his soldiers from looting, and reinforcements to assist the suppression of Clubmen bands.[67]

With that, the matter had to be shelved for the time being. The news now came in that Goring had raised the blockade of Taunton and was moving his army eastward through Somerset. The objective of the New Model now became to intercept and destroy it. On 5 July, hot and tired, it marched down from the chalk hills into the mid-Somerset lowlands, a country of many rivers, marshes, small lanes and enclosed fields. It was a notoriously difficult terrain over which to move armed forces, especially to catch and engage a nimble opponent. This was where Cromwell had been halted in the spring, and by the same dangerous adversary who faced him now, George Goring. The circumstances now, however, were completely different. Then, Cromwell and Waller had commanded a body of men only around equal to the royalist's, and composed almost wholly of horse and dragoons, while Goring also had foot. Now Cromwell and Fairfax had a much bigger army, especially superior in foot and of generally higher quality. They also had a massive advantage in morale. Naseby had changed everything. It had ensured that ever after, the king was going to be on the defensive and his forces inferior in numbers to their assailants. For the great majority of the population who wanted an end to the war above anything else, it seemed that the balance had now tipped decisively in Parliament's favour, and the swiftest and surest way to stop the fighting would increasingly be to back it. For the royalists, the New Model not only had numbers on its side but the huge prestige of Naseby, and nowhere dared they now face it in a formal pitched battle. All that they could do was to try to buy time, avoiding a straight fight and slowing it down and trying to hold territory, in the hope that new recruits would eventually be found to rebuild their numbers. This was the strategy that was now forced upon Goring. In late June his army had been reckoned by the leaders of the West Country royalist administration at around 5,000 horse and 5,000 foot.[68] This was not far short of the probable numbers of the New Model by this time, and if handled well it might well reduce the latter to a frustrating game of attrition in that cluttered landscape. Goring's men, however, would always be on the defensive, and always aware of facing a superior and hitherto victorious foe bent on their destruction; and that was not a predicament likely to bring out the best in soldiers who were not fighting to save homes and families.

Goring's main line of defence was the River Yeo, which was conveniently long and deep, and ran straight across the path of the New Model. On 7 July Cromwell and Fairfax took a party to find a crossing, but found all the bridges and fords guarded by the royalist army. Horse units from the two armies skirmished in the water meadows along the river. The weakness in Goring's position, however, was that the Yeo was *too* long for him to block every way over it, against an enemy with the numbers to pin down his men at the crossings which they held, while probing ever further upriver for an unguarded one. This is what Fairfax's council of war decided to do, and by the end of the day some of their soldiers had found a bridge at Yeovil which had been broken and then left unwatched. They repaired it and crossed, and the next morning, realizing that his flank was turned, Goring pulled back his whole army from the river and the New Model poured across it. Fairfax heard that his enemy was immediately sending a strong party of horse towards Taunton, apparently hoping to catch the town by surprise. He immediately despatched Edward Massey, with a larger brigade of horse and dragoons, to intercept it. On the next day, Massey caught the royalist force completely by surprise as it rested in a pasture, routing it and killing or capturing three hundred troopers. By now the New Model was marching westward down the valley of the Yeo, towards the small town of Langport, where Goring had established his new headquarters.[69] It stood on a hill above where the river joined another, the Isle, to make a bigger one, the Parrett, which flowed down through the large town of Bridgwater.

On the morning of 10 July the royalist general was pulling out of Langport as part of a change of strategy. With the New Model across the Yeo, and his attempt to seize Taunton foiled and his horse division reduced, Goring decided to retire to the apparent safety of Bridgwater, which had been fortified and garrisoned, and review his options. He accordingly sent off his baggage and artillery trains first with his infantry following, and despatched a rear guard to the far side of Langport to cover his retreat. The New Model was divided at this point, as Fairfax and Cromwell had sent Ireton's horse regiment and most of Okey's dragoons with Massey, and a foot brigade and more horse to reinforce him; and these were still on the wrong side of the Parrett. They still, however, had most of their cavalry and eight whole foot regiments and parts of three more: quite enough to take on Goring. A council of war was debating whether to attack him at once when his rear guard appeared, going into position on the New Model's side of Langport. Ironically, this precipitated a decision to launch an assault, on the grounds that the royalists themselves could be intending an attack.

Between the two forces lay a small valley, formed by a muddy stream called the Wagg Rhyne, which ran down to the Yeo. That stream was hardly an obstacle in itself, but it could only be approached by a narrow lane between hedged fields which led to a ford that only four horses abreast could cross at a time, after which the lane went uphill through a large fallow field, under pasture, in front of Langport. The weather was still hot and dry, the lane dusty. Goring tried to make best use of the ground, filling the hedges with musketeers and putting a body of cavalry and set of field guns onto the top of the fallow field. The plan was that the muskets and artillery would riddle an attacking force with shot as it came up the lane and the horsemen would charge it as it emerged, disordered, into the field. This scheme underestimated the speed, determination and firepower of the New Model. Fairfax drew his soldiers up on a ridge on the far side of the valley from Langport, which gave them a good view of the prospective battlefield between, and around noon trained his heavy guns on the royalist troopers and artillery in the field at the top of the far slope. A relentless bombardment forced the gunners to retire altogether and the horsemen to recoil in disorder. Then one and a half thousand musketeers drove their royalist counterparts back beyond the stream and into flight, opening the way for a charge across the ford by the horse.

Cromwell gave that task to the regiments of his relatives Whalley and Desborough, which had been formed out of his old one. He put the spearhead of it, the post of greatest honour, under the command of Christopher Bethell, whose troopers were giving Richard Baxter so much heartache. Baxter himself was watching them from the ridge where the army's senior officers were gathered, and so was somebody of whose religious policies he must have disapproved just as much, Cromwell's former protégé John Lilburne, who had turned up to ask Oliver for another favour. His disillusion with military life after his experience of service under the earl of Manchester had led him to return to a civilian existence, and now he was short of money, and needed a letter from his powerful friend asking that Parliament grant him the compensation it had discussed giving to him for his former sufferings at the hands of the royal government.

Bethell's men careered across the ford and uphill at full pelt into the enemy horsemen, breaking two bodies of them. A counter-charge drove back Bethell to the stream in turn, but by then Desborough's men were across and reinforcing him, the musketeers pouring fire into Goring's troopers and the rest of the New Model advancing from the ridge, and the royalists turned and fled. Next to Baxter, another cavalry officer with whose religious views the minister would have been uncomfortable, Thomas

Harrison, broke into rapturous praise of the Almighty at the sight. Cromwell and Fairfax agreed that it was one of the best cavalry actions they had ever witnessed. The retreating royalists set fire to Langport to stall pursuit, and Cromwell led a body of troopers along the burning main street to encourage the others to get through. The parliamentarians broke out of the town and found the retreating royalist foot in a large summer pasture on the far side of the Langport ridge, down among the marshes known as the Somerset Levels. Cromwell would have immediately recognized them as a miniature of his familiar Fens, a flat land mostly covered in floods in winter and lush grass in summer, veined everywhere with ditches that held water even in the dry season, and studded with pools. Across this landscape the royalist army broke and ran when it saw the strength of the enemy coming at it, and was chased almost as far as Bridgwater. Many of its horses fell into the ditches and were captured. Cromwell himself led the pursuit of a body of infantry towing two field guns, and captured the guns and most of the men; and he still found time that day to write Lilburne his letter. Parliamentarian sources claimed between nine hundred and two thousand prisoners, and the total defeat of the king's only remaining army, and Parliament itself decreed another day of national thanksgiving.[70]

They were not far wrong. Goring himself reported to the king that he had actually lost only just over three hundred men killed or captured, but the remainder were demoralized and fearful and the local Clubmen, seeing them defeated, were turning on them. Most of the western cavalry in his army had deserted, leaving him with only 2,500 horse and between three and four thousand foot, with which he could not face the New Model. Rather than be trapped in Bridgwater, he left a thousand of his foot soldiers to reinforce the town and fled west precipitately with his remaining men to Devon in the hope of picking up reinforcements from the south-west.[71] The partnership of Fairfax and Cromwell had succeeded in crippling the two remaining royalist armies within four weeks. The published accounts of the battle gave full credit to them both for this second victory, and also to Bethell and Desborough. Harrison was favoured by Fairfax by being ordered to carry news of the battle to the House of Commons, which rewarded him with the gift of two splendid horses, and Bethell with two hundred pounds.[72] Lilburne was less lucky. He claimed to have returned to Westminster not only with Cromwell's recommendation for his bid for arrears of pay, but more letters to MPs with accounts of the action; but his presbyterian enemies got him imprisoned on a charge of insulting the Speaker of the Commons.[73] Cromwell sent his own report on the battle, which was published as a tract. As usual, he gave a strong impression that the royalists had been more numerous, and he made sure that readers knew that he had given the directions for the successful cavalry charges across the brook while emphasizing repeatedly that God had decreed and decided the result.[74]

The New Model now quartered in the settlements of the Somerset Levels, and Fairfax immediately used the victory to get tougher with the Clubmen. When the leader who had earlier been allowed to take a petition to Parliament reappeared to demand punishment of the garrison at Lyme for fighting some of his men, and compensation, Sir Thomas arrested him. Those from the area around Langport and Bridgwater rose in great numbers on the day after the battle, in arms, and flying sheets and aprons from poles to provide the white banners which signified a yearning for peace. Fairfax and Cromwell marched up to them to receive their petitions for it and promise that the New Model's soldiers would pay for all provisions taken, and were cheered and given a salute of musket fire. In reality, the money provided at Leicester had run out, and the horse been given none for three weeks; so the promise would be hard to keep unless another convoy of cash arrived.

On the next day the two commanders went to look at Bridgwater and decide whether to besiege it. Cromwell had already made a speech at the head of the army about the need to cut communications with it along the river, and a horse party had been sent to do that. It was a tempting prize, containing Goring's siege train and baggage and strategically sited, but it also had many soldiers inside, was mostly surrounded by cannon-proof earthworks, and lay in a level valley. The Parrett flowed through the middle of the town, and water from the river had been diverted into the ditches outside the earthworks, to create moats thirty feet across, which were swelled twice daily by the incoming tide; and the tidal race in this part of the Bristol Channel is one of the fastest and highest in the world. Indeed, the two generals were struck by it on 13 July when they went onto the river in a boat to look at the town's waterside defences and were almost over-turned and drowned. They decided to put the question of an attack on Bridgwater to a council of war, which sat on two consecutive days and decided that it was equally dangerous either to leave it in the army's rear and follow Goring, or to settle down to a regular siege and give him time to rebuild his army. The only solution was the most difficult and dangerous course: to try to take the place by storm.[75]

During the following four days the army slowly surrounded Bridgwater, glad of the break in forced marches after having covered so much mileage so fast since June. An innovative technology was devised to overcome the problem of the water defences, of constructing wooden bridges between 30 and 40 feet long, which could be brought up to the moats on carts and laid across them. Morale was greatly raised by the arrival of the hoped-for money from London, enabling everybody to be paid. The day before the attack was a Sunday, and the soldiers were treated to sermons in morning and afternoon: the former by an independent minister and the latter by a presbyterian.[76] The former was a rising star among the more radical English clergy, a preacher returned from New England – the congregations of which provided the clearest model for a federated Church of independent units – called Hugh Peters. The listening men would have seen a fervently animated man in early middle age, with an unruly bob of hair, a round face and a pencil-line moustache.[77] Towards evening the army was drawn up for a final fierce exhortation by Peters, after which the soldiers went to their posts as night fell. At two o'clock in the morning, when the tide was low, three guns were fired as the signal for them to fall on both sides of the town. The attack on the western part, led by Massey, was intended as a diversion, and it was on the east that Fairfax and Cromwell were stationed and the serious action was intended.

For a moment it all seemed to go wrong. On the west side Massey's men did not assault the town as planned, while on the east only one of the mobile bridges worked, and some of the storming parties – made up of volunteers – were obliged to wade the moat. What saved them was that the defences were not yet complete on that side, and for a space the moat was the only protection. Bereft of anything behind which to shelter, some of the defenders there, inexperienced Welsh conscripts just sent over by the king, shot wildly over the heads of the enemy and then threw down their arms. The attackers seized their artillery pieces and turned them on the remaining royalists. The gate to the defences was captured and its drawbridge let down so that a party of horse could charge into the town. The rest of the defenders there now surrendered and the eastern half of Bridgwater was taken. The governor, however, pulled up the central section of the bridge across the Parrett, which connected the east and west parts of the town. He then ruthlessly fired grenades and red-hot slugs of lead into the eastern section and set it on fire. The following night, the commanders decided to try a diversion on the east and launch a proper attack on the west, but there Massey's men, lacking the resolution of the New Model, again failed to move. On the following after-noon, Fairfax allowed the governor to send out the women and children from his remnant of the town, and then copied the man's own tactic by firing explosive shells and heated slugs into that remnant so it began to burn. This was too much for the defenders, and they forced the governor to capitulate. What was left of Bridgwater was granted immunity from plunder, but the near two thousand soldiers who had been in it were all kept prisoner, and lost their weapons, horses, ammunition and personal possessions. Goring's artillery and his army's baggage were added to the spoil, and the sale of the goods taken was enough to award a five-shilling bonus to each man in the storming parties. Once again, Fairfax favoured a leading independent when sending his victory despatch to the Commons, for he chose Hugh Peters, whom the MPs rewarded with a hundred pounds.[78]

The fall of Bridgwater on 23 July was as great a victory as that at Langport. The New Model had driven a wedge through the West Country, as far as the sea, and split the royalists at Bristol, and the king on the far side of the channel, from Goring and those in the south-west. Moreover, its taking of such an apparently strong town, as its third striking achievement in a row, convinced many even formerly loyal royalists that their cause was lost. The South Welsh gentry turned on King Charles, refused to obey him any longer, and drove him and his cavalry out of their region, leaving them to wander around the Midlands and Yorkshire for a month.[79] In Devon, Goring's remaining foot soldiers mostly deserted, and he had neither money nor realistic prospects of victory and loot to entice replacements.[80] The gaining of the town had prevented either of the king's two last armies, both of which the New Model had just wrecked, from being rebuilt. As long as Cromwell, Fairfax and their fellows did not now make any mistakes, and unless the king could find any new sources of support, the war was won, and what remained would be an extended process of mopping up.

AUTUMN OF SIEGES

Immediately after taking Bridgwater, Fairfax himself had wanted to march west at once and destroy the remainder of Goring's army.[81] The majority of his officers were less keen on this. After so much rapid action, the army needed to be recruited and resupplied to bring it up to full strength, and there was a great risk in going into the south-western peninsula with a weakened force and powerful royalist fortresses left in its rear. Bristol in particular had a concentration of troops which could seriously menace the New Model from behind, and the king's garrisons in Wiltshire and Hampshire might cut the vital supply lines from London; as might the Clubmen. On 25 July, therefore, a council of war resolved to clear those communications before going any further west. The first target was to be Bath, which seemed an easy one and would handsomely enlarge the territory that the army controlled. On the 28th the New Model reached Wells, in another heatwave, and Nathaniel Rich was sent ahead the next day with a party to summon Bath to surrender and probe its defences. He did better than that, as there were fewer than two hundred soldiers defending the city and they had no more stomach for a fight than the Welshmen at Bridgwater. When Okey's dragoons stormed the bridge over the River Avon and set fire to the gate at its end, the governor immediately gave up on condition that he and his officers could depart to Bristol.[82]

When this good news came, the New Model was advancing on Bath across the bare limestone ridge of the Mendip Hills, pockmarked with lead workings. On receiving it, the army immediately turned south-east towards its next prey, the powerful castle of the medieval bishops of Salisbury at Sherborne on the northern edge of the Dorset chalk hills. It had long held an especially active and troublesome royalist garrison, and while nobody expected that to give in easily, to take it would clear a useful corridor between the West Country and London. Pushing across the south Somerset pasturelands again, the roadside grass now the golden hue of late summer, Fairfax reached the castle with his advance guard on 1 August. There he was back in the territory of the most numerous, highly organized and hostile of the Clubman associations, and word reached him that their leaders from across the region were to meet on the following day at Shaftesbury, the next town to the east along the edge of the hills. He decided to seize them, and so behead their whole organization, and he and Cromwell sent Fleetwood with a thousand horsemen to do the job. He came back with fifty prisoners, but that action only provoked a mass rising of the Clubmen on the next day, with the design of staging a rescue. The leaders of the New Model resolved that this was the time to attack and crush them, and Cromwell was chosen as the one with the necessary experience, energy and ruthlessness for the job.

On 4 August he set out with a strong force, making his way through the hills towards Shaftesbury. This was now the land of the High Chalk, of steep-sided hills divided by deep wooded valleys, and he was making his way along one of the latter when he saw flags waving from the top of a crest on one side, above the trees. He sent an officer to ask the business of the countrymen gathered under them, and was answered with a deputation demanding to know why the men at Shaftesbury had been taken. He replied that they had held illegal meetings, and now took the initiative, boldly going up the hill with the Clubman deputation and an escort of his soldiers. There he told the armed mass in front of him that if they returned to their homes, he would personally protect them against plunder and molestation, and this did the trick. Marching on, he reached the massif of Hambledon Hill, which was ringed with ancient earthworks. These still represented a serious barrier and were held by the main body of the Wiltshire and Dorset Clubmen, between two and a half and four thousand strong, who fired on the party that Oliver sent to parley with them. He formally issued them with three warnings, to no effect, and that now meant a real fight.

First he sent a frontal attack uphill, which the defenders resolutely beat back. Then he ordered in his own former troopers, the regiment directly led by Desborough, which rode round the back of the hill and charged into the countrymen from behind. This broke them, and most fled down a slope so steep that the horsemen could not pursue, leaving some dead on the hill and four hundred captives, including most of the leaders. Cromwell and his men noted, perhaps with sympathy and perhaps with contempt, the slogan written across one of their banners: 'If you offer to plunder or take our cattle, be assured we will give you battle.' Others had passages of Scripture, but these did not give their captors any sense of a common heritage, one later commenting that these were 'profanely applied' by the 'malignant priests' who had led out their parishioners to the hill. The prisoners were herded into a village church, where Cromwell cross-examined them on the following day and released those who promised to submit to Parliament. In the evening he was back at the siege of Sherborne Castle, having solved the Clubman problem in forty-eight hours.[83] He had done so, moreover, carefully and judiciously, making a distinction between outright enemies and proponents of peace and neutrality, acknowledging the right of rural folk to protection from looting soldiers, and officially treating the bulk of those he had found in arms as simple souls misled by unscrupulous or deluded leaders. It had worked, and he had completely crushed the Clubman organizations while avoiding a massacre. When the news reached Parliament, the Commons secured a further four months' extension of his commission as lieutenant-general when that came up for renewal in September.[84]

The defenders of Sherborne Castle proved as resolute as had been feared and continued to resist for almost two more weeks. They were only broken when heavier siege guns were brought up to the New Model and these blasted in some of the walls, and miners arrived from the Mendips to plant more explosives beneath other sections. Cromwell visited both the gunners and the miners with Fairfax, to encourage them. The place was stormed and yielded a huge trove of booty, which the soldiers mostly sold to the local people, in the marketplace of the nearby town of Sherborne. This was needed as a boost to morale, because the convoy of money which had arrived at Bridgwater had only represented two weeks' worth of pay for the army, and now another two weeks' worth arrived at Sherborne. Overall, this meant that the amount owed was sliding more than a month behind schedule. Likewise, the promised recruits were reaching the New Model, but numbered no more than 1,200, instead of the 4,000 which it had been told to expect.[85] This helped to inform the decision which a council of war reached after gaining the castle: to postpone a march against Goring once again, and continue the mopping-up operation in the West Country. Specifically, it seemed unwise to push into the south-west while Bristol remained untaken in the rear. Prince Rupert himself was in command there, and if he could strengthen himself might take the New Model in the rear; at the very least, he might cut its communications. It was therefore resolved to turn on Bristol itself.

It was a great prize, being England's third largest city (after London and Norwich) and the second largest seaport after the capital. Its capture would be a further huge blow to the king's cause, and it had been stormed once already, by Rupert himself in 1643, so it seemed vulnerable. Just two days after Sherborne Castle was taken, the army began moving north-west towards this new objective, and the day after that it was deep in eastern Somerset and Ireton had been sent ahead with two thousand horse and dragoons to drive in the garrison. On the evening of 20 August Cromwell and Fairfax led the vanguard of the New Model up to the top of the huge hogback of limestone known as Dundry Ridge, and their prospective prize lay before them.[86] Opposite, across the broad valley of one of England's three large rivers called the Avon, snaked another line of hills, running across the horizon all along the watching horsemen's front, and closing off the land to their left. At one point on that left hand the Avon cut through the hills in a huge gorge of bare limestone cliffs through which the port's shipping passed to and from the sea. In the centre of the valley sat the city, a huddle of grey church towers and spires, with a wood of ships' masts in the midst of them. That valley situation was its military weakness: in the words of Rupert's engineer, it lay 'in a hole', with high ground surrounding it on all sides.[87] On three of those, the hills were at a safe distance, but all along the north they came closer, and siege artillery positioned there could fire down easily into the city.

The only remedy was to push an encircling ring of new fortifications far out to the north so that it ran along the crest of the nearest ridges. That rendered Bristol safe from bombardment, but it resulted in a defensive perimeter five miles in circuit. To man this effectively needed over four thousand soldiers, which the city and its region could not easily support. Moreover, the high ground was made of hard limestone, so that the digging of ditches through it, and extraction of blocks to build ramparts, was extremely difficult. That was why the royalists had managed to get over the line in 1643. Since then, they had strengthened it in places and constructed or strengthened forts along it, but there were sections which remained weak. The worst was to the east, which had been especially neglected, and was only five feet high. Moreover, too many hedges and ditches had been left beyond it where an enemy might hide.[88] During daylight, the guns in the forts could rake along the approaches to the walls, but in darkness this advantage would be gone. To defend the whole precinct, Rupert had gathered 2,300 foot and

1,000 horse, but too many of the foot soldiers were raw Welsh conscripts of the kind who had proved useless at Bridgwater, and he could not rely on more than 1,500 of his soldiers. These were too few to defend a precinct of that size. To make things even worse, a serious outbreak of bubonic plague had occurred in the city, carrying off an increasing number of the inhabitants and the garrison, and reducing morale further.[89]

Initially, however, it was the strength and size of the defences which impressed the New Model as it took up its stations around the city. In the next ten days Rupert's best men sallied out six times to attack its regiments in their quarters. They came in both daylight and darkness, and on some nights Cromwell and Fairfax could get no sleep, but were riding round the billets of their men with horse contingents trying to assess the danger and damage and co-ordinate responses. To make matters worse, the weather turned wet and misty, literally dampening the spirits of the parliamentarians and giving further cover to the garrison's attacks. After such a run of victory, moreover, bad news was arriving from elsewhere. On 28 August it was heard that the king's cavalry, on their wanderings with him, had sacked Cromwell's original home town of Huntingdon, and then returned to Oxford, to gather more horsemen for a descent on the Scots or the New Model. In July the Scottish army had invaded the Welsh Marches in what was supposed to be the start of its campaign to catch and crush the remnant of the royal army in South Wales. Instead it had got stuck in a siege of Hereford, possessing neither the artillery to break a way into the city nor the determination to attempt a storm of it. It was still there all through August, when appalling tidings arrived from Scotland itself: the king's champion there, the marquis of Montrose, had managed to destroy the army retained by the Covenanter government to guard the kingdom, and was now dominant there and might invade England.

Immediately many of the best units of the Scottish army in England left for home to restore the situation there, which they swiftly did, and in their absence that army began to disintegrate before Hereford. When the king advanced upon it, its remaining members raised the siege on 4 September and fled the region. Charles entered the city in triumph and moved on to restore his authority in South Wales.[90] All this was relayed to the New Model as it sat in its wet quarters around Bristol, and even more worrying information arrived from the south-west, in a letter intercepted from Goring to one of the king's secretaries. Fairfax had detached Massey and his local army to keep the royalists in Devon pinned down, but once more they had failed in a mission, and Goring had now advanced into Somerset. The letter announced that within three weeks he would bring ten thousand men to Prince Rupert's relief. In reality, this was a pure bluff, like the advance itself, and almost certainly intended to fall into parliamentarian hands and shake the New Model's nerve. At any rate, the leaders of that army were now conscious of what seemed a real danger of being attacked simultaneously by the king, Goring and Rupert, in superior combined strength, when it was spread out around Bristol. The fear of this, however, had the opposite effect to that for which Goring had hoped: after a day of prayer and fasting to seek divine guidance, and a long debate, a council of war decided to take the risk of storming the city, as each new day outside it seemed to increase the danger of the army's position.

Preparations took almost two weeks, some of that time being spun out by a ploy of Rupert's, in offering to negotiate in order to buy time. Two thousand local sympathizers had appeared with weapons to reinforce the army, which made the assault all the more practicable. It eventually began in the dead of a fine autumn night, the weather having cleared: at one o'clock on 10 September. The great gold star of the season, Arcturus, would have hung in the western sky, and near it the pendant semicircle of the Corona Borealis. A huge bonfire of straw bales, left from the local corn harvest, was lit on a ridge to the north, and four cannon fired one after the other. At that the New Model attacked, and its size enabled it to do so from different sides of the defences at once, with scaling ladders, and logs to fill up the ditch. Almost everywhere they held, but at two places foot battalions got over the low eastern wall with little difficulty, and at a third with a harder fight: a total of nine regiments had converged on those points and so would have had overwhelming numbers. Once inside the line, they opened a gate and gap for some of Cromwell's horse regiments to enter, his old troopers in Desborough's and Whalley's units being once more part of the vanguard. They then provided cover as pioneers pulled down a whole section of wall for all the rest of the cavalry to enter.

The remaining defenders of the eastern perimeter were now surrounded and gave up or fled; the royalist horse, outnumbered, fell back, and the forts in that sector were isolated. That on Prior's Hill was attacked, and fought hard until some of the New Model's infantry got over its palisades and killed almost everybody inside. By now day was starting to break, and Cromwell and Fairfax climbed on top of the captured fort to survey the scene. A cannonball from the medieval castle at the end of the city centre grazed the roof next to them: like the shot or blow on Cromwell's neck at Marston Moor, it came very close to changing the course of history. Instead it was Prince Rupert's career which was coming to an end. He still held the city and the strongest forts on the northern sector, but this counted for little with his enemies occupying all the ground between that sector and the medieval walls. They could mount siege guns whenever they wished, and blast down those walls, which had never been designed to withstand cannon fire, at close range. With so many soldiers cut off, dead or demoralized, the prince would not be able to muster the strength to defend the breaches, and to shut himself in the castle would leave him trapped while his foes took over the city. He decided to surrender while he still had some bargaining power, and was allowed to march his surviving soldiers away without their weapons, while the citizens were granted immunity from plunder.

Cromwell and Fairfax moved into Bristol for a single night, appalled by the extent of the pestilence in it, the obvious poverty to which war had reduced it, and the stench of the streets, where plague and the demands of the fighting had caused the system of refuse collection to be abandoned. The following day they watched Rupert, clad flamboyantly in scarlet embroidered with silver lace, lead his men towards Oxford, as a crowd of local people from the area around shouted 'Give him no quarter': he had burned the neighbouring villages to deny the New Model shelter in them and driven their livestock into the city to feed it. The ashes of the villages were added to those of Langport and Bridgwater to mark the trail of the summer's fighting. The New Model had lost around a hundred killed and a hundred wounded. There were few casualties among the infantry officers who had led their men over the wall, but more among those leading in the first wave of horse. Their concentration among independents showed again how much Cromwell used these as shock troops and so gave them the best opportunities for glory. Ireton had an arm broken by two pistol shots, which left him in pain for months, while Christopher Bethell, the hero of Langport, who might now have looked forward to a splendid career, was dying. For all that, the damage to the army was minimal and the gain colossal. Parliament had won the capital of the West Country, and with it control of the Bristol Channel. The king promptly dismissed Rupert from his employment in disgrace, and he never held another command in the war. South Wales promptly slipped out of royal control once more, this time for good, Goring retreated helplessly back into Devon and the king moved away northward again. The military initiative had been returned decisively to the New Model.[91]

The fall of Bristol also had some impact on the continuing debate over the future form of English religion. In August, Parliament ordered the establishment of a presbyterian system in London and Westminster, with a provincial synod, divided into ten district 'classes' meeting monthly. This was to be a model to be extended later across the nation, with a national assembly to unite the synods. Ministers and congregations were to choose elders to serve on the classes, who had to take the Solemn League and Covenant, excluding both royalists and religious and political radicals. In the same month the traditional service book was outlawed and a new 'Directory of Worship' suited to broad Puritan tastes made mandatory in its place.[92] These measures, however, left open once again the burning question of the status of Puritans who chose no longer to worship inside the national Church, or who exhibited a divergence of opinion from the mainstream.

Cromwell used the conquest of the city to make a very public intervention in the matter, with Fairfax's support. Formally at the latter's command, Oliver wrote to the Commons to announce the victory, and followed this with the message 'presbyterians, independents, all had here the same spirit of faith and prayer, the same presence and manner, they agree here, know no names of difference, pity it is, it should be otherwise anywhere . . . As for being united in forms (commonly called uniformity) every Christian will for peace sake, study and do as far as conscience will permit; And from some brethren, in things of the mind, we look for no compulsion but that of light and reason.'[93]

It was, as usual, a clever statement. On one reading it could be taken as an expression of abhorrence for religious division, and an exhortation to unity without regard for faction. On the other, its conclusion did seem like a plea for the toleration of diverse opinions and an absence of legal sanctions enforcing orthodoxy upon true Christians. The House supported him once again, directing that another day of thanksgiving be held in all Parliament's territory on 5 October, and the letter read out at the services held upon it. It returned formal thanks to all Fairfax's officers, but singled Cromwell out for special regard.[94] Fairfax tactfully wrote to the Lords himself to describe the victory, in more detail than Cromwell and not seeking to draw any religious lesson from it.[95] Nonetheless, Oliver's letter immediately became partisan. When an official version of it was published, for use at the thanksgiving, the section concerning religion was omitted.[96] In response, the missing section was scattered round London on the night of 21 September, and the following month an ally of Lilburne's called William Walwyn, who was emerging as a notable radical thinker in the city, published an anonymous tract calling for liberty of conscience which used Cromwell's words as an exemplar of the case it was trying to make.[97] By that time the Scottish representatives in London were badly disillusioned, recognizing that their influence had declined because of the near-uselessness of their army in England all year. They considered the presbyterian system being established at London to be merely a nominal one, and commented that 'our wrestlings with devils and men are great'.[98] In October, also, Parliament passed an ordinance excluding from communion all who committed a long list of religious and moral offences and who did not hold a set of defined basic beliefs; but again it did not legislate against those who might not want to be in communion with the new Church anyway.[99]

Because of the epidemic in the city, after its fall the army was quartered in villages at a safe distance from it, to east and south.[100] When it had arrived outside Bristol the hedgerows would have been blushing with rose hips and hawthorn berries, and purple with elderberries and dark with blackberries. Now those were passing, the leaves on the turn and the weather cooling. It was the time when armies generally went into winter quarters, but neither the New Model nor its political masters were anxious to do so this year. Instead, there was a general wish to continue inflicting damage on the royalists, to deprive them of any opportunity to recover. For the time being, the New Model rested in its villages, waiting for more money and recruits to arrive from London. A council of war on 13 September decided to use the interlude to clear more enemy garrisons from the region around. The task of reducing those in northern Wiltshire was given by Fairfax to Cromwell, to honour him again and give him a fresh chance for glory and an extension of his command. He was allotted four foot regiments, this being the first time that he had ever led a substantial body of infantry, and a powerful siege train.[101]

Civil War artillery consisted of a series of different sizes of big, wheeled gun, firing balls weighing anything from six to forty-eight pounds. The lighter were useful as anti-personnel weapons, and could blow in gates and chop down battlements. To make a serious impact on fortifications, however, required a demi-cannon, firing balls twenty to forty pounds in weight, or a whole cannon, which used shot of forty-eight to eighty pounds. These weapons could smash a hole in a medieval castle or town wall. Even they, however, could be foiled if the defenders resorted to either of two remedies, both of which amounted to getting literally down and dirty. One was to construct low modern fortifications of earth around the whole position, with deep ditches and sloping banks, both studded with sharply pointed projecting wooden poles to deter storming soldiers. These works would include projecting bastions, the larger shaped like arrow heads and the smaller in semi-circles and triangles, to provide the defenders with flanking fire. Defences like these had foiled the parliamentarians at Donnington and Faringdon. The other remedy was to pack solid earth behind medieval stone walls, to their tops and at least to a width of fifteen feet. This would enable the stonework on the front to absorb the shock of even heavy shot, and if it crumbled then the mud bank behind would present an equally formidable barrier. Both measures were, however, extremely onerous and expensive, and in many places garrison commanders had gambled that an attack was unlikely and would not put in the extra effort to provide them; this was why Leicester had fallen to the king in May. Even a well-fortified position, however, might be reduced by mortars, which could lob their explosive shells up over the defences and down among the people inside. One mortar would make life unpleasant for the besieged, while a number would create conditions that were simply unendurable.[102]

Cromwell seems to have been given the best of the train which had been assembled to reduce Sherborne Castle, including a whole cannon, two demi-cannons and four mortars. They were accompanied by smaller guns, still formidable in weight, like five culverins which fired a fifteen to twenty-pound ball. These would work in a team with the giant wall-smashers, to crack masonry and topple parapets before the bigger shot broke a structure open. No Civil War army disposed of better firepower than Cromwell did now. In the third week of September great teams of men and animals – for each demi-cannon alone needed thirty to forty horses or oxen, or a hundred men to move it – dragged these monsters across the west Wiltshire clay lands towards the steep grassy scarp which was the edge of Salisbury Plain. There sat Devizes Castle, another fortress built by long-dead bishops of Salisbury, like Sherborne, on the brink of a range of chalk uplands; though it had now been a Crown property for centuries. It was the main royalist stronghold in the north and west of the county, and governed by a skilled engineer who had surrounded it with cannon-proof earthworks. Cromwell accordingly unleashed his mortars on it, as well as pounding the defences, day and night. After two days of this ordeal, unable to get his men any sleep and having his position blown to pieces around him and his powder magazine at risk, and with absolutely no hope of relief, the commander asked for terms.

Here a new policy of clemency became fully apparent on Cromwell's part, having already manifested itself in the measured and cautious way in which he had treated the Clubmen. It was not a personal initiative but part of a unified response which was now enacted by the whole New Model and which he was following. At Bridgwater, Fairfax had allowed the women in the town to leave before the final bombardment; at Devizes, Cromwell offered the same. When the governor asked to negotiate, he got the same terms which Fairfax had given Rupert at Bristol, being allowed to march out his men, to other garrisons if they wished, leaving their arms behind. It seems very much that the leaders of Parliament's army had decided that generosity would be more likely to persuade enemy commanders to capitulate than severity. It is also likely that after the treatment of the royalist women at Naseby a decision had been taken at some very high level to avoid further atrocities, because of reputational damage. On the day of the surrender of Devizes, 23 September, Cromwell sent three regiments to obtain the surrender of the small royalist force in the pretty manor house of Lacock Abbey, fashioned from a former medieval monastery. It gave in at once, and he honoured the force for its prudence by coming to watch it march away himself. With that his job in Wiltshire was done.[103]

Immediately, however, Fairfax gave him another, and tougher (and more glorious) task. On 23 September the Committee of Both Kingdoms asked Sir Thomas to advance south-west at last and occupy most of Devon, so finally ruining Goring's army by leaving it with too small a span of territory on which to subsist. The House of Commons endorsed this, and resolved to borrow a further forty thousand pounds in London and its area in order to pay the New Model during the campaign. It also desired the remnant of the Scottish army in England to make itself useful by besieging Newark.[104] The task of invading Devon meant a winter campaign, which was the hardest sort of soldiering and made a reliable supply line along which money, food, equipment and recruits could regularly arrive all the more imperative. The problem here was that communications between London, which would be the collecting point for all these supplies, and the south-west, were still cut by major royalist garrisons at Donnington Castle, Winchester and Basing House. A chaplain of Fairfax's described these in a memorable metaphor as 'vipers in the bowels'. Sir Thomas and his officers decided that while they marched towards Devon, Cromwell should take his present expeditionary force and first-class siege train eastwards, and reduce as many of these fortresses as possible. Oliver accordingly led his foot soldiers and his train around the edge of Salisbury Plain, and on over the rolling chalk uplands to Winchester, arriving there on 28 September.[105]

Immediately, he deployed his men to attack all the gates of the city, reasoning both that the garrison would be too few to defend such a widely spread perimeter and that the inhabitants would want a rapid surrender to avoid being looted. He was exactly right, for the defenders withdrew into the castle and the mayor admitted Cromwell's men on an assurance of protection for the citizens. The serious siege now started, of the castle which was one of the great royal fortresses of England and the legendary seat of King Arthur, whose reputed round table (actually a medieval fake) hung in its hall. The governor burned down the houses surrounding it to give his men a clearer field of fire. Those houses, however, had prevented the construction of protective earthworks, and nobody had bothered to stack earth inside the castle walls. As a result, when Cromwell planted his batteries the wretched men inside were given a masterclass in siege warfare. He bombarded twelve points at once. The mortar shells began to smash the interior, right down to the vaults, wrecking the defenders' dining chamber, and blowing up the mill which ground their flour and killing the horses which worked it. The cannon fired twelve hours a day and sent the stones of the castle walls flying in all directions, after eight days opening a gap through which thirty men could pass abreast. By now almost half of the garrison had deserted, slipping over the walls in the night, and the morale of the rest had plummeted. When the great breach was made, the governor finally asked for terms.

On the tariff of those that the New Model now seemed to operate, the governor got some less generous than those at Bristol and Devizes but more than at Bridgwater or Sherborne, as befitted the middle level of resistance he had shown. He and his officers were allowed to march away to join the king, but his men were dispersed and all the weapons, munitions and food stocks were seized. Once more the independent Hugh Peters was chosen to take the news of victory to the House of Commons, as a way of underlining the contributions of such men to the cause. Peters was careful in turn to pass on Oliver's thanks to the House for his leave of absence from it, implying with it the reminder that his service might be further extended. He also delivered a moving plea for money and supplies to be sent to the men of the New Model, including Cromwell's party. It included the news that the horse regiments were now twelve weeks behind in pay, and the foot were falling sick because they were reduced to eating raw roots and green apples.[106]

The day after the royalists left Winchester, Cromwell headed for Basing House. Of all the fortresses on his list, this was the most notorious, and expected to be the most formidable. Unlike all those which the New Model had attacked since June, it had regularly been besieged, for long periods, and held out against each attempt to reduce it. Furthermore, the garrison consisted of Roman Catholics, followers of a Church which the English in general, and Puritans in particular, regarded as the mortal enemy of their own religion and committed to its destruction. It was the seat of the marquises of Winchester, the fifth of whom was now the leader of the garrison, and consisted of two neighbouring great houses, an older castle with towers and battlements, and a sprawling new Tudor mansion with pepper-pot turrets, both built out of red brick. These had been surrounded by fourteen and a half acres of new defences, constructed of brick thickly lined with earth to stop cannonballs. These, and the resolution of the defenders, had kept out attackers hitherto, but Cromwell had three advantages over his predecessors in trying to take the place. The first was that it had been softened up before his arrival, by a local parliamentarian force which had surrounded it with over a mile of siege works with close approaches constructed to the defences. The second was that having joined his own men to that local force he deployed overwhelming numbers, several thousand men against three hundred defenders. The third was that previous besiegers had possessed, at best, a single demi-cannon, whereas Oliver brought a siege kit of unsurpassed power.[107]

He immediately released that power upon the defences, and cannily ignored the shot-proof new brick and earth works to concentrate on the precinct of the Tudor mansion, which had tall walls of brick that were more vulnerable. After three days his guns ripped two large breaches in them. The next morning, that of 14 October, was chosen for the assault. Cromwell spent the previous night in prayer, and chose as his text to inspire his men part of Psalm 115, a fierce ancient Hebrew diatribe against idolatry, which could now be deployed against the Papists in the fortress. At six o'clock, which at this season was still a time of darkness, they went into the gaps in the walls and attacked a third point as well. As they did so the defenders offered to surrender but the attacking soldiers, eager for blood and loot, refused to parley – which had also happened at Sherborne – and fought their way into both houses. Under these circumstances, and remembering that the garrison was mostly Catholic, it is remarkable that the slaughter was not greater than it was. The marquis was taken prisoner unharmed, and so was his chief military officer, and so were over two hundred other soldiers and civilians. Nobody seemed sure afterwards how many died, the rough figure being a hundred. The problem was that the new house caught fire during the fighting, and after twenty hours had burned down to the bare walls and chimneys. Some bodies were buried under the wreckage, and – much worse – more of the inhabitants took refuge in the cellars and were trapped there by the flames, crying out in vain for aid and mercy. One woman was killed outright, allegedly for berating the incoming soldiers, and eight or nine 'gentlewomen of rank . . . were entertained by the common soldiers somewhat coarsely, yet not uncivilly', whatever that means.

One reason for the survival of most of the royalists was that their assailants were more intent on plunder than killing, and the more anxious to lay their hands on it before the fire got to it first. Also, the garrison had some parliamentarian prisoners, who might be killed if their captors despaired of their own lives. The loot was certainly prodigious. One bed alone was worth £1,300, and a single soldier got 120 gold pieces and others plate dinner services and jewels. An unlucky infantryman secured three bags of silver, only to be stripped of all but one coin by his companions. When the valuables were taken, the wooden furniture and store of wheat were dragged out and sold off to the local people, and finally the lead was stripped from the buildings, including the gutters, and sold in turn. For Cromwell's ill-paid and hungry men, it was a prodigiously lucrative action.[108]

Tellingly, he once more gave Hugh Peters the honour of carrying the news to the House of Commons, which he did two days later. The House decreed a national thanksgiving for Oliver's string of victories, and ordered him to proceed at once to reduce Donnington Castle, the last royalist fortress west and south-west of London. Cromwell was very reluctant to do this, having already started his march back into the chalk hills to rejoin Fairfax. In a reply to the Commons he emphasized that the New Model badly needed him and his men to have the strength to confront Goring, and this makes sense: he urged the House to neutralize Donnington with a blockade by local forces. The House decided to allow him and Fairfax to dispose of their soldiers as they thought best; and they accorded Cromwell the practical reward for which he had apparently been hoping, of persuading the Lords to concur with a further extension of his office as lieutenant-general, into the following spring. Oliver marched on westward, and completed his tally of victories by accepting the surrender of the last royalist stronghold in Wiltshire, a country house near Salisbury called Langford: the garrison got the same terms as at Devizes and Winchester. He entrusted the account of this sent to the Commons to another independent, a former London artisan, now a lieutenant-colonel, called Paul Hewson, who was rewarded like Harrison with two excellent horses. As ever, Oliver was looking after his own.[109]

WINTER CAMPAIGN

Meanwhile Fairfax was leading the bulk of the New Model Army into Devon. On 19 October he opened the way into the centre of the county by taking Tiverton Castle, with a lucky shot as a cannonball severed the chain holding up the drawbridge. Oliver and his returning expeditionary force were then passing over the rolling chalk ridges, with their faded cornfields and withering sheep pastures, into Dorset. At Blandford he held a council of war which tried six of his troopers who were proved to have looted goods from royalist officers marching out of Winchester and Langford. As a gesture to advertise the probity of their army and their cause, he and his fellows returned the items concerned to their former owners according to the articles of surrender, and condemned the guilty men to death. One, who drew a fatal lot, was hanged before the soldiers the next morning, and the others were handed over to the royalists to do with as they pleased. Cromwell led his force on, and, having got into the south Somerset lowlands again, received an urgent summons to Fairfax's headquarters, leaving his foot soldiers and siege train to catch him up later. Late on the evening of the 24th he rejoined them in the market town of Crediton, situated south-west of Tiverton at a point from which the army could strike in any direction across Devon. He must have got a very warm welcome, as his victories had won glory for the whole army and he brought a much-needed reinforcement: allegedly, when Fairfax had informed the men at Tiverton that Oliver was on his way, they had burst into cheers.[110]

He had been summoned with such haste to attend another council of war, to decide on the next steps of the campaign. There were now several reasons against continuing a rapid attack on Goring. The weather had broken, in the manner of the season, becoming so wet that the lanes were suddenly deep in mud and the wagons of the army could not get along them. The men were worn out with their recent marches, and the increasing cold and rain were nurturing a serious outbreak of epidemic disease among them: probably influenza or typhus. There seemed no need for haste as the chances of the king mounting an attack against the New Model's rear were diminishing: at Crediton the news arrived that the last of his Northern Horse had been destroyed at Sherburn in Yorkshire.[111] Goring remained unable to recruit a force large enough to make a counter-stroke against the New Model from the two impoverished and exhausted counties of Devon and Cornwall.[112] To the south of the army's current position lay the city of Exeter, which blocked the main route in and out of Devon and was a royalist fortress containing over two thousand soldiers under determined leadership. Not even Cromwell's siege train was of any use against it, because it had two rings of brand-new defences around the medieval walls. The inner consisted of a ditch about seven feet deep and thirty feet wide, with an earthen breastwork for foot soldiers behind it and a counterscarp on the outer side angled to deflect cannonballs from hitting the breastwork. The outer ring consisted of at least three forts, also made of earthen banks and ditches proof against bombardment, the guns of which could rake soldiers trying to attack the breastwork and ditch. The suburbs had all been burned down to allow clear fields of fire to the defenders.[113] Exeter could therefore neither be taken by storm nor easily left in the rear of the New Model.

On 28 October Fairfax's council, including Cromwell, decided to retreat behind the city and put the army into winter quarters in the villages and small towns to the east of it, blockading it on that side and fortifying the mansions and crossings along the Rivers Exe and Clyst, to establish a defensible line about twenty-five miles long. This was achieved in eight days, the headquarters of Fairfax and Cromwell being established at the small market town of Ottery St Mary. After that the soldiers stayed put, as the East Devon landscape, one of small hills, woods and pastures, settled slowly into its midwinter colours of black, brown and olive green. They were protected in their billets from the storms and frosts, but these static and crowded quarters were perfect for the transmission of disease. During November half of some regiments were ill, and seven to nine people died daily. It must have been some consolation to the commanders that the House of Commons remained supportive throughout this period. It replenished Cromwell's cavalry division by directing that five hundred pounds be spent on new horses for the New Model immediately and two hundred a month henceforth: in this way it hoped to keep the troopers effective through the winter. When the Lords wanted to force Fairfax to march further into Devon immediately, the lower House refused to agree, and won his army the rest it needed. A stream of money was maintained from London, and to win over the local people, and provide good publicity in general, the soldiers were ordered to pay for everything they needed in the county, on pain of death.[114] The army consumed around seventeen thousand pounds of bread (often baked into biscuit to preserve it), seventeen thousand quarts of beer, and a proportionate amount of cheese and meat, per day. By now, with the roads from London cleared of enemy garrisons, and nearby seaports such as Lyme Regis sending on goods delivered by sea, these foodstuffs too were arriving from the capital with some regularity.[115]

On 2 December Fairfax moved the headquarters back to Tiverton, and pulled most of the New Model forward to it again, to find healthier quarters, start to establish fortified posts on the west of Exeter, and leave those on the east side to be manned by local parliamentarians. Some of the best of Cromwell's horse, including the regiments of Fleetwood, Whalley and Fairfax (under Desborough), had to be sent away to the Oxford area at Parliament's request, to keep the royalist horsemen from raiding at will out of that city. Those remaining under Cromwell skirmished regularly with Goring's troopers in Devon. Then with midwinter came a prolonged and intense period of cold, with blizzards and severe frosts, in which horses could not operate, and both sides were confined to their bases.[116]

In this period Cromwell was probably warmed spiritually by personal developments. Preparations were being made for the wedding of his daughter

Elizabeth, reputedly his favourite one and now aged seventeen, to John Claypole, the son of an old family friend based in Northamptonshire: Oliver was not yet making any dynastic alliances outside his traditional circle of kin. The ceremony took place in January, at Ely where his wife and children were still safely living; and he could not have attended as he was still on campaign in Devon.[117] He did allot a very generous dowry of £1,250 to the union, which was a distinct sign of how much he had risen in the world; but then another development that month made him capable of affording it. Until this point, he had been drawing his salary as a captain, colonel and general, though at a reduced rate and inadequately paid. He could expect, if all went well, to receive the arrears as a golden handshake after the war, and also in the same best-case circumstances to be repaid with interest the huge sums he had lent to support the reconquest of Ireland and Parliament's war effort in 1642. He had, however, no personal source of income on which to fall back when returning to civilian life, having liquidated all his assets so dramatically in 1640. On 1 December, however, the House of Commons debated the peace terms it would offer the king on what was now expected to be his final defeat; and the two soldiers whom the House thought had done most to bring about that defeat would both be well rewarded from the spoils. Fairfax was to be made an English baron (his father held a Scottish title), and granted lands worth five thousand pounds a year, while Cromwell was also to become a lord, and be given an estate worth two and a half thousand pounds a year. Skippon was to get a thousand a year. The former generals were not neglected: Essex would be made a duke and Manchester a marquis, and Waller would have the same package as Cromwell. Honours were also to be spread among a range of politicians from both the current parties, with more promotions in the Lords, and in the Commons the Presbyterians Denzil Holles becoming a viscount and Sir Philip Stapleton a baron, while the Independent Vane also got ennobled.[118] For Cromwell, the man who had worked as a tenant farmer and then risen back into the lesser gentry, this promised glory, comfort and security indeed; if the deal went through and he survived the rest of the war.

At the opening of 1646 the icy weather was continuing but both armies in Devon were preparing for action. Goring, shrewd soldier that he was, had decided that the royalist cause was doomed, and found excuses to depart to France. In his absence the council appointed by the king in the previous spring, to run the West Country with his son, the teenage prince of Wales, as figurehead, became a collective leadership by default. In late December this had set about organizing a relief expedition for Exeter, by uniting the militia of Cornwall, the regular Cornish and Devonian field soldiers, units from garrisons, and the horse regiments Goring had brought from the royal army. This promised an army just about big enough to challenge the New Model, if of rather doubtful quality. The royalist problem was the Dartmoor massif, that great high barren crown of granite rock which occupied the centre of the county and presented a major barrier to the assemblage of the new army. By the first week of January the horse units were quartered on the south-east side of the moor, and in the South Hams, the southern part of the county which jutted out into the English Channel. The regular Cornish foot was on the north side of Dartmoor and the rest of the infantry was assembling on the west side.[119] The New Model had a natural vested interest in attacking this scatter of units before it could unite.

By January it was both collected for action and ready for that: one more missing element in its provisions, vital for winter warfare – fresh stockings and shoes for the soldiers – had arrived from London. On 5 January the officers prayed for divine guidance and held private discussions, in preparation for a council of war the next day. That decided to attack the cavalry on the side of the moor and then advance into the South Hams to shatter the royalist position. On the 8th the main army advanced to Crediton again and sent an advance guard onward due west towards the Cornish. This was a feint, because that afternoon Cromwell led the cavalry southward towards Bovey Tracey, a little market town on the side of the moor where the nearest party of royalist horsemen was stationed. He delayed his attack until darkness had fallen and his victims settled into their billets for food, recreation and sleep.

It was another freezing winter night, and the constellations of the season – Orion with his jewelled belt and sword, and red upraised hand and blue-white foot, the great sparkling green eye of his dog Sirius, red-eyed Taurus the bull, the clustered shimmer of the Pleiades, and the ice-white heavenly twins, Castor and Pollux – would have shone above the parliamentarian troopers as they carried out the action. They were in the streets before their presence was suspected, and they captured 130 men and four to six hundred horses. Most of the royalist soldiers ran off into the dark countryside and the highest-ranking officers got away because they were playing cards in an upstairs room of a house when the attackers came into the street outside. With admirably quick wit the men in the room threw the money laid out as stakes down from a window, and escaped out of the back as the New Model's soldiers scrambled for it. Nonetheless, the main enemy outpost had been routed, and the next day Cromwell and Fairfax reunited their forces outside the town and pushed on through the still thick ice and snow into the South Hams. The royalist cavalry fled before them and the relief plan for Exeter was destroyed.[120] On 12 January the last royalist units retired into Cornwall, lifting the blockade of Plymouth, a major parliamentarian seaport which had been cut off by land for well over a year. On that day also, the New Model arrived outside the principal port of the South Hams, Dartmouth.

On the following day, muffled against the still bitter cold, Fairfax, Cromwell and their fellows viewed the town and decided that it could be stormed, despite the fact that their siege guns, which could not be pulled through the snow, had been left behind. Dartmouth had been taken by assault by the king's men in 1643, showing its vulnerability. There were strong forts on the landward side of town, but their guns did not cover the defences there comprehensively, and there were various weak points in the fortifications where a determined party might enter, especially in the dark. A parliamentarian squadron arrived off the harbour which could bombard that and draw off defenders. Five days were spent in preparations, which were delayed slightly by a sudden unexpected warming of the weather, producing a massive thaw and flooding. On 18 January the blood of the men was raised by sermons from Peters, and from a new man called William Dell, another independent who had replaced the presbyterian chaplain who partnered Peters before, and so strengthened that religious interest in the army. At eleven o'clock at night the attack began, and at one place the defenders fled at once, allowing the New Model's soldiers to get over the wall on their scaling ladders. After that, resistance in the town crumbled fast. The outlying forts were left isolated at daybreak, and surrendered, and so the New Model had notched up another important victory. Again Peters was sent to Parliament with the news. On hearing it, the Commons ordered that a clerical living be found for him, and gave thought to the practical business of how the income to be granted to Fairfax and Cromwell to support their forthcoming titles of nobility could be found. They referred the matter to a committee, but specified that some of the income for Cromwell be provided by granting him the Hampshire estates of the marquis of Worcester, a leading Catholic royalist. For good measure, they also obtained a further, whopping, six-month extension of his commission as lieutenant-general, pushing it well into the autumn.[121]

He now went with Fairfax and the bulk of the New Model back north and east to tighten the stranglehold on Exeter. This involved using infantry units to reduce the royalist outposts on the west of the city and drawing a circle of strongpoints all round it which would starve it out. Cromwell's horsemen gave this work cover. New regiments were raised from local volunteers, and news came in of the surrender of Chester, the king's last major sea port. Various councils of war were held to discuss either storming Exeter or marching west to finish off the royalist field army, but reached no settled plan.[122] As at times before, it was a royalist initiative which precipitated a decision. After the failure of the project to relieve Exeter, the prince of Wales had formally replaced Goring as commander-in-chief of the western royalist army, and at the start of February the prince appointed the veteran commander Ralph, Lord Hopton, to act as his lieutenant-general and gather that army for a fresh attempt to break the siege of the city. He could only collect 1,890 foot and 3,200 horse, the former reluctant and demoralized and the latter mutinous. Nonetheless, he dutifully advanced into North Devon on 6 February, and after four days reached the small hilltop town of Great Torrington, which he thought an easily defensible position and where he halted to await more ammunition and other supplies.[123]

The news of his advance reached the leaders of the New Model on 8 February, when they were holding another council to discuss strategy, and that resolved at once to march to meet him. On the 10th, Fairfax and Cromwell entered Crediton once more with the bulk of the army, and more contingents came up from the south of the county, with the latest welcome instalment of pay, which had been shipped to Dartmouth. That gave them seven foot regiments, five horse regiments and five companies of dragoons, which even at reduced strength would have provided a superiority of around three to one in foot but only a slight one in horse.[124] The weather was still mild, but this being the start of an English spring, mildness meant wind and rain, and so mud. Progress was therefore slow, and five more days were needed to get within sight of Torrington. The downpour had continued and the bridges over the little rivers of this land of hillocks had been broken by the royalists. On arrival, Fairfax sent an advance party under Cromwell's former major James Berry to alarm the royalists in the town while the rest of the army retired to quarters for the night, glad that the weather was at last clearing. Hopton's foot soldiers at the defences, however, opened fire on Berry's men. Despite Cromwell's efforts to restrain them, some of the New Model's infantry went in to help their comrades, and then Sir Thomas himself led in yet more to aid those. He ordered Cromwell to call up all the rest of the army to join the action, and so a regular battle developed in the moonlight which neither side had intended.

The royalists had hastily fortified the town with barricades made of earth and chopped-down trees, and opposed the attackers bravely across these with pikes and muskets for one to two hours. The defences were, however, both inadequate and incomplete, and could be outflanked. Slowly, superior numbers told, and eventually the New Model infantry got across and around the barriers and pulled them open to let in Cromwell's horsemen.

Hopton's fundamental problem now showed itself: his main strength, relative to his enemy, was in horsemen, but his were mostly gathered outside the town on the far side from the attackers and could not easily get into its streets, which were infantry country. Two hundred royalist horsemen were inside the town, and twice charged the parliamentarian foot soldiers in the main street and beat them back, only to be hit by a counter-charge of the New Model's troopers, which broke them in turn; and so the whole force of defenders began to run and Torrington was taken and plundered. As its occupation was completed, around eleven o'clock, Hopton's magazine of eighty barrels of gunpowder, which had been stored in the parish church, blew up. It shattered the building and strewed stones, timber, lead and ironwork across the whole town, inflicting terrible damage. The victors had penned two hundred of their prisoners into the building, and it seems one of those had ignited the store by accident, though parliamentarian propaganda held that a hired hand had been paid by Hopton to perform the deed. Debris crashed into the street where Cromwell and Fairfax were riding, but once again both escaped injury. Most of the defeated infantry, and almost all of the cavalry, escaped out of the town and into the night, but the foot soldiers threw away their weapons to speed their flight, leaving streets, and the lanes and fields beyond, full of pikes and muskets. When the news reached Parliament it ordered another thanksgiving.[125] At the same time the grant of the lands of the marquis of Worcester in Hampshire to Cromwell – three manors, including fine woods – was formally sealed, and the process began of making up the rest of his estate worth £2,500 a year, by signing over to him more land, with a large country house, that belonged to the captive marquis of Winchester.[126]

Hopton's frightened infantry had not done badly at Torrington: Fairfax thought it the hardest fight the New Model had known when storming a town. Moreover, Hopton managed to gather most of those who had got away and lead them and the horsemen to temporary safety, across the River Tamar into Cornwall. Fairfax himself was determined to give them no time to regroup, by sending Ireton with a force to blockade Barnstaple, the royalist stronghold in northern Devon, and taking the rest of the New Model into Cornwall to hunt down and destroy the last of Hopton's army. On 20 February another council of war, including Cromwell, unanimously agreed to this after a long argument. Speed seemed further compelled by the now regular arrival of rumours – actually false but believed by the New Model – that in another month a French royal army would land to rescue the king's cause. The conquest of Cornwall, however, seemed on first sight to be a daunting prospect. The county had provided some of the king's most ardent supporters at the opening of the war, who had raised a complete regional army, led by Hopton, which had taken most of the West Country in 1643. It had remained a great royalist recruiting ground ever since and had rallied to the king when Essex had invaded it in 1644, a factor which had played a significant part in his defeat there. It was a unique region, part English and part Celtic in culture and tradition, and at this period still preserving in its western parts its own Celtic language. During the previous hundred and fifty years it had repeatedly displayed an aggressive local patriotism and refusal to conform to metropolitan English policies.[127]

The leadership of the New Model had therefore agreed upon a charm offensive to win the Cornish over. All soldiers from that county who were captured at Dartmouth were released and given two shillings each to pay for their journey home, and now the same treatment was accorded to those taken at Torrington. Hugh Peters was sent to Plymouth, to contact the gentry of East Cornwall over the river and offer them friendship. Another four thousand pounds had arrived to pay the men, which made it easier to enforce a directive to them not to loot or abuse the common Cornish people.[128] On 23 February the advance guard of the New Model seized a crossing into Cornwall over the River Tamar, and two days later the bulk of the army drove the royalists out of the first town to be reached there, Launceston. Fairfax gave the prisoners the same deal as those at Dartmouth and Torrington. As March opened the next advance began, led by Cromwell and Fairfax, in battle order across Bodmin Moor, another large granite upland, of rock outcrops, bogs and rough grass, open to the elements. The season was turning, and the sap rising in the trees: in the valleys it was the time of catkins, elder buds and birdsong. The weather, however, had grown cold once more, and many of the infantry had to sleep on the open moor in a night of hard frost.

Cromwell had a worse time, because on the far side of the moor lay the largest town of East Cornwall, Bodmin, which was Hopton's current head-quarters. Another battle might be imminent, in which the open moor would give the numerous royalist horsemen some advantage, and that afternoon Oliver led forward his horsemen to reconnoitre, hearing that an outpost of New Model dragoons had already come under attack by them. He and his companions sighted two large bodies of enemy cavalry near the town. Those retreated, but for much of the night he and his men remained in the saddle, ranging the final slopes of the freezing moorland to block, and give warning of, an attack; they snatched brief periods of sleep on the icy grass. When the sun rose, it turned out that Hopton's army had fled westwards under cover of darkness, and the New Model was able to occupy Bodmin in its place. The policy of clemency, and the obvious weakness of the royalists, now began to bear fruit, as the locals of the eastern half of the county started to come into the town with weapons and offer their services. The real danger now was not that Hopton would fight, but that his cavalry, which still numbered in the thousands, would take advantage of the New Model's position on the south-east side of the moor to ride round the northern side, and away across the Tamar. They could then make for Oxford, to reinforce the king. To prevent this, Cromwell set off again that same morning, despite his lack of sleep, with a thousand horse and four hundred dragoons to occupy Wadebridge, which controlled the main river crossing on the north coast, and block the way eastwards. Two foot regiments and two more horse regiments joined him there the next day.[129] The king's army of the west was finally trapped.

After spending a week tightening the parliamentarian grip on east Cornwall, from his base at Bodmin, Fairfax moved in for the kill. Hopton's army was now quartered in and around Truro, the main town of west Cornwall, and the last point on the narrowing south-western peninsula of Britain which had space to accommodate it. This was the point from which he had launched his conquest of much of the West Country, over three years before, and now he was back there, defeated. The prince of Wales and his councillors had fled overseas, and when Hopton called a council of war on 2 March almost all of his senior officers said that their men were no longer willing to fight. On the 8th the New Model advanced to within seven miles of them, Cromwell coming down from Wadebridge to rejoin the main body, and the royalist general wrote to Fairfax offering to parley. The negotiations took four days, and ended in an agreement that Hopton's whole force would disband, the common soldiers handing over all their weapons and their steeds. This process lasted until the 20th, and by then the troopers who had been Goring's, and who had routed Cromwell's men at Newbury, peacefully capitulated, and thousands of cavalry horses came into the possession of their victorious foes; though hundreds of them were now in poor enough condition to be useless. In their reports to Parliament, Fairfax and his subordinates played up the drama of the achievement by crediting fresh rumours, that the king had made an alliance with the Irish rebels, and that the latter were about to land a large force of infantry in Cornwall to join Hopton's cavalry. This, the reports went, had been thwarted in the nick of time. Fairfax rewarded Peters for his service in winning over many of the Cornish by giving him his own main despatch again to take to Westminster.[130]

Cromwell and Fairfax had made a perfect team. Sir Thomas had employed a consultative style of leadership, with frequent councils of war to represent the views of his senior officers, in which Oliver played a full part. Cromwell had been given a series of missions and duties, from start to finish of the New Model's first campaign, which had enabled him to display his talents to the full and increase his reputation and his standing with Parliament. Just as important, Sir Thomas had shown consistent favour to the religious independents in the army, soldiers and ministers, who looked to Oliver as their natural patron. Fairfax had also countenanced presbyterians, but not to the same extent, and never in such a way as blocked or threatened the independents. For his part, Cromwell had been a consistently loyal, capable and reliable lieutenant, carrying out every duty assigned to him to perfection. The result had been that Parliament had won the Civil War, greatly assisted by the king's blunder in fighting at Naseby, and the two men now had the prospect of spending the rest of their lives as wealthy aristocrats. That prospect, however, would be heavily contingent on subsequent events, and that qualification weighed especially heavily in Cromwell's case because he was the more prominent and exposed politically.

ENDGAME

The day after the last of the western royalist army was disbanded, on 21 March, a body of newly recruited infantry, marching from Worcester to join the king at Oxford, was trapped and destroyed at Stow on the Wold in Gloucestershire. This was the last battle of the war, because it removed Charles's final chance to rebuild a field army in time for a summer campaign and left him completely helpless militarily. The mission of the New Model Army was now clear: to head for Oxford itself and besiege it into surrender, preferably with the king trapped inside it and forced to give himself up with his wartime capital. It set out on the very next day after the last of Hopton's regiments handed over its arms, and on 25 March Fairfax, Cromwell and the other senior officers crossed the Tamar again, to Plymouth, where three hundred guns were fired to welcome them. Two days later they rejoined the army halfway across Devon, and on the last day of the month surrounded Exeter again and summoned it to surrender. This time the governor, recognizing a hopeless situation, agreed to talk at once, and got generous terms in return, his men being allowed to join the Oxford garrison with their weapons or hand them over and go home. Barnstaple followed suit, and by 18 April Fairfax and Cromwell could continue the march on Oxford, leaving the whole of the west of England clear of royalist soldiers, save for a few coastal forts and castles which could be starved out by local forces. After two gruelling days they reached Salisbury, and from there Fairfax sent Cromwell to report to Parliament in person on the condi-tion in which the West Country had been left.[131]

The political atmosphere in London and Westminster, when Oliver returned there after his long absence, was as febrile as ever, and the tension still focused primarily on the impending Church settlement. In essence nothing had changed to resolve the instinctual opposition between those who were comfortable with a looser structure of discipline and belief and those who were not. Everybody recognized both that the New Model Army had been stunningly successful in achieving a decisive victory in the war, and that religious independents had been prominent in that achievement. Where people differed was over the logical consequences of those facts. Opinion occupied a spectrum running between those who felt that the independents, and the sectaries who were often allied to them, should be rewarded with a place in the reformed Church of England, and those who felt that to award such a place would negate the whole role of a "national religion, and that the temporary freedom granted to those with unorthodox opinions had been reward enough (and perhaps too much). The latter view was still strongly propounded by the Scots, increasingly allied with a dominant faction in the city of London and the Westminster Assembly, and the Presbyterian grouping in Parliament and its allies in the counties. The most potent force that the independents had on their side, other than the political Independents in and out of Parliament, was the New Model Army itself, and the awful logic of the latter's situation was that the closer it came to winning the war, the sooner it would have to disband.

Thus far, the Independents had continued to hold a precarious supremacy at Westminster and contain the problem. On 17 April the Commons issued a prospectus for reconstruction of the nation after the war. It tried to reassure presbyterians by promising to settle the Church according to the Solemn League and Covenant, and in a presbyterian form, and to keep the alliance with the Scottish Covenanters. It then offered hope to religious independents by reaffirming a will to 'give some ease to tender consciences', but left the nature of this unclear. Three days later the MPs trounced the

Westminster Assembly by declaring that it exercised no authority of its own and had purely an advisory role. The assembly had just pushed its luck by petitioning Parliament to entrust religious discipline ultimately to churchmen, and not to itself, and the Commons had voted this a breach of privilege. The motion had passed after a long debate by a dozen votes, in a classic division between Independents (the tellers for whom were Hesilrig and Sir John Evelyn) and Presbyterians (the tellers for whom were Holles and Stapleton, as usual); the latter opposing and being defeated.[132] Nonetheless, participants felt that the debate had sharpened the distinctions and animosities between the two parties, one MP noticing 'much joy that the independents should be bolted out of their burrows'.[133] Furthermore, having lost the vote, some of the Presbyterians went to the common council of London, the elected body of the city's government, and persuaded their allies there to agree to frame a protest to the Commons about the decision. There was talk of a refusal by the citizens to pay taxes until it was reversed.[134]

Through the winter, Cromwell had kept up his role and reputation as a leading political Independent and religious independent. During his army's immobilization in East Devon he wrote twice to John Lilburne, trying to tempt him back to join it, but Lilburne remained too disenchanted with military life to oblige.[135] There was a rumour in January that both Houses had canvassed Oliver to see if he were willing to leave the war in England to undertake the reconquest of Ireland, with the title of Lord Deputy. He was said to have refused because he wanted to see the Independents securely in charge of England before going abroad.[136] In February it was reported in London that one MP had called Cromwell the only true friend to religious independents in the House of Commons.[137] At that time his cousin and ally Oliver St John wrote to him despondently that their cause in Parliament had slid back to where it had been before the battle of Naseby had boosted it.[138] When Cromwell reappeared at Westminster, on 23 April, newspaper editors who favoured that cause hailed him as a returning hero. One called him 'active, pious and gallant' and claimed that he had come 'to advance . . . reformation', while another termed him 'ever renowned, and never to be forgotten'.[139]

Certainly he was graciously received by the Commons, with the public and formal thanks of the Speaker for all his services. Immediately his presence seemed to bolster the resolution of the House to deny the Scots a role in the forthcoming settlement of England, as it agreed after a hard dispute that the New Model Army should replace the Scottish army in reducing Newark, which had been blockaded all winter by the Scots but still not surrendered. The obvious argument that this could provoke a breach with the Covenanters was made but did not prevail. It is not known what part Cromwell himself played in this, but on the following day he was recorded as speaking, on purely military affairs, by asking the House to ensure that the soldiers left to conduct the remaining sieges in Devon and Cornwall were properly paid. On 25 April he was asked to take back to Fairfax the MPs' direction that any peace overture from the king to his army should immediately be forwarded to them without any attempt to answer. On the 28th he was added to the membership of a Commons committee again – on his old subject of Fen drainage – but seems already to have left Westminster, and his appointment to have been made in the expectation that he would return before long and resume his political career.[140]

On May Day, Fairfax opened the siege of Oxford,[141] but by then he and Parliament knew that the greatest prize he might have taken in it had already escaped, for the king had left the city in disguise before a blockade closed around it. The question of his destination was solved on 5 May, when it was reported to both Houses that he had surrendered himself to the Scottish army besieging Newark, in a blatant attempt to divide the allies. The Commons sat until ten o'clock at night and resolved to demand that the Scots hand him over immediately. Fairfax detached five thousand horse and dragoons from his army to march towards Newark to enforce this directive, and it looked as if war might be about to break out between the Scottish and English forces. If it did, the former would find many English sympathizers, as when the news of the king's union with the Covenanters broke, bonfires were lit all over London to celebrate it. Such a conflict was prevented by two factors. One was that King Charles, still devoted to the traditional Church of England, refused to agree to its replacement by a Scottish presbyterian system. The Scots therefore made him a prisoner, and sent hastily to Parliament to reassure it that his appearance had been completely unexpected and that they did not want a breach. When the king ordered his governor inside Newark to surrender, the Scots immediately handed it over to parliamentarian soldiers and retreated rapidly to Newcastle with their royal captive.

The other calming factor was that the House of Lords was more conciliatory, and a majority in it, mostly Presbyterian, voted not to agree with the Commons' demand for an immediate handover of the king. It also resolved to support a plea from the Scots to recall the force sent against them from the New Model. On 11 May the Commons moderated their stance to the point of demanding only that Charles order all his remaining adherents to lay down arms and abandon any alliance with the Irish. Holles and Stapleton acted as tellers for the majority to indicate that this was a Presbyterian initiative. However, the House then voted to snub the Lords by not seeking their concurrence with these terms, with two Independents telling the votes for the majority. On the 14th Holles and Stapleton were in a majority again, against an Independent minority with Hesilrig and Evelyn as tellers, in resolving against informing the Scots that they should have no part in the coming settlement of England. Four days later, by one vote, the Presbyterian peers confirmed this victory by resolving that Parliament should act with the Scots to present terms for a lasting settlement to the king. The Commons did, however, agree to offer their Scottish partners £150,000 to remove all their soldiers from England; only for the Lords to fail to support this.[142] The balance of power between the parties was dizzyingly even, but it seemed that Parliament had rejected the opportunity to exclude the Covenanters from a role in settling England, and so to reduce the possibility of ending up with a Church close to their model. Instead the Houses agreed to set up a huge national commission to establish the presbyterian Church system agreed upon in the spring, subsequently taking up to three years over the job.[143]

Meanwhile Cromwell, Fairfax and the New Model were proceeding with the reduction of the royalist capital. It was soon obvious that Oxford, like Exeter, had been turned into an impregnable fortress. It sat at the junction of two rivers, the Thames and Cherwell, which flowed around it on three sides and could not be bridged or waded. The fourth side, across the neck of the peninsula between the rivers, had been given defences of a strength and modernity which made them impervious alike to gunfire and storm parties. Inside the city were thousands of veteran infantry and a huge magazine of food and munitions. It could only therefore be starved out slowly or enticed out with good terms. These terms Fairfax set out to provide, with the full support of a council of war which included Cromwell, and on 20 June they were concluded. The garrison marched out four days later, to go home or overseas, while those whose property had been seized by Parliament would be allowed to regain it swiftly on payment of a fine.[144] Units of the New Model, under individual officers including Fairfax, would now disperse to reduce the remaining royalist fortresses across the nation, and on 29 June Sir Thomas appointed Cromwell to a council of officers empowered to decide who should tackle each siege.[145] Oliver himself, however, undertook none of them. For him the war really was over at last.

This final episode of it must have been one of the most pleasant parts of the whole conflict for him. He seems to have engaged in no military action, and enjoyed the society and discussions of his fellow officers.[146] Another of his daughters got married on 15 June, Bridget, and this time Oliver was very much present, because the ceremony was at his quarters, a country house near Oxford, and the bridegroom was none other than Henry Ireton. Once again the dowry was generous, the lease of a farm in the Isle of Ely. The clergyman who performed the ceremony was William Dell, the independent who was Fairfax's chaplain and one of the two main preachers in the army.[147] A week before the wedding Dell had delivered a sermon to the generals of the army, including Sir Thomas and Oliver, which denounced 'carnal Gospellers' who libelled the small but glorious number of 'saints' in England as independents, sectaries, schismatics and heretics. He predicted that these saints would build the true Church after the war, which was composed only of the godly. When this was reported at London it gave great offence, and Dell was obliged to publish his text with a preface claiming that he believed presbyterians to be among the godly, and abhorred party labels.[148] Nonetheless, the impression of the army as a hotbed of independent firebrands was strengthened, The Scottish clergy representing their Kirk in London and at the Westminster Assembly had come, moreover, to regard that army as being under Cromwell's control.[149]

The reception of Dell's sermon in London, and his hurried response to it, had much to do with the increasingly fraught religious atmosphere there. On 25 May the common council of the city had delivered its rebuke to Parliament, calling for a suppression of all congregations meeting outside the national Church, a purge from public office of any except presbyterians, the preservation of good relations with the Scots, a rapid offer of peace terms to the king, and the reduction of taxes (which meant the end of the New Model Army). Its acceptance would mean the end of all Cromwell's hopes. The Lords voted to agree with all its main points, against the opposition of their Independent minority. The Independents in the Commons tried to have it rejected, but the Presbyterians got a motion to consider it through by forty-three votes, Stapleton telling against Hesilrig and Evelyn for the majority. A week later many of the London religious independents delivered a petition to the Commons in reply to the council's one, thanking and praising them for their grace towards them to date. This time the Independents won a decision to thank them, by just four votes, the classic teller teams of Hesilrig and Evelyn, and Holles and Stapleton, being pitted against each other again. The common council voted the petition a scandal. The Commons therefore kept the balance between the religious factions, and without them the Lords could not act effectively and the common council was thwarted. Subsequently Fairfax seemed to snub the upper House by informing only the Commons of the surrender of Oxford, and he had to apologize to the peers after they sent a furious rebuke.[150] A tract published in London in late June called on readers to protect Fairfax and

Cromwell, 'our preservers', from being first demobbed and then 'rooted out' by the same people who were trying to destroy the sects. It called the Scots the true enemies of Parliament and its cause.[151]

Into this imbroglio came Cromwell in July, returning to civilian life properly at last from the comparative peace and security of the army's quarters in Oxfordshire. He did so with gusto, immediately settling back into the regular existence of a serving MP. On 11 July he was put on his next committee, and had been appointed to a total of twenty-one by the end of the year, for purposes small (such as a examining a writ for a particular parliamentary by-election, investigating the conduct of the English ambassador at the Turkish court, or deciding whether to approve a petition for a new parish church) and large (some of which will be mentioned later).[152] Likewise, he swiftly returned to service as a teller of votes in divisions, ten times before the year ended. Here too the matters debated ranged from the trivial (such as whether to sack a member of the committee which ran the Welsh country of Montgomeryshire for Parliament) to the nationally important.

Along this whole range, however, the divisions were still often partisan, Cromwell being partnered with a prominent Independent like Hesilrig or Sir Henry Vane against Holles and Stapleton and their Presbyterian allies, who now increasingly included the former general Sir William Waller.[153] One function which Oliver does not seem to have resumed on his return was to carry messages to the Lords or engage in conferences with them, presumably because he remained in bad odour with them. In case the peers needed a reminder of his quarrel with one of their most respected members, the earl of Manchester, a tract was published in London in July, to greet Cromwell's return, repeating his accusations against the earl in detail; the author was probably Lilburne, pursuing his own grudge against Manchester. The Lords ordered the tract to be publicly burned in both Westminster and London.[154]

Certainly his glorious military career had only enhanced Cromwell's confidence as a patron and defender of religious radicals. In late July he wrote to Thomas Knyvett, the Norfolk squire whom he had captured at Lowestoft and for whom he had subsequently interceded, to call in that favour. One of Knyvett's tenants was allegedly persecuting 'poor men' among his neighbours because of their 'consciences' (which presumably caused them to absent themselves from church or object to what went on there). Oliver asked the squire to lean on his tenant to stop this, adding pointedly that 'I am not ashamed to solicit for such as are anywhere under a pressure of this kind'.[155] He had truly become a national leader of nonconformist Puritans, at all levels of society. On the last day of July he clashed with Holles over this, in a debate over whether to send some of the New Model Army immediately to join the war against the Irish rebels. Cromwell spoke passionately against doing so, on the grounds that the English royalists were still dangerous enough to need to be held down; though another reason was that any weakening of the New Model's forces at home was likely to strengthen the proponents of an intolerant religious settlement. His side carried the matter by a single vote, and Holles delivered a long and passionate attack on him as a persecutor of presbyterians in the New Model. Cromwell insisted that only one presbyterian officer had been dismissed from it, and he had distributed Scottish propaganda in an attempt to get the army to put pressure on Parliament to establish a Church like that of Scotland.[156] The truth of the matter is lost.

The key development of the month was the presentation of the joint terms of Parliament and the Scots to the captive king at Newcastle on 13 July. They required him effectively to hand over most of his royal powers to the two Houses, some for decades and others for ever, to accept the punishment of a long list of royalists, and to agree to a reform of the Church of England which removed bishops and cathedral chapters (though the form of it in other respects was still left open). On 1 August Charles stunned both nations by rejecting them: he expressed his willingness to keep on talking, but said that he could not consent to that which was absolutely destructive of his hereditary rights.[157] In legal terms, this meant that the war continued and Parliament's rule lacked any validity in the eyes of a large number of the British people. The Scots representatives in London immediately saw that what one of them termed the king's 'madness' stood to benefit the Independents, whom they credited with a desire both to remove the king from government altogether and to make a breach with Scotland.[158] In this situation, the Covenanters decided to give up on Charles and cut their losses, offering to hand him over to Parliament and leave England if all the expenses of their intervention there were covered as had been promised. They initially put these at almost a million pounds, but in September a sum of £400,000 was agreed instead (pushed through by the Presbyterians against an Independent bid for a lesser amount), and the Scottish army prepared to pull out when the first half of that was paid at the end of the year.[159]

On learning of the Scottish intention to make a deal, Cromwell himself was far from sanguine. He complained to Fairfax that at Westminster 'we are full of faction and worse', begged for the return of his cousin and ally Oliver St John from a mission with the army to help with the situation, and expressed fear that Sir Thomas had now discarded Oliver himself.[160] He clashed again with Holles in the House on 14 August, when the latter won a majority vote that ministers to be ordained in the new Church should be recruited more broadly than from 'saints', and that Parliament should not have the whole power to discipline clergy. Later the same day, it was Oliver's turn to win a motion against another Presbyterian teller, to offer initially no more than £100,000 to the Scots for their expenses: his hostility to them remained intense. When the Commons realized that it had to quadruple the sum, he attempted and failed to slight the Lords by backing a motion to seek a loan to enable the first instalment to be paid on time, without seeking the concurrence of the peers.[161]

Meanwhile those opposed to his vision of the religious future responded with a proportionate animosity. In August a pamphlet was published denouncing the New Model Army for being increasingly hijacked by preachers such as Peters and Dell, and turned into a vehicle for 'irreligion'.[162] In the same month one of the publications of the presbyterian minister

John Vicars, who produced potted histories of each phase of the war with a religious commentary, brought out the latest instalment with a preface that ranked Cromwell twelfth in order of importance after a list of other military commanders which included some purely local figures.[163] Another tract from this period was a list of Parliament's victories, which gave Essex, Leven, Manchester and Sir Thomas Fairfax most credit, and ranked Cromwell equal among six lesser generals: in such ways a history of the war was already being formed which pushed Oliver into the sidelines.[164] This particular broadsheet is notable for providing what is apparently the earliest securely dated portrait of Oliver. It is a crude woodcut but so distinctive that it must reflect some kind of reality: he has the shortest hair of all the men portrayed, hanging over his ears but cut into a bob above his collar, the largest nose, and the thinnest moustache, above a small beard of severely formal cut. This image matches that provided by Sir Philip Warwick, of a man who disdained elegance and ornamentation in the manner of a stereotypical Puritan.

September brought the deal with the Scots, and the sudden death of the earl of Essex, who had become one of the leaders of the Presbyterian party. He was given a lavish public funeral for his services, but of the New Model Army only three officers attended, two of them rigid presbyterians in religion and one Philip Skippon, who had been the earl's loyal infantry commander; it was noted that Fairfax, Cromwell and Ireton stayed away, and in Cromwell's case that was the more glaring in that he was in the vicinity.[165] The question of a successor to the earl as lord lieutenant of Yorkshire provoked another heated wrangle between Holles and Cromwell, the former proposing a prominent civilian member of the current House of Lords, and the latter Lord Fairfax.[166]

The deepening autumn brought no easing of the atmosphere. In October some of the Commons rounded on the army, with 'some heat', to which Cromwell replied with a plea 'for them and for charity': the cause of the affair is not known.[167] It may have been incidents like this, and a general weariness with parliamentary life, that produced an alleged exchange long after recalled by Edmund Ludlow, a young Wiltshire gentleman who had fought through the whole war as a fervent parliamentarian and Puritan. He claimed that he had walked with Oliver in a garden at this time, and the latter inveighed bitterly against the Presbyterians, adding that 'it was a miserable thing to serve a Parliament, to whom let a man be never so faithful, if one pragmatical fellow among them rise up and asperse him, he shall never wipe it off'. He rued the contrast with life in the army, which had a general in charge whom everybody respected and obeyed.[168] Ludlow, who by the time of writing had become bitterly hostile to Cromwell, implied that the latter was already losing faith in Parliaments as custodians of the nation's affairs, but the remarks ring true simply as an outburst of frustration and impatience with the verbal war of attrition in which Oliver now found himself mired.[169] Some tang of the fatigue may perhaps be found in a rare surviving letter of his to one of his children, Bridget, sent in October to her at the Oxfordshire quarters where she was still established with her husband, Ireton. He told her that the latter was sending him long letters, to which he was too busy to reply, and added just that he hoped that marriage had inflamed her love of Christ.[170]

Progress was still made with the settlement. In October bishops were at last abolished in the Church of England, though this was impelled by the need to use their lands as security for the loan required to pay off the Scots. Cromwell was put on the committee to launch the sale of these.[171] By now even matters which should not, on the surface of things, have been partisan, had become so. A proposal to use a ballot box when determining how rewards would be handed out for service to Parliament, to prevent bribery, was contested between the Presbyterians, with Stapleton as one of the tellers, and the Independents, with Cromwell and Hesilrig acting for them.[172] Sir Thomas Fairfax finally arrived in mid-November, to receive the formal thanks of Parliament, but six Presbyterian peers, one of them Willoughby, tried to persuade their house to snub him by making no formal recognition of his arrival.[173] Parliament had now made the decision to keep up Fairfax's army for a further six months – until the early part of the next summer – while starting the calculation of the arrears of pay due to it which was the first major step towards disbanding it.[174] Cromwell was put onto a committee to find ways of paying the money due to the men.[175] He himself was owed a hefty sum in unpaid wages for his military service, but his contacts ensured that he was better treated than most: in late November the existing parliamentary committee for the supply of the army's needs, dominated by Independents, made him a whopping payment of five hundred pounds.[176]

As the dead of winter arrived, his position remained at once prominent and glorious, and insecure. He was a war hero to many, mostly Independents, but a figure of suspicion and menace to others, mostly Presbyterians. He had been promised the landed estate and title of a nobleman, but neither had yet been properly obtained. The departure of the Scots removed their influence from English politics, which had been personally hostile to him as well as generally so to his preferred form of religion. On the other hand, it also removed a major reason for the continued existence of the New Model Army, which was the best prop of that form. The refusal of the king to accept terms, even though now a prisoner, put any settlement in doubt. Parliament seemed to be edging towards the establishment of a presbyterian Church which allowed some toleration for independent congregations and was under parliamentary control rather than separate from the state as in Scotland. That toleration was, however, not yet guaranteed, and it was completely unclear whether it would encompass people who wished to worship outside a national Church altogether, the sectaries who also looked to Oliver for help and protection.

On 15 December 1646 the Lords turned the screws on unorthodoxy by completing an ordinance to forbid preaching by the laity, a practice that was a feature of many sects and which traditionally minded people – the vast majority of the nation – found especially offensive.[177] In the Commons, Cromwell and Hesilrig partnered again as tellers in favour of a compromise whereby lay people would be banned from preaching but allowed to 'expound' the Bible. If this term were thought to embrace discussion, it was something that Puritans had been doing in private ever since the Elizabethan period. It was doubtless familiar to Cromwell from his own experience as one of them in Huntingdonshire and Cambridgeshire in the 1630s and had apparently first brought him to the attention of those in Cambridge who had decisively relaunched his political career. It was a feature of those sections of the New Model Army which had been deplored by Baxter. Cromwell's side in the debate was, however, heavily defeated, two Presbyterians serving against him as tellers for the majority.[178] Another troubling straw in the wind was a further long petition from the common council of London, which reflected adversely on the army. Oliver reported it to Fairfax, adding resignedly that 'this is our comfort, God is in heaven and He doth what pleaseth Him'.[179] The annual elections in December to the common council swept out many Independents and brought in some former royalists: opinion in the capital was swinging further against a religious settlement of the kind Cromwell favoured.[180]

Oliver himself, of course, showed not the slightest inclination to be deterred by these omens, as midwinter began to pass and preparations for 1647 began. In his time the British still observed a calendar in which the number of the year changed on 25 March, but informally, and to the mass of the population, the passage from December to January was still regarded as representing the end of a major annual cycle and the opening of another. The rebirth of the sun, and the palpable lengthening of the daylight a week beyond the end of the solstice, continued to inspire a host of folk customs of purification, blessing and renewal at this season, and the first of January was still New Year's Day even if the date did not alter then.[181] Cromwell faced this one as a man utterly determined to see through his career as a parliamentary leader, and as a sign of this he had at some point in late 1646 taken the decisive step of moving his family, and his home life, to the capital. When attending Parliament in the previous few years he had lodged in Long Acre, which, as its name suggests, was and is one of the longest streets in the plush area that joined London to Westminster, within an easy walk of both. Now he bought a house in Drury Lane, part of the same new development in that area and with the same convenience of situation, with the great smoking, teeming city – already one of the largest in the world – to the east, and the seat of government, law and legislature an equal distance to the west. Elizabeth and their younger children duly arrived from Ely.[182] No longer was Cromwell a country town dweller, an East Midlander or East Anglian. Henceforth he was forever a resident of the metropolis, as befitted his role as a national figure, general and politician. However precarious his position remained, he was now, truly, made.

CONCLUSION

After the story that has been told here it may now be possible to understand better the apparent paradox of Cromwell's career and reputation: that he should seem so pious, selfless and high-principled in his own words yet so devious, ruthless and self-seeking to others. It may also perhaps be more easily understood why he was both so successful and effective, and so divisive and controversial.

His success may be attributed to a number of factors. One is that he was undoubtedly a superb leader, efficient, charismatic and inspiring, and this showed to best advantage as a soldier. Until his status as a general made it more effective to supervise and control large bodies of men from behind, he led from the front, with exemplary courage and determination. He instilled a fierce discipline into his troopers, which they displayed both on and off the battlefield, but he also encouraged them in a sense of common participation in a divinely ordained cause. He worked hard, mainly by getting money out of others but also by using his own reserves and credit, to make sure that his soldiers were properly paid and supplied, and he constantly showed his pride in them. They repaid this with fervent loyalty, standing by him in the heat of conflict and remaining obedient to him when they jibbed at the authority of others. He was not the man who won Parliament the English Civil War, for this was a collective achievement in which the Scottish intervention of 1644 was a crucial turning point, tipping the odds against the king. We know too little about what actually happened at critical points: for example, the precise role that Cromwell played in the victory of the allied left wing at Marston Moor, the moment, if ever there was one, when the war hung in the balance. There is also an intractable question of the counter-factual, of what would have happened had he not been in command at certain places, most notably at Marston Moor and Naseby. An incompetent commander, in his position, would probably have lost the day, but it is hard to say whether Vermuyden, if promoted to the same position, would have done worse at the former battle, or Fleetwood or another of the New Model's most experienced cavalry colonels at the latter.

He did not just possess virtues as a soldier, however, but as a parliamentarian. Plainly, he was an effective and persuasive speaker, employing an unusual and distinctive style, harsh, emotional, aggressive and bereft of elegance, polish or erudition. It may well have been instilled in him by the Puritan preachers to whom he listened in his home district before joining the Long Parliament. Initially he made some gaffes there, but these never seemed to have harmed him or weakened faith in him among those who shared his views and ideals. Consistently, he worked well with allies in the House of Commons and commanded the sympathy of a large number of its members, usually the majority. Part of this was his unwavering zeal for the cause of religious and (as an accompaniment to this) political reform which was embraced by each grouping that was dominant in the House for most of the time during the period between 1640 and 1646: first the 'Junto', then the war party, and then the Independents. As a defender of Parliament's cause during the war he was not only very effective but absolutely dependable, especially at that dreadful moment in 1643 when the West Riding, Gainsborough and Lincoln had all fallen and East Anglia seemed open to the earl of Newcastle's army. At that point Cromwell seemed to Parliament to be its most determined champion in the entire region.

He was helped in his success by a tremendous measure of good luck, or as he saw it, divine providence. It is one aspect of this that, as said, he happened to be part of, and useful to, the dominant set of people in Parliament at most times, and that increasingly the soldiers on whom the parliamentarian cause came to rely were also sympathetic to his views. It was also integral to his career that Charles I mismanaged his government of his kingdoms so badly in the period 1638–42 that somebody who opposed the royal religious policy as Cromwell did could be swept into Parliament and then kept there. The sequence of events, each so perfectly timed, which restored him to military command in 1645, is of the same magnitude of good fortune. The same benign luck or providence saved him from death or serious injury in any of his military actions, most notably when he fell from his dying horse into the path of an assailant at Winceby, when he was wounded in the neck at Marston Moor, when his fellow generals Ireton and Skippon were injured at Naseby, and when the tide almost overturned his boat at Bridgwater, the cannon shot passed beside him at Prior's Hill, and the falling lead crashed into the street near him at Torrington. It helped a lot that he almost always fought with an advantage of numbers, ground and timing, most spectacularly at Marston Moor and Naseby, but also at Gainsborough, Langport and Torrington, and probably at Belton. When he and his men were in difficulties at Winceby, Fairfax came in and decided the battle, and fate seems to have kept Cromwell out of the rout which was inflicted on most of the parliamentarian horsemen at Edgehill. In his career as a commander of sieges in late 1645, he disposed of the best artillery train ever given to a Civil War general. During the lap of victory of the New Model Army after Naseby, it was either facing demoralized foes who fled at once, or determined foes who could nonetheless be overpowered by superior numbers and firepower. Although already a middle-aged man by the time that he first mounted a war horse, he was supported by a wonderfully hardy and reliable body, capable of surviving the knocks at Winceby and Marston Moor with ease, and enduring rain, cold and fatigue on successive campaigns, and especially in the west in 1645–6, without once falling seriously ill. Nor did he ever contract one of the epidemic diseases that ravaged the armies in which he served.

For much of the war he was a soldier who made consummate use of his advantages when pitted against weaker and disadvantaged foes. This really matters, because excellent as his cavalry were, they were not invincible: the Newark royalist horse and Goring's cavalry surprised and crushed units of them on raids, and at Newbury they were defeated and put to flight when caught on difficult ground by equal or greater numbers, and only saved by supporting infantry on the right terrain. Rupert's and Goring's troopers, the Newark cavalry, and the king's Northern Horse, were all as good as Cromwell's men, and the latter emerged victorious over each in the end just because eventually they faced each with the odds heavily in their favour. Once the Scots came in on Parliament's side, the royalists could only survive, or even win, as long as they did not make serious mistakes; which in the end they did.

Although we know pitifully little about the first four decades of his life, it has been clear to most of Cromwell's biographers that the informing and defining experience of his life was his conversion to a passionate, Puritan, religiosity, which probably took place in the early 1630s. Until then he seems a genuinely undistinguished and unambitious provincial minor gentleman, content to be a big fish in the small pond of Huntingdon. It was apparently the shock of defeat, humiliation and degradation there which led to his exile in relative ignominy and obscurity at St Ives, and his remaking there. He found a new, supportive and ultimately admiring community among the local Puritans. Conversion also seems to have given him a new and supremely powerful father figure and patron, in the Christian God, on whom Cromwell remained fixated for the rest of his life, eclipsing either a personal devotion to Christ or a fear of the Devil. The effect of this, on an emotional, impulsive and intemperate man in his prime, was that of a magnet on iron filings – to align everything to a single direction and purpose. It was Cromwell's usual good luck – in having a wealthy, childless and forgiving uncle – which restored his financial fortunes, but his new-found piety both restored his sense of self-worth and purpose and opened the way to a better political career. It linked him to a national Puritan network, to key figures to whom he was already related by blood or marriage, and a regional one which was – it appears – to play the vital part in giving him the successful role in Parliament that was to accompany and enable his stellar one as a soldier.

We may therefore regard his fervent, born-again, religiosity – extreme even by the standards of a conventionally religious age – as absolutely genuine. It became implanted in the core of his being and identity; and, as said, in terms of apparent worldly outcomes, it worked. One consequence of his new persona as an (initially clandestine) opponent of official religious policy was his enduring sympathy with radical evangelical Protestants who were either actually persecuted by, or in danger of persecution by, the prevailing ecclesiastical establishment. This explains his intervention on behalf of John Lilburne as soon as the Long Parliament met, and his long-sustained support for that courageous, wayward and rather irritating man. It also accounts for his subsequent, and associated, steady championship and protection of those who wanted to meet for worship and religious discussion outside the formal and currently prescribed services of the Church, namely independents or sectaries. This made him into an exposed and potentially vulnerable figure, much detested by those of a more religiously conservative temperament; and those were a powerful lobby in the parliamentarian wartime cause: most of the House of Lords and many of the Commons, most of the initial set of generals and provincial commanders and administrators, and all of the Scottish Covenanters who came to Parliament's aid.

On the other hand, it also produced some excellent results, which would not have been obtained if a man of Cromwell's comparatively lowly position in the social elite had adopted a more conventional set of attitudes. It ensured him a set of able and committed allies in the Commons, who often exerted a prevailing influence there, and also in the Lords where they operated as an active and often influential minority. It also enabled him to build up a military clientele, of independents and sectaries who gave him their devoted allegiance, filled up his own regiment, and became ever more prominent in the armies which proved to be the most successful in Parliament's service. In other words, a regard for heterodox opinions on the part of godly Puritans gave him a distinctive power base which he could not otherwise have obtained: and so genuine instinct and political self-interest made a good match.

Here less attractive – and less often remarked – aspects of his personality come into play. One is his relentless pursuit of self-promotion. His advocacy on behalf of Lilburne was an intervention on behalf of somebody whom Cromwell had never met, but who had been a celebrated victim of the crackdown on Puritanism instituted by Charles I's Personal Rule. It was doubtless conducted, as has been said, with passionate sincerity, but it also immediately brought Cromwell to the attention of the House of Commons in a context which could reasonably be expected to win him sympathy and regard, and so it did. His parliamentary career developed steadily from there onward. His military career initially involved greater problems in attracting notice and glory, as his actions were for a long time minor, local and fought at a great distance from the capital. Oliver solved this problem, as other regional commanders had before him, by securing the attention of supportive journalists, who would trumpet his achievements in the capital. It seems impossible to tell whether he briefed these authors himself, or had a friend or follower who did the job for him, but in each of his early actions – at Lowestoft, Crowland and Belton – his own achievements were magnified over those of his fellow commanders. The very first achievement of his horse regiment, of quashing an attempted royalist uprising at St Albans, became part of his portfolio of successes even though he does not seem to have been present.

In his own accounts of military actions, he adopted a standard tactic, of according all glory to God and extolling the achievements of his side in the plural form, without mentioning names, save those of his immediate subordinates at Gainsborough: which served at once to give an appearance of modesty while completely eclipsing his commanders. At Belton he commanded jointly with John Hotham and at Gainsborough was under the leadership of John Meldrum; but both are completely invisible in his account. In Hotham's case, this could be taken as charity as his performance had been poor, but Meldrum must have decided on the bold uphill

attack and the battle on the summit which broke the main body of the
enemy; and yet he is never mentioned, though in his own despatch he gave
full credit to Cromwell for his part of the action. Moreover, Oliver was a
master of representing actions to emphasize their most positive aspects.
Belton was a drawn skirmish, at which he committed the elementary
mistake of abandoning the field to pursue a fleeing enemy wing before the
action was won: but in his (published) report it was a total, glittering,
victory. Likewise, Gainsborough ended in disaster, the relieving party
chased from the district by an approaching field army and the town invested
once more, this time without hope of survival. In Cromwell's account of it,
repeated to one set of recipients after another, it was explicitly a glorious
success, with full detail provided on his own actions and those of his
regiment in securing it. After Marston Moor he scorned the part played by
his Scottish allies in the achievement; and the historical record is such that
the justice of this can never be determined.

From there onward, he had less need to promote himself directly in this
way, because he had a reliable set of admiring journalists who could
normally be relied upon to eulogize him; and by the autumn of 1644 one
of them had provided a charismatic and enduring nickname for him,
'Ironsides', with the almost certainly invented story that it had been
bestowed by the most celebrated of the royalist generals. In his service with
the New Model Army there was no call for self-promotion at all, because
his actions in it were always represented with admiration in all the official
despatches to Parliament, as his prominence and effectiveness ensured. His
main failures were at Newbury and on the western spring campaign and
the Midland campaign of 1645: in the first case his men were routed on the
battlefield, and in the second and third, forced back by raiding royalist
troopers, each time belonging to George Goring. In the last two examples,
his lack of achievement was smothered in reports, and both cases (and
especially the Midland one) overshadowed by initial minor successes. After
Newbury, far more drastic action was needed in the face of a public outcry,
and he colluded with his fellow generals on that flank of the battlefield to

make a scapegoat of the commander on the other. Like most Civil War propagandists, on both sides, he also routinely gave the impression that in every action his enemies outnumbered his own men, so making the ensuing successes the more superlative. The rising Cromwell undoubtedly believed that the glory of God was best served by winning the maximum glory for himself.

This characteristic was accompanied by another, a tendency to demonize opponents, and to see the universe as a battlefield between good and evil powers, in which he was invariably ranged on the side of good, which meant that of his deity. In a sense this view of the cosmos is built into evangelical Christianity, and so was inevitably into Puritanism. In Oliver, however, it was apparently joined with brain chemistry: the unrestrained verbal violence with which he lashed out at his opponents on the corporation of Huntingdon, and which got him into such fatal political trouble, is an early example of this disposition. Soon after he manifested his religious conversion, at St Ives, he was already referring to the executors of royal religious policy as 'the enemies of God his truth'. This trait of course carried straight into the burgeoning political and then military crisis of the 1640s, for which he made a natural holy warrior, a Puritan jihadi. From the start, he was anxious not just to assist and protect Puritan victims of actual or apparent persecution but to obtain savage retaliation against their enemies, calling in 1640 to 1642 first for the prosecution of leading churchmen who had enacted royal policy and then for action against emerging defenders of the king.

When war erupted he was able to employ physical violence in place of legal action, and revelled in it, exulting over 'doing execution' on fleeing royalists at Belton and the killing of the helpless opposing commander at Gainsborough. The pamphlet which eulogized his campaign around Stamford in July 1643 exulted in the slaughter of the wretched countrymen near the town. All this led up to the prodigious massacre of the defeated royalists at Marston Moor, whom in his own account Cromwell systematically dehumanized in a pair of images which made them first mechanical and then demonic. This attitude to warfare was scripted by Old Testament accounts of genocide against heathen tribes, but these matched naturally with a savage streak in his own nature. In the campaign of the New Model, however, he restrained that, becoming apparently more aware of the propaganda rewards of clemency. He cannot be held responsible for the vile treatment of the royalist women after Naseby, as that was the work of the infantry and not of his troopers. That incident seems to have induced the New Model to adopt a standard new policy of restraint in dealing with defeated enemies, which Oliver followed to the letter. He imitated the dealings of Fairfax with the Dorset and Wiltshire Clubmen, in limiting bloodshed, imprisoning leaders and letting the rank and file go home. He applied punctiliously the tariff of terms accorded to governors of royalist fortresses who offered to negotiate terms, and which varied according to the point at which they did so. This held good even at the Catholic stronghold of Basing House, which was treated with the greatest severity because it attempted surrender after the attacking soldiers had got into the precinct. Even here, however, Cromwell cannot be held directly responsible for the limited slaughter that ensued because (allegedly) it was his men who refused to negotiate, being eager for the plunder which was a more important objective than bloodshed. On the other hand it could be said that Oliver had prepared the mindset of his soldiers for violence and retribution by addressing them before the storming of Basing House on a Biblical text which condemned idolatrous heathens.

The same tendency to polarize the world, and see ideological differences in terms of cosmological conflicts, was applied to his own wartime party and its allies. For the first year and a half of the fighting there was little sign of this, for the simple reason that it was not yet a feature of parliamentarian religious politics. As soon as the dispute between presbyterian and independent opened up at the beginning of 1644, however, Cromwell entered the fray firmly on the latter side. First he was concerned only to protect real or apparent religious radicals among his own troopers, but by the middle of the year he had gone over to the offensive. When he spoke of Marston

Moor as having been the victory of 'the party of God' there can be little doubt that he did not mean the allied cause as a whole, but the independent one. This is proved by the campaign which he then mounted for the rest of the autumn to remove rigid presbyterians from the army of the earl of Manchester. The policy of Manchester himself, of his presbyterian officers, and even of some of the Scottish presbyterians in England who became involved in the matter, was to try to accommodate both sides in the same army; but it was Cromwell who became increasingly obdurate. On this we have only the testimony of his opponents, but that is so unanimous and from such a range of sources, public and private, that it can be accepted.

In his own written words, however, Oliver himself cannily avoided setting forth this policy, and instead firmly, if vaguely, blamed those with opposing views for malevolence, intolerance and calumny. In the New Model Army this dual policy was maintained. There he had a much easier and more pleasant time of it, because there were far fewer rigid presbyterians in it, and independents were proportionately stronger. He did all that he could to encourage them there, and to extol their value as able soldiers and loyal parliamentarians before Parliament and the public. He was abetted in this tactic by his new commander, Fairfax, although the latter seems to have had much less of a personal zeal for the independent cause. Cromwell's public declarations, however, were carefully framed to avoid giving the impression of partisan independency, but spoke a language of mutual tolerance and forbearance, and unity, and common service in the cause of Parliament's and the nation's liberties. This was calculated to offset the picture of him as a crusader for religious independency, and woo the middle ground of opinion which still hoped for moderation, comprehension and reconciliation. He certainly seemed to become willing to accept the settlement of a presbyterian ecclesiastical system in England and Wales, as long as this allowed freedom to those who wished to worship outside it. That compromise, however, itself embodied a partisan position, which unified the Independents as a political force and was unacceptable to the great majority of the nation, including both royalists and most presbyterians.

Had Cromwell not been prepared to accept a presbyterian structure for the Church of England in 1645–6, his political position would simply have become untenable, and there is no sign that he regarded such a system as a good thing in itself, and no telling with how much reluctance he acquiesced in it.

His tendency to view his own ideological opponents as those of God was accompanied in turn by a readiness to dispose of members of his own wartime party who had become inconvenient. There was a preceding dramatic illustration of this trait in his nature – of removing people who were in his way – in his botched attempt to get his uncle declared a lunatic so that he could obtain immediate access to the old man's estate. Once the war was under way, he had better success with that trio of upper-class dimwits whom he found to be liabilities in 1643: Lord Grey of Groby, John Hotham and Lord Willoughby of Parham. Grey got off lightest, as Cromwell simply denounced him behind his back to fellow parliamentarians when he failed to co-operate soon enough. Hotham proved hostile and an ideological opponent as well as an incompetent commander, and so was arrested and charged with treachery, an act which had the unlooked-for consequence of pushing him over the brink into actual disloyalty and destroying him completely. Willoughby, the most capable and least culpable, was the hardest to dislodge, but Cromwell managed it by a campaign of defamation within Parliament in which he told blatant untruths. He was fortunate in that the lord's nerve broke and he gave way voluntarily.

That was not the case with Cromwell's last and most eminent victim in this context, the earl of Manchester. The tactic was identical, of a campaign of accusation waged within Parliament and its executive committee, to destroy the earl's reputation as a soldier, and also that as a reliable supporter of the war itself. Once more Oliver supported his charges with a catalogue of lies and misrepresentations, though this overlaid the basic truth that Manchester was a slow and cautious general whose instinct for a defensive war was accompanied by a growing wish for a compromise peace, some-thing that was anathema to Cromwell. The latter was also careful to gather a large number of supporters and allies for the attack. This time, however, Manchester fought back with unexpected determination and made equally damaging allegations against Oliver himself, the truth of which cannot now be established, at a time when Cromwell was becoming aware of other powerful enemies. Oliver's reaction was swift and decisive: to abandon the contest and support a solution which would set aside Manchester and himself with most of the existing generals.

Thereafter he felled no more colleagues in the war effort, not merely because he had made too many foes within his party and perhaps sustained too great a scare, but because he did not have to do so. His service as lieutenant to Sir William Waller was too brief for friction to develop between them, and Waller was at the time an important ally in the attack on Manchester. Fairfax, in turn, was the perfect commander for Oliver: capable and dynamic, popular with his officers, and prepared fully to support Cromwell's twin major aims of winning the war as swiftly and absolutely as possible, and promoting the cause of religious independency. These cases do make it clear that Cromwell suffered from no inherent inability to accept subordination to another's authority and no innate tendency to quarrel with anybody with whom he was partnered. Instead they drive home the conclusion that he targeted individuals who had become obstructive and inconvenient to him; and that he did so with a high degree of both ability and ruthlessness.

He also, however, bore grudges. One example of this trait is his treatment of Robert Bernard, the smooth lawyer who outmanoeuvred and humiliated him at Huntingdon and so precipitated his flight from the town. The petty and sustained malice with which Cromwell persecuted this man in wartime is revealing, as is the manner in which he then hounded the Hothams to their deaths. They were already ruined, as politicians and soldiers, but Oliver pressed on with his vendetta against them, first by testifying at the trial of the son (possibly again pushing past the truth of events, such as when recounting the action at Belton) and then by fighting attempts to postpone or reprieve the execution of the father. A concomitant to this remorseless pursuit of personal foes is his enduring loyalty to, and desire to promote, friends, subordinates and relatives who were loyal to him and shared his political and religious views. His kindness to Lilburne is one example, and others are his affection for his cavalry officers, especially those who had served under him in his own regiment and in the earl of Manchester's army.

This unwavering fixity of ideological commitment, and commitment to personal relationships with reliable and faithful people, was potently combined with a mental agility and an immense capacity for learning, above all on the job. At Belton, as said, he made the classic mistake of pursuing a defeated cavalry wing away from the field, leaving the rest of the action to be lost or drawn behind him. On the next occasion on which he fought a pitched battle, at Gainsborough, he deliberately avoided that very mistake, with initially spectacularly successful results. Thereafter he repeated his avoidance of it every time, and fortune gave him the superior numbers which made the retention of a body of horsemen for further action possible. When his attack on the earl of Manchester became difficult and dangerous, he changed tactics completely and so helped to break the deadlock and defuse the situation. In his first year as an MP he once proposed a motion and found himself unsupported on it. He never made that mistake again. He also learned to cope, admirably, in a theatre of parliamentary politics to which he was in many ways quite unsuited. Especially during his periods active in Parliament between 1644 and 1646, he found himself dealing with people who opposed him ideologically, and traded arguments with him publicly and vehemently, whom he could not fight physically and seemed to have no ultimate prospect of removing politically. To defeat them over particular issues, he had to rely on winning over a middle ground of MPs who tended instinctually to support moderation, compromise and common sense, though they could be fired up by slights to the honour of their House and threats to their cause, as well as inspired by conspicuous successes. The strain of this shifting and often indecisive war of verbal attrition told on Cromwell, especially in late 1646 when he seemed to be consigned to it indefinitely, and partisan identity, and rancour, seemed to be ever increasing. Yet he kept on engaging in it, without faltering, tiring or making any more apparent mistakes.

The same suppleness, and also his inherent deviousness, shows in Cromwell's letters, which are filled with the same rough, idiomatic eloquence that others attributed to his speeches. When approaching a difficult issue, and trying to persuade somebody of his case with respect to it, he would often employ what I have termed the 'scatter-gun' approach. By this, he would question whether a given situation was actually that which those with whom he differed supposed it to be, and then go on to show various different ways in which, *even if* their impression of it was correct, reasonable people should still react to it as he wished. He varied his tone to the occasion, warm and cajoling in one instance, frigidly courteous in another, excited, uplifted and exhortatory in a third, and occasionally menacing and bullying. Whether or not he was a master of persuasion – and in most cases the evidence from this period does not enable a conclusion to be drawn – he certainly attempted to be one.

Thus we have the man, aged in his forties and during this critical period which turned him from an obscure provincial into an enduring national figure. Even now, before his political track record stretched any further and the number of those disenchanted by him greatly increased, and that of people who were won over to him by his deeds and persona as a figure in power also burgeoned, the complexity of his nature is revealed. He was courageous, devout, resolute, principled, intelligent, eloquent, able, adaptable and dedicated, but also self-seeking, unscrupulous, dishonest, manipulative, vindictive and bloodthirsty: definitely not somebody to be taken simply at his word. There was no internal contradiction in this bundle of qualities, for they were all woven together, in a single seamless whole, at the centre of which lay an acquired sense of a special relationship with God, which informed and justified all.

NOTES

ABBREVIATIONS

BL British Library
Bod L Bodleian Library, Oxford
CJ *Journals of the House of Commons*, London, 1803
CSPD *Calendar of State Papers, Domestic Series*. The volumes used were edited by John Bruce, and then William Douglas Hamilton, in London between 1860 and 1891.
CSPV *Calendar of State Papers and Manuscripts Relating to English Affairs, Existing in the Archives and Collections of Venice*. The volumes used were edited by Allen R. Hinds, in London between 1925 and 1926.
HMC Historical Manuscripts Commission
L Library
LJ *Journals of the House of Lords*, London, 1803.
NA National Archives
RO Record Office

INTRODUCTION

1. Barry Coward, *Oliver Cromwell*, London, 1991; Peter Gaunt, *Oliver Cromwell*, Oxford, 1996; J. C. Davis, *Oliver Cromwell*, London, 2001; Martyn Bennett, *Oliver Cromwell*, London, 2006; and Ian Gentles, *Oliver Cromwell, Basingstoke, 2011*. The lull since 2011 may be due to the fact that many colleagues have been expecting a full-length treatment by John Morrill, and also awaiting the outcome of the hugely valuable project which John has been leading, of a new edition of Cromwell's letters and speeches.
2. The military studies are Simon Robbins, *God's General*, Stroud, 2003; Frank Kitson, *Old Ironsides*, London, 2004; and Martyn Bennett, *Cromwell at War*, London, 2017; the collections, John Morrill, ed., *Oliver Cromwell and the English Revolution*, London, 1990; Patrick Little, ed., *Oliver Cromwell: New Perspectives*, Basingstoke, 2009; and Jane A. Mills, ed., *Cromwell's Legacy*, Manchester, 2012.
3. This is also the Cromwell of John Morrill, and the contributors to his 1990 collection, and of the military studies cited. It was formulated for their generation by the essays of Blair Worden from the 1980s onward, collected by him in *God's Instruments*, Oxford, 2012; but Blair's Cromwell is also that of the great Victorian authorities, Thomas Carlyle, Samuel Rawson Gardiner and Charles Harding Firth.
4. For this see Mark Nixon, *Samuel Rawson Gardiner and the Idea of History*, Woodbridge, 2012, 132.

5. Wilbur Cortez Abbott, ed., *The Writings and Speeches of Oliver Cromwell*, Cambridge, MA, 1937, vol. 1, xiv.
6. Coward, *Oliver Cromwell*, 1.
7. Davis, *Oliver Cromwell*, 2–3.
8. John Morrill, 'Cromwell and his Contemporaries', in Morrill, ed., *Oliver Cromwell*, 259.
9. Patrick Little, 'Introduction', in Little, ed., *Oliver Cromwell*, 7–12.
10. Simon Healy, 'The Unmaking of Oliver Cromwell', in Ibid., 22.
11. Ronald Hutton, *The British Republic*, Basingstoke, 1990, 23–4, 58–78; *Debates in Stuart History*, Basingstoke, 2004, 93–131; *A Brief History of Britain 1485–1660*, London, 2010, 276–82.

CHAPTER ONE: THE PREHISTORIC CROMWELL

1. John Rutt, ed., *The Diary of Thomas Burton*, London, 1828, vol. 2, 529; Thomas Le Wright, *An Exact Character or Narrative Of The late right Noble and Magnificent Lord, Oliver Cromwell*, London, 1658, 3; *The Pourtraiture of his Royal Highness, Oliver Late Protector*, London, 1659, 7–8; Henry Fletcher, *The Perfect Politician*, London, 1660, 2.
2. The issue was well discussed by Antonia Fraser, *Cromwell: Our Chief of Men*, London, 1975, 24.
3. Robert Davies, ed., *The Life of Marmaduke Rawdon of York*, Camden Society, 1863, 112–13, testifies to the building as a tourist attraction in the mid-1660s.
4. The matter was discussed by Davies in his notes to the source cited above, and by Andrew Barclay, *Electing Cromwell*, London, 2011, 32; and the development of the assertion has been well studied by Laura Lunger Knoppers, '"Sing Old Noll the Brewer"', *Seventeenth Century* 15.1 (2000), 32–52.
5. Huntingdonshire RO, 3870/1, sub 1621 and 1628. See the discussion in Caroline Clifford and Alan Akeroyd, *Risen from Obscurity? Oliver Cromwell and Huntingdonshire*, Huntingdon, 2002, 23.
6. The reference number for the register is above, the entry sub 1599. Martyn Bennett, *Oliver Cromwell*, London, 2006, 3–4, seemingly first noticed this anomaly in it.
7. *CSPV (1655–6)*, 160–1.
8. The editor of the record above notes that other sources record a visit to London at this time by a rabbi from Amsterdam, not Antwerp, without mentioning any prior connection between that man and Cromwell. This compounds the likelihood that the Venetian was misinformed about that, as well as the home city of the visitor.
9. What follows is based on T. S. Willan, *River Navigation in England 1600–1750*, London, 1936; Peter Bigmore, *The Bedfordshire and Huntingdonshire Landscape*, London, 1979; Christopher Taylor, *The Cambridgeshire Landscape*, London, 1973; David Lack, *The Birds of Cambridgeshire*, Cambridge, 1934; H. C. Darby, *The Draining of the Fens*, Cambridge, 1940, 1–11, 23–8; J. R. Ravensdale, *Liable to Flood: Village Landscape on the Edge of the Fens AD 45 –1850*, Cambridge, 1974; Tom Williamson, *England's Landscape: East Anglia*, London, 2006, 198–202; Margaret Spufford, *Contrasting Communities: English Villagers in the Sixteenth and Seventeenth Centuries*, Cambridge, 1974; and Emily Cockayne, *Hubbub: Filth, Noise and Stench in England 1600–1740*, London, 2007, 200. Detail has been added from the author's own knowledge of the regions concerned, especially gained when working with the Cambridge Conservation Volunteers in the 1970s.
10. No picture of Huntingdon survives from Cromwell's time, but John Speed made a plan of it in 1610, which is reproduced on p. 212 of Bigmore, *The Bedfordshire and Huntingdonshire Landscape*.
11. Ibid., 211–14; Philip G. M. Dickinson, *Oliver Cromwell and Huntingdon*, Huntingdon, 1981.
12. Bigmore, *The Bedfordshire and Huntingdonshire Landscape*, 107–8; Mary Carter, ed., *Edmund Pettis's Survey of St Ives*, Cambridgeshire Records Society 16 (2002), 9–35.
13. Reg Holmes, *Cromwell's Ely*, Ely, 1975, passim.
14. For this in general see Sasha Handley, *Sleep in Early Modern England*, London, 2016.
15. Dickinson, *Oliver Cromwell and Huntingdon*, 16.

16. For a broad look at this, see Craig Koslofsky, *Evening's Empire: A History of the Night in Early Modern Europe*, Cambridge, 2011.
17. Mark Noble, *Memoirs of the Protectoral House of Cromwell*, 3rd edition, London, 1787, vol. 1, 1–123.
18. Diarmaid MacCulloch, *Thomas Cromwell*, London, 2018, 9–21, worked out the exact social relationship of the two families.
19. This has been well studied by Lloyd Bowen, 'Oliver Cromwell (alias Williams) and Wales', in Patrick Little, ed., *Oliver Cromwell*, Basingstoke, 2009, 168–94.
20. It hangs in the Cromwell Museum at Huntingdon.
21. The work begun by Noble in teasing these out was completed by Stanley J. Weyman, 'Oliver Cromwell's Kinsfolk', *English Historical Review* 6 (1891), 48–60.
22. Formerly known as Hinchinbrooke. It is now a conference and arts centre.
23. The portraits in the Cromwell Museum, long said to represent him and his wife, have been rejected as such, as not only is there a lack of any positive identification, but they show people of the wrong period, and – in Robert's case – the wrong age.
24. The syllabus was worked out by Dickinson, *Oliver Cromwell and Huntingdon*, 16.
25. The admission entry is on p. 151 of the college's first register. The other details are from Nicholas Rogers and Christopher Parish, *Cromwell and Sidney Sussex*, Cambridge, 1999.
26. The will was first tracked down, like so much else, by Noble, *Memoirs*, vol. 1, 82.
27. His family tried to get Oliver spared wardship altogether, and lost, so that the right to ward the estate was sold for £150 to two Crown officials: but the latter may have been acting for the Cromwell family and in any case Oliver came of age only a year later: the record is printed in Wilbur Cortez Abbott, ed., *The Writings and Speeches of Oliver Cromwell*, Cambridge, MA, 1937, vol. 1, 27–8.
28. See the comment on her by a Venetian ambassador in *CSPV* (1653–4), 284.
29. The register is in the Guildhall Library, MS 641912. The entry and the settlement of the jointure were of course found by Noble, *Memoirs*, vol. 1, 123–4.
30. A large version of it hangs in the Cromwell Museum.
31. Again, Mark Noble picked out the story from the parish register at Huntingdon: *Memoirs*, vol. 1, 132–57.
32. Ibid., 88–90.
33. Thomas Le Wright, *An Exact Character or Narrative Of The late right Noble, and magnificent lord, Oliver Cromwell*, London, 1658, 4–5; Samuel Carrington, *The History of the Life and Death of His Most Serene Highness, Oliver, Late Lord Protector*, London, 1659, 3–4; *The Pourtraiture of His Royal Highness*, 7–8; William Winstanley, *England's Worthies*, London, 1660, A4; J. H. Gent, *The History of the Life and Death of Oliver Cromwell*, London, 1663, 2–4; James Heath, *Flagellum*, 3rd edition, London, 1665, 4–11; Sir William Dugdale, *A Short View of the Late Troubles in England*, Oxford, 1681, 459; Sir George Bate, *Elenchus Motuum Nuperorum in Anglia*, London, 1685, vol. 2, 237.
34. E.g. BL, Harleian MS 991, f. 222 (he acts in a student play at Cambridge and impulsively puts a crown on his head); Heath, *Flagellum*, 7 (he ad-libs in a school play to crown himself); Carrington, *History*, 3–4 (he acts the part of a king in a play at Cambridge most convincingly); Gent, *History*, 2 (he acts in a student play at Cambridge, *The Five Senses*, and 'stumbled at a crown', which 'he had also dreamed he should wear'). Note that all these reports may be garbled versions of the same one, itself uncertain in provenance and value.
35. Carrington, *History*, 4.
36. John Morrill, 'The Making of Oliver Cromwell', in John Morrill, ed., *Oliver Cromwell and the English Revolution*, London, 1990, 19–25, sums up the evidence. Abbott, ed., *Writings and Speeches*, vol. 1, 46–52, prints the documents.
37. Good accounts of these events have been given over the years by Derek Hirst, *England in Conflict 1603–1660*, London, 1999, 79–129; Barry Coward, *The Stuart Age*, 3rd edition, London, 2003, 117–64; and Tim Harris, *Rebellion: Britain's First Stuart Kings*, Oxford, 2014, 63–278. My own can be found in my *Brief History of Britain 1485–1660*, London, 2010, 193–216.

38. Weyman, 'Oliver Cromwell's Kinsfolk', made the computation.
39. The records are printed in Abbott, ed., *Writings and Speeches*, vol. 1, 52–64, though he gets the speech wrong.
40. See Ibid., 52–4, for the parliamentary elections, and the entries by Richard Cust on the first Lord Montagu and Brian Quintrell on the first Earl of Manchester in the *Oxford Dictionary of National Biography*, vol. 38, 700–2 and 732–6.
41. Huntingdonshire RO, Accession 4880.
42. The papers with respect to this affair are calendared in *CSPD 1629–31*, viii–ix, and printed in Abbott, ed., *Writings and Speeches*, vol. 1, 67–8. There is further information in the copy of Thomas Beard's affidavit in Huntingdonshire RO, 2913/2/10/B/8. Bernard's character is displayed in his letters in the same record office, M28/1/31–4.
43. The final accord of the sale is in NA, CP 25/2/433/7 CHASITRIN.
44. This episode was fully studied by Brian Quintrell, 'Oliver Cromwell and Distraint of Knighthood', *Bulletin of the Institute of Historical Research* 57 (1984), 224–30.
45. The relevant documents are in the Huntingdonshire RO: the St Ives Manor Court Book 1632–61 (under 19 October 1633), and the Vestry Book 1626–1726 (entries 1633–34), supplemented by Noble, *Memoirs*, vol. 1, 103–4, 260. Carter, ed., *Edmund Pettis's Survey of St Ives*, 9–12, provides the administrative background.
46. The possibility of forgery was suggested by Clifford and Akeroyd, *Risen from Obscurity?*, 33. The earlier meeting was cited by Noble, *Memoirs*, vol. 1, 103–4. The two entries are extensively discussed in Bennett, *Oliver Cromwell*, 29–30.
47. The entries, like those for the baptisms of all Cromwell's previous children, are in the register of St John's parish church, Huntingdon, in the county record office.
48. The original record is in Mayerne's casebook, at BL, Sloane MS 2069, f. 96v.
49. Sir Philip Warwick, *Memoirs of the Reign of Charles 1*, London, 1813, 275–6.
50. It was Simon Healy who first cast doubt upon this source, in '1636: The Unmaking of Oliver Cromwell', in Patrick Little, ed., *Oliver Cromwell*, Basingstoke, 2009, 32–4. He still, however, credits Warwick's report.
51. F. N. L. Poynter and W. J. Bishop, eds, *A Seventeenth-Century Doctor and His Patients*, Bedfordshire Historical Record Society Publications 21 (1951), 76.
52. Noble, *Memoirs*, vol. 1, 105n.
53. The affair has been investigated by Healy, '1636', 26–30. The hostile posthumous sources were Dugdale, *Short View of the Late Troubles*, 459, and John Hacket, *Scrinia Reserata*, London, 1693, Part 2, 212.
54. Again, the will and its consequences are studied most carefully by Healy, '1636', 29–31.
55. Noble, *Memoirs*, vol. 1, 106–7. Holmes, *Cromwell's Ely*, 10, provides a detailed description of Cromwell's new home.
56. Ibid., 12. Abbott, ed., *Writings and Speeches*, vol. 1, 89–95, prints some of the documents. Cromwell's commission as a JP on 20 July 1638 is in Birmingham Reference L, Coventry MSS, Commissions of the Peace, no. 457.
57. Noble, *Memoirs*, vol. 1, 319.
58. The tax returns were noted by Morrill, 'The Making of Oliver Cromwell', 22.
59. Cromwell's compliance with Ship Money, and lack of apparent interest in national politics in the 1630s, has been noted by Morrill, 'The Making of Oliver Cromwell', 36; Barry Coward, *Oliver Cromwell*, London, 1991, 9; Peter Gaunt, *Oliver Cromwell*, Oxford, 1996, 36; and Bennett, *Oliver Cromwell*, 33–4.
60. This and what follows is based on Samuel Wells, *The History of the Drainage of the Great Level of the Fens*, London, 1830, 1–137; H. C. Darby, *The Draining of the Fens*, Cambridge, 1940, 3–57; L. E. Harris, 'Sir Cornelius Vermuyden and the Great Level of the Fens', *Proceedings of the Cambridgeshire Antiquarian Society* 45 (1952), 17–27; and *Vermuyden and the Fens*, London, 1953, 64–72; Keith Lindley, *Fenland Riots and the English Revolution*, London, 1982, 1–105, passim; Margaret Albright Knittl, 'The Design for the Initial Drainage of the Great Level of the Fens', *Agricultural History Review* 55 (2007), 23–50; and Eric S. Ash, *The Draining of the Fens*, Baltimore, MD, 2017, 192–3.

61. NA, SP 16/230, f. 151, summarized in *CSPD (1631–1633)*, 501.

62. Dugdale, *Short View of the Late Troubles*, 460.

63. Charles Firth, *Oliver Cromwell and the Rule of the Puritans in England*, New York, 1900, 33–4; Fraser, *Cromwell: Our Chief of Men*, 52–4; Roger Howell Jnr, *Cromwell*, London, 1977, 20.

64. Morrill, 'The Making of Oliver Cromwell', 37; Coward, *Oliver Cromwell*, 9; Bennett, *Oliver Cromwell*, 33–4; Barclay, *Electing Cromwell*, 75–96.

65. Lindley, *Fenland Riots and the English Revolution*, 96–105; Barclay, *Electing Cromwell*, 87.

66. Barclay, *Electing Cromwell*, 87, who draws attention to the importance of notes made by the bishop of letters he had sent, which mention Cromwell in connection with the riots and, though ambiguous, seem to imply that he was opposed to them. The documents concerned are Bod L, Rawlinson MS C368, ff. 12–13, and certainly read to me as if Cromwell were acting as the bishop's lieutenant: and this would fit well with his appointment as a JP.

67. BL, Additional MS 21422, f. 125.

68. Holmes, *Cromwell's Ely*, 7–9; Dickinson, *Oliver Cromwell and Huntingdon*, passim; Bigmore, *The Bedfordshire and Huntingdonshire Landscape*, 107–8; Noble, *Memoirs*, vol. 1, 5–17.

69. For my own summary of these matters and what follows, see my *Brief History of Britain*, 93–108, 198–201, 214, 221–4.

70. This is mainly inferred from the Civil War allegiances of its members, to be discussed below.

71. Rogers and Parish, *Cromwell and Sidney Sussex*, 1–2; Mark H. Curtis, *Oxford and Cambridge in Transition 1558–1642*, Oxford, 1959, 208–11; and Margo Todd, 'Samuel Ward', *Oxford Dictionary of National Biography* 57 (2004), 342–4.

72. Until 1990 it was generally assumed that Beard was a Puritan, and the major religious influence on Cromwell: the last publication to emphasize such influence seems to have been Judy Sproxton, 'From Calvin to Cromwell through Beard', *Journal of European Studies* 25 (1995), 17–33. Morrill, 'The Making of Oliver Cromwell', 26–8, correctly positioned him instead as a Calvinist conformist and pluralist, a line followed up by Alexandra Walsham's entry on him in the *Oxford Dictionary of National Biography* 4 (2004), 537–8. His role in Huntingdon's civic affairs is signalled in corporation documents printed in Abbott, ed., *Writings and Speeches*, vol. 1, 24–52. His books were *The Theatre of God's Judgements*, London, 1597, 1612 and 1631; *A retractive from the Romish Religion*, London, 1616; and *Antichrist the Pope of Rome*, London, 1625.

73. *CJ*, vol. 1, 929; Wallace Notestein and Francis Helen Relf, eds, *Commons Debates for 1629*, Minneapolis, MN, 1921, 139–40, 192–3.

74. The matter was meticulously pieced together by John Morrill in 'The Making of Oliver Cromwell', 26–30. He makes a strong case that Cromwell sided against Beard in the controversy, and that Beard then repaid him by siding with Cromwell's enemies in the quarrel over the charter, but the evidence is ultimately circumstantial.

75. A copy is in the Huntingdonshire RO, 2913/2/10/B/8.

76. This was first noticed and discussed by James Waylen, *The House of Cromwell*, revised by John Gabriel Cromwell, London, 1897, 22–4.

77. The letter is printed in Abbott, ed., *Writings and Speeches*, vol. 1, 80–1. Morrill, 'The Making of Oliver Cromwell', 39, identified the most plausible candidate for the imperilled lecturer as Walter Wells, at Godmanchester. In 'Rewriting Cromwell', *Canadian Journal of History* 38 (2003), 566, Morrill identified Storie as a young London cloth merchant who had visited the Puritan colony of Massachusetts and so at the least had strong Puritan sympathies.

78. The different sources were identified and analyzed by Robert S. Paul, *The Lord Protector*, Grand Rapids, MI, 1955, 399–400. The letter is printed in Abbott, ed., *Writings and Speeches*, vol. 1, 96–7.

79. Firth, *Oliver Cromwell*, 38–9, put it in 1628–36; Paul, *The Lord Protector*, 39–40, in 1626–35; Fraser, *Cromwell: Our Chief of Men*, 45, in 1631–5; Roger Howell, 'Cromwell's Personality',

Biography 1 (1978), 41–2, from 1628 on; Morrill, 'The Making of Oliver Cromwell', 34–5, in 1628–34; Coward, *Oliver Cromwell*, 13, by 1630; Gaunt, *Oliver Cromwell*, 36, by 1636; Davis, *Oliver Cromwell*, 16, seemingly after 1631.

80. Abbott, ed., *Writings and Speeches*, vol. 1, 50–1.
81. Noble, *Memoirs*, vol. 1, 105n.
82. This was worked out by Morrill, 'The Making of Oliver Cromwell', 34.
83. Mary Wagner, 'Puritans at St Ives, 1631–1643', *Records of Huntingdonshire* 1.10 (1980), 5–7; Carter, ed., *Edmund Pettis's Survey of St Ives*, 19; A. G. Matthews, *Walker Revised*, Oxford, 1949, 79. The dispute within the parish by 1640, over how communion could be taken (Downhall holding to the Laudian requirement that it be at a rail protecting a communion table at the east end of the church, and his critics wanting to continue Tookey's practice of bringing the table down into the nave) is described in NA, SP 16/444/79.
84. In 1990 John Morrill suggested this in 'The Making of Oliver Cromwell', 35.
85. In 2003 Morrill moved his opinion from that above to suggesting that Cromwell moved to St Ives already radicalized, in readiness to emigrate to a new Puritan settlement in Connecticut, of which Lawrence was a trustee: 'Rewriting Cromwell', 563. For Lawrence's early career, see Timothy Venning's entry in the *Oxford Dictionary of National Biography* 32 (2004), 823.
86. Carter, ed., *Edmund Pettis's Survey of St Ives*, 37.
87. It is possible, however, that Cromwell declined the office, either on appointment or at some later time. In the later seventeenth century a man who had known the churchman who had been dean of Ely at the time of Cromwell's residence there recorded (presumably quoting his friend) that Oliver 'would not act' in the office: Andrew Clark, 'Dr Plume's Notebook', *Essex Review* 15 (1906), 15. It is not certain how reliable this retrospective testimony is.
88. See Margaret Spufford, 'The Quest for the Heretical Laity in the Visitation Records of Ely in the Late Sixteenth and Early Seventeenth Centuries', in Derek Baker, ed., *Schism, Heresy and Religious Protest*, Cambridge, 1972, 223–30; and *Contrasting Communities*, 223–38, 266–71.
89. The entry was found by Noble, *Memoirs*, vol. 1, 319. His previous child, Mary, was baptized at his former parish church of St John's Huntingdon, in 1637, presumably because his mother still lived in the parish. She subsequently joined him in Ely, with his two unmarried sisters; hence the move to St Mary's for family rites: Noble, *Memoirs*, vol. 1, 106–7, 352.
90. Cf. Patrick Collinson, 'The English Conventicle', in W. J. Sheils and Diana Wood, eds, *Voluntary Religion, Studies in Church History* 23 (1986), 223–59. Joel Halcomb, 'Was Cromwell an Independent or a Congregationalist?', *Cromwelliana*, series 3, vol. 5 (2016), 29–35, positions him in such a milieu at this time.
91. Heath, *Flagellum*, London, 1665, 18, is the first of these and may be the origin point for all the rest: John Nalson, *The Prospect of Peace*, London, 1678, 47–54; *A Perfect Politician*, 2; and Dugdale, *Short View of the Late Troubles*, 459–60.
92. Hacket, *Scrinia Reserata*, Part 2, 212.
93. BL, Harleian MS 991, f. 13, notes made by Richard Symonds.
94. Andrew Barclay, in *Electing Cromwell*, 112–13; and 'Oliver Cromwell and the Underground Opposition to Bishop Wren of Ely', *Cromwelliana* series 3, vol. 1 (2012), 32–43, has made the most eloquent possible argument for crediting the reports that Cromwell attended a full-blown conventicle during his Ely years, but, fine historian that he is, he does not claim that it represents proof.
95. The growth of it is splendidly chronicled in J. W. Dean, 'The Reported Embarkation of Cromwell and His Friends for New England', *New England Historical and Genealogical Register* 20 (1866), 113–21.
96. The burial entry in the Felsted register, and its linkage to Cromwell's deathbed memory, were discovered by Waylen, *The House of Cromwell*, 22–4. The text is the Epistle to the Philippians, 4:11–13. This epistle really got to Cromwell in the 1630s. It is the most important of the sections of Scripture quoted in his letter to Elizabeth St John.

CHAPTER TWO: MEMBER OF PARLIAMENT AND CAPTAIN OF HORSE

1. The document is printed in Wilbur Cortez Abbott, ed., *The Writings and Speeches of Oliver Cromwell*, Cambridge, MA, 1937, vol. 1, 109.
2. James Heath, *Flagellum*, London, 1665, 18–22.
3. Andrew Barclay, *Electing Cromwell*, London, 2011, 13–74.
4. BL, Additional MS 28930, ff. 2, 5.
5. Barclay himself has modestly summed up his achievement in drawing attention to this source as being possibly 'to replace some speculation about Cromwell's election based on no documentary evidence at all with more extensive speculation based only on documentary evidence of the most debatable quality': *Electing Cromwell*, 177. As will be suggested, his argument that Cromwell was elected as an anti-Laudian at Cambridge, being put forward by the town's Puritans with whom connections across the shire had brought Oliver into contact, can be supported from other sources.
6. J. H. Gent, *The History of the Life and Death of Oliver Cromwell*, London, 1663, 4–5.
7. John Twigg, *The University of Cambridge and the English Revolution, 1625–1688*, Woodbridge, 1990, 11–41.
8. Sir William Dugdale, *A Short View of the Late Troubles in England*, London, 1681, 459–60.
9. See the sources listed in nn. 65–7 of the previous chapter. In particular, Andrew Barclay has made a forthright argument that Dugdale was simply wrong in stating that Cromwell owed his election at Cambridge to his championship of Fenlanders: *Electing Cromwell*, 75–96.
10. The documents for the election are in Abbott, ed., *Writings and* Speeches, vol. 1, 109–11. It is discussed in detail in Barclay, *Electing Cromwell*, 116–21.
11. For the development of the Covenanter rebellion and the ensuing wars, see David Stevenson, *The Scottish Revolution*, Newton Abbot, 1973; Peter Donald, *An Uncounselled King*, Cambridge, 1990; John Morrill, ed., *The Scottish National Covenant in its British Context*, Edinburgh, 1990; Allan I. Mcinnes, *Charles I and the Making of the Covenanting Movement*, Edinburgh, 1991; Kevin Sharpe, *The Personal Rule of Charles I*, New Haven, CT, 1992; and Mark Charles Fissel, *The Bishops' Wars*, Cambridge, 1994. For English politics 1640–2, the main works are Conrad Russell, *The Fall of the British Monarchies*, London, 1991; Austin Woolrych, *Britain in Revolution 1625–1660*, Oxford, 2002, 85–188; David Cressy, *England on Edge*, Oxford, 2006; John Adamson, *The Noble Revolt*, London, 2007; and Tim Harris, *Rebellion: Britain's First Stuart Kings*, Oxford, 2014, 373–488. See also now Jason Peacey, 'The Outbreak of the Civil Wars in the Three Kingdoms', in Barry Coward, ed., *A Companion to Stuart Britain*, Oxford, 2003, 296–306.
12. The financial implications of the sale have been examined by Patrick Little, 'Cromwell and Ireland before 1649', in Patrick Little, ed., *Oliver Cromwell*, Basingstoke, 2009, 138; and Barclay, *Electing Cromwell*, 101–7.
13. Abbott, ed., *Writings and Speeches*, vol. 1, 111–12.
14. These elections have been analyzed by Morrill, 'The Making of Oliver Cromwell', 43; and Barclay, *Electing Cromwell*, 123–43.
15. This portrait is based on the woodcut on the title page of *A Perfect Diurnall of the Passages in Parliament* 38 (27 February to 6 March 1643), with details added from Caroline Shenton, *The Day Parliament Burned Down*, Oxford, 2012, 10, 28–9; and J. P. D. Cooper, 'The Elizabethan House of Commons and St Stephen's Chapel Westminster', *Parliamentary History* 38 (2019), 34–59.
16. See the introduction to Wilson H. Coates et al., ed., *The Private Journals of the Long Parliament: 3 January to 5 March 1642*, New Haven, CT, 1982.
17. Jason Peacey, 'Disorderly Debates: Noise and Gesture in the 17th-Century House of Commons', *Parliamentary History* 32 (2013), 60–78.
18. Hence the illustration in *A Perfect Diurnall of the Passages in Parliament*, above.
19. Paul Seaward, 'Tellers and Management in the 17th-Century House of Commons', *Parliamentary History* 32 (2013), 79–102.
20. Calculated from Coates et al., eds, *The Private Journals of the Long Parliament: 3 January to 5 March 1642*.

21. It is represented in William Capon's watercolour from 1799, 'The Painted Chamber in the Palace of Westminster', owned by the Society of Antiquaries; see also Shenton, *The Day Parliament Burned Down*, 200–2.

22. Shenton, *The Day Parliament Burned Down*, 10; David Dean, 'Parliament', in Susan Doran and Norman Jones, eds, *The Elizabethan World*, London, 2011, 122–3. The dimensions of the chambers are given in the drawing of the Palace of Westminster made in the 1550s by Anthonis van der Wyngaerde, kept in the Ashmolean Museum.

23. All this is depicted in Claude de Jongh's oil painting, 'The Thames at Westminster Stairs', c. 1630, at the Yale Center for British Art.

24. Shenton, *The Day Parliament Burned Down*, 8, 14.

25. Shown best in the oil painting of c. 1670 in the House of Lords collection, 'Old Palace Yard and Westminster Hall'.

26. Mary Frear Keeler, *The Long Parliament, 1640–1641*, Philadelphia, PA, 1954, 15–19, 26–7.

27. Stanley J. Weyman, 'Oliver Cromwell's Kinsfolk', *English Historical Review* 6 (1891), 48–60.

28. *CJ*, vol. 2, 24; Wallace Notestein, ed., *The Journal of Sir Simonds D'Ewes from the Beginning of the Long Parliament to the Opening of the Trial of the Earl of Strafford*, New Haven, CT, 1923, 18–19.

29. There is a later source which identified him firmly as involved with the group from before the meeting of the Long Parliament, having been introduced to it by St John: BL, Additional MS 4460, f. 74v. This is, however, a piece of gossip recorded in the 1690s, and its reliability is seriously in doubt. It was discussed by Morrill, 'The Making of Oliver Cromwell', 44–5.

30. Sir Philip Warwick, *Memoirs of the Reign of Charles I*, London, 1813, 277–8. This is my reading of the phrase, based on its apparent reference to riding while tilting a lance at a target.

31. Edward, Earl of Clarendon, *The History of the Rebellion*, ed. W. Dunn Macray, Oxford, 1888, vol. 4, 305.

32. This computation was first made by Stephen Roberts, '"One that Would Sit Well at the Mark": The Early Parliamentary Career of Oliver Cromwell', in Little, ed., *Oliver Cromwell*, 47. This seems the best study of Cromwell's activities in the Long Parliament between 1640 and 1642 to date.

33. E.g. *CJ*, vol. 2, 44, 52, 91, 117, 200.

34. Warwick, *Memoirs*, 273–4. Warwick described this scene as belonging to the first days of the Long Parliament, in November 1640, so it is probably Cromwell's speech on behalf of Lilburne. However, Warwick said that it was for a servant of another celebrated Puritan critic of the regime, William Prynne, and a servant of Prynne was the subject of a later debate on 3 December at which Cromwell was present as it got him put onto another committee: *CJ*, vol. 2, 44. Perhaps Warwick confused the two events.

35. G. S., *A letter from an ejected Member of the House of Commons to Sir John Evelyn*, London, 1648, 6. The subject of Cromwell's plea is identified here as Alexander Leighton, and the timing may have been that of the debate on his case on 21 April 1641, for which see Maija Jansson, ed., *Proceedings in the Opening Session of the Long Parliament: House of Commons: Volume Four*, Rochester, NY, 2003, 35–6, or the one at the opening of the Long Parliament which established the committee to which Cromwell was appointed on 9 November 1640, as in n. 28 above.

36. *CJ*, vol. 2, 56–7, 120, 126, 146, 162, 193, 199.

37. Samuel Rawson Gardiner, ed., *The Constitutional Documents of the Puritan Revolution*, Oxford, 3rd edition, 1906, 137–44.

38. *CJ*, vol. 2, 54.

39. Notestein, ed., *The Journal of Sir Simonds D'Ewes*, 339–42.

40. Jansson, ed., *Proceedings in the Opening Session of the Long Parliament: House of Commons: Volume Four*, 320.

41. *A Collection of Speeches Made by Sir Edward Dering*, London, 1642, 62–3.

42. Maija Jansson, ed., *Proceedings in the Opening Session of the Long Parliament: House of Commons: Volume Six*, Rochester, NY, 2005, 382, 635, 688.
43. Gardiner, ed., *Constitutional Documents of the Puritan Revolution*, 197–8.
44. Warwick, *Memoirs*, 193–4.
45. Abbott, ed., *Writings and Speeches*, vol. 1, 125.
46. Notestein, ed., *The Journal of Sir Simonds D'Ewes*, 196–7.
47. Jansson, ed., *Proceedings in the Opening Session of the Long Parliament: Volume Four*, 181. For an excellent study of the nature and impact of the Protestation, see John Walter, *Covenanting Citizens*, Oxford, 2017.
48. *CJ*, vol. 2, 44.
49. Maija Jansson, ed., *Proceedings in the Opening Session of the Long Parliament: House of Commons: Volume One*, Rochester, NY, 2000, 578–83; *Volume Two*, Rochester, NY, 2000, 228, 464, 486.
50. Ibid., *Volume Four*, 679; *Volume Five*, Rochester, NY, 2005, 68, 72.
51. Edward, Earl of Clarendon, *The Life of Edward, Earl of Clarendon*, Oxford, 1857, vol. 1, 73–4, 87–8.
52. Hyde's autobiography was commenced after 1668. For his unreliability as a historian, see Ronald Hutton, 'Clarendon's *History of the Rebellion*', *English Historical Review* 97 (1982), 70–88.
53. Jansson, ed., *Proceedings in the Opening Session of the Long Parliament: Volume Five*, 68.
54. The significance of this case was spotted, and its details teased out, by Roberts, '"One that Would Sit Well at the Mark"', 42–3.
55. The entry from D'Ewes's diary is printed in Abbott, ed., *Writings and Speeches*, vol. 1, 133–4.
56. Also noted in Abbott, ed., *Writings and Speeches*, vol. 1, 134.
57. Three between 28 August and 1 September, to consider a series of petitions: *CJ*, vol. 2, 276, 280, 284.
58. This was first noticed by Alfred Kingston, *East Anglia and the Great Civil War*, London, 1902, 28.
59. *CJ*, vol. 2, 298; William Havelock Coates, ed., *The Journal of Sir Simonds D'Ewes from the First Recess of the Long Parliament to the Withdrawal of King Charles from London*, New Haven, CT, 1942, 40, 51–4.
60. Clarendon, *History*, vol. 1, 419–20.
61. Coates, ed., *Journal of Sir Simonds D'Ewes*, 80, 236, 357–9.
62. Compiled by combing *CJ*, vol. 1, 440–683; Wilson H. Coates et al., eds, *The Private Journals of the Long Parliament: 3 January to 5 March 1642*, New Haven, CT, 1982; and Vernon H. Snow and Anna Steele Young, eds, *The Private Journals of the Long Parliament: 7 March to 1 June 1642*, New Haven, CT, 1987; and *The Private Journals of the Long Parliament: 2 June to 17 September 1642*, New Haven, CT, 1992.
63. *CJ*, vol. 2, 591–2; Snow and Young, eds, *Private Journals: 7 March to 1 June*, 382.
64. Snow and Young, eds, *Private Journals: 7 March to 1 June*, 103–4.
65. Coates et al., eds, *Private Journals*, 255–7, 264, 293.
66. Snow and Young, eds, *Private Journals: 7 March to 1 June*, 403–69, passim.
67. *CJ*, vol. 2, 453, 463, 468, 480, 536, 569, 571, 588, 590, 594, 599, 610, 627, 629, 672, 683; Coates et al., eds, *Private Journals*, 180, 304, 370–1, 395; Snow and Young, eds, *Private Journals: 7 March to 1 June*, 268, 372, 375–6, 384, 400–1, and *Private Journals: 2 June to 17 September*, 14, 126, 134, 140, 245–50.
68. Abbott, ed., *Writings and Speeches*, vol. 1, 164–5; Karl S. Bottigheimer, *English Money and Irish Land*, Oxford, 1971, 45–6, 70.
69. Coates et al., eds, *Private Journals*, 67; C. H. Firth and R. S. Rait, eds, *Acts and Ordinances of the Interregnum*, London, 1911, vol. 1, 1–5.
70. *CJ*, vol. 2, 620; Coates et al., eds, *Private Journals*, 101, 114, 177–8; Snow and Young, eds, *Private Journals: 7 March to 1 June*, 8–9.
71. *CJ*, vol. 2, 555, 582–3, 585, 591–2, 596, 598, 606–7, 609, 622, 625, 627, 629–32, 634, 641–2, 647–8, 653–4, 660, 665, 676, 680; Snow and Young, eds, *Private Journals: 7 March to 1 June*, 112–13, 236–7, 382, 398–9; and *Private Journals: 2 June to 17 September*, 61, 80–2, 106, 231, 249.

72. The list is in Bod L, Tanner MS 63, f. 57.
73. Firth and Rait, eds, *Acts and Ordinances*, vol. 1, 6–9.
74. Ibid., 14–16.
75. Roberts, "'One that Would Sit Well at the Mark'", 55–8, computes the men most often named to committees with Cromwell, and finds that three were in particular: his relatives Sir Gilbert Gerard and Sir Thomas Barrington, and the Herefordshire Puritan Sir Robert Harley. It is difficult, however, to tell how far this represented systematic co-operation, and how much it was coincidence. Likewise, on many committees he sat with members of 'the Junto', but his relations with them are not elucidated thereby, even though he must have known them well.
76. Snow and Young, eds, *Private Journals 7 March to 1 June*, 236–7; *CJ*, vol. 2, 620.
77. Gardiner, ed., *Constitutional Documents*, 2478.
78. Roberts, "'One that Would Sit Well at the Mark'", 39.
79. The documents are printed in Charles Henry Cooper, *Annals of Cambridge*, Cambridge, 1845, vol. 3, 3258; and F. J. Varley, *Cambridge during the Civil War 1642–1646*, Cambridge, 1935, 736. Varley comments that the college accounts show that only £735 was sent, but this does not seem to accord with the king's response, and the accounts may be incomplete.
80. The sum reported by the Venetian ambassador in a despatch reprinted in Varley, *Cambridge*, 75.
81. Ibid., 778.
82. Cooper, *Annals*, vol. 3, 326–7.
83. *CJ*, vol. 2, 673–5.
84. *LJ*, vol. 5, 226. The man was William Welbore, reporting, with friends, the royalist speech of a militia muster master at Fowlmere on 28 June.
85. *LJ*, vol. 5, 248–50.
86. HMC 8th Report, Appendix, Part 2, 59.
87. David Cozens, 'Family Loyalties', *Records of Huntingdonshire* 3.7 (1999), 33–42.
88. BL, Additional MS 15672, ff. 1, 14. 32–4; and NA, SP 20/1, f. 106v, contain the depositions of witnesses.
89. The witness statements are in NA, SP 23/80, ff. 649–55. Dowcra's release is in *CJ*, vol. 1, 952.
90. *CJ*, vol. 2, 720.
91. Thomas William Bramston, ed., *Autobiography of Sir John Bramston*, Camden Society 32 (1845), 85–6.
92. *CJ*, vol. 2, 720, 731; *LJ*, vol. 5, 334.
93. Bod L, Tanner MS 62, f. 116.
94. Peter Barwick, *Life of the Reverend John Barwick*, London, 1724, 22–7; *Querela Cantabrigiensis*, London, 1647, 4–5.
95. NA, SP 24/30; and SP 23/99, ff. 713–15.
96. Varley, *Cambridge*, 79.
97. Of the early historians of the affair, Charles Cooper was convinced that most of the plate got past Cromwell (*Annals*, vol. 3, 328), while Frank Varley was determined to prove that none did (*Cambridge*, 79). Twentieth-century historians have generally credited Oliver with near or total success, and Susan Sadler seems to have been the first scholar to point out the contradictory and confused nature of the sources: 'Cambridgeshire Society during the First and Second Civil Wars' (Anglia Ruskin University, PhD thesis, 1998), 74–80; and 'From Civilian to Soldier', *Cromwelliana*, series 3, vol. 1 (2012), 44–60.
98. Indeed, it was said that Dowcra was shown an order of Parliament against the conveying of the plate when he arrived in Cambridge, but replied that he had the king's warrant to carry it off: NA, SP 23/80, f. 655.
99. *CJ*, vol. 2, 717, 721, 723–4, 726, 728–9, 743; *LJ*, vol. 5, 306–7.
100. *A true Relation of the manner of the taking of the Earl of Northampton . . .*, London, 1642; *A True Relation of the late expedition into Kent . . .*, London, 2 September 1642; *Remarkable*

Passages from Nottingham . . ., London, 1 September 1642; *Querela Cantabrigiensis*, 4–5; *Joyfull Newes from the Isle of Ely*, London, 2 September 1642; *Mercurius Rusticus*, Oxford, 1646, 114–15; John Walker, *The Sufferings of the Clergy during the Great Rebellion*, Oxford, 1862, 147.

101. *England's Memorable Accidents* (19–26 September 1642), 20; *LJ*, vol. 5, 341.

102. *CJ*, vol, 2, 754.

103. NA, SP 28/1A, f. 271. The money, a total of £104, was handed over the next day.

104. The warrant was first cited by C. H. Firth, 'The Raising of the Ironsides', *Transactions of the Royal Historical Society*, NS 13 (1899), 18–19. It is reprinted in Abbott, ed., *Writings and Speeches*, vol. 1, 201.

105. *A Perfect Diurnall*, reprinted in Abbott, ed., *Writings and Speeches*, vol. 1, 201.

106. *Theaurauiohn High Priest to the Iewes*, London, March,1652, 6.

107. The first portrait I have been able to date, a woodcut on *A perfect List of all the Victories obtained (through the blessing of God) by the Parliaments Forces . . .*, London, August 1646, shows all these characteristics, which recur in the later and more famous paintings.

108. This is prescribed in detail in Robert Ward, *Animadversions of warre*, London, 1639, Book 1, 282–3. Other manuals – such as John Cruso, *Militarie instructions for the cavallrie*, London, 1632, and John Vernon, *The young Horse-man*, London, 1644, state more briefly what Ward describes, so his directions may be taken as standard.

109. Ward, *Animadversions*, Book 1, 292. That this equipment was indeed routine is confirmed by the reports of it in Civil War actions, which are brought together in C. H. Firth, *Cromwell's Army*, London, 1962, 116–18.

110. Ward, *Animadversions*, Book 1, 283–5.

111. Firth, 'The Raising of the Ironsides', 17–19, 38–40, cites the list of Essex's horse captains, including Cromwell, to whom £1,104 each was paid, and also reckons up the prices of different items. Martyn Bennett, *Cromwell at War*, London, 2017, 36–9, matches the payments to the prices and concludes that the shortfall of money was probably covered by getting the troopers to buy their own boots and buff coats.

112. Firth, *Cromwell's Army*, 118, notes that Cromwell's horsemen were not equipped with them by 1643–4.

113. Thomas Le Wright, *An Exact Character Or Narrative Of The Late Right Noble and Magnificent Lord, Oliver Cromwell*, London, 1658, 3–4.

114. The best recent account of the battle is Christopher L. Scott et al., *Edgehill*, Barnsley, 2004, with logistical additions by Aaron Graham, 'The Earl of Essex and Parliament's Army at the Battle of Edgehill', *War in History* 17 (2010), 276–93.

115. Nathaniel Fiennes, *A most True and Exact Relation of Both the Battels . . .*, London, 9 November 1642, 2–3, 8.

116. Sir William Dugdale, *A Short View of the Late Troubles in England*, Oxford, 1681, 110; *Memoirs of Denzil Lord Holles*, London, 1699, 17.

117. Of previous biographers, Abbott, ed., *Writings and Speeches*, vol. 1, 204, kept open both possibilities. Sir Charles Firth proposed each at different times: 'The Raising of the Ironsides', 19; and *Oliver Cromwell and the Rule of the Puritans*, New York, 1900, 83–4. Lady Antonia Fraser, Peter Gaunt, Frank Kitson, and the team of Christopher Scott, Alan Turton and Eric Gruber von Arni, have backed that of Cromwell missing most of the battle: Antonia Fraser, *Cromwell: Our Chief of Men*, London, 1973, 96; Peter Gaunt, *Oliver Cromwell*, Oxford, 1996, 44; Frank Kitson, *Old Ironsides*, London, 2004, 42–3; Scott et al., *Edgehill*, 58, 64, 146. Martyn Bennett stated simply that his role at Edgehill is unknown: *Oliver Cromwell*, London, 2006, 57. The view put forward here, from a fresh look at the evidence, is therefore the majority one.

118. The speech, from 13 April 1657, is reprinted in this context, in Abbott, ed., *Writings and Speeches*, vol. 1, 204.

119. The warrant, and Cromwell's covering letter, are printed in Abbott, ed., *Writings and Speeches*, vol. 1, 208.

CHAPTER THREE: THE CAVALRY COLONEL

1. For all this, see C. H. Firth and R. S. Rait, eds, *Acts and Ordinances of the Interregnum*, London, 1911, vol. 1, 38–52; *CJ*, vol. 2, 865–92, passim; *LJ*, vol. 5, 505; Clive Holmes, *The Eastern Association in the English Civil War*, Cambridge, 1974, 62–4; and Lynn Beats, 'The East Midland Association, 1642–1644', *Midland History* 4 (1978), 160–75.
2. For which see especially in recent years the work of Jason Peacey, above all *Politicians and Pamphleteers*, Farnham, 2004; and *Print and Public Politics in the English Revolution*, Cambridge, 2013.
3. Julius Hutchinson, *Memoirs of the Life of Colonel Hutchinson* ed., Lucy Hutchinson, revised by C. H. Firth, London, 1906, 101–2.
4. The recent scholarly study of Sir Thomas is Andrew Hopper, *Black Tom*, Manchester, 2007. The pamphlet concerned is *The Rider of the White Horse and His Army*, London, 1643.
5. *CJ*, vol. 2, 932; Dawson Turner, 'Letter from Sir Philip Stapleton to Oliver Cromwell', *Norfolk Archaeology* 2 (1848), 43–60; Bod L, Tanner MS 64, f. 125.
6. *CJ*, vol. 2, 917.
7. *CJ*, vol. 2, 924, 932; NA, SP 28/128/3, ff. 1–3.
8. I have here followed the detailed account in the *Kingdomes Weekly Intelligencer* 3 (10–17 January 1643), 24, backed up by the papers in NA, SP 23/82, ff. 775–7. There are slighter references in *Mercurius Aulicus* 3 (15–21 January 1643), 31; and *Certaine Informations From severall parts of the Kingdome* 1 (16–23 January 1643), 3–4. There is a suspect later version in John Vicars, *God in the Mount*, London, 1644, which looks like an embroidery on the story in the *Kingdomes Weekly Intelligencer*.
9. BL, Harleian MS 7048, f. 38v.
10. Wilbur Cortez Abbott, ed., *The Writings and Speeches of Oliver Cromwell*, Cambridge, MA, 1937, vol. 1, 210.
11. Sir Philip Warwick, *Memoirs of the Reign of Charles I*, London, 1813, 277–8. For the allegiances of Sir Oliver and his son, see David Cozens, 'Family Loyalties', *Records of Huntingdonshire* 3.7 (1999), 33–42.
12. Alan Everitt, ed., *Suffolk and the Great Rebellion 1640–1660*, Suffolk Records Society 3 (1960), 39–42; BL, Additional MS 28930, ff. 1–2.
13. *A Perfect Diurnall of the Passages in Parliament* (by John Grismond) (6–13 March 1643) and (13–20 March 1643); *Certaine Informations From severall parts of the Kingdome* 7 (26 February–6 March 1643), 53–4; *Speciall Passages and Certain Informations from severall places* 30 (28 February–7 March 1643), 244, and 31 (7–14 March 1643), 257.
14. Andrew Clark, 'Dr Plume's Notebook', *Essex Review* 15 (1906), 16. This entry was made in the later seventeenth century, presumably from the testimony of an eyewitness as the details are so precise.
15. *Mercurius Aulicus* 10 (5–11 March 1643), 126–7; Warwick, *Memoirs*, 280.
16. *Querela Cantabrigiensis*, London, 1647, A3–4; Peter Barwick, *The Life of the Reverend Dr John Barwick*, London, 1724, 27–31.
17. *LJ*, vol. 5, 636; Charles Henry Cooper, *Annals of Cambridge*, Cambridge, 1845, vol. 3, 340.
18. The documents are printed in Alfred Kingston, *East Anglia and the Great Civil War*, London, 1902, 91–3.
19. See the sources at n. 13.
20. The dating and nature of the troops are analyzed in Laurence Spring, *The Regiments of the Eastern Association*, Bristol, 1998, vol. 1, 17–26. In his memoirs, written decades later, the Puritan minister Richard Baxter stated that when Cromwell was at Cambridge with his original horse troop, his officers had proposed making it a 'gathered church', i.e. a sectarian religious group meeting outside the national Church, and invited Baxter – then a promising young Puritan minister in Worcestershire – to be its minister. Baxter said he had refused, giving Cromwell a lasting grudge against him: Matthew Sylvester, ed., *Reliquiae Baxterianae*, London, 1696, 51. There is something wrong with this account. Cromwell's original horse troop would only have been at Cambridge for a brief while around the beginning of September 1642 – if it was there at all – and this seems too early for a unit of the parliamentarian

forces to want to form such a sectarian church. Baxter's memory seems faulty, and his later intense dislike of Cromwell to be helping to falsify it. It may be, however, that the same West Midlands connection which secured Berry for the regiment generated an invitation to Baxter to serve as the regimental chaplain: Baxter and Berry were friends (*Reliquiae Baxterianae*, 57), and it would make sense for the one to be invited in around the same time as the other.

21. The accounts are in Bod L, Tanner MS 62, ff. 348, 352, and MS 66, ff. 1–2.
22. BL, Harleian MS 164, ff. 340–1. Grey's policing action in and around Norwich is in *Certaine Informations* 8 (6–11 March 1643), 59; and *A Perfect Diurnall of the Passages in Parliament* 40 (13–20 March 1643), n.p.
23. The list of losses is printed in Alfred Suckling, *The History and Antiquities of the County of Suffolk*, London, 1846, vol. 2, 48–9.
24. Bertram Schofield, ed., *The Knyvett Letters 1620–1644*, Norfolk Record Society 20 (1949), 33–7, 107–14.
25. Bod L, Tanner MS 62, f. 317.
26. It was accepted by R. W. Ketton-Cremer, *Norfolk in the Civil War*, London, 1969, 179–86; and John Morrill, *The Revolt of the Provinces*, London, 2nd edition, 1980, 95–7.
27. Ketton-Cremer, *Norfolk*, 185–6.
28. BL, Harleian MS 164, ff. 340–1.
29. *The Kingdomes Weekly Intelligencer* 13 (21–28 March 1643), 101.
30. *A Continuation of certain Speciall and Remarkable Passages* 37 (16–23 March 1643), n.p.
31. *A Perfect Diurnall* 40 (13–20 March 1643), n.p.
32. Ketton-Cremer, *Norfolk*, 187–91.
33. Firth and Rait, eds, *Acts and Ordinances of the Interregnum*, vol. 1, 85–100, 106–17.
34. *Querela Cantabrigiensis*, 10–14.
35. BL, Harleian MS 7048, f. 39v.
36. This expedition is considered in Peter Young and Richard Holmes, *The English Civil War*, London, 1974, 106; Holmes, *The Eastern Association*, 69–70; and Malcolm Wanklyn, *The Warrior Generals*, London, 2010, 47.
37. Abbott, ed., *Writings and Speeches*, vol. 1, 220–1; *A Perfect Diurnall*, by Pecke 43 (3–10 April 1643), n.p.; *Certaine Informations* 11 (27 March–3 April 1643), 83–4, and 12 (3–10 April 1643), 92.
38. Everitt, ed., *Suffolk and the Great Rebellion*, 51–7.
39. Newcastle's own viewpoint on these events is in Margaret, Duchess of Newcastle, *The Life of William Cavendish, Duke of Newcastle*, ed. C. H. Firth, London, 1906, 13–17.
40. *Mercurius Aulicus* 13 (26 March–2 April 1643), 155–6, and 16 (16–22 April 1643), 193–4; *A Relation of a Fight in the County of Lincoln . . . Neere Ancaster*, York, 1643; *Speciall Passages and Certain Informations from severall places* 33 (21–28 March 1643), 273–4, and 36 (11–18 April 1643), 295–6; *A Continuation of certain Speciall and Remarkable Passages* 38 (23–30 March 1643), 4–5; *The Kingdomes Weekly Intelligencer* 15 (4–11 April 1643), 120, and 16 (11–18 April 1643), 125.
41. *Mercurius Aulicus* 15 (9–15 April), 185–6; *Speciall Passages and Certain Informations* 35 (4–11 April), 285.
42. The passivity of most in the war was established by K. J. Lindley, 'The Part Played by Catholics in the Civil War in Lancashire and Monmouthshire' (Manchester University MA thesis, 1965).
43. P. R. Newman, 'Catholic Royalists of Northern England, 1642–1645', *Northern History* 15 (1979), 88–95.
44. William Sheils, 'English Catholics at War and Peace', in Christopher Durston and Judith Maltby, eds, *Religion in Revolutionary England*, Manchester, 2006, 137–57.
45. Andrew Hopper, 'The Popish Army of the North', *Recusant History* 25 (2000–1), 12–28.
46. The order is in BL, Stowe MS 807, ff. 117–18.
47. *Speciall Passages and Certain Informations* 36 (11–18 April 1643), 294–6; *A Continuation of certain Speciall and Remarkable Passages* 41 (13–20 April 1643), n.p; *A Perfect Diurnall of the Passages in Parliament* (by Samuel Peake) 45 (17–24 April 1643), n.p.

48. Abbott, ed., *Writings and Speeches*, vol. 1, 225.

49. *Speciall Passages and certain Informations* 36 (11–18 April 1643), 294–6. Either just before or just after it passed through Wisbech (probably before), Cromwell took steps both to secure this town and to make sure that an ally of his was put into it, by persuading the commander of a Cambridgeshire dragoon unit, with whom he had been co-operating, to march to it and fortify it; see the statement by this man in John Bruce and David Masson, eds, *The Quarrel Between the Earl of Manchester and Oliver Cromwell*, Camden Society N.S. 12 (1875), 73. There is a manuscript copy of this printed account, perhaps the original for it, in Huntingdonshire RO, M80/Acc 3343. The dragoon commander concerned was almost certainly William Dodson, who had tried to prevent the king's declaration being read at Ely in August 1642, as argued by Clive Holmes, 'The Identity of the Author of the "Statement by an opponent of Cromwell"', *English Historical Review* 129 (2014), 1,371–82.

50. *A Perfect Diurnall of the Passages in Parliament* (by John Grismond) 46 (17–24 April 1643), n.p.; *Certaine Informations* 15 (24 April–1 May 1643), 220.

51. The damage is reported in detail in Bruno Ryves, *Mercurius Rusticus*, London, 1685, 212–16; Simon Gunton, *The History of the Church of Peterborough*, London, 1686, 92–8 and plate 2; and *Mercurius Aulicus* 17 (23–29 April 1643), 218. The inscription in the returned book was printed in Abbott, ed., *Writings and Speeches*, vol. 1, 226. All these records agree with each other, and the first two are very detailed, while differing enough to suggest that they were not copying from each other. Moreover, they accord of what is known of the fabric of the church, before and after the war. I am therefore inclined to accept them.

52. The siege has recently been considered by Michael Byrd, 'The Reverend Robert Ram and the Siege of Crowland, 1643', *Cromwelliana* (2002), 43–5; and Peter Gaunt, 'Learning the Ropes in "His Own Fields"', *Cromwelliana* (2003), 27–39. The primary sources are *Divers Remarkable Passages of God's Good Providence*, London, 3 June 1643; *Speciall Passages and Certain Informations* 37 (18–25 April 1643), 303; and 39 (2–9 May 1643), 317; and *Certaine Informations* 16 (1–8 May 1643), 113.

53. *A True Relation Of A great Victory obtained by the Parliament forces in Lincolnshire*, London, 27 May 1643. As this book was in the press, Clive Holmes kindly sent me, with some useful comments on this chapter, his article in the current (2020) issue of *Cromwelliana*, pp. 72–7, 'Oliver Cromwell in the News, April–May 1643', which independently concludes that Cromwell's role in the fall of Crowland was exaggerated in a parliamentarian newspaper.

54. *Speciall Passages and Certain Informations* 38 (25 April–2 May 1643), 313; *Certaine Informations* 16 (1–8 May 1643), 113.

55. See the statement by a critic of his, almost certainly William Dodson, in Bruce and Masson, eds, *The Quarrel Between the Earl of Manchester and Oliver Cromwell*, 73. S. L. Sadler, '"Lord of the Fens"', in Patrick Little, ed., *Oliver Cromwell*, Basingstoke, 2009, 71–3, has apparently been the only scholar to note this, and the discrepancy between the apparent reality and the press reports, though she still thinks that Cromwell directed the operation.

56. *Mercurius Aulicus* 19 (7–13 May 1643), 237.

57. *Querela Cantabrigiensis*, 15. Like all the accounts of the sufferings of the university repeated here, this is a local report, not official royalist propaganda. As these are detailed observations made by people on the spot, I am inclined to accept them.

58. Alan Thompson, ed., *The Impact of the First Civil War on Hertfordshire 1642–1647*, Hertfordshire Record Society 23 (2007), 64, 137–8.

59. Firth and Rait, eds, *Acts and Ordinances*, vol. 1, 138, 155–6.

60. Mary Anne Everett Green, ed., *Letters of Queen Henrietta Maria*, London, 1857, 197–9.

61. *CJ*, vol. 3, 52, 82.

62. Abbott, ed., *Writings and Speeches*, vol. 1, 228.

63. Ibid., 228–9; *CJ*, vol. 3, 75; HMC Portland MSS, appendix, vol. 1, 706–8; BL, Harleian MS 164, f. 383.

64. *Mercurius Aulicus* 19 (7–13 May 1643), 236.

65. *A Perfect Diurnall*, by Pecke, 48 (8–15 May 1643), n.p.

66. This is my formula, which accords with the view in David Scott, 'John Hotham', *Oxford Dictionary of National Biography* 28 (2004), 259–61.
67. It is calendared in the HMC Portland MSS, appendix, vol. 1, 87–109, passim, and 699–707, passim; and printed in John Langton Sandford, ed., *Studies and Illustrations of the Great Rebellion*, London, 1858, 553–5.
68. For a different, but complementary, view of the Hothams' behaviour, see Andrew Hopper, *Turncoats and Renegades*, Oxford, 2012, 170–4.
69. Robert Ward, *Animadversions of warre*, London, 1639, Book 1, 280–1, 294–316; with material added from Ward's imitator and successor John Vernon, *The young Horse-man*, London, 1644, 43.
70. Abbott, ed., *Writings and Speeches*, vol. 1, 230; *A True Relation Of A great Victory obtained by the Parliament forces in Lincolnshire*, London, 27 May 1643.
71. Samuel R. Gardiner, *History of the Great Civil War*, 2nd edition, London, 1897, vol. 1, 142–3. The fullest account of the action is A. C. E. Welby, 'Belton Fight', *Lincolnshire Notes and Queries* 13 (1915), 38–47, but this is an over-imaginative one based on an intense admiration for Cromwell and lacking precise references.
72. This is Martyn Bennett, *Oliver Cromwell*, London, 2006, 63, the other scholar being Robert S. Paul, *The Lord Protector*, Grand Rapids, MI, 1955, 59.
73. The second royalist garrison was Gainsborough: *Mercurius Aulicus* 21 (27 May 1643), 267–8; and *Special Passages and Certain Informations* 41 (16–23 May 1643), 335–6. *A Perfect Diurnall* 48 (8–15 May 1643), n.p., states that when Hotham and Cromwell met, the former alone had fifteen horse troops and Cromwell another two thousand men (which would make sixteen troops at full strength). *Speciall Passages and Certain Informations* 41 (16–23 May 1643), 335–6, says the parliamentarians at Belton were fifteen troops against twenty-five. *The Kingdomes Weekly Intelligencer* 19 (9–16 May 1643), 150, and *Mercurius Civicus* 2 (11–18 May 1643), B3, state just that the royalists had sixteen troops.
74. John Rushworth, *Historical Collections*, London, 1721, vol. 4, 744–9.
75. The single exception, to my knowledge, is Clive Holmes, *Seventeenth-Century Lincolnshire*, Lincoln, 1980, 166–7, and he seems to have been ignored ever since.
76. William Hamper, ed., *The Life, Diary and Correspondence of Sir William Dugdale*, London, 1827, 50.
77. Sources are those cited at nn. 70 and 73, plus *Certaine Informations* 18 (15–22 May 1643), 139.
78. *CJ*, vol. 3, 102.
79. Robert Bell, ed., *Memorials of the Civil War*, London, 1849, vol. 1, 45; *CSPV (1642–1643)*, 283; *Speciall Passages and Certain Informations* 42 (23–30 May 1643), 343.
80. *Mercurius Aulicus* 19 (7–13 May 1643), 249.
81. Abbott, *Writings and Speeches*, vol. 1, 234–5; Green, ed., *Letters of Queen Henrietta Maria*, 208–15; Bell, ed., *Memorials of the Civil War*, vol. 1, 46; *CSPV (1642–1643)*, 292; *Speciall Passages and Certain Informations* 43 (30 May–13 June 1643), 348, and 44 (6–13 June 1643), 355; *Certaine Informations* 23 (19–26 June 1643), 181; *A Continuation Of certain Speciall and Remarkable Passages* 48 (1–8 June 1643), n.p.; *Mercurius Aulicus* 25 (18–24 June 1643), 327, and 26 (25 June–1 July 1643), 339; *Mercurius Civicus* 7 (16–23 June 1643), 52; Rushworth, *Historical Collections*, vol. 5, 274; BL, Harleian MS 165, f. 112; Hamper, ed., *The Life, Diary and Correspondence of Sir William Dugdale*, 51–3.
82. Individual reports claimed various exploits for him in June, in raiding, and winning engagements, across Lincolnshire and Leicestershire, but as none seems to be corroborated in any other source, they can probably not be admitted to history: *Certaine Informations* 22 (12–19 June 1643), 173; *A Continuation of certain Speciall and Remarkable Passages* 49 (8–14 June 1643), 2–3; Hamper, ed., *The Life, Diary and Correspondence of Sir William Dugdale*, 51; *Mercurius Civicus* 7 (16–23 June).
83. *Mercurius Aulicus* 24 (11–17 June), 312; and 25 (18–24 June 1643), 328; BL, Additional MS 15903, ff. 28, 40; Essex RO, D/Y/2/7/8; Bell, ed., *Memorials of the Civil War*, 54–6.

84. This was reported in *Mercurius Civicus* 6 (5–16 June 1643), 47. The accounts of the Norfolk officials in Bod L, Tanner MS 66, ff. 1–27, show that the money was indeed collected and attempts were made to send it to Cromwell, matching those of the association treasury at Cambridge, in Tanner MS 62, f. 113.

85. For the situation at Nottingham, see Hutchinson, *Memoirs of the Life of Colonel Hutchinson*, 122. The way free quarter was supposed to work, with special reference to Cromwell's regiment, is explained in C. H. Firth, 'The Raising of the Ironsides', *Transactions of the Royal Historical Society* N.S. 13 (1899), 50–1.

86. Abbott, ed., *Writings and Speeches*, vol. 1, 247; Thomas Bailey, *Annals of Nottinghamshire*, London, 1852–5, vol. 2, 682.

87. Cromwell Museum, Huntingdon, Elizabeth Cromwell to William Welbore, 3 July 1643.

88. Abbott, ed., *Writings and Speeches*, vol. 1, 235–6; BL, Egerton MS 2646, f. 267.

89. Essex RO, D/Y/2/7/8.

90. For this and what follows, see *CJ*, vol. 3, 138–53; Hutchinson, *Memoirs of the Life of Colonel Hutchinson*, 121–3; Green, ed., *Letters of Queen Henrietta Maria*, 221–3; BL, Egerton MS 2647, f. 9; *State Papers Collected by Edward, Earl of Clarendon*, Oxford, 1773, vol. 2, 181–5; *Certaine Informations* 23 (19–16 June 1643), 128; 24 (26 June–3 July 1643), 190; and 25 (3–10 July 1643), 196; *A Continuation of certain Speciall and Remarkable Passages* 50 (29 June–6 July 1643), 2–3; *The Parliament Scout* 1 (20–27 June 1643), 8; *More Plots found out*, London, 1643; Sandford, *Studies and Illustrations of the Great Rebellion*, 556–7.

91. *CJ*, vol. 3, 162.

92. *Certaine Informations* 26 (10–17 July 1643), 106; Mike Osborne, *Cromwellian Fortifications in Cambridgeshire*, Huntingdon, 1990, passim.

93. *Wednesday's Mercury* 1 (19 July 1643), 7.

94. *The Parliament Scout* 5 (20–27 July), 35; BL, Egerton MS 2647, ff. 41, 51; HMC Seventh Report, appendix, 555; *A True Relation of Colonell Cromwells Proceedings against the Cavaliers*, London, 1643; BL, Harleian MS 165, f. 129.

95. *A True Relation of Colonell Cromwells Proceedings*; BL, Egerton MS 2647, f. 61; *The Parliament Scout* 5 (20–27 July 1643), 35; and 6 (27 July–3 August 1643), 43–4; Ketton-Cremer, *Norfolk*, 203. The latter prints a letter from Sir Edward Astley to his wife about the siege, which was one of a number by him then held at the Astley home of Melton Constable, Norfolk. Clive Holmes subsequently used them for his book *The Eastern Association*, cited in n. 1. Since then that home has been sold, and the documents concerned have apparently disappeared: I am grateful to the staff of the Norfolk Record Office, the Northumberland Record Office (to which many of the papers from the house were sent), and to Delaval Astley, the current Lord Hastings, for confirming this. It is shocking that valuable primary source material for the Civil War can still seemingly be lost even in very recent times. For Burghley and its inhabitants, see Lady Victoria Leatham et al., *Burghley House,* Derby, 2000.

96. BL, Egerton MS 2647, f. 61; Ketton-Cremer, *Norfolk*, 203.

97. *The Parliament Scout* (above); *Certaine Informations* 28 (24–31 July 1643), 224. The committee at Cambridge also heard the news as 'Cromwell's success': BL, Additional MS 22619, f. 90.

98. Hutchinson, *Memoirs of the Life of Colonel Hutchinson*, 120–1. See also *Mercurius Aulicus* 30 (23–29 July 1643), 402–3.

99. E.g. *Certaine Informations* 28 (24–31 July 1643), 217–19; and the later development of the story in John Vicars, *Gods Ark*, London, n.d., 6–7, and Bulstrode Whitelock, *Memorials of the English Affairs*, Oxford, 1853, vol. 1, 209. There is no sign that Willoughby's action was part of any cohesive strategy by parliamentarians in the East Midlands: he himself, in Bod L, Tanner MS 62 f. 208, stated that he was acting alone and on his own initiative.

100. *CJ*, vol. 3, 179.

101. See the classic description in C. H. Firth, *Cromwell's Army*, London, 1902, 123–8, which is borne out by all the actions described in the present book.

102. Abbott, ed., *Writings and Speeches*, vol. 1, 240–6; Bod L, Tanner MS 62, f. 205; *Mercurius Aulicus* 31 (30 July–5 August 1643), 31; Hutchinson, *Memoirs of the Life of Colonel*

Hutchinson, 126–9; Newcastle, *The Life of William Cavendish*, 26–8; *A Perfect Diurnall Of Some Passages in Parliament* 6 (31 July–7 August 1643), 41–2.

103. Compare Meldrum's much briefer despatch, in which he sums up all the events of the day and singles out Cromwell for special praise, entrusting him, not wholly wisely, with the sending of a more detailed account: Bod L, Tanner MS 62, f. 205.

104. For the royalist side of this, see Newcastle, *The Life of William Cavendish*, 26–7; and *Mercurius Aulicus* 31 (30 July–5 August 1643), 31. The latter claims that Cavendish fought with sixteen troops against twenty-four, which would if true explain why his generally excellent cavalry was broken. Cromwell actually agreed that the attacking force numbered twenty-four troops, and was not specific about the royalist strength, while giving the impression that it was superior: Abbott, ed., *Writings and Speeches*, vol. 1, 243. *Mercurius Aulicus* accords with Cromwell's account of Cavendish's death, save for the detail that it asserted that after he had been cut from his horse, his fatal wound was inflicted by two shots rather than a stab. Long after, in 1674, a chaplain to his family preached a sermon in which he claimed that Cavendish had died because he had refused quarter, recorded in John Aubrey, *Brief Lives*, Woodbridge edition, 1982, 66–7. He also claimed that Cavendish refused to flee as well, something clearly untrue as he was killed doing just that, so the sermon's portrait can be dismissed as a piece of heroic mythologizing.

105. *CJ*, vol. 3, 187; Bod L, Tanner MS 62, f. 188.

106. *CJ*, vol. 3, 186.

107. *Wednesday's Mercury* 3 (25–28 July 1643), 22. It may be noted that no one particular paper or journalist, or set of them, consistently led the praise of Oliver.

108. BL, Egerton MS 2647, ff. 89–125.

109. James Waylen, *The House of Cromwell*, revised by John Gabriel Cromwell, London, 1897, 26–7.

110. For mortar warfare in general, see Ronald Hutton and Wylie Reeves, 'Sieges and Fortifications', in John Kenyon and Jane Ohlmeyer, eds, *The Civil Wars*, Oxford, 1998, 205–6.

111. Bod L, Tanner MS 62, ff. 208, 232; *Mercurius Aulicus* 31 (30 July–5 August 1643), 415; *The Kingdomes Weekly Intelligencer* 29 (1–8 August 1643), 222–3.

112. Green, ed., *Letters of Queen Henrietta Maria*, 224–5.

113. Abbott, ed., *Writings and Speeches*, vol. 1, 251–3.

114. *The Parliament Scout* 9 (17–24 August 1643), 9–10.

115. Newcastle, *The Life of William Cavendish*, 28–30; Green, ed., *Letters of Queen Henrietta Maria*, 224–5; Sir Philip Warwick, *Memoirs of the Reign of Charles I*, London, 1813, 235; Daniel Parsons, ed., *The Diary of Sir Henry Slingsby*, London, 1836, 99; Bod L, Fairfax MS 36, f. 12; Edward, Earl of Clarendon, *History of the Rebellion and Civil Wars in England*, ed. W. Dunn Macray, Oxford, 1888, vol. 3, 145. In late August and early September 1643 the king formally appointed Newcastle Lieutenant-General in Lincolnshire, gave an East Anglian command to a cavalry officer, and made a set of local gentry, including Sir Oliver Cromwell and his son Henry, civilian administrators for Huntingdonshire: Bod L, Dugdale MS 19, ff. 26–8. All this suggests a plan for conquest.

116. Firth and Rait, eds, *Acts and Ordinances*, vol. 1, 180–242; Lawson Nagel, 'The Militia of London, 1641–1649' (King's College London, PhD thesis, 1982), 115–25.

117. *CJ*, vol. 3, 187–99; Firth and Rait, eds, *Acts and Ordinances*, vol. 1, 242–73.

118. *LJ*, vol. 5, 174: his commission, signed by Essex on the 12th, is in HMC Seventh Report, appendix, 59.

119. This character sketch is based on the events to be related in much of the remainder of this book.

120. This is the much-reproduced one by Sir Peter Lely.

121. Spring, *The Regiments of the Eastern Association*, vol. 1, 48–59, 100–2.

122. Holmes, *The Eastern Association*, 149–67.

123. I. G. Philip, ed., *The Journal of Sir Samuel Luke: Volume Two*, Oxfordshire Record Society, 1950, 137.

124. BL, Egerton MS 2647, ff. 197–241: quotation from f. 241.

125. Spring, *The Regiments of the Eastern Association*, vol. 1, 17–26.
126. Gavin Robinson, *Horses, People and Parliament*, Farnham, 2012, 133–4.
127. Ibid.; Abbott, ed., *Writings and Speeches*, vol. 1, 264–5.
128. Spring, *The Regiments of the Eastern Association*, vol. 1, 17–26. The troop was given to Robert Swallow, who like most of the other new captains – Adam Lawrence, William Patrick, Ralph Margery and William Ayres – seems to have had no previous connection with Cromwell. Little is known of their previous lives.
129. The correspondence is in Abbott, ed., *Writings and Speeches*, vol. 1, 256–62; quotations on p. 256.
130. The terms were already used, of the members of the assembly, in *Mercurius Aulicus* 35 (27 August–2 September 1643), 481.
131. Abbott, ed., *Letters and Speeches*, vol. 1, 258.
132. Bruce and Masson, eds, *The Quarrel*, 73.
133. Abbot, ed., *Writings and Speeches*, vol. 1, 258.
134. Bod L, Tanner MS 62, f. 349.
135. Abbott, ed., *Writings and Speeches*, vol. 1, 258–65.
136. BL, Egerton MS 2643, ff. 138–9.
137. Ibid., ff. 181–6.
138. Ibid., ff. 209, 216, 223.
139. *Certaine Informations* 34 (4–11 September 1643), 263–4 (which has the report of the screams), and 35 (11–18 September 1643), 273; *Mercurius Civicus* 16 (7–14 September 1643), 125; *The Parliament Scout* 12 (7–15 September 1643), 92; *A Perfect Diurnall of Some Passages in Parliament* 7 (28 August–4 September 1643), 51, and 8 (4–11 September 1643), 59.
140. *A briefe and true Relation of the Siege and Surrendering of Kings Lyn*, London, 1643; BL, Egerton MS 2643, f. 266; *The True Informer* 1 (23 September 1643), n.p. Cf. Susan Yaxley, *The Siege of King's Lynn 1643*, Dereham, 1993.
141. Samuel Rawson Gardiner, *Constitutional Documents of the Puritan Revolution,* 3rd edition, Oxford, 1906, 267–71; Firth and Rait, eds, *Acts and Ordinances*, vol. 1, 311–15.
142. Ibid., 291–8, 309–10; *CJ*, vol. 3, 250, 260, 268; *LJ*, vol. 5, 261, 285.
143. *Mercurius Aulicus* 38 (17–22 September 1643), 509.
144. *Certaine Informations* 38 (25 September–2 October 1643), 291.
145. Abbott, ed., *Writings and Speeches*, vol. 1, 261–2; *Mercurius Aulicus* 40 (1–7 October 1643), 550; BL, Egerton MS 2643, f. 286; House of Lords RO, HL/PO/JO/10/1; Bod L, Fairfax MS 36, f. 13.
146. BL, Egerton MS, ff. 286–96. Just as the Astley letters have disappeared from the knowledge of historians during the past forty years, so has most of the earl of Manchester's archive. During the 1960s its Civil War papers were deposited in the then Public Record Office, where they were profitably used by Clive Holmes for his book on the Eastern Association. Then they were withdrawn and sold, and are unavailable, leaving scholars with a Victorian calendar in the appendix to the Eighth Report of the Historical Manuscripts Commission.
147. BL, Egerton MS 2643, f. 286; *The Parliament Scout* 15 (29 September–6 October 1643), 133–4, and 17 (13–20 October 1643), 147; *The True Informer* 3 (30 September–7 October 1643), 19.
148. *The Scottish Dove* 1 (13–20 October 1643), 2.
149. For this and my account of the battle which ensued, see *LJ*, vol. 5, 255–6; *Mercurius Aulicus* 43 (22–28 October 1643), 600–1; BL, Egerton MS 2643, f. 319; *Certaine Informations* 40 (16–23 October 1643), 309–10; George Bell, ed., *Memorials of the Civil War*, London, 1849, vol. 1, 162–5; *The Parliament Scout* 17 (13–20 October 1643), 147–50; *A Perfect Diurnall of Some Passages in Parliament* 14 (16–23 October 1643), 105–6; *The Scottish Dove* 1 (13–20 October 1643), 2; *A True and Exact Relation Of The great Victories obtained by the Earl of Manchester*, London, 19 October 1643; *A True Relation of the Late Fight Betweene the Right Honourable The Earle of Manchesters Forces . . .*, London, 1643; Bod L, Fairfax MS 36, f. 13; and HMC Hastings MSS, 105. Peter Young and Richard

Holmes, in *The English Civil War*, 154–8, provided a very detailed and influential narrative of the battle, matched exactly to particular local terrain and with confident figures for the strength of the armies, which I cannot substantiate from the original sources.

150. *Certaine Informations* 40 (16–23 October 1643), 309–10.
151. *A True and Exact Relation Of The great victories* . . .
152. *LJ*, vol. 5, 255–6.
153. *A True Relation of the Late Fight* . . .
154. Newcastle, *The Life of William Cavendish*, 31.
155. *Certaine Informations* 41 (23–30 October 1643), 319, and 42 (30 October–6 November 1643), 323; *The True Informer* 65 (21–28 October 1643), 42–3; *The Scottish Dove* 2 (20–27 October 1643), 15.
156. For these events and the subsequent parliamentary measures, see BL, Egerton MS 2643, ff. 337, 346, 356; *Certaine Informations* 41 (23–30 October 1643), 42 (30 October–6 November 1643), 323; *The Parliament Scout* 18 (20–27 October 1643), 155–6, and 19 (27 October–3 November 1643), 163–4; *A Perfect Diurnall of Some Passages in Parliament* 15 (23–30 October 1643), 114, 16 (30 October–6 November 1643), 123; *The True Informer* 6 (21–28 October 1643), 42–3; Clarendon, *History of the Rebellion*, ed. Macray, vol. 3, 232–3.
157. Bod L, Dugdale MS 19 f. 36v.
158. HMC Seventh Report, Appendix, 567. Rich's men did get quite a lot of pay, though clearly not enough for their needs, receiving £2,341 of the £3,502 due to them between 1 September and 31 December 1643: NA, SP 28/20, f. 109.
159. Newcastle, *The Life of William Cavendish*, 31.
160. *Certaine Informations* 46 (27 November–4 December 1643), 362; *The Kingdomes Weekly Intelligencer* 35 (28 November–5 December 1643), 262, and 37 (19–26 December 1643), 282–3; *Mercurius Civicus* 25 (9–16 November 1643), 199, and 30 (14–21 December 1643), 338; *The Parliament Scout* nos 20–8, covering 3 November 1643 to 5 January 1644, passim; *A Perfect Diurnall of Some Passages in Parliament* nos 16–23, covering 30 October 1643 to 1 January 1644, passim; *The Scottish Dove* 4 (3–10 November 1643), 30–1; NA, SP 28/267, ff. 52–6; Bod L, Carte MS 74, ff. 159–60; *LJ*, vol. 6, 353.
161. Clements R. Markham, *Life of Robert Fairfax of Steeton*, London, 1885, 182–3.
162. John Lilburne, *Innocency and Truth Justified*, London, 1646, 41–6.
163. Bruce and Masson, eds, *The Quarrel*, 73–5.

CHAPTER FOUR: THE LIEUTENANT-GENERAL

1. C. H. Firth and R. S. Rait, eds, *Acts and Ordinances of the Interregnum*, London, 1911, vol. 1, 368–71.
2. *CJ*, vol. 3, 373.
3. The commission, once again, has not survived, but Sir Charles Firth dated it by discovering that the warrants by which Cromwell's salary for the post was paid started on that day: 'The Raising of the Ironsides', *Transactions of the Royal Historical Society* NS 13 (1899), 53.
4. Firth and Rait, eds, *Acts and Ordinances*, vol. 1, 381–2.
5. *CSPD* (1644), 18–19.
6. BL, Harleian MS 165, f. 233.
7. Clive Holmes, *The Eastern Association in the English Civil War*, Cambridge, 1974, 100.
8. *The Parliament Scout* 30 (12–19 January 1644), 253. The preacher was Stephen Marshall.
9. This is to accept the account of events by John Adamson, 'The Triumph of Oligarchy', in Chris R. Kyle and Jason Peacey, eds, *Parliament at Work*, Woodbridge, 2002, 101–27. The appointment of Cromwell to the committee is in *CJ*, vol. 3, 391–2.
10. BL, Harleian MS 165, f. 280r.
11. *LJ*, vol. 6, 405, 409, 414–15, 512, 524, 626, 531, 538, 555, 575, 605; *CJ*, vol. 3, 500; *The Parliament Scout* 33 (2–9 February 1644), 279; *Mercurius Aulicus* (31 March–6 April

1644), 918–19. See Clive Holmes, 'Colonel King and Lincolnshire Politics, 1642–1646', *Historical Journal* 16 (1973), 451–71

12. Holmes, *The Eastern Association*, 130–7, 186–94.
13. John Twigg, *The University of Cambridge and the English Revolution*, Woodbridge, 1990, 88–102.
14. *The Weekly Account* 36 (29 February–6 March 1644), A2.
15. Peter Edwards, *Dealing in Death*, Stroud, 2000, 32.
16. Gavin Robinson, 'Horse Supply and the Development of the New Model Army 1642–1646', *War in History* 15 (2008), 133.
17. Bod L, Tanner MS 115, f. 42.
18. Laurence Spring, *The Regiments of the Eastern Association*, Bristol, 1998, vol. 1, 33–6.
19. See Essex's jealous outburst in *LJ*, vol. 6, 505–6.
20. Spring, *The Regiments of the Eastern Association*, vol. 1, 33–6, 48–56.
21. Ibid., 17–26; Holmes, *The Eastern Association*, 176.
22. NA, SP 267, f. 96.
23. Holmes, *The Eastern Association*, 175.
24. John Langton Sandford, *Studies and Illustrations of the Great Rebellion*, London, 1858, 582.
25. NA, SP 16/500/31–2.
26. Perhaps the best recent summary of these divisions is Hunter Powell, *The Crisis of British Protestantism*, Manchester, 2015.
27. David Laing, ed., *The Letters and Journals of Robert Baillie*, Edinburgh, 1841, vol. 2, 142–3.
28. This is Crawford's account of the affair, recorded in John Bruce and David Masson, eds, *The Quarrel Between the Earl of Manchester and Oliver Cromwell*, Camden Society NS 12 (1875), 59.
29. Wilbur Cortez Abbott, ed., *The Writings and Speeches of Oliver Cromwell*, Cambridge, MA, 1937, vol. 1, 277–8.
30. This is to assume that the Lieutenant Packer suspended by Crawford was the Lieutenant William Packer who took over Valentine Walton's troop in July.
31. John Lilburne, *Innocency and Truth Justified*, London, 1646, 41–6; *The Iust Mans Iustification*, London, 1646, 1–20; and *The Resolved Mans Resolution*, London, 1646, 34–5; *Articles Exhibited against Colonel Edward King*, London, 1644; John Bastwick, *A Iust Defence of John Bastwick*, London, 1645, 32.
32. This is to judge from the order of Cromwell to a man at Ely in March to pay a sum direct to his wife: Abbott, ed., *Writings and Speeches*, vol. 1, 282. For the fortifications, see Mike Osborne, *Cromwellian Fortifications in Cambridgeshire*, Huntingdon, 1990.
33. Abbott, ed., *Writings and Speeches*, vol. 1, 370.
34. *A Continuation of certain Speciall and Remarkable Passages* 3 (10–27 January 1644), 41–2.
35. *Certaine Informations From severall parts of the Kingdome* 53 (15–22 January 1644), 416–17; *The Parliament Scout* 30 (12–19 January 1644), 253.
36. *Mercurius Civicus* 34 (34 (11–18 January 1644), 371–2; *A Perfect Diurnall of Some Passages in Parliament* 22 (18–25 December 1643), 172.
37. The campaigns in the north-east of England between January and April 1644 are well described in Peter Newman, *The Battle of Marston Moor 1644*, Chichester, 1981, 13–33; and John Barratt, *The Battle of Marston Moor 1644* (Stroud, 2008), 22–36.
38. *CSPD* (1644), 23–33.
39. *Mercurius Civicus* 41 (29 February–7 March 1644), 422; H. G. Tibbutt, ed., *The Letter Books of Sir Samuel Luke 1644–45*, Bedfordshire Historical Record Society 42 (1963), 19, 589, 623–9; *Mercurius Aulicus* (3–9 March 1644), 867; *The Scottish Dove* 21 (1–8 March 1643), 166; *The Kingdomes Weekly Intelligencer* 46 (29 February–6 March 1644), 372–3; Bulstrode Whitelock, *Memorials of the English Affairs*, Oxford, 1853, vol. 2, 242; Bod L, Tanner MS 62, ff. 591–2; William Hamper, ed., *The Life, Diary and Correspondence of Sir William Dugdale*, London, 1827, 62. Comparison of these accounts shows how differently journalists even on the same side could spin a story. I have taken the figure for the garrison from the report sent by its survivors: the parliamentarian press gave higher numbers. There

is also a puzzle about a possible massacre committed in the storming of the house. None of the royalist sources mention any unusual bloodshed, even though *Mercurius Aulicus* milked the event for all possible sympathy by speaking of women and children being plundered of their clothes and prisoners driven along barefoot: it puts the death toll at sixty, which would be high given the size of the garrison but not unexpected in a hard fight, and as said the newspaper does not comment on it. Nor did the prisoners taken in the house, writing subsequently to their superiors for aid, mention anything untoward. The parliamentarian newspapers, however, boast of the slaughter of a group of French or Walloon soldiers in the garrison – foreign Catholic mercenaries whose presence would besmirch the king's cause – of a number put variously from 30 to 140. *The Scottish Dove* specifically attributes the order to show no mercy to any who resisted to Cromwell, although it was Crawford's infantry who stormed the building, and Cromwell should not have been directly involved. The presence and fate of the foreigners therefore remain an unsolved question.

40. Abbott, ed., *Writings and Speeches*, vol. 1, 276–7; HMC Seventh Report, Appendix, 472; *CSPD* (1644), 45–63; *A Continuation of certain Speciall and Remarkable Passages* 9 (21–28 February 1644), 7–8.
41. *The Parliament Scout* 39 (15–22 March 1644), 329–30.
42. Lucy Hutchinson, *Memoirs of the Life of Colonel Hutchinson*, ed. Julius Hutchinson and revised by C. H. Firth, London, 1906, 181; *Mercurius Aulicus* (17–23 March 1644), 893–900; and (24–30 March 1644), 913–14; *The Military Scribe* 6 (26 March–2 April 1644), 45–6.
43. *CSPD (1644)*, 35–88.
44. *LJ*, vol. 6, 522–3.
45. HMC Eighth Report, Appendix, 60.
46. David Laing, ed., *The Letters and Journals of Robert Baillie*, Edinburgh, 1841, vol. 2, 144–55.
47. *A Catalogue of remarkable mercies conferred upon the seven Associated Counties*, London, 1644; NA, SP 28/223/5.
48. William Goode, *A Particular Relation Of The Several Removes, Services and successes of the Right Honourable the Earle of Manchesters Army* (London, 1644).
49. *CSPD (1644)*, 101–32.
50. Ronald Hutton, *The Royalist War Effort 1642–1646*, London, 1982, 135.
51. HMC Fourth Report, Appendix, 265; *The Parliament Scout* 43 (4–11 April 1644), 396.
52. *CSPD (1644)*, 128–38.
53. For the payment of the army, see Holmes, *The Eastern Association*, 143–5.
54. Goode, *A Particular Relation; A Continuation* 18 (25 April–2 May 1644); *Mercurius Civicus* (two issues 25 April–9 May 1644), 487; *The Parliament Scout* 44–47 (3 issues 11 April–2 May 1644); *A Perfect Diurnall Of Some Passages in Parliament* 39 (22–29 April 1644), 309; *The Kingdomes Weekly Intelligencer* (2 issues 16 April–7 May 1644); Bod L, Carte MS 74, ff. 159–60; Bod L, Firth MS C7, f. 59; Tibbutt, ed., *The Letter Books of Sir Samuel Luke*, 630; *The Scottish Dove* 30 (3–10 May 1644), 239.
55. *A True Relation Of The Taking of the City, Minster, and Castle of Lincolne*, London, 1644.
56. *The Parliament Scout* 47 (9–16 May 1644), 391; *The Weekly Account* 37 (8–15 May), 82–3; NA, SP 28/24, f. 390.
57. Firth and Rait, eds, *Acts and Ordinances*, vol. 1, 432–4; *CJ*, vol. 3, 481, 490; *LJ*, vol. 6, 536–7, 553.
58. *A Continuation* 19 (9–16 May 1644), 3; *The Parliament Scout* (3 issues 9–30 May 1644); *A Perfect Diurnall* 42 (13–20 May 1644), 331; *The Kingdomes Weekly Intelligencer* (2 issues, 7–28 May 1644).
59. W. A. Day, ed., *The Pythouse Papers*, London, 1879, 8.
60. Hutton, *The Royalist War Effort*, 141.
61. *A Diary, or an Exact Iorunall* 3 (31 May–6 June 1644), 22; *The Kingdomes Weekly Intelligencer* 57 (28 May–4 June 1644), 460; *The Parliament Scout* (2 issues, 30 May–12 June 1644); Simeon Ash and William Goode, *The Continuation of True Intelligence From the Right Honourable the Earl of Manchester's Army*, London, 1644.

62. *CJ*, vol. 3, 539–40; *CSPD 1644*, 138–87, passim.
63. Bod L, Fairfax MS 36, f. 14.
64. The standard work on the siege is Peter Wenham, *The Great and Close Siege of York*, Kineton, 1970.
65. *CSPD 1644*, 190–1, 202–3; HMC Tenth Report, Appendix, 152.
66. Ash and Goode, *The Continuation of True Intelligence*.
67. *CSPV (1643–1647)*, 110.
68. Simeon Ash and William Goode, *A Particular Relation Of the most Remarkable Occurrences From The United Forces in the North*, London, 1644; Tibbutt, ed., *Letter Books*, 662.
69. Holmes, *The Eastern Association*, 155–6.
70. Ash and Goode, *The Continuation of True Intelligence*; and *A Particular Relation*.
71. *The Parliament Scout* (4 issues, 30 May–27 June 1644); Henry W. Meikle, ed., *Correspondence of the Scottish Commissioners in London, 1644–1646*, Edinburgh, 1917, 32.
72. *CSPD (1644)*, 246; *The Parliament Scout* (3 issues 5–27 June 1644); *An Exact Relation of the Siege before Yorke*, London, 1644; Ash and Goode, *The Continuation of True Intelligence*; Daniel Parsons, ed., *The Diary of Sir Henry Slingsby*, London, 1836, 108–9; *Newes From the Siege before Yorke*, London, 24 June 1644.
73. [David Buchanan], *A Short And True Relation of Some main passages*, London, 1645, 34; and *A Explanation Of Some Truths*, London, 1646, 11–12; Laing, ed., *Letters and Journals of Robert Baillie*, vol. 2, 186.
74. Bruce and Masson, eds, The Quarrel, 60, 76.
75. Thomas Carte, ed., *A Collection of Original Letters and Papers*, London, 1739, 52–4; W. Beaumont, ed., *A Discourse of the War in Lancashire*, Chetham Society OS 62 (1864), 50–3; C. H. Firth, ed., 'The Journal of Prince Rupert's Marches', *English Historical Review* 13 (1898), 736; Peter Young, *Marston Moor*, Kineton, 1970, 212–13 (printing of 'Prince Rupert's Diary'); E. B. Saxton, 'Losses of the Inhabitants of the Town of Liverpool', *Transactions of the Historic Society of Lancashire and Cheshire* 91 (1940), 181–92; Bod L, Carte MS 10, f. 664; *Mercurius Aulicus* (2 issues, 2–15 June 1644); George Ormerod, ed., *Tracts Relating to Military Proceedings in Lancashire*, Chetham Society (1844), 199–201.
76. *CSPD (1644)*, 206–66, passim.
77. These events are told from Charles's point of view in Hutton, *The Royalist War Effort*, 146–7.
78. Eliot Warburton, ed., *Memoirs of Prince Rupert, and the Cavaliers*, London, 1849, vol. 1, 415, 437–9; Bod L, Carte MS C7, ff. 116, 122.
79. Ibid., f. 124.
80. Ibid., ff. 125–6; Firth, ed., 'The Journal of Prince Rupert's Marches', 736.
81. HMC Fourth Report, Appendix, 268; *A True Relation Of The Late Fight Between the Parliament Forces and Prince Rupert*, London, 1644; Simeon Ash, *A Continuation of True Intelligence from the English and Scottish Forces Before York*, London, 1644.
82. *CSPD (1644)*, 286–99.
83. This is to follow the meticulous reconstruction of the Civil War landscape, made from local records, by Newman, *The Battle of Marston Moor 1644*, 48. I spent many happy hours walking the battlefield with Peter Newman, who lived beside it, in the 1980s.
84. This is the number that has generally been accepted by historians. *A Continuation Of certaine Speciall and Remarkable Passages* 5 (13–20 June 1644), 35, gives 21,500 foot (6,000 under Manchester, 2,500 under Fairfax and 13,000 Scots) and 10,000 horse (5,000 led by Cromwell, 2,000 by Sir Thomas Fairfax and 3,000 Scots), which accords well with other totals claimed earlier in the summer for the respective forces. The 2,000 men sent to reinforce the town of Manchester should, however, probably be deducted from this number, if they departed after the report was sent.
85. We shall never know the certainty of this: much larger figures have been quoted for armies in Roman and medieval times, but these are not reliable.
86. Ash, *A Continuation of True Intelligence*; Stockdale's narrative, printed in C. H. Firth, 'Marston Moor', *Transactions of the Royal Historical Society* NS 12 (1898), 73–6; Rupert's

'Diary', printed in Peter Young, *Marston Moor*, Kineton, 1970, 213 ; Parsons, ed., *The Diary of Sir Henry Slingsby*, 110–11; Robert Bell, ed., *Memorials of the Civil War*, London, 1849, vol. 1, 111; *A More Exact Relation of the Late Battell Neer York*, London, 1644.

87. Firth, 'Marston Moor', 73–6; *A More Exact Relation of the late Battell Neer York*; Bod L, Fairfax MS ff.14–15 (I have used this version of Sir Thomas Fairfax's 'memorials', but they have also been published in *Stuart Tracts 1603–1693* in 1903, and the Marston Moor section in Young, *Marston Moor*, 242); *LJ*, vol. 6, 626; *The Glorious and Miraculous Battell At York*, Edinburgh, 1644.

88. Day, ed., *The Pythouse Papers*, 19.

89. Rupert's 'Diary' in Young, *Marston Moor*, 213; Parsons, ed., *The Diary of Sir Henry Slingsby*, 110–11; C. H. Firth, ed., 'Two Accounts of the Battle of Marston Moor', *English Historical Review* 18 (1890), 347.

90. Margaret, Duchess of Newcastle, *The Life of William Cavendish, Duke of Newcastle*, ed. C. H. Firth, London, 1886, 75–6.

91. Meldrum and the earl of Denbigh probably had, as said, 5,000 between them, while the northern royalists now on the march to York numbered 1,300, the figure noted in accounts of Rupert's retreat to them after the battle. The royalist historian Clarendon believed and repeated Newcastle's story that the allies were preparing to disperse, which has given it a spurious authority: Edward, Earl of Clarendon, *History of the Rebellion and Civil Wars in England*, ed. W. Dunn Macray, Oxford, 1888, vol. 378–80.

92. Ash, *A Continuation of True Intelligence*.

93. Ibid.; *LJ*, vol. 6, 626; Ash, *A Continuation of True Intelligence*.

94. Parsons, ed., *The Diary of Henry Slingsby*, 10–11.

95. Ogden's narrative in Firth, 'Marston Moor, 71–2.

96. Parsons, ed., *The Diary of Henry Slingsby*, 10–11.

97. Rupert's 'Diary', in Young, *Marston Moor*, 213; Firth, 'Two Accounts of the Battle of Marston Moor', 347; Ogden's narrative in Firth, 'Marston Moor', 71–2.

98. This action is only noted by one commentator, in *A Full Relation of the late Victory Obtained by Gods Providence*, London, 1644, so it is hard to tell how significant it was to the battle which followed. Certainly, had the royalists lodged on the ridge then they would have turned the flank of their enemies' position, but a party of the size sent, given the strength and determination of the opposition, stood no chance of success. Peter Newman identified the place concerned as Bilton Bream, a rabbit warren on the western end of the ridge, and that has generally been followed since: *The Battle of Marston Moor*, 53–4.

99. *CSPD (1644)*, 311; Ash, *A Continuation of True Intelligence*.

100. *Mercurius Britannicus* 43 (8–15 July 1644), 335–6; Ash, *A Continuation of True Intelligence*; *A Full Relation of the late Victory*.

101. The parliamentarians at Nottingham, who were well acquainted with those on the field, reckoned the total at 5,000: Hutchinson, *Memoirs of Colonel Hutchinson*, 184. As shown in n. 84, the Eastern Association Horse had been put at 5,000 a month earlier, and now had the Scottish detachment as well. Robert Douglas's Diary has the Eastern Association horse at 3,000 instead, to which the Scots horse and dragoons would probably have added at least 1,000 more: Charles Sanford Terry, *The Life and Campaigns of Alexander Leslie*, London, 1899, 280–3. Of recent historians, Peter Newman has estimated Cromwell's wing at over 5,000 (*The Battle of Marston Moor*, 71); Ian Gentles the same (*The English Revolution and the Wars in the Three Kingdoms*, London, 2007, 216–19). Stuart Reid preferred 3,500 horse and 500 dragoons (*All the King's Armies*, Staplehurst, 1998, 136); and John Barratt 4,000 horse and 500–1,000 dragoons (*The Battle of Marston Moor 1644*, Stroud, 2008, 72).

102. Grifen's letter, printed in Young, *Marston Moor*, 240; W. H., *A Relation of the good successe of the Parliament's forces*, Cambridge, 1644; Terry, *The Life and Campaigns of Alexander Leslie*, 280–3; *A Full Relation of the late Victory*.

103. On the problems of visibility from the moor, see Firth, 'Two Accounts', 347.

104. Newcastle, *The Life of William Cavendish*, ed. Firth, 76–9; Firth, 'Two Accounts', 348.

105. *A More Exact Relation.*
106. BL, Additional MS 16370, ff. 64–5.
107. *A True Relation of the late Fight Between the Parliament Forces and Prince Rupert*, London, 8 July 1644, puts its strength at around 18,000, while Rupert's engineer Bernard de Gomme gave 17,500: BL, Additional MS 16370, ff. 64–5. So these parliamentarian and royalist accounts agree. Lionel Watson's parliamentarian estimate of 23,000 is way out of line with them: *A More Exact Relation.*
108. On the prince's arcane reputation, see Mark Stoyle, *The Black Legend of Prince Rupert's Dog*, Exeter, 2011.
109. The sun must have shone at periods between the showers or it would not have featured in the accounts as a factor giving advantage to the parliamentarians, as the sources make clear.
110. Their singing of psalms is noted in Parsons, ed., *The Diary of Henry Slingsby*, 114.
111. Arthur Trevor's assertion that the allies attacked as soon as they saw Newcastle's foot arriving from York is contradicted by the royalist accounts of the debate which took place between Rupert, and Newcastle and his commanders, after their foot arrived. That of Edmund Ludlow, in C. H. Firth, ed., *The Memoirs of Edmund Ludlow*, Oxford, 1894, 98–9, that the battle was provoked by a spontaneous and local engagement between Cromwell's wing and the royalists opposite, which turned into a general one, is hardly credible. Ludlow was not there, and writing decades later, and the accounts of all eyewitnesses agree that the generals ordered the attack, led by Leven.
112. *A More Exact Relation* has 7 p.m.; Ash has 6 to 7 p.m.; Robert Douglas reports 7 p.m.; Stockdale gives 7.30 p.m.; the allied generals, in *CSPD (1644)*, 311, near 7 p.m.; and W. F., in *A Relation of the good success of the Parliament's forces*, between 7 and 8 p.m.
113. Ash, *A Continuation of True Intelligence.*
114. Ibid.; *A More Exact Relation.* The account of the battle in John Vicars, *Gods arke*, London, 1645, relies mainly on Ash, but adds from an unknown source the detail that at the moment of the attack there was a sudden fierce storm of hail, thunder and lightning (on p. 479). This is not found in any eyewitness account, so can probably be discarded. Vicars' books were really sermons delivered on texts consisting of newspaper and pamphlet reports of parliamentarian successes, with embellishing and unreliable details, and should not be treated as primary sources for military actions.
115. These reflections are based on thirty years of experience of recreations of Civil War musket actions in the Sealed Knot Society. The impact of volleys on ear pressure can be painful even in blocks of a few dozen, let alone the hundreds who would have been firing together on Marston Moor. As for the other effect, there is a common proverb among late medieval and early modern reenactment societies: 'never follow a gunner into a portaloo'.
116. Musket balls are the most common find on Civil War battlefields, in varying stages of splay according to whether they had struck anything or not. Peter Newman collected scores from Marston Moor, and I have a smaller collection of my own.
117. *A Full Relation of the late Victory; Mercurius Britanicus* 43 (8–15 July 1644), 335–6.
118. Manchester's chief scout, Lionel Watson, said that the action lasted 'a pretty while' (*A More Exact Relation*). Sir Thomas Fairfax stated that it took a while but that victory was achieved 'at last': Bod L, Fairfax MS 36, ff. 14–15. Edmund Ludlow agreed that the rout came 'after an obstinate dispute': Firth, ed., *The Memoirs of Edmund Ludlow*, vol. 1, 99. The author of *Vindiciae Veritatis*, London (?), 1654, 81, said Rupert's men stood 'like an iron wall' for a significant time.
119. This charge is found in three sources. The earliest is Thomas Fuller, *The Story of the Worthies of England*, London, 1662, vol. 3, 224–5. The others are Rupert's 'Diary', which is a set of notes on the prince's military and political career compiled at some point after 1662, and the memoirs of the later king James II, from the 1690s, both handily printed in Young, *Marston Moor*, 214–15. James knew Rupert well at court in the 1660s and 1670s.
120. Sir Hugh Cholmley, the royalist governor of Scarborough, took care to collect and compare accounts of the battle from royalists who had been there, in a manner worthy of a true

historian, and none of them mentioned Byron's alleged action: Firth, ed., 'Two Accounts', 348. See also Slingsby's diary. These earlier royalist views find their scapegoat in a Scottish turncoat, Sir John Hurry, for his bad ordering of the units on the wing and the alleged fact that his troop broke first. Virtually all historians to write about the battle from C. V. Wedgwood, *The King's War*, London, 1958, 319, to Ian Gentles, *The English Revolution and the Wars in the Three Kingdoms*, London, 2007, 220; David Cooke, *The Road to Marston Moor*, Barnsley, 2007, 131–6; and Ian Roy and Joyce Malcolm, 'Why Did Prince Rupert Fight at Marston Moor?', *Journal of the Society for Army Historical Research* 86 (2008), 253, accepted that Byron ruined Rupert's dispositions on the right wing and so contributed significantly or decisively to the royalist defeat, though Stuart Reid, *All the King's Armies*, Staplehurst, 1998, 150–1, extenuated his alleged action as justifiable. John Tincey, *Marston Moor 1644*, Oxford, 2003, 60, did the same, while being apparently the first writer to point out the retrospective and untrustworthy nature of the accounts of Byron's rash attack. Malcolm Wanklyn, *Decisive Battles of the English Civil War*, Barnsley, 2006, 127–8, did the same, and Peter Gaunt, *The English Civil War*, London, 2014, 188, at last flatly stated that it was unproven.

121. Ash, *A Continuation of True Intelligence*; *A More Exact Relation*.
122. James, 11th Lord Somerville, ed., *Memoires of the Sommervilles*, Edinburgh, 1815, vol. 2, 343–52; (Buchanan), *Truth Its Manifest*, 34; *Mercurius Britanicus* 43 (8–15 July 1644), 335–6; *The Scottish Dove* 39 (5–13 July 1644), 307; *A Full Relation of the late Victory*; Douglas's diary in Terry, *The Life and Campaigns of Alexander Leslie*, 280–3.
123. BL, Additional MS 33084, letter from Henry Shelley, 9 July 1644; Bulstrode Whitelocke, *Memorials of the English Affairs*, Oxford, 1853, vol. 1, 277; *A More Exact Relation*.
124. This account is found in the *Memoirs of Denzil Lord Holles*, London, 1699, 15–16, who says that Crawford took over the horse and led them to victory while Cromwell was being tended.
125. *Vindiciae Veritatis*, 81.
126. Most of the large number of authors who have written about the battle have credited the allies' numerical superiority with playing some part in their victory. They differ, however, over how far also to emphasize Byron's alleged stupidity, or Cromwell's genius, or the action of the Scots in taking the royalist horse in the flank, as the decisive factor, selecting among these according to personal taste. The contention here is that we can never know what actually tipped the balance, or whether Rupert's dispositions could ever have compensated for his comparative weakness in numbers, had his right wing been differently led. The best-based conclusion, which was drawn by royalist commentators at the time, is that Rupert should not have fought at Marston Moor at all, given the size of the army which he faced and the high quality of much of it. It is tempting to project contemporary accounts of Cromwell's fight with Rupert's horsemen onto De Gomme's plan of the royalist battle order, to describe how specific royalist units fared, but such an exercise seems too speculative to be worthwhile. Malcolm Wanklyn, *Decisive Battles of the English Civil War*, Barnsley, 2006, set a good example by pointing out how difficult it often is to decide the details of actions in Civil War battles, including Marston Moor.
127. Ogden's narrative, in Firth, 'Marston Moor', 71–2, confirms that the prince was separated from his life guard and had to break through his enemies to avoid death or capture. The bean-field story first appears in Ash, *A Continuation of True Intelligence*.
128. Newcastle, *The Life of William Cavendish*, ed. Firth, 79.
129. Ash, *A Continuation of True Intelligence*.
130. Bod L, Fairfax MS 36, ff. 14–15; Clements R. Markham, *The Life of Robert Fairfax of Steeton*, London, 1885, 19–20; *A Full Relation of the Late Victory*; Stockdale's narrative, in Firth, 'Marston Moor', 74; *A More Exact Relation*.
131. Ludlow (Firth, ed., *Memoirs*, vol. 1, 99; Slingsby [Parsons, ed., *The Diary*, 114]; and Cholmley [Firth, 'Two Accounts', 349]) say all three generals fled, and *Vindiciae Veritatis*, 81, confirms Leven and Fairfax. Manchester's loyal chaplain, Simeon Ash, had the earl rally 500 fugitives and lead them back to the battle, which seems to be an admission that he

had himself left the field for a time: *A Continuation of True Intelligence*. A Scot called Robert Douglas claimed credit in his diary for having retrieved the fleeing Manchester and brought him back with other fugitives: printed in Terry, *The Life and Campaigns of Alexander Leslie*, 281–3.

132. There is no account of this discussion except the embittered and unreliable one later left by Crawford and preserved in the *Memoirs of Denzil Holles*, 15–16.

133. Stockdale's account in Firth, 'Marston Moor', 75; Parsons, ed., *The Diary of Sir Henry Slingsby*, 115–16; *A More Exact Relation*; *A Full Relation*; Ash, *A Continuation of True Intelligence*; *William Lilly's History of His Life and Times*, London, 1822, 177–9; Fuller, *The Story of the Worthies of England*, vol. 3, 224–5;

134. Ash, *A Continuation of True Intelligence*.

135. Ibid.

136. Sanford, *Studies and Illustrations of the Great Rebellion*, 610–11.

137. Ash, *A Continuation of True Intelligence*.

138. *LJ*, vol. 6, 636.

139. Rupert's 'Diary', in Young, *Marston Moor*, 214; Newcastle, *Life of William Cavendish*, ed. Firth, 80–1; Carte, ed., *A Collection of Original Letters*, vol. 1, 57–8; Cholmley's narrative in Firth, 'Two Accounts', 350; Ogden's and Stockdale's in Firth, 'Marston Moor', 72, 76.

140. Ash, *A Continuation of True Intelligence*; *A Full Relation*; *CSPD (1644)*, 311; Somerville, ed., *Memoire of the Somervilles*, vol. 2, 351–2; *The Kingdomes Weekly Intelligencer* 63 (9–16 July 1644), 510; *A Continuation Of certain Speciall and Remarkable Passages* 2 (10–17 July 1644), 8.

141. *LJ* vol. 6, 626; *CJ*, vol. 3, 556–7; *CSPD (1644)*, 311.

142. Shropshire RO, 445/4277.

143. Laing, ed., *The Letters and Journals of Robert Baillie*, vol. 2, 209.

144. Ibid.; *LJ*, vol. 6, 636; *CJ*, vol. 3, 558; *A Full Relation*.

145. BL Harleian MS 166, ff. 87–90; *A More Exact Relation*.

146. Ash, *A Continuation of True Intelligence*; and *A Continuation of true intelligence From the Armies in the North, from the 10 day to the 27 of this instant July*, London, 1644.

147. Laing, ed., *The Letters and Journals of Robert Baillie*, vol. 2, 209, 211, 218.

148. Joyce Macadam, 'Soldiers, Statesmen and Scribblers', *Historical Research* 82 (2009), 92–113, is an excellent analysis of the politics of the parliamentarian press in general during mid-1644.

149. *A Continuation of certain Speciall and Remarkable Passages* 1 (3–10 July 1644), 7; *The Kingdomes Weekly Intelligencer* 62 (2–9 July 1644), 497–9; *The Scottish Dove* 29 (5–13 July 1644), 307; *Mercurius Britanicus* 43 (8–15 July 1644), 335–6; *The Glorious and Miraculous Battell at York*, Edinburgh, 1644, is a Scottish pamphlet which makes the same case.

150. *The Parliament Scout* 55 (4–11 July 1644), 440; *A True Relation Of The Late Fight Between the Parliament Forces and Prince Rupert*, London, 8 July 1644.

151. *A Dogs Elegy*, London, 17 July 1644.

152. *The Weekly Account* 45 (4–11 July 1644), A2.

153. Abbott, ed., *Writings and Speeches*, vol. 1, 287–8.

154. Waller's memoirs, in Wadham College, Oxford, MS A18.14, consist of reflections on a list of divine providences which he had believed he had received. The famous letter (to the royalist Sir Ralph Hopton) in which he uttered the phrase about the war was discovered by Mary Coate, and published in her *Cornwall in the Great Civil War and Interregnum*, Oxford, 1933, 77. It was mislaid for some years and rediscovered by me at Prideaux Place, Cornwall, in 1985.

155. *The Parliament Scout* 57 (19–25 July), 554; HMC Fourth Report, Appendix, 269.

156. Parsons, ed., *The Diary of Sir Henry Slingsby*, 115–16; *CSPD (1644)*, 311.

157. Parsons, ed., *The Diary of Sir Henry Slingsby*, 116, recorded that the surrender of York was hastened by the drying up of the ditches in front of the fortifications for lack of rain.

158. Bruce and Masson, eds, *The Quarrel*, 1; *A Perfect Diurnall Of Some Passages in Parliament* 52 (22–29 July 1644), 414.

159. *CSPD (1644)*, 361–2. A sampling comparison of these Victorian calendars with the original letter books in the National Archives has shown that the former do contain the information from the latter relevant to the concerns of this book.

160. Bod L, Carte MS 12, f. 14; and Clarendon MS 28, f. 129; Beaumont, ed., *A Discourse of the War in Lancashire*, 54; Firth, ed., 'The Journal of Prince Rupert's Marches', 737.

161. *CSPD (1644)*, 385–6, 409; William Goode, *A Continuation Of True Intelligence From The Army, under the Command of . . . the Earl of Manchester . . . from July 27 to August 16th*, London, 1644.

162. *A Continuation of certain Speciall and Remarkable Passages* 4 (24 July–1 August 1644), 7; *Mercurius Civicus* 62 (25 July–1 August 1644), 590; Ash, *A Continuation of True Intelligence From the Armies in the North*; Bruce and Masson, eds, *The Quarrel*, 60–1.

163. Bruce and Masson, eds, *The Quarrel*, 2; *A Diary, or an Exact Iournall* 10 (25 July–2 August 1644), 78–9; *Mercurius Civicus* 62 (25 July–1 August 1644), 590; Ash, *A Continuation of true Intelligence From the Armies in the North*.

164. Lilburne's account is in his pamphlet, *Innocency and Truth Justified*, London, 1646, 22–6, echoing that which he gave to the committee to examine charges against Manchester in December 1645. Cromwell's terse endorsement of it is in Bruce and Masson, eds, *The Quarrel*, 303, and that of Colonel John Pickering in *CSPD (1644–1645)*, 150. For another example of Cromwell intervening to help Lilburne in a dispute at this time, see another of the latter's pamphlets, *The Resolved Mans Resolution*, London, 1646, 34–5.

165. Bruce and Masson, eds, *The Quarrel*, 1–5; *CJ*, vol. 3, 577.

166. Bruce and Masson, eds, *The Quarrel*, 5–20; *CSPD (1644)*, 409–10.

167. Hutton, *The Royalist War Effort*, 148.

168. Bruce and Masson, eds, *The Quarrel*, 16–21.

169. The campaign is described in detail in *A Journal, Or A True and Exact Relation of Each Dayes Passage . . . of that Party . . . under the Command of . . . Major General Crawford*, London, 1644, of which the various newspaper accounts are shorter versions. The record of marches of the force is in Bod L, Carte MS 74, ff. 159–60. See also Bruce and Masson, eds, *The Quarrel*, 5–7; and Goode, *A Continuation of True Intelligence*.

170. Goode, *A Continuation Of True Intelligence*. It is notable that the presbyterian Goode made a full report of the humiliation of Cromwell's cavalry. See also *The Parliament Scout* 62 (22–29 August 1644), 495, for Cromwell's subsequent duties.

171. Abbott, ed., *Writings and Speeches*, vol. 1, 292.

172. *LJ*, vol. 6, 674–5.

173. Laing, ed., *The Letters and Journals of Robert Baillie*, vol. 2, 211, 218.

174. Bruce and Masson, eds, *The Quarrel*, 61–2.

175. Samuel Rawson Gardiner, 'A Letter from the Earl of Manchester to the House of Lords . . .', *Camden Miscellany* 8 (1883), item 5.

176. This was John Crew, in HMC Eighth Report, Appendix, 61.

177. Abbott, ed., *Writings and Speeches*, vol. 1, 292.

178. Bruce and Masson, eds, *The Quarrel*, 2–12; *CSPD (1644)*, 409. For Cromwell's pay, see Patrick Little, 'Cromwell and Ireland before 1649', in Patrick Little, ed., *Oliver Cromwell: New Perspectives*, Basingstoke, 2009, 121.

179. Holmes, *The Eastern Association*, 158–64.

180. *CJ*, vol. 3, 620; *LJ*, vol. 6, 699; *CSPD (1644)*, 22–6.

181. *LJ*, vol. 6, 700; Bod L, Carte MS 74, ff. 159–60; *The Parliament Scout* 64 (5–13 September 1644), 512.

182. Alan Thompson, ed., *The Impact of the First Civil War on Hertfordshire 1642–1647*, Hertfordshire Record Society 23 (2007), 123–8.

183. HMC Eighth Report, Appendix, 61.

184. *A Perfect Diurnall Of Some Passages in Parliament* 59 (9–16 September 1644), 470.

185. Bruce and Masson, eds, *The Quarrel*, 27–8.

186. Ibid., 62; Gardiner, 'A Letter from the Earl of Manchester'; *The E: of Manchesters narrative in ye house of Peeres*, manuscript in George Thomason's hand among the British Library Thomason Tracts.

187. *CSPD (1644)*, 499.

188. Their attendance of the committee is recorded in *CSPD (1644)*, 499–517.

189. *CJ*, vol. 3, 626.

190. BL Harleian MS 166, f. 113r; Bod L, Carte MS 80, f. 196.

191. Laing, ed., *The Letters and Journals of Robert Baillie*, vol. 2, 226–35.

192. Bruce and Masson, eds, *The Quarrel*, 27–30.

193. Ibid.

194. It appears in issue 70 (19–26 September 1644), 658.

195. Sources at n. 199; plus Bod L, Carte MS 12, ff. 461–2.

196. Bruce and Masson, eds, *The Quarrel*, 31–47; *CSPD (1644–1645)*, 21–32; *CJ*, vol. 3, 634–5, 641–2, 658–9; Firth and Rait, eds, *Acts and Ordinances*, vol. 1, 520–1, 526–8, 530; *The Parliament Scout* (3 issues 27 September–17 October 1644); *A Perfect Diurnal Of Some Passages in Parliament* (3 issues 16 September–October 1644); Tibbutt, ed., *The Letter Books of Sir Samuel Luke*, 357–8.

197. Sir Edward Walker, *Historical Discourses upon Several Occasions*, London, 1705, 106–9; Charles Edward Long, ed., *Diary of the Marches of the Royal Army during the Great Civil War*, Camden Society 74 (1859), 141–2; BL, Additional MS 18981, f. 303; and Additional MS 18982, f. 8; Bod L, Firth MS C7, f. 207.

198. BL, Additional MS 70108, 'Misc. 31'.

199. Walker, *Historical Discourses*, 103, gave 3,000 as the total strength of Waller's force when the king's cavalry routed it at Andover with a forward strike on the march to Donnington Castle. Royalists were not inclined to understate the numbers of their defeated enemies. In a letter to Rupert, the king's secretary of state Lord Digby stated that Waller's force had been composed of his own horse, that of the earl of Essex, and eight troops which Manchester had sent ahead from his army to help Sir William: Bod L, Firth MS C7, f. 207. This precise information, with the number of the force, was presumably gained from prisoners taken during the attack. Manchester's troopers need therefore to be deducted from the size of the party Waller would have had in Dorset.

200. Malcolm Wanklyn reached similar conclusions, though with a different starting point and slightly different numbers, in 'A General Much Maligned', *War in History* 14 (2007), 133–56.

201. Cromwell himself estimated the total size of the combined parliamentary force as 8,000 horse and dragoons and 11,000 foot (Abbott, ed., *Writings and Speeches*, vol. 1, 306), while the opposed royalists thought it 8,000 horse and 8,000 foot (Walker, *Historical Discourses*, 110). Of historians writing since 2000, Ian Gentles has suggested 22,000 parliamentarians altogether, facing 9,000 royalists (*The English Revolution and the Wars in the Three Kingdoms*, 241); Malcolm Wanklyn, 10,000–11,000 parliamentarian foot and 7,000–8,000 horse, facing 5,500 royalist foot and 5,500 horse (*The Warrior Generals*, London, 2010, 129); and Peter Gaunt, 15,000–18,000 parliamentarians altogether, facing 9,000–10,000 royalists (*The English Civil War*, London, 2014, 197). Part of the uncertainty is due to the fact that we are not sure if the lower totals given by contemporaries include officers.

202. Rain fell for three days and nights on end between 21 and 24 October: HMC Portland MSS, Appendix, vol. 1, 188–9.

203. Bod L, Carte MS 74, f. 160.

204. Food, especially the staples of bread and cheese, was in short supply from the beginning: see the source at n202.

205. Despatch to the Committee of Both Kingdoms printed in Walter Money, *The First and Second Battles of Newbury*, 2nd edition, London, 1884, 156.

206. Despatches printed in Ibid., 156–7; HMC Tenth Report, Appendix, 155.

207. There is an excellent plan of the fortifications and account of the sieges in the West Berkshire Museum guide *Donnington Castle* (its Heritage Guide no. 2, n.d.).

208. Cromwell's testimony in Abbott, ed., *Writings and Speeches*, vol. 1, 306; John Rushworth, *Historical Collections*, London, 1721, vol. 5, 772–3; Simeon Ash, *A True Relation of The*

Most Chiefe Occurrences, at and since the Late Battell at Newbery, London, 1644; Bruce and Masson, eds, *The Quarrel*, 48–9, 63; BL, Harleian MS 166, ff. 139–40; BL, Additional MS 70108, 'Misc. 3i'.

209. BL, Additional MS 18981, f. 312; *LJ*, vol. 7, 40–1.

210. This, and the general account of the battle given below, is based on *LJ*, vol. 7, 40–1; Walker, *Historical Discourses*, 111–15; Sir Richard Bulstrode, *Memoirs and Reflections upon the Reign and Government of King Charles Ist and K. Charles the IInd*, London, 1721, 117–18; Long, ed., *Diary of the Marches of the Royal Army*, 144–6; Rushworth, *Historical Collections*, vol. 5, 722–3; HMC Fourth Report, Appendix, 297; Ash, *A True Relation*; Bruce and Masson, eds, *The Quarrel*, 49–52; Peter Young and Norman Tucker, eds, *Military Memoirs: The Civil War*, London, 1967, Memoirs of John Gwyn, 56–7; *Mercurius Aulicus* (27 October–2 November 1644), 1,231–42; *Mercurius Civicus* 75 (24–31 October 1644), 696–7; *A Letter Sent to the Honourable William Lenthall . . . wherein is truly Related the great Victory . . . by the Parliament Army . . . neer Newbery*, London, 29 October 1644; BL, Harleian MS 166, ff. 139–41. The overwhelming majority of the sources agree that the action started around 3 or 4 p.m.

211. *William Lilly's History of His Life and Times*, 182–3.

212. The effect of the bombardment is emphasized in Bruce and Masson, eds, *The Quarrel*, 49–50; *A Letter Sent to the Honourable William Lenthall*; and BL, Harleian MS 166, ff. 140–1 The garrison itself had only four pieces of artillery, but Walker makes clear that the royal train had reinforced these, and that would have delivered serious firepower.

213. Wadham College, Oxford, L, MS A18.14, f, 20.

214. Bruce and Masson, eds, *The Quarrel*, 63–4.

215. BL, Harleian MS 166, f. 140; Bod L, Carte MS 80, f. 715.

216. Walker, *Historical Discourses*, 114, testifies to this incident, which seems to contradict Ash's assertion, in *A True Relation*, that Manchester could not hear the royalists retreating.

217. This was the estimation of Ludlow, in his *Memoirs*, ed. by Firth, vol. 1, 101–6.

218. Abbott, ed., *Writings and Speeches*, vol. 1, 307; Bruce and Masson, eds, *The Quarrel*, 64; *CSPD (1644)*, 82–3.

219. *The Scottish Dove* 54 (25 October–1 November 1644), 419–20; *A Letter Sent to the Honourable William Lenthall*; *Mercurius Civicus* 75 (24–31 October 1644), 696–7.

220. *CJ*, vol. 3, 680–2; Laing, ed., *The Letters and Journals of Robert Baillie*, vol. 2, 240.

221. Walker, *Historical Discourses*, 116; *Mercurius Aulicus* (27 October–2 November 1644), 1,240–2; *The Weekly Account* 62 (31 October–6 November 1644), 489; Bod L, Firth MS C7, f. 223.

222. *CSPD (1644)*, 89–96.

223. *LJ*, vol. 7, 46.

224. Bruce and Masson, eds, *The Quarrel*, 52–3, 65; Ash, *A True Relation*; *CSPD (1644–5)*, 146–61 (Sir James Harrington's relation); *The Weekly Account* 63 (6–13 November 1644), sig. Rrr; Bod L, Carte MS 74, f. 60.

225. Tibbutt, ed., *The Letter Books of Sir Samuel Luke*, 670–1; Walker, *Historical Discourses*, 117; Long, ed., *Diary of the Marches of the Royal Army*, 147; BL, Additional MS 16370, ff. 60–1. Again the lower totals of the possible size of the royal army may be due to not counting the officers.

226. *LJ*, vol. 7, 61; Abbott, ed., *Writings and Speeches*, vol. 1, 309; Bruce and Masson, eds, *The Quarrel*, 65–7; BL, Harleian MS 166, f. 141; BL, Additional MS 25465, f. 21.

227. The account which follows of the actions on 9 and 10 November, sometimes called the Third Battle of Newbury, is based on *LJ*, vol. 7, 61–2; Walker, *Historical Discourses*, 117–20; Abbott, ed., *Writings and Speeches*, vol. 1, 308–10; Firth, ed., *The Memoirs of Edmund Ludlow*, vol. 1, 105–6; Long, ed., *Diary of the Marches of the Royal Army*, 147–51; Rushworth, *Historical Collections*, vol. 5, 730–6; Ash, *A True Relation*; Bruce and Masson, eds, *The Quarrel*, 55–6, 66–7; Eliot Warburton, ed., *Memoirs of Prince Rupert and the Cavaliers*, London, 1849, vol. 3, 31–2; Tibbutt, ed., *The Letter Books of Sir Samuel Luke*, 387–8; *Mercurius Aulicus* (10–16 November 1644), 1,252–3; *CSPD (1644–5)*, 146–61; *Perfect Passages of Each*

Day's Proceedings in Parliament 4 (6–13 November 1644), 18; *The Weekly Account* 63 (6–13 November 1644), Sig. Rrr; *The E: of Manchesters narrative in ye house of Peeres* (in Thomason Tracts); BL, Harleian MS 166, f. 141; BL, Additional MS 16370, ff. 60–1.

228. Walker, *Historical Discourses*, 120; Bruce and Masson, eds, *The Quarrel*, 57–8, 70; Abbott, ed., *Writings and Speeches*, vol. 1, 311; Long, ed., *Diary of the Marches of the Royal Army*, 152–4; Ash, *A True Relation; CSPD (1644–5)*, 125–38; *The E: of Manchesters narrative in ye house of Peeres:* BL, Harleian MS 166, ff. 142–4; Bod L, Carte MS 74, f. 160; Bod L, Firth MS C7, f. 233.

CHAPTER FIVE: BORROWED TIME

1. The *Kingdomes Weekly Intelligencer* 82 (19–26 November 1644), 639–40; *A Perfect Diurnall Of Some Passages in Parliament* 66 (11–18 November 1644), 537–8; *The Scottish Dove* 56 (8–15 November 1644), 436–7.
2. *Mercurius Civicus* 79 (21–28 November 1644), 731.
3. *The Parliament Scout* 74 (14–21 November 1644), 583.
4. *A Perfect Diurnall* 66 (11–18 November 1644), 537–8.
5. *The Scottish Dove* 56 (8–15 November 1644), 436–7.
6. Keith Lindley and David Scott, eds, *The Journal of Thomas Juxon 1644–1647*, Camden Society 5th series 13 (1999), 60–3.
7. *CJ*, vol, 3, 696–7; *Memoirs of Denzil Lord Holles*, London, 1699, 27; *A Perfect Diurnall* 66 (11–18 November 1644), 541; BL, Additional MS 31116, f. 174.
8. Bulstrode Whitelocke, *Memorials of the English Affairs*, Oxford, 1853, vol. 1, 327.
9. BL, Harleian MS 166, f. 166; BL, Additional MS 31116, f. 175; *CJ*, vol. 3, 703–4.
10. Strictly speaking, no record of this pivotal speech survives. Instead we have a written repetition of that part which concerned Manchester, submitted later during the ensuing row, which is printed in Abbott, ed., *Writings and Speeches*, vol. 1, 302–11. The injustice of his charges has been exposed by Malcolm Wanklyn, in 'A General Much Maligned', *War in History* 14 (2007), 133–56, though that perhaps underestimates the strength of Manchester's resistance to his orders in late September and early October 1644, and the friction this produced with the Committee of Both Kingdoms and Parliament. Professor Wanklyn has also reflected adversely on Cromwell's representation of the campaign and that of his supporters (discussed below) in 'Oliver Cromwell and the Performance of Parliament's Armies in the Newbury Campaign', *History* 96 (2011), 3–25. More of the speech is described in Lindley and Scott, eds, *The Journal of Thomas Juxon*, 67. For his weeping, see *William Lilly's History of His Life and Times*, London reprint, 1822, 182–3.
11. Lindley and Scott, eds, *The Journal of Thomas Juxon*, 67.
12. *Perfect Occurrences of Parliament* 16 (22–29 November 1644), 2–3.
13. *Perfect Passages of Each Day's Proceedings in Parliament* 6 (20–27 November 1644), 47.
14. Lindley and Scott, eds, *The Journal of Thomas Juxon*, 66.
15. *Memoirs of Denzil Lord Holles*, 27.
16. *CJ*, vol. 3, 703–5.
17. The *Kingdomes Weekly Intelligencer* 82 (19–26 November 1644), 640; *Mercurius Civicus* 79 (21–28 November 1644), 731; *Perfect Occurrences of Parliament* 16 (22–29 November 1644), 2–3; *The Weekly Account* 65 (20–26 November 1644), n.p.; *The Scottish Dove* 58 (22–29 November 1644), 453. Bulstrode Whitelocke echoed the recurrent phrase that Cromwell had given 'great satisfaction' to the House in his *Memorials of the English Affairs*, vol. 1, 343.
18. *The Parliament Scout* 75 (21–28 November 1644), 601–2; see also 76 (28 November–4 December 1644), n.p.; *A Perfect Diurnall Of Some Passages in Parliament* 70 (25 November–2 December 1644), 553–4; *Perfect Passages of Each Day's Proceedings in Parliament* 6 (20–27 November 1644), 47; *Mercurius Britanicus* 60 (2–9 December 1644), 474.
19. Lindley and Scott, eds, *The Journal of Thomas Juxon*, 67.

20. *LJ*, vol. 7, 73, 76. Three different versions of Manchester's defence survive, which agree on the main points: Bod L, Tanner MS 61 f. 205, printed by Samuel Rawson Gardiner, ed., 'A Letter from the Earl of Manchester to the House of Lords', Camden Miscellany 8 (1883), item 5; *The E: of Manchesters narrative in ye house of Peeres*, copied out by George Thomason and in the BL's Thomason Tracts; and BL, Additional MS 70108, 'Misc. 31'.

21. *LJ*, vol. 7, 76. The committee consisted of the earls of Essex, Warwick, Northumberland, Pembroke and Salisbury and Lord North.

22. *LJ*, vol. 7, 76–80; *CJ*, vol. 3, 713–18; BL, Additional MS 31116 f. 178; Lindley and Scott, eds, *The Journal of Thomas Juxon*, 67–8.

23. David Laing, ed., *The Letters and Journals of Robert Baillie*, Edinburgh, 1841, vol. 2, 243–5; Henry W. Meikle, ed., *Correspondence of the Scots Commissioners in London, 1644–1646*, Edinburgh, 1917, 51–2.

24. See Juxon's comments in his *Journal*, eds Lindley and Scott, 67–8. The Venetian ambassador thought that Essex supported the attack on Manchester, but this is contradicted by Juxon and Whitelocke, and the ambassador was usually less well informed than those: *CSPV* (1643–1647), 159–60.

25. Whitelocke, *Memorials of the English Affairs*, vol. 1, 343–8.

26. These testimonies are famously calendared in *CSPD (1644–1645)*, 146–61.

27. *The Parliament Scout* 77 (5–12 December 1644), 617.

28. John Bruce and David Masson, eds, *The Quarrel Between the Earl of Manchester and Oliver Cromwell*, Camden Society N.S. 12 (1875), 59–76; Simeon Ash, *A True Relation OF The Most Chiefe Occurrences, at and since the Late Battell at Newbery*, London, 1644. Dodson's identity as the anonymous critic of Cromwell is argued almost decisively in Clive Holmes, 'The Identity of the Author of the "Statement by an opponent of Cromwell"', *English Historical Review* 129 (2014), 1371–82. What may be the original copy of his deposition is in the Huntingdonshire RO, M80/Acc3343.

29. In broad terms, I accept the account of Civil War parliamentarian politics provided by David Scott, 'Party Politics in the Long Parliament, 1640–8', in George Southcombe and Grant Tapsell, eds, *Revolutionary England c. 1630–c. 1660*, Abingdon, 2017, 32–54.

30. Whitelocke, *Memorials*, vol. 1, 349–50.

31. His words are recorded in John Rushworth, *Historical Collections*, London, 1721, vol. 6, 4; Edward, Earl of Clarendon, *History of the Rebellion and Civil Wars in England*, ed. W. Dunn Macray, Oxford, 1888, VIII.193–6; and *Perfect Occurrences of Parliament* 18 (6–13 December 1644), sub. 9 December. The words attributed to him in those three sources are unique to each, which made Wilbur Cortez Abbott believe that they referred to different speeches (*Writings and Speeches*, vol. 1, 315), but it could be that each record echoes different parts of one or two speeches: Oliver's usual practice was to make one, lengthy, oration. These sources also preserve other information about the debate, for which also see *A Perfect Diurnall* 72 (9–16 December 1644), 567–8.

32. The royalist Clarendon asserted long afterward that the ordinance was a ruse by the Independents to get rid of their enemies, but there is no means of testing the quality of his sources and he may have been speaking from mere prejudice: Clarendon, *History of the Rebellion*, ed. Macray, VIII.197, 201. The Venetian ambassador saw it at the time as a bipartisan measure; *CSPV (1643–1647)*, 163–5. Whitelocke, who was opposed, simply said that the ordinance passed the Commons because of 'envy and self-interest': *Memorials*, vol. 1, 353. Of historians, Samuel Rawson Gardiner thought the ordinance a cross-party measure (*History of the Great Civil War*, 2nd edition, London, 1897, vol. 2, 89–92), followed by A. N. B. Cotton, 'Cromwell and the Self-Denying Ordinance', *History* 62 (1977), 211–31. John Adamson has argued that it was launched by the group around Cromwell, Vane, Sir John Evelyn and Viscount Saye ('Cromwell and the Long Parliament', in John Morrill, ed., *Cromwell and the English Revolution*, London, 1990, 62–3), followed by Barry Coward (*Oliver Cromwell*, London, 1991, 36–8). Ian Gentles likewise views it as a move against the earl of Essex, which would make it largely an Independent initiative ('The Politics of Fairfax's Army', in John Adamson, ed., *The Civil Wars*, Basingstoke, 2008, 176–80).

33. There has been majority agreement on this among historians since Samuel Rawson Gardiner argued it in the 1890s.
34. *The Kingdomes Weekly Intelligencer* 84 (3–10 December 1644), 675–7; *The Parliament Scout* 77 (5–12 December 1644), 617; *A Perfect Diurnall* 72 (9–16 December 1644), 567–8; *The Weekly Account* 67 (4–11 December 1644), sub 9 December; *The Scottish Dove* 60 (6–13 December 1644), 466–7; and see the comments in Lindley and Scott, eds, *The Journal of Thomas Juxon*, 69.
35. *CJ*, vol. 3, 721–9; Lindley and Scott, eds, *The Journal of Thomas Juxon*, 70.
36. *CJ*, vol. 4, 13, 17; *LJ*, vol. 7, 127, 129; *The Kingdomes Weekly Intelligencer* 88 (7–14 January 1645), 703–4.
37. *CJ*, vol. 4, 26, 31; *LJ*, vol. 7, 135; *A Perfect Diurnall* 78 (20–27 January 1645), 615–22.
38. *CJ*, vol. 4, 40, 42–4, 48–51; *LJ*, vol. 7, 192; C. H. Firth and R. S. Rait, eds, *Acts and Ordinances of the Interregnum*, London, 1911, vol. 1, 630–46.
39. *CJ*, vol. 4, 2, 6, 15–16, 18, 20.
40. *CJ*, vol. 4, 25–7, 46–7; *CSPD (1644–1645)*, 263, 269.
41. *CJ*, vol. 3, 734; and vol. 4, 4; Rushworth, *Historical Collections*, vol. 5, 744–9; *The Kingdomes Weekly Intelligencer* 83 (20 November–3 December 1644), 667–8; *Mercurius Civicus* 81 (5–12 December 1644), 749–50; *A Perfect Diurnall* 72 (9–16 December 1644), 571–6; *Perfect Occurrences of Parliament* 18 (6–13 December 1644), sub 9 December.
42. For one on a relatively minor matter, see *CJ*, vol. 3, 728.
43. *CJ*, vol. 3, 725, 729.
44. As well as those mentioned, see *CJ*, vol. 3, 724; and vol. 4, 42, 52.
45. *CSPD (1644–1645)*, 172–323 passim; *CJ*, vol. 7, 37, 51.
46. *CJ*, vol. 4, 7, 11–12, 20, 28; *The Parliament Scout* 84 (23–30 January 1645), 670–1.
47. *CJ*, vol. 4, 20, 36.
48. *CSPD (1644–1645)*, 291–2; HMC Portland MSS, Appendix, 208–9.
49. The best parliamentarian account is Peter Ince, *A Brief Relation of the Surprise of the Forts of Weymouth*, London, 1645; a royalist one in Eliot Warburton, ed., *Memoirs of Prince Rupert and the Cavaliers*, London, vol. 3, 58–9. See also H. G. Tibbutt, ed., *The Letter Books of Sir Samuel Luke*, Bedfordshire Historical Record Society 42 (1963), 442. There is a lively local account of the affair: Mark Vine, *The Crabchurch Conspiracy 1645*, privately published at Weymouth in 2013.
50. *CJ*, vol. 4, 46–7; *Mercurius Civicus* 90 (6–13 February 1645), 821–2.
51. *CSPD (1644–1645)*, 303–4; Tibbutt, ed., *The Letter Books of Sir Samuel Luke*, 442.
52. NA, SP16/106/20, 50–8.
53. *A Diary, or an Exact Iournall* 42 (27 February–6 March 1645), n.p.
54. Tibbutt, ed., *The Letter Books of Sir Samuel Luke*, 420.
55. *CSPD (1644–1645)*, 304–8; *A Perfect Diurnall* 82 (17–24 February 1645), 650; Lindley and Scott, eds, *The Journal of Thomas Juxon*, 74; R. N. Dore, ed., *The Letter Books of Sir William Brereton*, Lancashire and Cheshire Record Society 123 (1984), 48; Whitelocke, *Memorials*, vol. 1, 389. The mutineers formally made their apology to the House of Commons, and were forgiven, on 20 March: *CJ*, vol. 4, 89.
56. *A Diary* 42 (27 February–6 March 1645), n.p.; *Perfect Passages of Each Day's Proceedings in Parliament* 17 (12–19 February 1645), 131.
57. *CJ*, vol. 4, 63.
58. *CSPD (1644–1645)*, 323.
59. *CJ*, vol. 4, 67.
60. *A Diary* 43 (6–13 March 1645), n.p.
61. Ince, *A Brief Relation*.
62. *Mercurius Civicus* 95 (13–20 March 1645), 858; *A Diary* 44 (13–20 March 1645), n.p.; *The Kingdomes Weekly Intelligencer* 91 (11–18 March 1645), 733–4.
63. *The Kingdomes Weekly Intelligencer* 92 (18–25 March 1645), 740; and 93 (25 March–1 April 1645), 744.
64. Bod L, MS DON d. 57, ff. 8–9.

65. BL, Sloane MS 1519, f. 66; Bod L, Tanner MS 60, ff. 15–16.
66. *Mercurius Aulicus* (23–30 March 1645), 1526; and (6–13 April 1645), 1540–2; *A Diary* 46 (27 March–3 April 1645), n.p.; *The Kingdomes Weekly Intelligencer* 93 (25 March–1 April 1645), 744; and 94 (1–8 April 1645), 762; *Mercurius Civicus* 97 (27 March–3 April 1645), 876; and 98 (3–10 April 1645), 881; *A Perfect Diurnall* 87 (24–31 March 1645), 692; and 88 (31 March–7 April 1645), 700; Bod L, Tanner MS 60, ff. 27–8, 38–9; Bod L, Clarendon MS, ff. 71–5, 83, 95, 99, 105, 107, 113, 119; Sir Richard Bulstrode, *Memoirs and Reflections upon the Reign and Government of Charles I and II*, London, 1721, 120.
67. Bod L, DON d, 57, ff. 8–9.
68. Abbott, ed., *Writings and Speeches*, vol. 1, 336–7; *The Kingdomes Weekly Intelligencer* 95 (8–15 April 1645), 762; *The Moderate Intelligencer* 8 (17–24 April 1645), 622; William Salt L, Stafford, Salt MS 45, ff. 58r, 47r, 40r; Bod L, Clarendon MS 24, ff. 113, 117, 119, 121, 123, 125, 127.
69. *CSPD (1644–1645)*, 393, 415.
70. For what follows I accept the views of Robert K. G. Temple, 'The Original Officer List of the New Model Army', *Bulletin of the Institute of Historical Research* 59 (1986), 50–77; Ian Gentles, *The New Model Army in England, Ireland and Scotland 1645–1653*, Oxford, 1992, 15–24; 'The Choosing of Officers for the New Model Army', *Historical Research* 67 (1994), 264–85; and *The English Revolution and the Wars in the Three Kingdoms*, London, 2007, 251–2; and Andrew Hopper, *Black Tom*, Manchester, 2007, 62–6.
71. The text is in Samuel Rawson Gardiner, *The Constitutional Documents of the Puritan Revolution*, 3rd edition, Oxford, 1906, 287–8.
72. *CJ*, vol. 4, 97.
73. HMC Tenth Report, Appendix, 450.
74. Sir Charles Firth and Godfrey Davies, *The Regimental History of Cromwell's Army*, Oxford, 1940, vol. 1, 57–9.
75. Joshua Sprigg, *Anglia Rediviva*, Oxford edition, 1854, 11.
76. *CSPD (1644–1645)*, 419.
77. *LJ*, vol. 6, 339–40; Rushworth, *Historical Collections*, vol. 6, 24. The royalist horse party consisted of parts of three regiments, while Cromwell had with him the two formed from his old one, and parts of five more.
78. William Hamper, ed., *The Life, Diary and Correspondence of Sir William Dugdale*, London, 1827, 78–9.
79. Abbott, ed., *Writings and Speeches*, vol. 1, 341–2. Like his previous despatch, this one was much quoted and paraphrased in the newspapers.
80. *CJ*, vol. 4, 128.
81. Abbott, ed., *Writings and Speeches*, vol. 1, 344–5; *Mercurius Aulicus* (27 April–4 May 1645), 1570–3.
82. *CSPD (1644–1645)*, 445.
83. Bod L, Firth MS C7, f. 318; BL, Additional MS 18982, ff. 48–50; Bod L, Clarendon MS 24, ff. 134–6.
84. Clarendon, *History of the Rebellion*, ed. Macray, IX.28; Georges Bernard, ed., *Life of Sir John Digby*, Camden Miscellany 12 (1910), 110.
85. Sprigge, *Anglia Rediviva*, 17–18; *A Diary* 51 (1–8 May), n.p.; *The Kingdomes Weekly Intelligencer* 99 (5–12 May 1645), 794; *The Moderate Intelligencer* 11 (8–15 May 1645), 85; *A Diary, or an Exact Iournal* 51 (1–8 May 1645), n.p.
86. Sir Edward Walker, *Historical Discourses upon Several Occasions*, London, 1705, 125–7; Hamper, ed., *The Life, Diary and Correspondence of Sir William Dugdale*, 79; BL, Harleian MS 7379, f. 43; for the Worcestershire campaign, see Ronald Hutton, *The Royalist War Effort 1642–1645*, London, 1981, 173–4.
87. R. N. Dore, ed., *The Letter Books of Sir William Brereton*, Lancashire and Cheshire Record Society 123 (1984), 432–4.
88. *LJ*, vol. 7, 350.
89. Abbott, ed., *Writings and Speeches*, vol. 1, 348.

90. *CJ*, vol. 4, 138; *LJ*, vol. 7, 364; Firth and Rait, eds, *Acts and Ordinances*, vol. 1, 684.
91. *The Weekly Account* 19 (7–14 May 1645), n.p.; BL, Additional MS 31116, f. 207.
92. Dore, ed., *The Letter Books of Sir William Brereton*, 400, 414–15, 447–8; Sprigge, *Anglia Rediviva*, 15–16; *Perfect Occurrences of Parliament* 20 (9–16 May 1645), n.p.
93. Dore, ed., *The Letter Books of Sir William Brereton*, 473–4.
94. *LJ*, vol. 7, 390–2, 397–8; Leven's despatches printed in Charles Sanford Terry, *The Life and Campaigns of Alexander Leslie, First Earl of Leven*, London, 1899, 349–60.
95. Warburton, ed., *Memoirs of Prince Rupert*, vol. 3, 97–8.
96. *CSPD (1644–1645)*, 476–534; *The Moderate Intelligencer* (2 issues, 15–29 May 1645).
97. Philip Tennant, *Edgehill and After*, Stroud, 1992.
98. *CJ*, vol. 4, 142; Sprigge, *Anglia Rediviva*, 15–16; *CSPD (1644–1645)*, 30–1.
99. *CSPD (1644–1645)*, 486–528.
100. Dore, ed., *The Letter Books of Sir William Brereton*, 460.
101. Meikle, ed., *Correspondence of the Scottish Commissioners*, 75.
102. Sprigge, *Anglia Rediviva*, 23; *CSPD (1644–1645)*, 485–519; Dore, ed., *The Letter Books of Sir William Brereton*, 497; H. G. Tibbutt, ed., *The Letter Books of Sir Samuel Luke 1644–45*, Bedfordshire Historical Society 42 (1963), 540; *The Kingdomes Weekly Intelligencer* 102 (27 May–3 June 1645), 815–16.
103. Hamper, ed., *The Life, Diary and Correspondence of Sir William Dugdale*, 79.
104. Walker, *Historical Discourses*, 128.
105. *CJ*, vol. 4, 155–6; *CSPD (1644–1645)*, 533–58.

CHAPTER SIX: THE GLORIOUS YEAR

1. J. Whinnell, *Matters of Great Concernment*, London, 1646, 16.
2. Wilbur Cortez Abbott, ed., *The Writings and Speeches of Oliver Cromwell*, Cambridge, MA, 1937, vol. 1, 352–4; *CSPD (1644–1645)*, 558; *The Kingdomes Weekly Intelligencer* 103 (3–10 June 1645), 103; *The Moderate Intelligencer* (2 issues 29 May–12 June 1645); *Mercurius Civicus* 106 (29 May–5 June 1645), 956.
3. *CJ*, vol. 4, 163; *LJ*, vol. 7, 411–12.
4. *CSPD (1644–1645)*, 564, 571, 572, 580; *LJ*, vol. 7, 403–4.
5. Robert Bell, ed., *The Fairfax Correspondence*, London, 1849, vol. 1, 228.
6. Joshua Sprigge, *Anglia Rediviva*, Oxford edition, 1854, 30–2.
7. Keith Lindley and David Scott, eds, *The Journal of Thomas Juxon 1644–1647*, Camden Society 5th series, 13 (1999), 79.
8. Sprigge, *Anglia Rediviva*, 32; *The Moderate Intelligencer* 15 (5–12 June 1645), 118.
9. Sprigge, *Anglia Rediviva*, 32–3, for the council. The letter is in *LJ*, vol. 7, 421.
10. *CJ*, vol. 4, 169–70; *LJ*, vol. 7, 421.
11. John Rushworth, *Historical Collections*, London, 1721, vol. 6, 39.
12. See *Mercurius Britanicus* 86 (5–16 June 1645), 780; and *Mercurius Civicus* 107 (5–12 June 1645), 107, which did not doubt that the appointment of 'such religious and faithful commanders' would earn the blessing of God. *The Moderate Intelligencer* 14 (29 May–5 June 1645) had already just called Cromwell 'our right hand'.
13. Tibbutt, ed., *The Letter Books of Sir Samuel Luke,* 564–71; NA, SP 28/171–3, for the accounts submitted by officers for the free quarter.
14. *CJ*, vol. 4, 167, 172; *LJ*, vol. 7, 414, 424, 428; Firth and Rait, eds, *Acts and Ordinances of the Interregnum*, vol. 1, 696–7, 700–2.
15. Rushworth, *Historical Collections*, vol. 6, 40.
16. Sir Edward Walker, *Historical Discourses upon Several Occasions*, London, 1705, 128–30; Eliot Warburton, ed., *Memorials of Prince Rupert and the Cavaliers*, London, 1849, vol. 3, 100, 214; BL, Additional MS 62084(B), f. 25.
17. Sprigge, *Anglia Rediviva*, 33–4; Tibbutt, ed., *The Letter Books of Sir Samuel Luke*, 574–5; *The Moderate Intelligencer* 16 (12–19 June 1645), 124; Sir Henry Ellis, ed., *Original Letters Illustrative of English History*, London, 3rd series, 1846, vol. 4, 243–4.

18. Walker, *Historical Discourses*, 129–30; Daniel Parsons, ed., *The Diary of Sir Henry Slingsby, of Scriven*, London, 1831, 143–4; 'Iter Carolinum', printed in *Somers Tracts*, 2nd edition by Sir Walter Scott, 1811, vol, 5, 270. The royalist historian Clarendon, in Edward, Earl of Clarendon, *History of the Rebellion and Civil Wars in England*, ed. W. Dunn Macray, Oxford, 1888, IX.37, later asserted that the destination of the royal army was Leicester, where it would await the reinforcements from Newark. This is not found in the accounts of those present at the time, but perhaps the route of the king's soldiers was to be through Leicester.

19. Sprigge, *Anglia Rediviva*, 34.

20. 'Iter Carolinum' puts the time at 2 a.m., Sprigge, 11 p.m.

21. Walker, *Historical Discourses,* 129–30; BL, Additional MS 62084(B), f. 25. A version of this meeting, presumably from the testimony of royalist prisoners, is given in Sprigge, *Anglia Rediviva*, 34, where it is said that most of the military men present were against fighting. Some parliamentarian sources – Sprigge; *A more exact and perfect Relation of the great victory . . . Being a letter from a gentleman in Northampton*, London, 1645; *A True Relation Of A Great Victorie obtained by Sir Thomas Fairfax*, London, 1645; and *A Glorious Victory obtained by Sir Thomas Fairfax*, London, 1645 – assert that the royalists were compelled to fight because the New Model was so close on their heels. This story gave greater lustre to it in enforcing the battle, but the reason is not cited in any royalist source, though it would have excused the decision more, and so a historian who repeats it as fact may be falling for a piece of parliamentarian propaganda.

22. 'Iter Carolinum'.

23. The quotation is from *A more Particular and Exact Relation . . . Being two letters*, London, 16 June 1645.

24. *A more exact and perfect Relation*; Parsons, ed., *The Diary of Sir Henry Slingsby*, 149–50; Walker, *Historical Discourses*, 130; Sprigge, *Anglia Rediviva*, 34.

25. The terrain is described by Slingsby and Sprigge; and by *A more Particular and Exact Relation*; Richard Symonds, in Charles Edward Long, ed., *Diary of the Marches of the Royal Army during the Great Civil War*, Camden Society 74 (1859), 192–3; *A more exact and perfect relation*; and *An Ordinance Of The Lords and Commons . . . For . . . a day of Thanksgiving . . . for the great Victory near Knasby*, London, 17 June 1645. The sun is mentioned by Parliament's commissioners to the army, in *LJ*, vol. 7, 434. There are particular studies of the landscape in Martin Matrix Evans et al., *Naseby 1645*, Barnsley, 2002, 171; Glenn Foard, *Naseby*, Barnsley, 2nd edition, 2004, 209–15; and Mandy de Belin, 'Naseby', in Andrew Hopper and Philip Major, eds, *England's Fortress*, Farnham, 2014, 71–93.

26. For example, the royalist Lord Belasyse estimated the royal army at 12,000 and the New Model at 15,000, in his memories as recorded by his secretary Joshua Moone in 1688 (printed in Peter Young, *Naseby 1645*, London, 1985, 320–2); but the king's secretary Sir Edward Walker put the royal army at 3,500 foot and 4,100 horse, in *Historical Discourses*, 130, echoed by Clarendon, *History of the Rebellion*, IX.37; and Rupert's engineer Bernard de Gomme calculated 3,5000 foot and 4,000 horse: Warburton, *Memoirs of Prince Rupert*, vol. 3, 73–4. We do not know, however, if the last two sets of figures included officers. Among recent experts, Stuart Reid calculated the royal army at around 5,000 foot and 5,000 horse, and the New Model at around 7,000 foot and 6,000 horse (*All the King's Armies*, Staplehurst, 1998, 199–200). Alan Marshall made the king have almost 4,000 foot and 4,010 horse, and the New Model over 7,000 foot, and 7,200 horse (*Oliver Cromwell, Soldier*, London, 2004, 140–2). Glenn Foard estimated 4,500 royalist foot and 5,200 horse, and up to 7,500 foot, 6,600 horse and at least 5,000 dragoons in the New Model (*Naseby*, 197–209). Malcolm Wanklyn reckoned a royal army of over 5,000 horse and under 5,000 foot, and a New Model Army of 7,000 or 8,000 foot and 6,200 to 6,500 horse (*Decisive Battles of the English Civil War*, Barnsley, 2006, 173). Ian Gentles has 15,000 to 17,000 in the New Model Army (*The English Revolution and the Wars in the Three Kingdoms 1638–1652*, London, 2007, 265); and put the king's at 9,000 (*The New Model Army in England, Ireland and Scotland, 1645–1653*, Oxford, 1992, 55–60). Martin Matrix Evans preferred a royal army of 4,610 foot and 5,590 horse, and a New Model Army of 9,144 foot and 6,078 horse in theory, but probably reduced to a total of 13,700 in practice (*Naseby 1645*,

32). Peter Gaunt made the king's army 10,000 and the New Model 14,000 (*The English Civil War*, London, 2014, 109–10). Finally, Mandy de Belin settled at 7,000 to 12,000 royalists and 12,000 to 17,000 in the New Model ('Naseby', 80), figures which span all those proposed above both at the time and recently, and which I therefore echo myself.

27. Sprigge, *Anglia Rediviva*, 34.
28. *A more Particular and Exact Relation.*
29. This is based on the famous map of the battle formations by Robert Streeter, for Sprigge's *Anglia Rediviva,* which is supported by *A more Particular and Exact Relation.*
30. *The Copie of a Letter sent from a Gentleman of publicke employment in the late service neere Knaseby*, London, 1645; *LJ*, vol. 7, 434.
31. Analyses of the Northern and Newark Horse at Naseby include Young, *Naseby 1645*, 242–4 (1,700 men in 21 regiments, facing Cromwell with 3,900 men in his wing), who is echoed by Marshall, *Oliver Cromwell, Soldier*, 140–2; Martyn Bennett, *Traveller's Guide to the Battlefields of the English Civil War*, Exeter, 1990, 155–9 (fewer than 2,000 in the Northern and Newark Horse together, facing 3,500 under Cromwell); Reid, *All the King's Armies*, 199–201 (1,700 Northern Horse and 800 Newark Horse, facing 3,000 to 4,000 under Cromwell); Evans, *Naseby 1645*, 32 (1,710 Northern Horse with a reserve of perhaps 1,300 including the Newark men). Frank Kitson also gives Young's figures, but attributes 25 regiments to the Northern Horse: *Old Ironsides*, London, 2004, 116–17. Malcolm Wanklyn and Frank Jones, *A Military History of the English Civil War*, Harlow, 2005, 246, make the king have over 3,000 horse on *both* wings together, and Cromwell over 3,000 on his wing *alone*, but estimate a royalist horse reserve of 1,000 altogether, including the Newarkers.
32. The basic narrative of this action is taken from Sprigge, *Anglia Rediviva*, 40–2, which is compatible with the other records. Every contemporary account of the battle agrees that the right wing of the New Model, Cromwell's horse, routed the royalist horse opposite, and that this was the turning point of the battle. Sir Henry Slingsby says in his *Diary*, ed. by Parsons, 151, that the front line of the Northern Horse held until Cromwell's second line came up and overwhelmed it, and emphasizes the ability of Cromwell's men to outflank their opponents, as does Walker, *Historical Discourses*, 131. Belasyse, printed in Young, *Naseby 1645*, said that the royalist wing was 'routed without any handsome dispute', but this is contradicted both by the other accounts and by the list of wounded men in the regiments in the parliamentarian front line, counted by Wanklyn, *Decisive Battles*, 179, and Evans, *Naseby 1645*, 71–4.
33. *A more Particular and Exact Relation.*
34. Walker, *Historical Discourses*, 131.
35. Rupert's role as leader of the right-wing attack is attested by parliamentarian sources, Streeter's plan and Sprigge, *Anglia Rediviva*, 50, but also by a royalist one in BL, Additional MS 62084B, f. 25.
36. The primary sources for all this are those already cited in notes 18–30 above. The textual evidence for the final stages of the battle does not agree with the archaeological evidence, especially the concentrations of musket balls. Wanklyn, *Decisive Battles*, 183, and *The Warrior Generals*, London, 2010, 165, prefers the written sources, Foard, *Naseby*, 275–82, and Evans et al., *Naseby 1645*, 111–19, the material evidence; and there is no apparent way of determining the matter.
37. *A more Particular and Exact Relation.*
38. Bulstrode Whitelocke, *Memorials of the English Affairs*, Oxford edition, 1853, vol. 1, 448.
39. *The Copie of a Letter.*
40. Wanklyn and Jones, *A Military History*, 247–8, repeated by Wanklyn, *Decisive Battles*, 162–4, have suggested that Rupert had intended, after routing Ireton's wing, to sweep behind the rear of the New Model Army to attack Cromwell's men from behind; but that his way was blocked first by the sheer mass of the New Model's infantry, greater than expected, and then by its well-guarded baggage train. He apparently came up to the train with his troopers and was beaten off by the musketeers protecting it: as reported in *The Copie of a Letter sent from a Gentleman.* The hypothesis is therefore plausible but unprovable.
41. BL, Additional MS 62084B, f. 25.

42. Walker, *Historical Discourses*, 130. This was, however, the plan at the start of the day, and may not have been executed like this in the field.

43. This issue was first noted by Peter Young, in *Naseby 1645*, 268–72.

44. Thomas Carte, ed., *A Collection of Original Letters and Papers*, London, 1739, vol. 1, 126–30; *An Ordinance Of The Lords and Commons*.

45. The best study of this episode is Mark Stoyle, 'The Road to Farndon Field', *English Historical Review* 123 (2008), 895–1,015.

46. Carte, ed., *A Collection of Original Letters*, 126–30.

47. *The Copie of a Letter; A more Particular and Exact Relation; LJ*, vol. 7, 434; Sprigge, *Anglia Rediviva*, 253–5.

48. *An Ordinance Of The Lords and Commons*.

49. Sprigge, *Anglia Rediviva*, 56–8, which summarizes the reports of the contemporary newspapers. See also *LJ*, vol. 7, 439.

50. E.g. *The Copie of a Letter; A more exact and perfect Relation; A more Particular and Exact Relation . . . Being Two Letters; LJ*, vol. 7, 434; *A more particular and exact relation; Mercurius Britanicus* 87 (16–23 June 1645), 791.

51. *A True Relation of a Victory obtained over the King's Forces by the Army of Sir Thomas Fairfax*, London, 1645. In general, this work is the least valuable of the sources for the battle, being the work of a hack recycling, sometimes inaccurately, information taken from others.

52. *LJ*, vol. 7, 434.

53. *LJ*, vol. 7, 433–4.

54. *LJ*, vol. 7, 434.

55. Whitelocke, *Memorials*, vol. 1, 451; *CJ*, vol. 4, 176, 178, 186; *A Perfect Diurnall Of Some Passages in Parliament* 99 (16–23 June 1645), 783, 786,

56. The campaign of the New Model Army between July 1645 and June 1646 is exceptionally well documented, by sources which barely conflict with each other, in a manner not known for any previous comparable period of the war, and has accordingly been well recounted by successive historians in a generally consensual manner. My aims when treating of it are to bring out Cromwell's own role in the events, and to show more clearly why particular actions had particular results.

57. I am quite willing to acknowledge that I am myself less assured when dealing with religion, and especially with theology, than with war and politics. Having said that, there is a real lack of evidence during this period for Cromwell's own theological opinions, and his webs of connection in religious affairs; aside from his consistent support for independency and liberty of conscience. I am not prepared to try to fill this gap with back-projection and conjecture.

58. This has already been commented on in Chapter Three, n. 20.

59. A warning against necessarily believing Baxter has been delivered by Joel Halcomb, 'Was Cromwell an Independent or a Congregationalist?', *Cromwelliana* series 3.5 (2016), 29–35.

60. Matthew Sylvester, ed., *Reliquiae Baxterianae*, London, 1969, Part 1, 50–4.

61. Sprigge, *Anglia Rediviva*, 59–61.

62. Ibid., 61; *CJ*, vol. 4, 186; *LJ*, vol. 7, 439–62; *CSPD (1644–1645)*, 611, 617. Edward Wogan's account, in Carte, ed., *A Collection*, vol. 1, 130, seems garbled.

63. Philip Tennant, *Edgehill and Beyond*, Stroud, 1992, went through the relevant accounts and claims.

64. Sprigge, *Anglia Rediviva*, 61; Edward Bowles, *The Proceedings of the Army Under The Command Of Sir Thomas Fairfax, From the first of July to the sixth*, London, 9 July 1645.

65. The best overall survey of the movement remains that in John Morrill, *The Revolt of the Provinces*, London, 2nd edition, 1980. At the local level, there is also enduring merit in the chapter in George Anthony Harrison, 'Royalist Organisation in Wiltshire 1642–1646', (London University PhD thesis, 1963), 381–92.

66. For the king's overture, and that of Sir Lewis Dyve, see their letters in Bod L, Ashmole 1071.22. For the Prince of Wales's, see Bod L, Clarendon MS 24, f. 175. For Rupert's meetings, see Bod L, Firth MS C8, f. 27.

67. Sprigge, *Anglia Rediviva*, 62–6; Bowles, *The Proceedings of the Army . . . From the first of July; LJ*, vol. 7, 484–6.

68. Bod L, Clarendon MS 24, f. 192.

69. Sprigge, *Anglia Rediviva*, 66–71; *A Letter Sent to the Right Honourable William Lenthall, Esquire . . . Concerning the raising of the Siege of Taunton*, London, 10 July 1645; *A more full Relation of the great Battell fought betweene Sir Tho: Fairfax and Goring*, London, 1645; *The Proceedings of the Army . . . from the first of July*; Bod L, Firth MS C8, ff. 301–2; Edward Bowles, *An Exact and Perfect Relation of the Proceedings of the Army under the Command of Sir Thomas Fairfax, From the sixth of this instant July to the eleventh of the same*, London, 14 July 1645. Sprigge's account was not written until 1647, as a defence of the New Model in the political crisis of that year, but he was another of Fairfax's chaplains, and his narrative is not only detailed and comprehensive but contains information which is not in the contemporary newspapers and pamphlets. Indeed, I have hardly cited the former here, because almost all of what they say about the campaign is in Sprigge or the tracts.

70. Sprigge, *Anglia Rediviva*, 71–4; *CJ*, vol. 4, 207; *LJ*, vol. 7, 496; Baxter, *Reliquiae Baxterianae*, Part 1, 54; John Lilburne, *Innocency and Truth Justified*, London, 1646, 63–4; *A More full Relation of the great Battell fought betweene Sir Tho: Fairfax and Goring*, London, 1645; *Three Letters From Sir Thomas Fairfax His Armie*, London, 1645; Capt. John Blackwell, *A More Exact Relation Of The Great Defeat Given to Goring's Army in the West*, London, 1645; Bowles, *An Exact and Perfect Relation of the Proceedings of the Army*; Sir Richard Bulstrode, *Memoirs and Reflections upon the Reign and Government of Charles I and II*, London, 1721, 136–40; *The Coppie Of A Letter From Sir Thomas Fairfax his Quarters . . . concerning . . . Langport*, London, 1645; *A True Relation of a Victory obtained over the Kings Forces, by the Army of Sir Thomas Fairfax: Being Fought neere Langport*, London, 1645.

71. Warburton, ed., *Memoirs of Prince Rupert*, vol. 3, 137–9.

72. *CJ*, vol. 4, 208.

73. Lilburne, *Innocency and Truth Justified*, 43–4; *A more full Relation of the great Battell*. See M. A. Gibb, *John Lilburne the Leveller*, London, 1947, 127–8.

74. *Good Newes out of the West*, London, 1645.

75. Sprigge, *Anglia Rediviva*, 74–5; Edward Bowles, *A Continuation of the Proceedings of the Army under the Command of Sir Thomas Fairfax*, London, 26 July 1645; *The Coppie Of A Letter*.

76. The presbyterian was Fairfax's chaplain Edward Bowles, who wrote the weekly account of the army's progress for publication: see the entry on him by Stephen Wright in the *Oxford Dictionary of National Biography*, vol. 6, 959–60.

77. As represented in the print attached to his sermon *Gods doings and mans duty opened*, London, 1646.

78. Sprigge, *Anglia Rediviva*, 76–8; *CJ*, vol. 4, 220; *LJ*, vol. 7, 511; Bell, ed., *Memorials of the Civil War*, vol. 1, 239; Edward Bowles, *A Continuation of the Proceedings of the Army under the Command of Sir Thomas Fairfax*, London, 29 July 1645; *A Brief Relation Of The taking of Bridgewater*, London, 25 July 1645; *III Great Victories*, London, 1645; *A Fuller Relation From Bridgewater*, London, 26 July 1645; Edmund Wyndham, *A True Declaration Concerning the Surrender of Bridgewater*, London, 1646; Warburton, ed., *Memoirs of Prince Rupert*, vol. 3, 147. These accounts disagree about the efficacy of the bridges, the 'official' versions such as Sprigge and Bowles holding that they all worked, but the less official parliamentarian narratives agree with the royalist one that some failed, and I have followed those.

79. Ronald Hutton, *The Royalist War Effort 1642–1646*, London, 1982, 183–5.

80. Bod L, Clarendon MS, ff. 19, 21, 31, 37, 122, 127, 149.

81. This seems proved by his letter to his father in Bell, ed., *Memorials*, vol. 1, 240.

82. Sprigge, *Anglia Rediviva*, 83–5; Edward Bowles, *A Continuation of the Proceedings of the Army under the Command of Sir Thomas Fairfax*, London, 4 August 1645; *A Fuller Relation of the Taking of Bath*, London, 1645.

83. Sprigge, *Anglia Rediviva*, 85–91 (where the banners are noted); Wilbur Cortez Abbott, ed., *The Writings and Speeches of Oliver Cromwell*, Cambridge, MA, 1937, vol. 1, 368–9; Bell, ed., *Memorials*, vol. 1, 244–5; Edward Bowles, *A Continuation of the Proceedings of the Army under the Command of Sir Thomas Fairfax*, London, 11 August 1645; *Two Great Victories. 1. One obtained by Colonel Fleetwood*, London, 1645.

84. *CJ*, vol. 4, 234; *LJ*, vol. 7, 532–5; Whitelocke, *Memorials*, vol. 1, 492–3.
85. Sprigge, *Anglia Rediviva*, 91–6; HMC Portland MSS, vol. 1, 242–3; *The Proceedings of the Army under the Command of Sir Tho. Fairfax*, London, 18 August 1645; *Sir Thomas Fairfax's Letter To the Honorable William Lenthall . . . Concerning the taking of Sherborn Castle*, London, 19 August 1645; *A True Relation Of The taking of Sherborn Castle*, London, 18 August 1645.
86. Sprigge, *Anglia Rediviva*, 99.
87. Warburton, ed., *Memoirs of Prince Rupert*, vol. 2, 236.
88. Both these last details are in De Gomme's report in *A Declaration of His Highnesse Prince Rupert*, Oxford, 1645, 9–10.
89. Warburton, ed., *Memoirs of Prince Rupert*, vol. 3, 167.
90. These events are recounted in Hutton, *The Royalist War Effort*, 185–6.
91. This account of the siege and taking of Bristol is compiled from Sprigge, *Anglia Rediviva*, 97–131; *LJ*, vol. 4, 584–6; Carte, ed., *A Collection*, vol. 1, 133–4; *CSPD (1645–1647)*, 96; HMC Portland MSS, vol. 1, 268–9; *A True Relation of the Storming Bristoll*, London, 13 September 1645; *Two Letters Sent to the Honorable William Lenthall . . . concerning the Seige at Bristoll*, London, 1645; Warburton, ed., *Memoirs of Prince Rupert*, vol. 3, 166–80. Extra material has been added from Hutton, *Royalist War Effort*, 186–8.
92. C. H. Firth and R. S. Rait, eds, *Acts and Ordinances of the Interregnum*, London, 1911, vol. 1, 749–57.
93. *LJ*, vol. 7, 584–5.
94. *CJ*, vol. 4, 277.
95. *LJ*, vol. 7, 585–6.
96. *Lieutenant-General Cromwell's Letter . . .*, London, 1645.
97. *The Conclusion of Lieutenant-General Cromwell's Letter, to the House of Commons*, London, 1645; *Strong Motives*, London, n.d. The attribution of the latter to Walwyn seems clinched by David R. Como, 'An Unattributed Pamphlet by William Walwyn', *Huntington Library Quarterly* 69 (2006), 353–82.
98. David Laing, ed., *The Letters and Journals of Robert Baillie*, Edinburgh, 1941, vol. 2, 319–20.
99. Firth and Rait, eds, *Acts and Ordinances*, vol. 1, 789–97.
100. Bristol RO, 8029(9).
101. Sprigge, *Anglia Rediviva*, 132–3.
102. For all this, see Ronald Hutton and Wylie Reeves, 'Sieges and Fortifications', in John Kenyon and Jane Ohlmeyer, eds, *The Civil Wars*, Oxford, 1998, 195–233. For manuals, see *Enchridion of Fortification*, London, 1645; William Bourne, *The Arte of Shooting in Great Ordnance*, London, 1643; and Robert Norton, *The Gunners Dialogue*, London, 1643.
103. Sprigge, *Anglia Rediviva*, 132–6; *A Letter Concerning The Storming and Delivering up of the Castle of the Devises*, London, 25 September 1645; *Mercurius Civicus* 122 (18–25 September 1645), 1,076.
104. *CSPD (1645–1647)*, 157; *CJ*, vol. 4, 283, 292, 298.
105. Sprigge, *Anglia Rediviva*, 138–9.
106. Bod L, Clarendon MS 26, ff. 114–16; Abbott, ed., *Writings and Speeches*, vol. 1, 381–2; Sprigge, *Anglia Rediviva*, 141–4; *A Coppie OF Lieut. Gen. Cromwels Letter; Concerning the taking of Winchester Castle*, London, 9 October 1645.
107. The structure and previous history of the place are summed up in David Allen and Alan Turton, *Basing House*, published by Hampshire County Council, 2010, which also has a good reconstruction of the Civil War defences. The earlier sieges and the context for Cromwell's are narrated in G. N. Godwin, *The Civil War in Hampshire*, London, 1904, 26–7, 109–18, 221–70, 345–7.
108. Abbott, ed., *Writings and Speeches*, vol. 1, 386–7; *The full and last Relation, Of all things concerning Basing-House*, London, 1645 (Hugh Peters's relation, from which the quotations are taken); *A Continuation of certaine Speciall and Remarkable Passages* 4 (10–17 October 1645), 4–5; *The Weekly Account* 41 (8–15 October 1645), n.p.

109. *The full and last Relation; CJ*, vol. 4, 309, 312, 315; *LJ*, vol. 7, 656; Abbott, ed., *Writings and Speeches*, vol. 1, 387–9.

110. *The Moderate Intelligencer* 35 (23–30 October 1645), 174–6; *A Packet of Letters From Sir Thomas Fairfax his Quarter*, London, 30 October 1645; *The taking of Tiverton*, London, 23 October 1645; *LJ*, vol. 7, 657.

111. *A Packet of Letters*; Sprigge, *Anglia Rediviva*, 159–60.

112. Bod L, Clarendon MS 25, ff. 204–37; and MS 26, ff. 3–51.

113. Mark Stoyle, *The Civil War Defences of Exeter and the Great Parliamentary Siege of 1645–46*, Exeter, 1990.

114. Sprigge, *Anglia Rediviva*, 160–2; *CJ*, vol. 4, 318, 355; *A Continuation of certaine Speciall and Remarkable Passages* (2 issues, 14–28 November 1645); Carte, ed., *A Collection*, vol. 1, 135; BL, Additional MS 18979, f. 207.

115. Aryeh J. S. Nusbacher, 'The Triple Thread Supply of Victuals to the Army under Sir Thomas Fairfax' (Oxford University D.Phil. thesis, 2001).

116. *CSPD (1645–1647)*, 235, 244; Sprigge, *Anglia Rediviva*, 170–5; *Mercurius Academicus* (15–20 December 1645), 4–5; Bell, ed., *Memorials*, vol. 1, 261–5.

117. Abbott, ed., *Writings and Speeches*, vol. 1, 398.

118. *CJ*, vol. 4, 360–1; Whitelock, *Memorials*, vol. 1, 541.

119. Clarendon, *History of the Rebellion*, ed. Macray, IX.106–17; Bod L, Clarendon MS 26, ff. 61, 81, 101, 108, 182, 191; P. H. Hardacre, 'The End of the Civil War in Devon: A Royalist Letter of 1646', *Report and Transactions of the Devon Association* 85 (1953), 97–102; Bulstrode, *Memoirs*, 150–2; *CSPD (1645–1647)*, 282–3; HMC Portland MSS, vol. 1, 332–4.

120. Sprigge, *Anglia Rediviva*, 176–8; *A Continuation of certaine Speciall and Remarkable Passages* 17 (9–16 January 1645), 2–5; Carte, ed., *A Collection*, vol. 1, 136; *A Perfect Diurnall Of Some Passages in Parliament* 129 (12–19 January 1645), 1,035–6; Bell, ed., *Memorials*, vol. 1, 274–5; *The Parliament's Severall late Victories In the West*, London, 21 January 1646; *An Exact and True Collection Of The Weekly Passages, from the First of January last*, London, 1646; Hardacre, 'The End of the Civil War in Devon'; *History of the Rebellion*, ed. Macray, Clarendon, IX.117.

121. Sprigge, *Anglia Rediviva*, 179–82; *A Continuation of certaine Speciall and Remarkable Passages* 18, 16–23 January 1645, 4–5; *Sir Thomas Fairfax's Letter to Both Houses of Parliament*, London, 24 January 1646; *LJ*, vol. 8, 121–2, 127; *CJ*, vol. 4, 414–15; Carte, ed., *A Collection*, vol. 1, 137–8; Bell, ed., *Memorials*, vol. 1, 276–7; *Mr Peters Message Delivered in Both Houses . . . With The Narration of the Taking of Dartmouth*, London, 1646; *A Full and Exact Relation Of The Storming and Taking of Dartmouth*, London, 23 January 1646.

122. Sprigge, *Anglia Rediviva*, 185–9; *A Continuation of certaine Speciall and Remarkable Passages* (3 issues, 23 January–13 February 1646); Bell, ed., *Memorials*, vol. 1, 281–3; *Powtheram Castle At Exeter . . .*, London, 1646; *Sir Thomas Fairfax's Proceedings About the Storming of Exeter*, London, 9 February 1645.

123. Bod L, Clarendon MS 27, ff. 5, 18, 21; Carte, ed., *A Collection*, vol. 1, 109–11.

124. Most of the parliamentarian sources exaggerate the royalist strength, which was recorded with precision and in detail by Hopton, in Carte, ed., *A Collection*, vol. 1, 109–10. Fairfax himself recorded the number of regiments and companies that he took to the battle, in *Sir Thomas Fairfax Letter . . . Concerning Torrington*, London, 14 February 1646. Hopton estimated the New Model's numbers at 6,000 foot, 3,500 horse and 500 dragoons, which matches Fairfax's statement well.

125. Sprigge, *Anglia Rediviva*, 190–7; *Sir Thomas Fairfax Letter*; Carte, ed., *A Collection*, vol. 1, 111–14, 140–3; Bell, ed., *Memorials*, 285; *A Fuller Relation Of Sir Thomas Fairfax's Routing All The Kings Armies in the West*, London, 21 February 1646; *A True Relation Concerning the late Fight at Torrington*, 20 February 1646; *A more Full Relation Of The Continued Successes of His Excellency Sir Thomas Fairfax*, London, 1646; *Sir Thomas Fairfax Letter to the Honorable William Lenthal I . . . Concerning . . . Torrington*, London, 24 February 1646; *A Famous Victorie Obtained By Sir Thomas Fairfax, against the Lord Hopton*, London, 20 February 1646; Bulstrode, *Memoirs*, 152–3; *CJ*, vol. 4, 449. There is a good local history of the engagement in John Wardham, *The Forgotten Battle: Torrington 1646*, Bideford, 1996.

126. BL, Additional MS 4292, f. 249.

127. For the role of ethnic identity in the Civil War, see especially Mark Stoyle, *Soldiers and Strangers*, London, 2005. For early modern Cornish separatism, see the same author's *West Britons*, Exeter, 2002.

128. Sprigge, *Anglia Rediviva*, 185; *Two Letters Sent To The Honorable William Lenthal I . . .*, London, 2 March 1646.

129. Sprigge, *Anglia Rediviva*, 206–16; Bell, ed., *Memorials*, vol. 1, 286. *Sir Thomas Fairfax his victorious proceedings in the taking of Launceston*, London, 4 March 1646; *The late victorious Proceedings Of Sir Thomas Fairfax Against the Enemy in the West*, 9 March 1646; *Sir Thomas Fairfax's Proceedings In The West*, London, 7 March 1646; *A Letter Sent To The Hono:ble William Lenthal I . . . Concerning Sir Tho: Fairfax;s gallant Proceedings In Cornwall*, London, 7 March 1646; *The Westerne Informer*, London, 7 March 1645; *Master Peters Message From Sir Thomas Fairfax*, London, 22 March 1645.

130. Sprigge, *Anglia Rediviva*, 212–36; *LJ*, vol. 8, 210–13, 230; Bell, ed., *Memorials*, vol. 1, 288; Carte, ed., *A Collection*, vol. 1, 115–23; *A more Full and Exact Relation (Being the Third Letter To the Honorable William Lenthal . . .)*, London, 18 March 1645; *His Majesties Whole Army in the West Conquered*, London, 15 March 1645; *Two Letters Sent to the Honorable William Lenthal I . . . Concerning the Total Disbanding Of Sir Ralph Hoptons Army*, London, 27 March 1645.

131. Sprigge, *Anglia Rediviva*, 239–53; Bell, ed., *Memorials*, vol. 1, 289–91; *Several Letters To the Honoble William Lenthal I . . . Concerning The Gallant Proceedings of Sir Tho: Fairfax Army in the West*, London, 13 April 1646; *Barnstable agreed to be surrendered to Sir Thomas Fairfax*, London, 16 April 1646.

132. For these votes see *CJ*, vol. 4, 506, 513–14, 518; Margaret F. Stieg, ed., *The Diary of John Harington, M.P. 1646–53*, Somerset Record Society 74 (1977), 15–21; Lindley and Scott, eds, *The Journal of Thomas Juxon*, 113–14.

133. Stieg, ed., *The Diary of John Harington*, 21.

134. Lindley and Scott, eds, *The Journal of Thomas Juxon*, 114.

135. John Lilburne, *Jonahs cry out of the whales belly*, London, 1647, 12–13.

136. Thomas Carte, *The Life of James, Duke of Ormond*, Oxford edition, 1851, vol. 6, 351–2.

137. Lindley and Scott, eds, *The Journal of Thomas Juxon*, 104.

138. BL, Additional MS 4292, f. 249.

139. *Mercurius Civicus* 152 (23–30 April 1646), 1229–30; *A Perfect Diurnall* 143 (20–27 April 1646), 1,147.

140. Stieg, ed., *The Diary of John Harington*, 22; *CJ*, vol. 4, 523, 528; Bulstrode Whitelocke, *Memorials of the English Affairs*, Oxford edition, 1853, vol. 2, 10.

141. Sprigge, *Anglia Rediviva*, 255; *Sir Thomas Fairfax Facing Oxford*, London, 4 May 1646.

142. *CJ*, vol. 4, 538–51, 573; *LJ*, vol. 7, 308–19; Stieg, ed., *The Diary of John Harington*, 25–6.

143. Firth and Rait, eds, *Acts and Ordinances*, vol. 1, 852–5.

144. Sprigge, *Anglia Rediviva*, 256–84. The modern study is Frederick John Varley, *The Siege of Oxford*, Oxford, 1932.

145. Whitelock, *Memorials*, vol. 2, 44.

146. Ibid., 19–20.

147. Mark Noble, *Memoirs of the Protectoral House of Cromwell*, 3rd edition, London, 1787, vol. 1, 358.

148. William Dell, *The Building and Glory of the truely Christian and Spiritual Church*, London, 1646.

149. Laing, ed., *Letters and Journals of Robert Baillie*, vol. 2, 343–76, passim.

150. *CJ*, vol. 4, 555–69; *LJ*, vol. 7, 332, 392, 414; Lindley and Scott, eds, *The Journal of Thomas Juxon*, 124–5.

151. *Conscience Caution'd*, London, 1646.

152. *CJ*, vol. 4, 528, 570, 615–16, 632, 641, 644, 663, 666, 671, 681, 695, 696, 708, 727, 730, and vol. 5, 6, 10, 11, 17, 28.

153. *CJ*, vol. 4, 631–2, 640, 665, 680, 690, 700, 713, 726, and vol. 5, 12, 34–5; Stieg, ed., *The Diary of John Harington*, 32.

154. *LJ*, vol. 7, 427. The tract was *The Summe Of The Charge Given by Lieutenant-General Cromwell* . . ., London, n.d., but collected by George Thomason on 10 July. It refers to some of Lilburne's works and is in his style.

155. Abbott, ed., *Writings and Speeches*, vol. 1, 408.

156. Stieg, ed., *The Diary of John Harington*, 30.

157. Samuel Rawson Gardiner, ed., *The Constitutional Documents of the Puritan Revolution*, Oxford, 3rd edition, 290–308.

158. Laing, ed., *The Letters and Journals of Robert Baillie*, 392.

159. Anglo-Scottish relations in general at this period, as well as this negotiation, are well treated in David Stevenson, *Revolution and Counter-Revolution in Scotland*, London, 1977, 62–77. The details of the agreement are in *CJ*, vol. 4, 654–5, 665.

160. Abbott, ed., *Writings and Speeches,* vol. 1, 410.

161. Stieg, ed., *The Diary of John Harington*, 32; *CJ*, vol. 4, 665.

162. James Cromford, *Plain English*, London, 1646.

163. John Vicars, *Magnalia Dei Anglicana*, London, 1646.

164. *A perfect List of all the Victories obtained (through the blessing of God)* . . ., London, 1646.

165. Noted by Mark A. Kishlansky, *The Rise of the New Model Army*, Cambridge, 1979, 143.

166. Stieg, ed., *The Diary of John Harington*, 37.

167. Ibid., 42.

168. C. H. Firth, ed., *The Memoirs of Edmund Ludlow*, Oxford, 1894, vol. 1, 144–5.

169. Samuel Rawson Gardiner, *History of the Great Civil War*, Oxford, 1893, vol. 3, 35, thinks this conversation probably took place in March 1647, but it makes perfect sense where Ludlow dated it, in the autumn of 1646.

170. Abbott, ed., *Writings and Speeches*, vol. 1, 416.

171. Firth and Rait, eds, *Acts and Ordinances*, vol. 1, 879–904; *CJ*, vol. 4, 730.

172. *CJ*, vol. 4, 690; *The Moderate Intelligencer* 84 (8–15 October 1646), 689.

173. *LJ*, vol. 1, 563.

174. For the developing problem, see Ian Gentles, 'The Arrears of Pay of the Parliamentary Army at the End of the First Civil War', *Bulletin of the Institute of Historical Research* 48 (1975), 52–63.

175. *CJ*, vol. 5, 9.

176. NA SP 28/41/4, f. 377v. The composition and nature of the committee have been studied by John Adamson, 'Of Armies and Architecture', in Ian Gentles et al., eds, *Soldiers, Writers and Statesmen of the English Revolution*, Cambridge, 1998, 36–67.

177. *LJ*, vol. 7, 605.

178. *CJ*, vol. 5, 34.

179. Abbott, ed., *Writings and Speeches*, vol. 1, 420–1.

180. Lindley and Scott, eds, *The Journal of Thomas Juxon*, 144.

181. I examined these calendar customs in *The Stations of the Sun*, Oxford, 1996, 42–53.

182. I shall give this last footnote to Lady Antonia Fraser, whose *Cromwell: Our Chief of Men*, London, 1973, yet remains the study of him most likely to be found in bookshops. Her treatment of his move is on p. 179.

◆

BIBLIOGRAPHICAL NOTE

The edition of Cromwell's letters and related documents which I have used has consistently been that by Wilbur Cortez Abbott, which is the fullest to date. It also, however, has distinct short-comings, which have been valuably highlighted by John Morrill ('Textualizing and Contextualizing Cromwell', *Historical Journal* 33, 1990, 629–39), and in some respects the Carlyle-Lomas edition is better. My preference for Abbott has been due simply to the fact that his happens to be the edition available in my own university library, which I could borrow, study and transcribe at leisure: we in the provinces do not have the choices available to those with college and copyright libraries at their doors. That has not been a problem in practice, because for the precise period which I have tackled, the Carlyle-Lomas edition presents the text of Cromwell's letters seemingly as Abbott's does (according to the sample I have checked) and it is not much superior in its notes. Like so many others, I have long and eagerly been awaiting the major new Oxford University Press edition of the letters and speeches overseen by John Morrill; but it was not ready in time for the writing of this book.